CLIVE

The Life and Death of a British Emperor

CLIVE

THE LIFE AND DEATH OF
A BRITISH EMPEROR

Robert Harvey

Hodder & Stoughton

For Antonella, Abdullah, Badia, Abdullilah, and Hasen

Copyright © 1998 by Robert Harvey

First published in 1998 by Hodder and Stoughton
A division of Hodder Headline PLC

10 9 8 7 6 5 4 3 2 1

British Library Cataloguing in Publication Data
A CIP catalogue record for this title is available from the British Library

ISBN: 0 340 65440 6

Designed by Behram Kapadia
Typeset in 11 on 13pt Palatino by
Hewer Text Limited, Edinburgh
Printed and bound in Great Britain by
Clays Ltd, St Ives plc

Hodder and Stoughton
A division of Hodder Headline PLC
338 Euston Road
London NW1 3BH

Acknowledgements

I owe a huge debt to a great many people who have assisted me in the preparation of the first major biography of Clive in two decades. Since boyhood I have been an admirer of Clive, and Macaulay's famous Essay ignited a real admiration towards this extraordinary figure. Two books that came out in my youth, Mark Bence-Jones's *Clive of India* and Michael Edwardes's *Plassey*, re-kindled my enthusiasm.

Bence-Jones's work, one of the two best biographies of Clive, is a masterpiece of scholarship and elegant writing, while Edwardes's book is direct and militarily compelling, and to them I owe heartfelt thanks for indicating some of the direction that my research should follow – although in most cases the conclusions and judgments are very different from theirs and are no one's responsibility but my own. Sir John Malcolm's detailed *Life of Lord Clive* remains, of course, the most fruitful treasury of correspondence and papers, but the meticulously kept and helpful India Office library in London, the National Library of Wales, the National Army Museum in Chelsea, and other letters and documents still in private hands such as those provided by Christopher Stainforth provide a fertile field for original research. I am grateful to them all.

I am also enormously indebted to the Earl and Countess of Plymouth, as well as Viscount and Lady Windsor, for their hospitality and help; likewise to Michael and the Hon Mrs Michael Woodbine Parish, Robin and the whole family, who quite apart from specific help, exposed one at an early age to the cheerful aura of a major Clive house; to the Rector of Moreton Saye; to Countess Bina Sella Di Monteluce, Deepak Vaidya and Indian friends too numerous to mention; to Peter Holt, a descendant of Clive's and gifted chronicler of his travels; to Dr Martin Scurr, for his invaluable advice on Clive's health; to Paul and Maureen Marriott, whose early enthusiasm for Clive always communicated itself to me as did that of Phyllis and Joce Humphreys for India; to Raleigh Trevelyan, whose advice and clear, penetrating insights into India are among the best there are; to Dr David Atterton, for his encouragement; to Lawrence James, whose tours de forces on the British Empire risk becoming definitive; to Andrew Williams, who knows India so well; to Dr Jonathan Wright of Christ Church, who steered me in one significant part of my research; and to Powys Castle, which contains many interesting relics of Clive. I also owe a huge debt to my former headmaster, Michael Phillips of Elston Hall, and my former Modern Tutor at Eton, John Peake, who instilled in me a passion for history.

I am personally vastly indebted to my brilliant agent Gillon Aitken; to my enthusiastic and painstaking assistant, Jenny Thomas, and her historian husband Geoffrey; to my gifted and warmly encouraging editors Roland Philipps and Angela Herlihy; to my mother and sister, always founts of love and support; and above all, as always, to my darling Jane and Oliver, who have to endure the hard slog, moodiness and single-mindedness of a writer's life, always restoring cheerfulness.

I am very grateful to Mark Bence-Jones, Raleigh Trevelyan, Lawrence James and Peter Holt for permisson to quote from their books. For the picture credits I am grateful to the Oriental and India Office Collections, the National Trust and the Hon Mrs Michael Parish.

Contents

CONTENTS

List of Illustrations

'Am I not rather deserving of praise for the moderation which marked my proceedings? Consider the situation in which victory at Plassey had placed me. A great prince was dependent on my pleasure; an opulent city lay at my mercy; its richest bankers bid against each other for my smiles; I walked through vaults which were thrown open to me alone, piled on either hand with gold and jewels! Mr Chairman, at this moment I stand astonished at my own moderation!'

Robert Clive

'No oath which superstition can devise, no hostage however precious, inspires a hundredth part of the confidence which is produced by the "yea, yea," and "nay, nay" of a British envoy.'

Lord Macaulay, *Essay on Clive*

'Whilst I could easily understand the reaction of a new generation to the imperial mystique . . . I knew that it had not all been hypocrisy, exploitation, lust and plunder, but that there had also been a degree of selflessness among a great many who had served in India and given their lives to it.'

Raleigh Trevelyan, *The Golden Oriole*

BOOK ONE

BORN A SOLDIER, 1725–1756

CHAPTER 1

Burial at Dusk

A moody, grey-grim, prematurely frosty evening in late November in the mid-eighteenth century, in one of the most obscure parts of central England. The buttress-hedged, snow-covered dirt-tracks are devoid of traffic, the window-coverings of the farmers' and artisans' cottages in place to keep in the warmth of the blazing, smoky fires and expel the ferocity of the cold. It is dusk, and the last light is fading. Anxious faces can be seen occasionally peeping from the windows. Ploughmen returning home, the odd venturesome older child, are outside, watching the road from the safety of thickets and copses of trees.

Some noble carriages have already passed up to the church. Some of the more confident and wealthy members of the farming community have walked there to pay their last respects.

Through the murk the sparking clatter of wheels on the rough stones of the lane can be heard approaching. The hidden watchers stiffen. Horses' hooves pound into earshot; there is not one carriage, but several, as though a small army were riding into battle. Those farthest down the lane first witness the spectral procession through the dusk. A huge carriage, draped entirely in black, is at its head. The carriage denotes a man of immense power and wealth. Behind follows a succession of seven or eight carriages, the ones at the front equally splendid, funereal, spectral, the last bearing servants in livery.

It is a terrifying sight for remote country folk, the passage of a black prince and his retainers to his funeral after nightfall. This was the burial, in Macaulay's phrase, of a 'great wicked lord who had ordered the walls around his house to be made so thick in order to keep out the devil'.

The thundering black carriages sped past the gawping onlookers like ghostly apparitions. Further on, they slowed and adopted a more respectful pace. As the procession clattered along the road, through the encroaching darkness, the glint and polish of magnificent coaches and liverymen dressed in black must have seemed awesome to the silent, hidden watchers.

Finally, the procession reached the very slight rise on which the then very humble church of Moreton Saye was perched, and the coaches disgorged their occupants, the women in the ample veils and black finery of loud mourning, the men stiffened in respect. The servants, with their black costumes and impassive faces, looked like the outriders of death. The huge wooden coffin was borne in, defying ecclesiastical regulations that burials must not take place after dusk.

Gloom, sadness and secrecy pervaded. It was a burial in a hurry, and in shame; ostensibly that of a suicide who by canon law could not be buried in the consecrated ground of a graveyard, never mind in church itself. The funeral was solemn, subdued, punctuated by the sobbing of some of the women present and the silent grief of the men.

When the coffin was laid in its vault, the secret, private mourners of the night departed in all their sepulchral finery. It was left to the gravediggers and stonemasons to cover the resting place, and then pave it over. No stone was erected over it, no tomb constructed, no memorial inscribed, no name carved. The floor was restored as it was, as though no one lay there.

As a strong-willed, troublesome boy, the deceased had worshipped in this simple chapel, in the family pew. The ancient rough-hewn silver communion cup and fine wooden balcony, erected in 1634, offset the building's rudeness. Fourteen years after the burial, in 1788, it was to be renovated in the Wren style into a respectable eighteenth-century edifice – by the standards of a provincial church. Nearly a hundred years later fine box pews were added. A tiny plaque was placed on the wall to the right facing the altar – not above the grave, but within the presbytery. It read: 'Sacred to the Memory of Robert Lord Clive KB buried within the walls of this church. Primus in Indis.' That is all the memorial that remains.

This century, a parquet floor was laid by workmen who discovered bones about two-thirds of the way up the aisle on the right. It is believed they were Clive's, and were laid to rest again. Yet this spectral apparition of the night, buried like Mozart in haste and secrecy (although, unlike the composer, at great expense), in an anonymous grave, was one of Britain's greatest and richest sons, far more deserving of a tomb in Westminster Abbey than most that rest there.

The great crags and moss-coloured granite bleakness of mid Wales give way as they reach England to lower hills sliced by deep wooded trenches in the east, at last spending themselves in the gentler ridges and valleys of western Shropshire. There, two up-lands stand out: the Stiperstones, a series of angular rocks supposed to have been a medieval gathering place for witches; and the pencil-precise escarpment of Wenlock Edge. Where these two meet over-looks a broad, fertile plain dominated by the small market town of Bishop's Castle. On the English side of this there lies a valley dominated by a large, graceful, classical eighteenth-century coun-try house set back behind a lake in extensive parkland.

There, more than 220 years ago, as the November evening drew in while fires fought to keep at bay the encroaching winter cold, a man was seated alone, having taken his leave of his family for the day. He wore the dress of a very wealthy nobleman, the most expensive silk shirt, gold-embroidered coat and black waistcoat that money could buy. He was of middle height and medium build, with a face rendered haggard by sickness. The features were uneven: pinched, slightly skewed, bushy browed and large nosed, he was not a handsome man.

But the stern expression, weathered and darkened by long exposure under a foreign sun, set him apart from the general run of wealthy country magnates. It was a proud, anguished face, the eyes decisive and piercing, the mouth curiously vulnerable, yet set in fierce determination. To modern eyes, the mixture of sensitivity and command conveyed by his portraits recalls that of Winston Churchill. He was about to turn 50. He remained possessed of the vigour of his prime. As so often these past months, he was silent and shrouded in his thoughts. None dared interrupt him.

Few encountering this taciturn squire in the windy gloom of an English country evening would have suspected that he had once been a continental emperor, a man who had built up, from almost nothing, a dominion to rival those of Alexander the Great, Augustus

Caesar, Genghis Khan and Tamerlane. His achievement had been far greater than those of the Spanish conquistadors. He had overcome a people ten times as numerous as Cortés did in Mexico, confronting huge armies equipped with primitive artillery, firearms, horses and elephants belonging to one of the greatest and most advanced civilisations in the world. By contrast, the Aztecs had no firearms and regarded men on horseback as supernatural monsters.

After securing a continent by the time he was only 35, this remarkable man had set down the administrative foundations of an empire that was to last two centuries. An even greater – although perhaps impossible – challenge beckoned. The government in London was considering appointing him to command the British forces resisting the uprising of the American colonists.

No feat, it seemed, was beyond him. If anyone could save America for Britain, it was surely Robert Clive. That summer, the East India Company's tea had been thrown into Boston Harbour. But with his withering perspicacity and realism, Clive believed that American independence was inevitable. Two years earlier he had written, with some exaggeration, 'that the Americans will sooner or later master all the Spanish possessions and make Cape Horn the boundary of their empire is beyond a doubt'.

Clive was a restless man, given to pacing up and down the magnificent drawing room, with its splendid ceilings, at Walcot. He gazed out as the light faded that autumn evening upon the spectre of the great oaks and ashes in the extensive parkland that fell away below the house as they shed the final glory of their red and brown leaves.

Nature put on its finest display of colour as death approached and the skeletons of the winter trees beckoned. To Clive the approach of English winter, the receding light of evening along the Welsh borders, the pervasive grey skies, green parkland and damp meadows seemed very different to the heat and dust of southern India. Yet there was a touch of Bengal here, in the subtle play of light through cloud and suffocating greenery. Only the chill in the air was in cold contrast to the suffocating humidity of the Ganges basin.

He was proud of his huge estate at Walcot. He had bought the estate from Charles Walcot, a young MP, heir to a deeply indebted father, for the staggering price of some £90,000 ten years before.

Unusually – for Clive, impoverished in youth, was careful with his money – he had got the worse of the deal. In the ten years he had owned it he had employed Sir William Chambers, one of the most celebrated architects of his generation, to enlarge it, adding a simple yet impressive Doric portico to the east front, to create a new entrance; the previous one had been on the north side. Elegant sash windows were introduced; and the ceilings of the main rooms had been decorated with friezes of bows and arrows as well as musical instruments.

An exotic lake was laid out in the formal gardens he had designed. Behind Walcot, Clive had begun an extensive arboretum as a gift to posterity which he relished planning and walking about in. The house was large, yet its design was classical simplicity itself: the new porch gave on to a beautifully proportioned hall with a magnificent staircase. To the left the drawing room beckoned, to the right the dining room. Outside, no excessive fripperies or adornments spoilt the symmetry of the façade. Built to human proportions, Walcot was light, straightforward and comfortable, set under a hill that dominated the surrounding landscape. The tiny hamlet of Lydbury North, mostly lived in by estate workers, trailed wisps of chimney smoke across the centre of this vast panorama.

It was one of three great houses, and a number of smaller ones, owned by one of the first men in English history who had risen from genteel poverty to awesome wealth through his own efforts without benefit of inheritance or royal patronage. Clive was by now certainly one of the richest men in England, with a fortune estimated conservatively at £1 million (around £400 million at today's prices).

Clive was to be reviled and sneered at for his nouveau riche love of ostentation and luxury. Yet his taste in houses could hardly be described as loud or vulgar. While no expense was spared on the interiors – yet for the most part they were within the bounds of good taste – his residences were more notable for subdued charm and elegance along classical lines than showiness.

Claremont, when completed, was compact, beautifully propor-tioned, ostentatious only in its enormous columns. Walcot, much older, was more streamlined still. Oakly, more modest, was full of charm. His Berkeley Square house was no palace, but the dwelling of a London gentleman. When he refurbished Styche Hall, his ancestral home, he did so with restraint, turning a very unassuming Elizabethan country pile into a fine Georgian one.

It was in October 1774, as he had helped to direct major alterations to Oakly in a downpour by a steep slope overlooking the swollen River Teme, that he had caught a bad cold and catarrh, precipitating an attack of his old illness, which in turn seems to have rendered Clive's sensitive mind defenseless. An intellect that was usually courageous, optimistic and creative in outlook was now at the mercy of every demon of regret and disappointment throughout an extraordinary life. Here, in his last evening in Walcot, they would have come rushing at him like the dancing patterns of the shadows from the flames of the great fire on the hearth.

Chapter 2

Rebel without a Cause

R obert Clive was born in an unmemorable house, Styche Hall, near the village of Moreton Saye close to the town of Market Drayton some 25 miles east of Walcot and 35 miles from Oakly in his beloved Shropshire on 29 September 1725.

Shropshire is one of England's loveliest counties, a concentration of lush green farmland through which little lanes wind like streams up to unexpected, remote, solitary farms and hamlets. Unlike the western part of the county, where Clive was to live later, his birthplace was in one of the flatter parts of the country, characterised by occasional slight rises in an area crisscrossed by hedges and fields.

Clive's life was to be surrounded by myths, and two were present even at his birth: that he came of humble stock; and that his formative years were spent in Shropshire. In fact the family, although by no means aristocratic, was from a respectable country gentry background. Not rich, the Clives were not poor. When only two years old the child ceased to live at Styche Hall, and was transferred to more comfortable and cosmopolitan surroundings.

The Clive family was probably named after the village of Clive, north of Shrewsbury. Its origins are recorded as going back to at least the twelfth century, when Henry II, slayer of Thomas à Becket, was on the throne. In the 1500s Sir George Clive was a considerable government official, knighted for his service, while the boy's grandfather, Robert Clive, was a noted and feared commander of the parliamentary forces in the following century.

Almost certainly, Clive's father, Richard, was fiercely committed to the anti-Jacobite, pro-parliament forces, and was committed to the Hanoverian king in later years, as were most, although by no means all, of the minor country gentry. Richard Clive was a man of unbendingly forceful views, stubborn, obstinate and probably a difficult father although – again contrary to legend, which has it that he was ashamed of his son in his teens – devoted to Robert in a kind of chivvying, hectoring fashion. He was also said to be irascible and fond of drink. Clive's mother, on the other hand, was sensitive.

In common with many poorer gentry, Richard found it difficult to stoop to the business of making money, something his limited circumstances made necessary. His income from renting land was a comfortable £500 a year, but he borrowed heavily on the estate to support his lifestyle and large family. He qualified as a lawyer, and moved to London to practise there when Clive was an infant.

The boy was his firstborn. Before he was three he was taken under the guardianship of his mother's sister, Elizabeth (born a Gaskell, of a respectable Manchester gentry family), and her husband, Daniel Bayley, who had only one son, while his father struggled to make ends meet in London. Contrary to myth again, Clive's early years were happy and spoilt. Soon after his third birthday, he fell seriously ill with a fever but through tender nursing recovered and one day descended to the parlour talkative and 'very merry and as good as it is possible'. The kindness of the household shines through: according to one account, his uncle remarked, 'with reluctance Bob this afternoon suffered his Aunt Bay to go to chapel'.

Clive as a young child was from the first a mixture of talkative precociousness, sensitivity and frequent alternation between cheerfulness and a fast and furious temper. He adored fighting and was very close to his cousin. At the age of six, his uncle commented with concern that 'he is out of measure addicted to fighting', which gave his temper 'a fierceness and imperiousness that he flies out on every trifling occasion; for this reason I do what I can to suppress the hero that I may help forward the more valuable qualities of meekness, benevolence and patience'.

The Bayleys' house, Hope Hall, was more comfortable than Styche, and Manchester at that time was a very pleasant small town inhabited by 'reserved and purse-proud' people compared with the 'free and open' inhabitants of the nearby port of Liverpool. At the age of nine, tragedy struck: Clive's surrogate mother, the gentle 'Aunt May' died, and his distraught uncle proved unable to look after the boy. Clive was sent for a while to his father's small lodgings in London. Soon afterwards the family returned to Styche.

Clive now lived in less comfortable surroundings; his father was not rich, and the eldest boy had to share with several other children. The house was of no great size, although adequate: it was a small Elizabethan country house, set on a hill, with a central block and two modest timbered wings. This he shared, eventually, with no fewer than five girls (two of his sisters died in infancy), and a baby boy who was only two when he left home (one brother was born four years later and his four other brothers died in infancy).

As the eldest, and only boy, in the household for most of his youth, he was almost certainly overindulged and surrounded by feminine influences, which helped further to develop his sensitive and egotistical nature. Yet from about this time can be dated his increasingly sullen and rebellious personality, which may have been prompted by the move from his doting uncle and aunt, where he was the centre of attention, to a household filled with others under the considerably less sentimental tutelage of his gruff and opinionated father. His mother, by contrast, appears to have been even-tempered and hard-working.

Robert had spent the last two years in Manchester at a well-known prep school, Dr Eaton's at Lostock in Cheshire, and on his return to Shropshire he went to the humbler Market Drayton grammar school. This was a comedown and may have contributed to his resentful attitude. He was an early rebel without a cause.

There is no reason to disbelieve the popular local story that he led a gang from the school that threatened to smash local shop windows unless paid protection money, or that he climbed the church spire at Market Drayton, to the horror of a crowd of locals, and refused to climb down unless he was paid. At school he seems to have been bored and inattentive.

His delinquency, combined with a modest improvement in the family fortunes, resolved Richard Clive to send him to Merchant Taylors', a tough, minor public school in London. Again, his conduct and work there were far from impressive and it is possible he was even expelled to a kind of cross between a modern 'crammer' and technical college, at Hemel Hempstead in Hertfordshire, to acquire some skills useful in life.

By the end of his schooling, although popular with his contemporaries, who looked upon him with fear and respect, he was dismissed by his teachers as little more than a rough-hewn country lad, with low to middling prospects in life. In addition, by his late teens, his temperamental but previously cheerful and egotistical personality had been hammered, probably by school life, into that of a rather shy, graceless young man of few words.

Styche Hall offered no prospect of providing a living from the land: and Richard Clive, while constantly chiding him for his defects, nevertheless wanted him to get the best out of life. Rebellious as he was, Clive seems to have been in awe of his father and determined to please him throughout life; the old man's personality must have been overwhelming to the teenager.

The Britain into which Robert Clive was born was by any standards on the threshold of a golden age that was to last some two centuries. For a millennium the country had been a marginal player on the European stage. For all its qualities, the middle-sized land mass off the shores of Europe had had only a peripheral impact on the mainstream of continental politics: no great religious, political, cultural or artistic movements had washed over from Britain to affect the swirl of European civilisation.

Rather the reverse: Britain's culture, borrowed from ancient Rome and Italy, and to a lesser extent France and Spain, was essentially second-hand. Its only significant religious movement had emerged from a schism born of a king's desire for a second wife. Its very people were European cast-offs – Iberians and Celts, in the distant past; Angles, Saxons, Jutes, Danes and Normans more recently. The Normans had imbued it with its first serious post-Roman cultural heritage, before the country had plunged into an obscurantist power struggle between kings and nobles which preceded an even more arcane series of dynastic wars.

When dynastic cohesion, renaissance splendour and, at last, real cultural achievement – in literature – belatedly flowered in the sixteenth century, England still appeared to be a somewhat backward European cousin. Only with its extraordinary political leaps from absolutist monarchy to parliamentary republic, military dictatorship, back to shortlived absolutism and then forward to constitutional monarchy did the country suddenly steal a huge march on its superficially more dazzling continental rivals.

Political absolutism and centralism clung on through most of Europe long after the societies beneath them had begun to bubble with social transformation. In Britain, for a variety of reasons, the political development which was to permit religious tolerance (at least by comparison with everywhere else), participation, free expression and the blowing off of steam among the newly emergent classes was in place before they had even emerged.

Instead of social change becoming dammed behind an absolutist system, and then spectacularly overwhelming it, transformation flowed smoothly into already constructed channels. Better still, that very grudging individualism, pragmatism, resistance to central control and suspicion of dogma which rendered absolutism so short-lived in Britain helped to nourish traditions which encouraged an astounding growth of science, literature, criticism and scepticism that were to underpin the industrial revolution a century later.

Clive was born into a country that was already the most politically sophisticated in Europe; which was among the most effective militarily; and whose economy was beginning to take off. Culturally and even perhaps economically India's inferior, Britain was politically and constitutionally several centuries more advanced. Little more than two decades before Clive was born, Britain attained dynastic stability under a family whose direct descendants are still sitting on the throne today. Under the constitutional settlement the power of the monarch was subordinated not to a handful of powerful nobles, but to a mixture of aristocracy, country gentry and middle-class merchants and professionals. Just ten years before Clive's birth and twenty years afterwards there occurred the last armed challenges to an edifice that has now stood the test of three centuries.

Britain in 1725 was a country at constitutional peace with itself for the first time in its history. More: it was a culture teeming with opportunity, change and innovation. The eighteenth century has been viewed as a kind of decadent, languid interlude between the civil wars and revolutions of the seventeenth century and the industrialisation and modernisation of the Victorian era. This is entirely wrong: every major social change usually ascribed to the nineteenth century in fact had its origins in the eighteenth; and they began because of a unique coincidence of social, economic, intellectual and artistic development that made the century a joy for many to live in.

Even beneath the surface of the continent's apparently static absolute monarchies, change was stirring: it was the failure of those monarchies to adapt that brought about their downfall. In British politics the essential changes had already taken place in the seventeenth century that provided the stable foundations for a much more far-reaching transformation of society.

It was a good time, too, to live in because at least until the last decade of the century the darker aspects of industrialisation were not to blight the land or its people. On the whole, living standards for the poor were to rise steadily from a low base throughout the century. Only in the nineteenth century did conditions start to deteriorate once more under the impact of rapid population growth and breakneck industrialisation.

Gentility, the rule of law, domestic peace, unprecedented prosperity, social change without massive upheaval, a sense of *noblesse oblige*, vigorous political, intellectual and artistic life largely uninhibited by state intimidation or the inanities of mass culture a century later – all these were to combine to make the period Clive grew up in one of the most attractive of social environments, before or since. England was prosperous, and at peace. While monarchy and aristocracy presided, the country was in fact governed by the middle classes. The Clives were deeply representative of the higher reaches of these. What this held out for the boy was the prospect of a life of peace, independence and comfort – though not luxury – and opportunity.

When Clive was less than two years old, George II, amiable, shrewd, German-speaking and more concerned with the fate of Hanover than that of England, came to the throne and embodied the new political continuity by retaining, instead of, as was customary, dismissing, his father's prime minister, Sir Robert Walpole, a skilful, manipulative and corrupt provincial politician whose chief goal was to entrench the dynasty and who had himself emerged from the ranks of the country gentry to supplant the Whig grandees of the age before him.

Under Walpole's skilful stewardship, the king was a figurehead.

George II spent long periods in Hanover and was treated with open contempt in the gutter press. His sexual habits and temper were mocked. In the winter of 1736, when he nearly died in a storm travelling from Hanover to London, no one seemed to care. The British were committed to the Protestant succession, not to the king himself.

Walpole's chief opponent, the brilliant Lord Bolingbroke, was hopelessly outmanoeuvred. Only in 1742, the very year that the 17-year-old Clive set sail for India, was Walpole deposed in the wake of a general election result which was seen as censuring him for his conduct of the war with Spain. A prime minister had for the first time been held accountable to his middle-class electorate. The bourgeois-mannered king and his bourgeois-born minister ruled a country where political power was for the first time decisively in the hands of the middle classes.

No class was more socially conscious, as the literature of the time, which reached its apogee in Jane Austen, was to show. The historian Paul Langford writes:

> The stratification of the middle class was almost infinite, corresponding as it did to the innumerable gradations of income and snobbery on which contemporary analysts frequently commented. But this was true of all classes. The acrimony invested in trivial quarrels between different ranks of the peerage, for instance in the periodic disputes as to the precise status of Irish peers in England, matched any of the petty social wars which social satirists recorded among the nouveaux riches. It may also be doubted whether any class had a stronger sense of its own importance than the respectable artisans and small farmers who dreaded nothing more than descent into the ranks of the truly poor.

The dominance of the middle class was undeniable: compared to an aristocracy of around 2,000 families, there were about 40,000 upper-middle-class families earning more than £200 a year (£40,000 at today's values), about 85,000 in the middle earning more than £80 a year (£16,000) and 155,000 lower-middle-class families earning some £50 a year (£10,000). Beneath them were 425,000 families who earned more than £25 a year (£5,000). Below that were some 72,000 families on the lowest incomes, although rarely at starvation levels. The Clives were comfortable members of the upper middle class.

The career alternatives, for a boy of limited academic calibre, seemed to be a job with one of the merchant houses of London or – far more romantic – one with the East India Company overseas. The Company was by that stage a major power in the city. It alone accounted for around a fifth of Britain's overseas trade and controlled the three most prosperous English settlements in the globe – Bombay, on the west coast of India, and Calcutta and Madras on the east. It occupied a position of responsibility and closeness to government second only to that of the Bank of England. The yearly value of calico, chintz hangings and bedspreads, silks, china and tea imported by the company averaged £1 million. In 1744 the Company even lent the government a similar sum.

Richard Clive knew one of the directors, an exalted connection; and at the age of 17, the tough, unruly wide boy of Market Drayton had the humbling experience of attending an interview at the Company's formidable headquarters in Leadenhall Street, where he passed muster as a 'writer' – a clerk, to be sent to Madras. The appointment was in fact highly prestigious, in one of Britain's most powerful commercial organisations, however lowly the actual first foot on the ladder.

Emerging from his successful interview into the bustling, cramped streets of what was essentially still a medieval city, Clive felt a surge of youthful exuberance and anticipation. He strolled through the labyrinthine passages, dodging the livestock destined for the city slaughterhouses and the cattle markets, negotiating the cracked and potholed paving stones, reeling from the stench of sewage and rubbish that oozed down a channel in the middle of the road, avoiding the water cascading from the spouts of the gutters above and ducking under the dangerous street and house signs that jutted out from the side.

Clive was on the threshold not just of the great adventure of adulthood but of a lengthy overseas journey: soon he would be away from the tranquillity of a Shropshire market town, the disciplinary drudgery of Merchant Taylors', even the tumult of London to a life several thousand miles away that he could only imagine, in a land that boasted a civilisation of great antiquity, wealth and barbarism.

Three months later, Clive said goodbye to his gruff, self-possessed father, doting mother and clutch of younger sisters, who, such were mortality rates overseas, feared they might never see him again, and left for London to embark on the great adventure of his life. How great no one could possibly have foreseen. The tall, thin young man, with his plain clothes, anxious yet determined expression, dark heavy brow, large nose, sensitive and determined mouth and piercing but vulnerable and intelligent eyes climbed from East India Dock aboard the *Winchester*, one of the biggest and most modern ships of the Company, a 500-tonner that seemed capable of withstanding the worst the oceans could inflict.

Clive's mood was a mixture of youthful defiance, pugnacity, apprehension and pride at having joined the world of men in such an adventurous and important fashion. As a writer, however young, he was one of the Company's anointed, treated with respect by the crew, expected to do no work aboard. The thrill of being aboard such a splendidly streamlined barque, with its mighty sails billowing above, at the head of a small convoy as it progressed down the Channel, invigorated a soul long repressed by the smallness of Market Drayton.

The voyage was due to last six months; yet youth, enthusiasm and the spirit of adventure kept at bay the bitter cold on deck at the beginning of the voyage, the stench of his cramped quarters below deck, the tedium of life aboard. The sea, while often choppy, was rarely heavy and, after the initial thrill of passing from the Thames into the Channel and from there into the Atlantic, hardly alarmed someone of Robert's restless temperament.

A ship of the times was a tiny, enclosed microcosm of the English social structure – the ship's officers and senior Company officials enjoying an idle if restricted passage, the junior officials like Clive socialising among themselves with little to do, the crew and functionaries below them, each in their watertight social containers, exchanging only orders, formalities and pleasantries.

Clive – aloof, shy, prickly, energetic – was unpopular among his contemporaries and spent much of his time alone; his few friends among the new clerks had gone aboard another ship. The food was poor, while delicacies and drink were expensive to someone of Clive's meagre resources. Life on board quickly settled into a monotony as routine as the rise and fall of the Atlantic swell.

The ship passed the tip of Brittany and crossed the choppier expanse of the Bay of Biscay, sighting the northern tip of Spain and the Portuguese coast. Finally, the west coast of Africa was sighted, which the vessel clung to like a limpet. As the climate grew steadily hotter Clive preferred to spend his time, and even to sleep, on deck rather than in his cramped and foetid quarters below. As time passed, frustration gave way to resignation. He was dreamy and distantly detached much of the time, looking out to sea or studying the few books he had brought on his future trade. Clive could relax and even become jovial after a few drinks in the evening. He disliked the captain, Gabriel Seward, a loud-mouthed, grasping man.

Off the westernmost tip of Africa, in increasingly stifling heat, the *Winchester* prepared to zig the Atlantic to the easternmost tip of Brazil, where it would pick up the trade winds that would zag it across down under the rump of Africa, the Cape of Good Hope. The buoyant security of the great East Indiaman had given Clive not a moment of apprehension since leaving London. Now the ship bucked and groaned in heavier seas near the Cape Verde Islands. As he looked towards the protuberances on the skyline, the last land before the deep ocean crossing, shouts suddenly reverberated around him.

One of the half-dozen ships accompanying the *Winchester* was in difficulties. It appeared to have stopped dead in the open sea. Huge waves broke over it. It had run aground on a hidden reef. The wind was strong and attempts by the *Winchester* and other ships to veer closer to her – while keeping clear of the murderous rock – proved hopeless; they were driven away, and the small schooner went down with all hands.

A fortnight later, as the seas calmed and the climate grew suffocatingly hot, the *Winchester* and its escort vessels crossed the Equator. After many days without sight of land, Clive had his first glimpse of a new continent – South America.

Jubilation was short-lived. After a day or two gazing at the flat, sandy beaches and dense foliage of the level land beyond, where the steamy and exotic smell of damp vegetation blew across to the *Winchester* at night and the moist-laden air left Clive in a continual bathe of sweat, the soothing rise and fall of the vessel suddenly ceased with a juddering crunch as it made contact with sand or rock.

Initial alarm, after witnessing the fate of the *Winchester*'s sister ship near the Cape Verde Islands, subsided quickly: the day was a fine one, the sea not too heavy, the ship plainly not floundering. It had run aground, under incompetent navigation. Boats were making their way from shore. Those aboard, however, had panicked, and all male hands joined in throwing off anything heavy in an effort to float the ship before the pounding of the sea began to break it up. Many of Clive's own belongings were thrown off.

He was taken safely off in one of the boats; and thus he landed for the first time on a strange continent: Brazil, a province of Portugal, where the ship's company was housed uncomfortably for a few days. After the damage had been inspected in calmer waters, a few minimal repairs made and water pumped out of the hull, Captain Seward decided the ship could be floated off. Clive and the others returned aboard.

Frustration followed; the *Winchester* could certainly not proceed without major repairs, and the weather had turned bad – too severe to try and reach the safety of the nearby port of Pernambuco. The ship was well anchored, far enough from land to prevent it being driven ashore, but close enough to give it a good chance of rescue in the event of another disaster.

Clive at first had been both alarmed and enthused by the adventure. But as the days turned into weeks the severity of the travellers' predicament became apparent. They were at the mercy of the often rough, sometimes stormy, seas, unable to move, secured only by anchors as they were buffeted. Frustration battled with fear as the boat bucked, was swept by torrential rains and hit by violent electrical storms, all in a tropical humidity that left them drenched day after day.

The weeks stretched into months, and still the ship could not move. The teenager of no importance and little patience could only fret along with the others until one day, as he gazed out to sea from the poop in a particularly violent squall, the ship suddenly rolled violently, and he was toppled overboard. Captain Seward, standing nearby, immediately grabbed a bucket that had been tied to a rope on deck. Soaked, dragged down by water-laden clothing, struggling to stay afloat in huge waves before being dragged away from the ship's side, Clive seized the bucket and was hauled back, losing his hat, wig and shoes in the swell.

After that, Clive's dislike of Seward, who had saved the youth's life, vanished, in spite of the latter's poor seamanship and grasping nature. Clive was to become a grateful debtor. It was the first of his many brushes with death.

The monotony and occasional alarm of the enforced wait continued for four months altogether. Only in September did the seas calm enough for the *Winchester* to raise anchor and make for Pernambuco, accompanied by a hearty cheer from the ship's company. The houses crowded along the undulations of the shoreline beckoned to Clive and his companions.

They had spent six months now on board, the last four under gruesomely stressful and trying conditions, the equivalent of being marooned – except constantly buffeted by storms, rough seas and high winds. They were still less than a third of the way to India. For weeks, they had lived with boredom and the fear that their ship might be lost. Now at last they would have a respite ashore, and could soon proceed on their voyage.

Pernambuco was a major port, a colourful maze of dazzlingly tiled colonial buildings arranged along narrow cobbled streets in the Portuguese fashion. In place of the order of England was the disorder, ease and exoticism of the tropics. Pernambuco's inhabitants had different shades of dark skin, only the tiny élite of the port being white, the rest a mixture ranging from mulatto to brown to black. It was a bustling, thriving centre of commerce, its usual vigour rendered listless at midday by the intense heat, its life awoken by the cool of equatorial early dusk at around 6 p.m. all year round when the beat and bustle of music and trade would resume.

To a young man just turned 18, the first taste of a tropical lifestyle seemed racy and exciting after the frozen and orderly structure of society in eighteenth-century England. The Portuguese colony was different even from a British colony: more relaxed, extraordinarily free in matters of sex, the Portuguese being largely unconcerned about intermarrying with the local Indian population or even with the imported black slave community.

Clive was to become more accustomed to it than he expected. It took a further five months for the *Winchester* to become seaworthy again, and it was not to put to sea again until February. Berthed aboard ship in the port, Clive had the freedom of the town and would wander to its perimeters, where baked beaches and azure seas stretched as far as the eye could see. Behind the town lay a great expanse of scrub and arid desert – the sertao.

The climate, while much more humid than he was to experience at Madras, provided his first acclimatisation to the intense heat of his soon-to-be-adopted country. Thus Clive of India's first acquaintance with the tropics was a long spell not in India, but in Brazil, where he learnt bastardised Portuguese; ironically he was never to learn any Indian language.

As a very junior member of the privileged class of writers and a sprig of the English squirearchy, he was occasionally invited to the social events of the local aristocracy, more relaxed than those of their Indian counterparts. He may have been introduced to some of the young ladies of local society – although Clive was so awkward at this stage that it is hard to believe any conversation would have got far.

Otherwise he had time on his hands, and we know that he spent all of his money, some presumably on clothing to replace what he had lost in the near-disaster at sea – he was always extravagant and fastidious in matters of dress – and some on the drink he had already become fond of in the small taverns of the port. It seems probable that he was first exposed to sexual temptation here: the mixed-race girls of eastern Brazil were famous for their beauty, and the port notorious for its easy morality. To an awkward teenager accustomed to the restricted life of the country gentry in eighteenth-century England, the laxity of local morals came as a shock.

He had soon exhausted the £54 he had been given for the journey to India – which had already taken twice as long as expected. He resorted to borrowing from his grasping life-saver, Captain Seward, accustomed to performing such a role for his passengers, with the promise that Clive's father would redeem the debt. Stiff and awkward with his fellow travellers, and one of the youngest among them, he got on well enough with the local people to converse with them, which was to stand him in good stead among the sizeable Portuguese Indian community, many of whom were later to soldier for him.

At last, in February, the ship sailed again: the bronzed young man, his first experience of tropical life behind him, was already very different from the gawky youth that had set out from London a year before. For five weeks, the *Winchester* sped before favourable trade winds across the inhospitable emptiness of the South Atlantic, the climate growing mercifully cooler and more temperate. As it approached the African continent a ferocious gale, worse than any Clive had yet endured, struck. Hurricane-force winds battered the ship, which bounced helplessly yet buoyantly about in giant seas. When the storm passed, serious damage had been done to the rigging and sails, and the *Winchester* was forced to make another unscheduled stop – at Cape Town.

It took eleven days to repair the damage. The little Dutch settlement was quite different to Pernambuco: to Clive it resembled a summery version of Manchester set against the dramatic backdrop of Table Mountain. It was a place of orderliness, neat and tidy straight streets, pleasant gardens and social order and preference. The rebellious teenager's only anxiety in this little corner of Calvinist Holland was his growing indebtedness.

The ship left to cross the reputedly more dangerous Indian Ocean, with its sudden squalls, rocks and pirates, on the last leg of the long journey. But the trip proved unexpectedly uneventful. On 1 June, the surly youth, thoroughly bored and weary of life on board, saw the continent that was to change his life – and he its destiny.

CHAPTER 3

Coromandel

T hey arrived off the Coromandel Coast in late afternoon. From the ship Clive could see that the land extended flat in both directions as far as the eye could see: a shimmer of heat haze lay over the sand. They reached Madras Harbour in darkness and Clive watched the lights of the colonial settlement from the deck of the *Winchester* with a mixture of intense excitement and apprehension. He was a long, long way from home. A yearning for the familiar hearth of Styche Hall, for his peppery father, loving mother and doting, quarrelsome sisters was later to overwhelm him, as his letters testify. He would not see them again for years, if ever.

Ahead lay the unknown, his destiny; he knew nothing of how to survive on this vast continent. He had never taken advice in his life; now he would have to from those with experience of India if he was to survive and prosper. There was the glittering prospect of making his fortune. There was the possibility of death by disease. In a confusion of emotions he went below.

Waking and dressing at dawn, he reached the side of the ship in time to hear the guns of Madras boom their welcome. Before him stretched a flotilla of small ships with varying sizes of hulls, masts and sails – clippers, dhows, bulky East Indiamen, tiny fishing boats bobbing at anchor like a species of exotic insect. The beach was one of the longest and finest in India. Dominating the shoreline was the 500-yard-long low wall of a magnificent fort, nonchalantly stretched out, its line of battlements running from the buttressed towers at the corners. A single sea gate was visible.

Even by the architectural standards of the time it was an unusually elegant specimen: within, the tops of other fine buildings could be seen, including the steeple of St Mary's Church, the ornate, impressive bulk of the Company's main warehouse and the rococo splendour of the governor's palace. To the right of this dazzling array of white buildings lay a sprawl of squalid, jumbled, colourful housing and streets peopled, it seemed, by a mass of humanity: the 'black', or Indian, town.

To the left were the pretty, decaying remains of the old Portuguese settlement. Flat-bottomed, coconut-fibred boats took Clive and the new arrivals ashore. He was carried the last few yards on the back of an Indian. He was immediately surrounded by a crowd at the sea gate of Fort St George. The smell was indescribable: a mixture of excrement, curry, spices and humanity, the odour had an almost physical presence.

As he strove to regain his dignity in the throng and made his way through the gate, he had a real sense of entering an enclave of Little England. Huddled together within the walls were the offices and warehouses of the Company, the barracks for its troops, the two churches (St Mary's and the baroque Portuguese Catholic church) and a host of merchant houses. To accommodate the climate, most of the buildings were large and airy, with columns and shutters.

Shrugging off the small army of Indians volunteering to be his *dubash* – valet – he was welcomed along with the other new arrivals by Company officials and taken to his new quarters at the hostel: a couple of rooms, which were reasonably light with high ceilings because of the climate. They were dirty and somewhat Spartan, but adequate for an 18-year-old. He slept on board ship until his rooms were cleaned and whitewashed.

The Company's welcome was warm, if shortlived. He and the new arrivals were taken around the settlement and then shown outside the fort to experience the crowded hubbub of the 'black town' and admire the villas or 'garden houses' of the governor and the wealthier Company traders. He glanced over the near-desert beyond, which extended, seemingly without limits, to the horizon.

He was taken to the offices and shown the desk he would work at. The approach of his new superiors was businesslike, friendly, not overwhelming. His supervisor seemed amiable enough, if loud and a little too bossy for Clive's taste. He was now in the real world, where he would have to earn his living, not enjoying the enforced indolence of life on board the *Winchester*, or the sheltered rebelliousness of his youth. When the surly adolescent arrived in the hostel, and the exuberance of having escaped from the confines of the ship slowly ebbed away, the first of the black depressions he was to experience throughout his life began to engulf him.

Clive was at first miserably unhappy at Fort St George. After the initial relief of landing and discovering the pleasures of a new world, the reality of deep loneliness and drudgery sunk in. Over in the 'black town' there was bustling life amid all the smells, joss-sticks and putrefaction. Here in Fort St George, there was the orderliness of a tiny expatriate community where everyone knew everyone, there was one employer and an almost militaristic structure of social hierarchy. Fort St George resembled nothing so much as a minor public school, the kind of existence Clive had rebelled against as a boy – but rebellion here would ruin his career.

His job was tedious in the extreme. Clad only in shirt, breeches and suncap, he filed figures and added them, inspected cloth, prepared ledgers, checked inventories, made orders and argued with Indian suppliers about quality and quantity. He was a glorified apprentice shopkeeper. He deeply disliked his pompous and bossy overseers.

His pay was performance-related: he earned only £5 a year, but his lodgings were free and he had an allowance of about £3 which paid for his candles, three servants and lodgings. In terms of modern purchasing power in India, he had living expenses of around £600 a year and a salary of some £1,000 a year. The rest had to be earned from his work, in which he was privileged above local merchants.

The conditions took a great deal of acclimatisation. His lodgings were plagued with mosquitoes, giant ants and constant coatings of dust from periodic dust storms. He was often bathed in sweat from the heat, particularly if there was any urgent hurrying to and from office to warehouse. The mixture of English and Indian food took time to get used to.

His three servants provided some consolation. Fortunately the heat was dry, unlike the suffocatingly humid atmosphere he was to experience in Bengal, but its intensity was oppressive nonetheless. In his boredom he may have relished the terrifying typhoons that periodically ravaged the enclave.

He wrote miserably to his cousin: 'I have not enjoyed one happy day since I left my native country. I am not acquainted with any one family in the place, and have not assurance enough to introduce myself without being asked. If the state I am now in will admit of any happiness it must be when I am writing to my friends. Letters were surely first invented for the comfort of such solitary wretches as myself.'

Pathetically he pleaded, 'If there is any such thing which may properly be called happiness here below, I am persuaded it is in the union of two friends who each love each other without the least guile or deceit, who are united by a real inclination, and satisfied with each other's merits . . . when you write me, I beg it may be carelessly and without study, for I had much rather read the dictates of the heart than of the understanding.'

Just three months after he arrived he wrote dutifully to his father, 'I can assure you my stay in this place is in every respect pleasant, and as satisfactory to me, as it is blessed with the hopes (if it please God to preserve my life) of being able to provide for myself and also of being of service to my relations.'

Yet Clive's desperation at discovering that all his dreams of excitement and prosperity in India amounted to no more than finding himself at the bottom rung of a long and very English ladder eventually showed through even to Richard Clive. A few months later his son wrote: 'The world seems to be vastly debased of late and interest carries it entirely before merit, especially in this service, though I should think myself very undeserving of any favour were I only to build my foundation on the strength of the former.'

Needing his father's financial support – debts were frowned upon by the Company – he became ingratiating. 'I think myself not only very happy, but infinitely obliged to you for my education, and as it has rendered me in a fair way of improving my talent, I flatter myself with the hopes of enlarging tenfold. I shall always make it my duty to behave truly and deserving of your confidence and esteem and am willing to give up all pretensions to your favour in case I don't behave with that sobriety and diligence which is expected.'

He begged his father for money, favours and a transfer to Bengal, where the opportunities were reported to be much greater. The once insolent teenager waxed positively prissy in seeking to justify his requests for drink: 'I hope you'll be so kind as not to take exception

26

at the wine as there are no other sort of drinkables here but that, and punch, and as I shall always drink it with water, intend to make it serve me a whole year.'

To his devoted Uncle Bay he was more honest: 'The pleasant and delightful days which I have spent with my kind relations and friends in Lancashire, refreshed and entertains my mind with very agreeable ideas. I must confess at intervals when I think of my dear native England it affects me in a very particular manner, however knowing it to be for my own welfare rest content and patient, wishing the views for which my father sent me here may in all respects be fully accomplished.'

Surprisingly, for one who was an obvious and rebellious leader of boys, and soon to be so of men – he was later to enjoy an enormous circle of friends – he seems to have shunned company in India at first. Tall, gangling and shy, he was not at first close to the three fellow writers he knew from England – his cousin, William King, John Pybus and John Walsh – the latter the natural leader of the pack, self-confident and well-off with a considerable fortune of some £2,000 after the death of his parents. Walsh knew India well, having been brought up in Madras. Clive may have resented Walsh's natural leadership at this early stage.

Clive felt himself to be in a community of suffocating incestuousness, comprising only 400 people. He was well aware that his survival and promotion depended on self-discipline; for the first time in his life he was trapped into conventionality and he hated it. Resentful and sometimes insolent to his superiors, he was forced to apologise on one occasion for his rudeness to the secretary of Fort St George. The rigidity of life there was underlined by the fact that he, like all writers, had to attend church twice a day.

There were just three consolations. The first was typical of a young writer confined to the village of Fort St George: acquiring the local habits. Clive took up chewing betel-nut and smoking hookah. Second, he took up drinking wine in a serious way; particularly outside the confines of the fort, there were many drinking parlours where it was acceptable to while away one's spare time over a bottle of wine.

However, any closer association with the locals would have been frowned upon. There was a rigid distinction between the two communities; in particular, there is no evidence at this stage of his frequenting the brothels of the 'black town', whatever his later activities. For a young clerk in his social position that would almost certainly have been unacceptable to the stodgy hierarchy of the settlement.

His third consolation was the most unlikely of all. His father had furnished him with an introduction to the Governor of Madras – who, however, had already left before Clive arrived after his interminable journey. The new governor, Nicholas Morse, a pleasant if ineffectual man, nevertheless invited Clive to dinner on his arrival – a considerable boost to his status – and offered him access to the huge library at Government House.

The previously unacademic Clive passed many hours of his free time reading on a huge variety of subjects. During those two years, he acquired a genuine breadth of scholarship that he was to prove much too busy to pursue in later life. His education was being completed in the rather Spartan finishing school of Fort St George.

The surly rebel without a cause, the undisciplined, unlettered youth of Market Drayton, improbably, was becoming a bookish intellectual under the crushing pressure of expatriate, small-town boredom. Prickly, sensitive, intellectually inquisitive, dreamy, ambitious – Clive was unrecognisable from the young thug of the past.

Often Clive would wander by himself to the outskirts of the settlement, to gaze at the seemingly endless expanse of the Choultry Plain and the arid, near-desert Carnatic beyond. He tried to come to terms with what lay beyond, with the vastness of the subcontinent. Madras was just a pimple upon its cheek. The British had barely scratched the surface of India.

His contact with the Indians, the respect they showed all Europeans, made him wonder whether there were much greater opportunities at hand than were being exploited by the stuffy, unimaginative functionaries of Fort St George. The Indians had been a people oppressed so long, often by outsiders; they were accustomed to subservience. Why not to the English?

He was a dreamer, but he could only dream: he was merely a junior clerk not yet out of his teens. As the great fireball of the sun plummeted with perceptible speed from the dark blue sky to the level land horizon, drawing down the curtain of darkness, he would turn disconsolately away: he knew so frustratingly little about the lands and people out there.

A life of unrelieved tedium as a minor merchant in India, slowly rising to greater authority and the power to tell young clerks what to do in turn, lay ahead, Clive supposed. According to Malcolm, the best informed if most pedantic of his biographers, writing fifty years after the event, he retired to his quarters one night, took out a pistol, and held it to his head; there was only a click. He repeated the attempt, with the same result. 'I am reserved for something!' he is said to have exclaimed. His explosive, unconventional energy and nature had been shut up in a bottle, and he preferred self-destruction to continued existence as one of the lowliest cogs in a genteel, confined village at the back of beyond.

Clive's modern biographer, Mark Bence-Jones, doubts this story; yet it is hard to believe that Clive, from whom it must have come, made it up, prone though he was to exaggeration sometimes. Suicide was frowned upon at the time much more than today, even regarded as cowardly. The story hardly reflects well upon a great leader of men. Almost certainly the incident is a polished version of something that really occurred.

Robert Clive endured this imprisonment of his restless nature for just two years; then his spirit was freed by violent action of a kind that, for the complacent burghers of Fort St George, threatened disaster. It was little consolation that the fateful turn of events that was to result in the razing of the comfortable little English settlement and its placid, self-aggrandising way of life, transforming Clive into a leader of men, was largely the English traders' fault.

The English – and indeed the European – presence in India had begun as an exclusively commercial one. The four English enclaves – Bombay on the west coast, Fort St George (Madras) and Fort St David on the south-east coast, and Fort William (Calcutta) in the north – were just that. Although possessed of garrisons, their main raison d'être was as entrepots for the European markets. The East India Company had been founded in 1599, primarily to trade in spices and undermine the Portuguese monopoly.

Over the next hundred years, however, the Portuguese were gradually beaten back by the Dutch, who also forced the English out of Indonesia and back to India, where they had to do battle with the Portuguese again. The first real toehold was established when the British promised to protect the then Mogul Emperor from attacks by Portuguese warships in exchange for trading enclaves. Sir Thomas Roe, the father of this early stage of British intervention in India, argued that 'if you will profit, seek it . . . in quiet trade; for without controversy it is an error to affect garrisons and land wars in India'.

In 1641 Fort St George was founded; in 1674 Bombay followed; and in Bengal the entrepôts at Hugli and Kasimbazar were established – although Calcutta, with its deep-water port next to tropical swampland, was soon to replace the first. In 1686 the English, with 600 men and 10 ships, declared war on the Mogul Empire and were forced out of Bengal. Only in 1690 were they allowed to return, chastened, in a purely trading role. However, within their enclaves, they soon exercised virtually all administrative powers, collected taxes and even administered justice.

In the late seventeenth century, the French set up their own small trading centres, the biggest being in Bengal at Chandernagore, about 16 miles from Calcutta up the Hugli river, and at Pondicherry, a town some three-quarters of the way between the British Fort St George and Fort St David on the Coromandel Coast. The French presence was small, however, and when war broke out between France and Holland, the latter captured Pondicherry and held on to it for six years. The British were dismissive of French efforts.

But in 1720 the French government suddenly decided to take over the French East India Company, increase its resources and effectively turn it into an instrument of national colonial expansion. The French company became in effect a branch of the state, while the British one remained primarily a commercial enterprise. The French now began to engage in serious commercial rivalry with the British.

When war broke out over the Austrian succession in Europe between Britain and France in 1744, the year Clive arrived in India, the French attempted to maintain their neutrality, fearing that they were militarily inferior. The British East India Company, however, saw a chance to make inroads into the lucrative French trade in saltpetre, indigo, silks, cotton and spices which had made such a dent in their own commerce. The East India Company asked the British government to send out a fleet to attack the French.

In 1745 this reached the Coromandel Coast and attacked a number of French ships, some belonging to the Governor of

Pondicherry, Joseph-François Dupleix, who lost a large part of his personal fortune. Incensed but powerless, Dupleix called on his government to send its own fleet; this eventually arrived under the command of Admiral Bernard La Bourdonnais and engaged the British fleet in July 1746.

The able and adventurous British naval commander, Commodore Barnett, had died a few months before. Poorly led, the British ships broke away from an indecisive battle with the French and made for repairs in Ceylon; La Bourdonnais's ships, which had suffered much worse damage, took advantage of the respite to flee for Pondicherry for repairs. Two months later the French fleet sailed out again to engage the British. Astonishingly, the English fleet chose not to fight and fled for Bengal. Dupleix now had his chance of revenge.

But first it was necessary to indulge in a little local politics. Both the French and British settlements were nominally subject to the local ruler, the Nawab of the Carnatic, even though they effectively administered their own territories. In order to prepare the way for their attack on Madras, the French promised that the enclave would be turned over to the Nawab when it was seized. The Nawab acquiesced in this, although he was nominally at peace with the British and mistrustful of the French. La Bourdonnais was then ordered to proceed by the ebullient French governor, who had heard false reports of the success of the French-backed Jacobite uprising in England, which had apparently deposed the English king.

Clive, like any inhabitant of Fort St George, was aware of the first indecisive naval engagement; when the British fleet sailed away, anxiety turned to panic in the 'village' of Fort St George. Nicholas Morse, the well-meaning governor, knew full well how exposed he was. Commodore Barnett, before his death, had written of the fort's defences, 'The works seem rather built by chance than design; the bastions are placed contrary to all the rules . . . if I was governor, I should never sleep soundly in a French war if there were 500 Europeans in Pondicherry.' The garrison consisted of some 300 men, about half of them 'Europeans' and half Indians, none with any experience of fighting.

On 7 September 1746, Clive awoke to find Fort St George in a state of turmoil. Out to sea, several French ships could be seen; troops were being landed. The women and children of the settlement were rushed to safety and civilians to positions of shelter. Clive, like the other young clerks, took up a vantage point from which to watch events. Within hours, he first heard the sound that was to become a constant companion through the rest of his life: the boom of cannon. He watched the chaos of the fort, the small and ragged garrison manning their positions, their striking red uniforms in place, the governor and senior Company officials watching anxiously.

The first explosions had no apparent effect, and by nightfall the garrison had been lulled into a sense of false security. It seemed the threat was more apparent than real. Before turning in, Clive and his friends gazed out on the twinkling lights of the French fleet at sea, and the glittering fires of the French encampment on shore, cursing roundly the cowardice of the fleet that had left Madras to its fate but confident that the assault would be seen off.

At dawn the young writers were woken again by the sound of cannon. This time sudden explosions just off the fort and within the walls showed that the gunners had found their range. Fire and destruction, although limited, induced panic among the inhabitants of Fort St George. The offer of Clive, like all his able-bodied companions, to help was gratefully accepted. As the day wore on, men on the battlements, before Clive's eyes, were injured and killed. He saw them borne away on stretchers as he helped to ferry ammunition to the defenders.

A total of four Indian and two English soldiers were killed that day, and several more wounded. The garrison seemed incapable of responding to this fire from two sides – land and sea. It had no plan, beyond firing back ineffectually. Its commander was an old man. As the relentless, if hardly overwhelming, barrage went on, the soldiers began to abandon their stations and disobey orders.

A French shell burst open one of the warehouses containing liquor. The terrified, insubordinate soldiers, always openly despised by their civilian counterparts in times of peace, seized the supplies and began to drink. Clive watched contemptuously with his friends as drunken soldiers roamed the small town shouting and laughing and the civilians sheltered indoors.

Alcohol and fear had taken over, and the women and children were at risk; the garrison was more of a threat than the French. The pompous, slow pace of this stodgy bourgeois settlement had been shattered in an instant, and a passionate 20-year-old could not but wonder at the shambles wrought by his superiors, coldly gazing upon the worst that can befall any army: indiscipline among the troops.

The following day, desperate to put an end to the breakdown in order among his own men, Governor Morse sued for peace and secured astonishingly favourable terms for the British. The French would occupy the fort and take over the Company's stores while the English would remain 'on parole' – that is to say, free men. For a ransom still to be agreed, the British would be handed back the town. It was to be a punitive expedition, but no more.

That would not have been apparent to Clive and the other apprentices: there was nothing more humiliating to these burning, angry young men than the disintegration in a single day of British resistance to the hated French, and the handover of their hard-won commercial stores and gains.

On 10 September Clive watched as the blue-tunicked French entered the gates of the citadel, La Bourdonnais at their head, disarming the garrison brusquely and beginning to remove the stores, while treating the civilians with tolerable civility. The women and children were now bold enough to come out of their lodgings. Distraught East India Company officials watched in horror as their possessions were confiscated. The British flag was lowered and the French raised high.

Proud and passionate, Clive felt the humiliation of his country bitterly; he had no role, and there was nothing he could do; he was now unemployed and subject to the swagger of foreign domination. For several days Clive and his followers hung about, drinking idly, encountering stray French soldiers, being barked at by them, longing to pick a fight but too wise to try.

Meanwhile a furious row had broken out between the French commanders. Dupleix was angry that La Bourdonnais had conceded such favourable terms; the former's objective was nothing less than the permanent French annexation of Madras. La Bourdonnais insisted he would not go back on his word to the English and, with his 1,200 French soldiers and formidable firepower, his view for the time being prevailed – although it seemed at one stage that Dupleix was planning to attack Fort St George to wrest it from his fellow countryman. The English could only watch in helpless horror as their once cherished citadel threatened to become a battleground between warring French factions.

In mid-October, after Madras had been occupied for a month, Clive awoke to a new sound: the ferocious, relentless drumming of tropical rain. The skies above were overcast and laden. He gloried for a moment in the refreshing luxury of the downpour, so welcome after the heat and dust of the searing summer. Later that day, with the rain, came the wind too, also mercifully cooling. Then followed the shout from John Walsh, the effective leader of the small group of writers in the fort. 'The French ships! They're leaving by God!'

Clive and his friends rushed to the roof of the hostel and observed the vessels weigh anchor and begin to move away from the coast, remaining within sight of the land. The watchers were transfixed by the spectacle. Over the next few hours the wind grew steadily stronger, and slowly transformed itself into a violent gale. Huge waves crashed up the beach and battered the very walls of the fort. The surf foamed out to sea, while dense sheets of rain concealed the distant craft bucking helplessly about in the distance.

As Walsh, Clive and their friends celebrated on the roof, furious French soldiers below shouted at them to get off, waving their muskets. The writers drank themselves to sleep. The following morning the tempest had passed. The horizon was absolutely clear: there were no French ships to be seen. La Bourdonnais's fleet had been mauled by the storm far more effectively than by any naval engagement, and had gone. Four ships had been sunk, four were dismasted, and another blown nearly to Ceylon. The French naval force on the Coromandel Coast had been cut by a third. If the English could only get reinforcements they would be safe.

But the storm offered little cause for celebration. The French troops in Fort St George remained and, later the same day, their new commander rode in: François Dupleix, labouring under the mixed emotions of being rid of his rival, La Bourdonnais, but also having lost many ships.

Small, vigorous and disdainful, with a dreamy expression that concealed a quick intellect and ability to take decisions, prone to middle-aged spread, Dupleix made a magnificent and haughty sight in his finery on his white horse. The gentlemanly occupation of Fort St George was over.

The inhabitants of the town, including Clive, were brusquely ordered by the French troops into the square. Governor Morse and the senior traders of the town were surrounded by a large armed guard and marched away to be paraded in triumph through the streets of the French capital, Pondicherry, in an effort to impress upon the Indians the crushing of British arms.

The French commanders asked the remaining British for their word that they would not bear arms against the French; if they gave it, they would be expelled from the fort and set free to fend for themselves as best they could. Clive and his headstrong companions flatly refused and were returned to the hostel under French guard.

There were four inseparable companions now: Walsh, always languid and cheerful; John Pybus, quiet and sensible; a more recent arrival at Fort St George, Edmund (Mun) Maskelyne, easygoing, witty, convivial, given to irresponsible japes, intelligent, a cousin of Walsh; and the headstrong, determined Clive himself. They were about to embark on the first serious adventure of their lives.

Once cooped up they immediately set about plotting their escape; all four were determined to fight the French. Observing how lightly they were guarded, by a single sentry who often left his post or dozed, they borrowed Indian clothing from their servants, darkened their faces and put on leggings to make their bare legs appear black. Clive wore the dress of his native servant.

It was unprecedented for Europeans to debase themselves to the level of Indians, and they had little trouble when they took advantage of the sentry's absence in crossing the confused citadel under occupation. As they glanced furtively about they observed the French ordering the Indians to loot Fort St George and pile up wooden furniture in preparation for setting fire to the fort. In the chaos Clive and his companions passed through the main gate with barely a second glance from the soldiers supposedly guarding it. They crossed the bridge in front of the portals.

There, disaster struck. The Indian crowd beyond began to 'jabber in their language' at the party, quickly realising that they were not Indian. Clive and his friends hurriedly pushed through, fearful that a local would seek to ingratiate himself with the French by giving them away. Amid the babble, to which the French soldiers by the gate paid no attention, they slipped away into the darkness. It was night by the time they had put Fort St George behind them. Flames from the burning citadel illuminated the clear night sky behind them.

The final destination of the four friends was Fort St David, the sole remaining British settlement in the Carnatic some 50 miles to the south across hostile country, beyond the French stronghold of Pondicherry. The journey was a long, circuitous one, skirting the French forces. It took all of three days, keeping to the main road when no one was about, hiding in ditches or marching parallel to it when they saw movement along it.

They walked chiefly by night, resting during the heat of the middle of the day. They skirted the main settlements and did not dare to ask for shelter; Pondicherry was given a wide berth. They were exhausted by the time they reached the fertile and wooded country further south. The sentries at Fort St David were incredulous when they challenged these 'natives' and were answered in impeccable English accents.

CHAPTER 4

Dupleix

François Dupleix would not have cast a second glance at the smouldering eyes fixed upon him by the tall, well-built, determined-looking youth that had passed him in the square days before. The French commander, in his mid-forties at the time, at the height of his powers, was a formidable personality and one who believed that his most ambitious dream – establishing himself at the head of a French empire in India – was within his grasp.

Dupleix's personality was as complex as Clive's. A man of considerable education and sophistication, literary and erudite, born of a civil service haute bourgeois background, he was typical of the higher kind of French government servant. He was the son of the director-general of the French East India Company. Studious and scientific as a boy, he had been sent to the east and the Americas at the age of 17, firing his imagination and ambition. By the age of only 23 he was on the governing council of Pondicherry. He was an excellent trader and administrator, if inclined to be a little severe with his men, and had a huge capacity for hard work. As an organiser, particularly in military matters, he was second to none. During this first campaign, the excellent state of French defences was rudely to expose the amateur nature of British preparations for war.

In addition, Dupleix was flexible and practical; every time he suffered a setback, he did not panic, but moved on to an alternative plan, patiently reorganising his forces. An apparently stern and contemptuous man, he was nevertheless fond of partying and fripperies in private life. He was vainglorious to a degree that exceeded even Clive in later life: parties, fireworks and pomp attended his victories. The usual explanation – that such shows of splendour impressed Indian princes – was only half true: Dupleix appears to have had an unusual degree of *folie de grandeur*, and from an early stage harboured the ambition necessary to bolster his pretensions.

He was encouraged in his vision by his wife, Johanna Begum, a remarkable beauty with 'the eyes of a lemur', who had Indian and Portuguese, as well as French, blood. Reputedly free in her relations with men, she was highly intelligent, conspiratorial and worked tirelessly for her husband's interest, feeding his ambitions. At a time when Clive could hardly have imagined he was destined for anything more than life as a trader, Dupleix had conceived the idea of a French empire in India, with him as its viceroy.

He came very close to succeeding and the British, through their lack of preparation and initial incompetence, to being driven out of India. That this did not happen was due to the emergence of a single English figure with a degree of boldness, leadership and guile that exceeded his: Robert Clive.

Dupleix's immediate problem, after securing and burning Fort St George, was not the British outpost at Fort St David, but a large army of some 10,000 men assembled by the Nawab of the Carnatic, Unwar Ud-Din, to press the French to honour their promise to hand over Madras to him. This powerful Indian prince was based at Arcot some 70 miles inland; he was himself a vassal of the formidable Nawab of the Deccan. The decision of his nominal French subjects suddenly to march on his English ones was dangerous and potentially threatening.

Dupleix chose to meet the threat head on, sending 450 of his French forces equipped with two field guns as well as muskets under the command of an able Swiss engineer, Captain Louis Paradis. In two brief engagements, the disciplined French force stood its ground, provoking confusion among the large Indian army with its swords, matchlocks, pistols and pikes. It was the first time a small European army had encountered a large Indian one in battle, and the lesson was not lost on Dupleix.

He now turned his attention to the last pocket of English resistance. He might have been forgiven, after the walkover at Fort St George, for believing Fort St David to be an easy prey. Yet the latter, although smaller, was a tougher proposition: although close to Pondicherry, it had stronger defences, was sited on a rise and was surrounded by an outer perimeter – the 'Bounds Hedge' – of spiky cactuses and other vegetation.

Governor Hinde was a more practical, far-sighted man than Morse at Fort St George; he had laid up provisions for a six-month siege (including wine from Pondicherry) and had hired 2,000 Indians ('sepoys' – after the Persian word) to supplement his small garrison of 200 European soldiers and 100 half-castes. In addition, the Nawab of the Carnatic, smarting from betrayal and defeat by the French, had sent some 2,500 cavalry under the command of his younger son, the formidable Muhammad Ali, to help the British.

On arrival at Fort St David, Clive had been confronted with the choice of continued idleness, a return to his profession as a writer (clerk) or enlistment. A natural fighter, prickly, young and still smarting from the humiliation of witnessing British defeat and enemy occupation, he and his friend Mun Maskelyne enlisted as soldiers – nominally a step downwards for one of the Company's servants. His decision ensured that he would not have to watch again in frustration when the French attacked while incompetents manned the defences.

The next few weeks were spent in rudimentary training, while scouts at the outer edge of the Bounds Hedge, which also protected the 'black town' of Cuddalore and the luxurious villas of the senior Company merchants, kept a watch on French movements; Clive was enthusiastic, determined and unflagging. It was a time of acute anxiety: the French were believed to be much stronger than they actually were, and their main base of Pondicherry was only 12 miles away. The elimination of the British presence in southern India was a real possibility. The garrison seemed set to repeat the fate of Governor Morse, paraded through the streets of Pondicherry in humiliation (although he was treated quite well afterwards). The best that could be expected was that the French would allow their defeated captives to return to Britain. Anxious appeals were made for the British fleet to return from Bengal.

On 9 December, in the comparative cool of the Carnatic winter, the French forces, led by Dupleix, advanced from Pondicherry and within a day had broken the rough outer perimeter, driving the British back from the Bounds Hedge. After dark, Governor Hinde sent a company of Indian soldiers to attack the French camp, but they were driven off.

At around seven the following morning, making short work of the outer defences, the French occupied the governor's villa, the Garden House, just two miles from the fort itself. This was a magnificent two-storey building set in ample grounds, where they decided to bivouac for the night and prepare supper.

Hinde despatched about half his forces in a desperate gamble to launch a joint attack with Muhammad Ali's cavalry. The enemy were taken completely by surprise as the two forces sprung upon them, the Indians led by Muhammad Ali on an elephant. The French fled, leaving most of their belongings. Clive is not believed to have taken part in this attack. This successful sally did much to restore British morale: it showed that they were capable of fighting back after all. Remarkably, the French withdrew to Pondicherry.

The next three months were spent preparing the defence of the fort – although Hinde had cause for anxiety as his provisions ran low. A further worry was that Dupleix had made his peace with the local ruler, the Nawab of the Carnatic, handing to him the over-lordship of Madras for a week, allowing him to fly his flag over the settlement, and showering presents upon him. The British could no longer count on the help of Muhammad Ali.

On 11 March, Paradis, a much more effective field commander than Dupleix, led a large French force forward. This time the British, among them Clive, were ready and met them at the outer perimeter: after bitter exchanges of fire, the British were compelled to fall back that evening. The position, though not desperate, was serious.

After a short night's sleep, Clive awoke the following day to find the garrison in a state of high excitement. Rushing to a vantage point, he joined in the cheering that had broken out below: the sails of the English fleet, which had returned at last from Bengal, could be seen on the horizon. A few hours later, there was renewed cheering: Clive and his fellow soldiers, preparing for a renewed attack, could see the French withdrawing. With the arrival of the fleet, the tables had been turned: the British were now numerically superior to the French.

The young man and his friends were exultant over the next few days, all the more so when he heard that Hinde had written to the Company directors in London: 'Mr Robert Clive, Writer in the Service, being of a Martial Disposition, and having acted as a Volunteer upon our Late Engagement, we have granted him an

Ensign's Commission upon his application for the same.'

Exhilaration soon turned to boredom: the weeks dragged past, then the months. The fleet lacked enough men to launch an attack on Pondicherry, although it deterred any further attack on Fort St David. The stalemate continued until the arrival in July 1748 of Major Stringer Lawrence, a professional military commander at last. A veteran of Culloden, he was a tubby, tough fighter, with a stubborn, irascible, yet benign expression, adored by his men with whom he enjoyed drinking off-duty. He was known affectionately by them as the Old Cock. Of no great intelligence or imagination, he was exactly what he seemed: an experienced, brave and professional soldier.

Fifty years old and of humble origins, also in Shropshire, he seems to have taken a shine to the youthful but higher-born Clive from the first: he immediately set about strengthening the defences of the fort and training the troops. The days of inaction for Clive and Mun Maskelyne were over. Lawrence was too experienced not to realise that they would have to wait for reinforcements before launching any attack on the French.

Nearly eight months later, support arrived at last from England: Admiral Edward Boscawen reached Fort St David with a large flotilla carrying twelve companies of troops, half untrained. The garrison was swollen to 4,000 Europeans and 20,000 Indians. The British were now in a dominant position, with the opportunity not just to reverse their recent humiliation at the hands of the French, but to expel the latter from India.

After so many months of apprehension, the garrison at Fort St David was now exultant. The English could break out of their enforced state of inertia in that cramped enclave and inflict upon the French the drubbing they deserved. Boscawen, confident, prissy, wrong-headed and haughty, made it plain that he would advance immediately; Lawrence pleaded with him in vain to show caution. A couple of days later the British moved forward to engage the French head on.

A small French fort stood between them and Pondicherry. Boscawen ordered his forces to lay siege to it. Day after day this continued, while the tiny French garrison held out doggedly. A senior British officer was killed. Then disaster struck: Lawrence, leading an assault, was captured by a French party of soldiers and taken to Pondicherry. After eleven futile days this tiny obstruction of no strategic significance was taken for the loss of the best British commander on the ground.

Boscawen then spent several days building up the fort's defences before moving on to the main French garrison at Pondicherry. Clive was to write later despairingly:

> How very ignorant we were of the art of war in those days. Some of the engineers were masters of the theory without the practice, and those seemed wanting in resolution. Others there were who understood neither, and yet were possessed of courage sufficient to have gone on with the undertaking if they had known how to go about it. There was scarce an officer who knew whether the engineers were acting right or wrong, till it was too late in the season and we had lost too many men to begin an approach again.

Boscawen, deprived of Lawrence's advice, dug in at a position 'fraught with every disadvantage that could attend a siege': on one side there was marshland, on the other open space, making the British vulnerable to French fire. The English heavy guns could not be brought up for days, while the fleet was kept away from Pondicherry by strong winds.

Dupleix supervised the defence, and is said to have bravely encouraged his men from the ramparts (contrary to the allegation that he was a cowardly leader), while Madame ran her network of scouts reporting on the British position. Enemy fire was accurate and in several sorties from the town, the French inflicted serious injuries. The British cannonades caused some damage but failed to inflict many casualties.

Dupleix's deputy, Paradis, launched a major assault on the British position in October. Clive was holding a trench, in command of one of three forward platoons. The other two broke ranks and fled as the French attacked, while Clive kept his men steady. As an eyewitness described it: 'All the company's troops had an affection for this young man, from observing the alacrity and presence of mind which always accompanied him in danger; his platoon, animated by his exhortation, fired again with new courage and great vivacity upon the enemy.'

The French infantry reached shelter only ten yards from Clive's position, and rained fire down on his men, piercing his hat and coat, but failed to draw blood. Although his men were pinned down, Clive ran back to get ammunition. The French at length withdrew.

As the raiding party pulled back towards Pondicherry, Paradis was fatally shot. This to some extent made up for the loss of Lawrence. But the monsoon broke soon afterwards. Dense rains and fierce winds swept the British position. The fleet was forced to retire. Boscawen raised the siege on 6 October, and the troops marched sodden and dejected back to Fort St David. In Pondicherry, loud cheers could be heard from the battlements. The Te Deum was celebrated and wild parties were held at which Dupleix and Madame regaled their friends with champagne and party games.

The first encounter between the British and French in India had ended with a victory for the French on points: Madras was still under their control while the British with a superior force had failed to dislodge them from Pondicherry. The defence of Fort St George had been a fiasco, the attempt to seize Pondicherry a failure. The British had nothing to be proud about.

In December the news of peace between Britain and France at the Treaty of Aix-la-Chappelle reached India; under this agreement, Madras was to be returned to the British. Lawrence was released, having been treated well by Dupleix, and rejoined the garrison at Fort St David.

The 23-year-old Clive had now begun to make his mark. It was not only Lawrence who held a high opinion of the young man. He had become a forceful personality that others envied and tangled with at their peril. At a game of cards in Fort St David, a notorious bully among the officers there won game after game, transparently cheating. Clive accused him openly, while the others present stayed silent. The officer called him out, there and then.

Clive had the first shot; he missed. The officer, a notoriously good marksman, told him to withdraw the accusation of cheating, and he would be spared. Clive is said to have declared, 'Fire and be damned. I said you cheated, I say so still and I will never pay you.' The officer raised his gun, then lowered it, and his adversary was spared. Clive, much relieved, made no formal complaint against the other.

After the engagement outside Pondicherry another officer, Allen, who had seen him run away from his post to get ammunition, called him a coward behind his back. One day in Fort St David, Clive shouted to him and Allen, as he passed, hit Clive on the arm from behind. Clive turned and hit him on the head with his cane, saying, 'You are too contemptible a coward even for a beating.' Allen then had to apologise in front of the troops – 2,000 men – and resign his commission.

In 1749, Clive took on no less a figure than the chaplain of Fort St David, an embittered reprobate, the Reverend Francis Fordyce, who had the power to create serious trouble for the young officer. In his previous parish, St Helena, he had seduced a planter's daughter and had been compelled to flee her father's anger. In Fort St David, he bitterly criticised the governor and his council, threatening violence upon them. The impressive Governor Hinde had been succeeded by the easygoing, amiable, card-addicted Floyer, who took no action against Fordyce.

After the Pondicherry fiasco, Fordyce heaped contempt on the performance of the forces. Clive was furious. The clergyman, who had already threatened to thrash one member of the council and slit the nose of another, told those emerging from a church service that he would 'break every bone in his [Clive's] body and half a dozen more of them!' Shortly afterwards Clive encountered him in the street and hit him a couple of times with his cane. The enraged – but courageous – Fordyce attacked Clive, and it took three men to separate them.

The churchman decided to complain to the council about Clive's 'violence and riot', and sought to have the matter brought before the Company in England. Before he could, however, he publicly insulted the governor and was dismissed. Clive was exonerated by the council as being 'generally esteemed a very quiet person and no ways guilty of disturbances'.

It was clear from this curious affair that the shy, unhappy, sat-upon youth of Fort St George was no more. Having distinguished himself in fighting he was at the age of only 23 capable of standing up to one of the most senior officials in the status- and hierarchy-obsessed colony. He must have commanded considerable respect in a quiet way.

Life in the settlement was now much more enjoyable than when he had first arrived. He had several friends. He was respected. He enjoyed the esteem of the military commander, Lawrence. He was lodged in a small house at Bandlipollam on hilly ground to the west, which he vastly preferred to the writers' lodgings at Fort St George. This he shared with an extrovert, often drunk, good-looking lieutenant of the marines, John Dalton.

The two of them spent much of their spare time in the brothels of Cuddalore, where they caught gonorrhoea at least twice. More genteely, they attended the endless and pleasant social life of the settlement, dining frequently with the governor and at the homes of other senior officials, of which Mrs Prince, who possessed a huge house and a large retinue of servants, was the most celebrated. There were a number of English girls in town, on the lookout for eligible bachelors like Clive, among them Eliza Walsh, John's sister, who enjoyed being carried about on a palanquin by four servants, with an armed soldier in front and a boy on hand to smooth her petticoats. Life was pleasantly relaxed and agreeable now that the French threat had passed.

With the conclusion of peace between Britain and France the considerable garrison at Fort St David was now unemployed; but Lawrence was not long in finding a suitable case for military intervention. There was no evidence whatsoever that this was part of a grand strategy of English intervention in Indian affairs. Lawrence lacked the vision or ambition for such a role; and the East India Company servants were determined to go ahead with trade and avoid, wherever possible, military engagements, which they feared and abhorred. The merchant class dominated the settlements, and regarded soldiers as second-class citizens, and warfare as an unwelcome interruption to trade.

However, the lure of a petty local conflict proved irresistible to the idle forces in Fort St David. Lawrence was well aware that his garrison would be much reduced, as the merchants were pressing, unless he could find something for it to do. In 1739 the Rajah of Tanjore had been deposed, and he had now come to the British to seek help. The region was only some 30 miles inland from Fort St David and was prosperous, pretty and strewn with pagodas. Quite why the British decided to help him remains a mystery. In exchange for restoring him to his throne, they demanded the expenses of the expedition and control of the fort of Devikottai on the Coleroon river, a place devoid of strategic significance.

In March 1749, Clive, now promoted to the rank of lieutenant, accompanied Captain John Cope on the expedition to restore this obscure prince to his throne. It marked his first journey into the interior, about which he had so long dreamed. The aim was to attack by land and sea. An appalling storm ravaged the footsoldiers; the company failed to make contact with the naval forces off the coast.

When the British finally encountered the enemy, they were not supported by the local people, as the rajah had said they would be. Instead, in Clive's words, they were 'a little staggered' by the sheer size of the Tanjore army. Wisely, Cope retreated, but not in an orderly manner. Pursued in desultory fashion by the colossal but clumsy local army, the British force lost around 400 Indian soldiers and most of its baggage as it crossed a small river.

The expedition had been a fiasco. The military reputation of the British in India had sunk to a new low. Lawrence was well aware of the grumbles from Company officials about the cost of the British military presence. He determined to try again. He took the risk of himself leading the entire garrison up the Coleroon river and landed on a mudflat opposite the fort of Devikottai.

Clive, the most promising of the younger commanders, was given the job of leading the assault on the fort by a force of 30 British soldiers and 700 Indians. With extraordinary bravado, he set the British a furious pace across the river and up towards the fort, where they became separated from the Indian soldiers still struggling to cross the river.

His small force was suddenly surrounded by a group of cavalry, slashing wildly at Clive and his men; to the young commander's horror, he realised that he and his men were unsupported from the rear. As the others were cut down beside him, a horseman rode up to Clive, raising his sword; Clive narrowly escaped being cut down, and with three or four survivors ran back to the river where his Indian troops were drawn up in a precarious position with their backs to the water. They looked like being overwhelmed. But Lawrence, across the river, understood Clive's difficulties and ordered his forces forward. They crossed successfully and rein-forced the foothold on the bank; fearing they had been lured into a trap, the attacking forces pulled back.

When the British reached the fort it was deserted. They climbed its ramparts and saw a huge army of some 15,000 men retreating across the plain. It had been a salutary demonstration: first, of how reckless and inexperienced the young Clive was; and, second, of how a seemingly irresistible force of Indians could be put to flight merely by a display of aggression, discipline and boldness by a much smaller force.

The usurping ruler of Tanjore promptly offered peace: the British could have the fort and their expenses, and the old rajah be given compensation. The British accepted these terms. Clive, who might have expected a reprimand for his foolhardy conduct, was complimented by Lawrence for 'his early genius . . . he behaved in courage and in judgment much beyond what could be expected from his years'.

Lawrence appointed Clive his quartermaster when the French formally handed back Madras. The small British contingent was despatched to Pondicherry, where they were received civilly by their arch-enemy, Dupleix, and his wife. The young soldier was fascinated to meet the man who had already tried to drive the British out of southern India, and who would soon become his most formidable opponent.

Dupleix, for his part, was more interested in shaking hands with his adversary Lawrence. The disdainful French intellectual made a striking contrast to the tubby, earthy, swashbuckling little Englishman. Clive was impressed by the beauty of the little French town, with its classical and stately baroque architecture. Its magnificent embellishments and columns were a little showy for British tastes, but were certainly impressive.

A few weeks later, a larger contingent of British soldiers and civilians retraced their way along the road to Madras, which they found ruined and deserted. Clive was deeply depressed. Having achieved so much militarily, reality was now returning. If the war was truly over, he had no alternative but to return to his old profession as a writer.

He had sought the rank of captain, but the Company seniors, with the short-sightedness and parsimony that was to mark their actions time and again, were determined to reduce military spending, having learnt nothing from the sack of Madras. With Lawrence's backing, he sought promotion; and was granted the job of Steward of St George, in charge of food supplies for the garrison town, as well as furnishings and fittings. It was potentially a highly lucrative job, with a commission on every supply to the garrison. Clive was now rising fast within the Company.

Within a few weeks he was struck down for the first time by severe illness – this time the fever endemic to the Carnatic. In January 1750, he went to Bengal to recuperate. Although Calcutta was suffocatingly humid in summer, unlike the Carnatic, it was quite fresh and cool in winter. As the ship docked after a few days' voyage, Clive was in good spirits in spite of his sickness. Calcutta was a city of wealth and elegance by comparison with the attractive, but provincial and nepotistic, enclaves along the Coromandel Coast.

Fort William, the British settlement, was a magnificent Italianate fortress with a low, heavily buttressed wall which extended for a mile and directly overlooked the Hugli river. Beautifully designed public buildings rose over the parapets and peered over the water-front where ships with elegant masts and puffed sails bobbed quietly at anchor. Magnificent merchant houses extended in both directions beside the fort, testaments to wealth and taste. The steamy climate made their white façades look faded and stained. Of all the English settlements in India, Fort William was the most exotic.

Yet there was also a sense of complacency and decay about it. Its basis was trade, and military activities counted not at all there. As Clive gazed from the ship at the wide mouth of the Hugli, surveying the damp, malarial swamp about him, the huge river snaking away as far as the eye could see from this astonishing piece of Italianate eighteenth-century glory, he felt a profound sense of adventure, as though arriving at an outpost of man on a distant planet. The dark interior of India beckoned upriver.

Bishop Heber's description of the 'black town' of Calcutta half a century later already applied: It was

> deep, black and dingy, with narrow-crooked streets, huts of earth baked in the sun, or of twisted bamboos, interspersed with ruinous brick bazaars, pools of dirty water . . . a crowd of people in the streets, beyond anything to be seen in London, some dressed in tawdry silks and brocades . . . religious mendicants with no clothing

but their long hair and beards in elf locks, their faces painted white or yellow, their beads in one ghastly lean hand, and the other stretched out like a bird's claw, to receive donations . . . a constant clamour of voices, a constant creaking of cart wheels, which are never greased in India . . . add to all this a villainous smell of garlic, rancid coconut oil, sour butter and stagnant ditches.

Clive by now considered himself a trader first and a soldier second. He had glimpsed the possibilities of acquiring immense wealth. His main aim was to make a fortune, not to indulge in ill-paid military adventuring. It was clear that he had no real interest in fighting for fighting's sake; he was a young man on the make. For the time being, though, he was recuperating; and his position immediately opened the doors of Calcutta society. He spent his enforced idleness being entertained to lavish meals, or listening to the harpsichord in the cool of the evening.

He made a friend in Robert Orme, effeminate, vain, intelligent and difficult, a 20-year-old who was to become Clive's biographer. Impulsively he expressed the desire to stay in Calcutta permanently; but as his health improved it was obvious that he must return to where he had made the beginnings of a reputation. He left that strange and exotic outpost at the mouth of a tropical river with regret: his fascination for Bengal dated from the visit.

CHAPTER 5

The Return of the French

A ny idea that Clive was a man of destiny, and still less that he was plotting to conquer Bengal, would have seemed ludicrous.

One other man, though, was plotting to do just that and his ambition was to spur Clive to his own destiny. François Dupleix, the Frenchman he had seen twice, first strutting as a conqueror in Fort St George, then as lofty peacemaker in the ornate town of Pondicherry, was preparing a more ambitious scheme than any yet conceived for India.

Dupleix had had the imagination, even genius, to have understood two things about India long before Clive. The first was that relatively small, well-trained, well-equipped European armies could defeat the colossal, ill-trained, ill-equipped moving townships that constituted Indian armies. Although Dupleix did not realise it, this was because of the essentially different nature of Indian warfare.

Indian armies, whenever possible, barely engaged each other. It was enough that one side was overwhelmingly superior, and proved it in a brief cannon duel, an infantry clash or cavalry battle, for the other to give way. The banners, tents, elephants, camels, music, weaponry, colour and sheer size of these forces were intended to intimidate the other side into submission. Sometimes major battles occurred; on other occasions, magnificence was enough. Musket fire was itself as much for display as death: the noise and flashes were terrifying, but even British bullets fell to the ground after a hundred yards.

Dupleix's second insight was that the ferocious infighting between Indian princes permitted a European force decisively to tilt a battle one way or the other, and so acquire a wholly disproportionate influence. Clive's success in India and the establishment of the British Raj was due to his own grasping of the two lessons learned by Dupleix.

India in the mid-eighteenth century was a truly astonishing civilisation. It was at once one of the most powerful, literate, artistically endowed, developed, sophisticated and economically advanced societies on earth, yet at the same time contained the seeds of its own destruction. One visitor, James Forbes, who later became Governor of Bombay, considered that India possessed 'eloquence, poetry, painting and architecture, in a considerable degree of perfection'.

Four major influences had shaped this continent of 180 million people, one-third of them Moslem, two-thirds Hindu or other sects. The first and most visible were the Mogul Emperors, direct descendants of Tamerlane through a ferocious fighter and heir of the Mogul, Barbar. In 1526 he had conquered most of the subcontinent. The Moguls were in fact Turks, their civilisation was Persian, and their culture an exquisite blend of Persian and Indian styles. Above all the Moguls were Moslems, fierce and imperious, but never able to do more than make a surface impression on their Hindu subjects – the vast majority of Indians, whose main pursuit was commerce, and whose own civilisation was also far developed.

Lawrence James captures the magnificence of the Moguls:

India's official architecture was a backdrop for the traditional public rituals of state. The formal processions in which a ruler presented himself to his subjects and undertook his devotions and the durbars [assemblies] where great men met, exchanged gifts and compliments and discussed high policy, required settings appropriate to what was, in effect, the theatre of power. At the heart of the Emperor Shahjahan's great palace, now called the Red Fort, in Delhi are the great audience halls, one a vast open courtyard, the other enclosed and reserved for foreign ambassadors and other elevated visitors. Both are now stripped of their awnings and wallhangings and the private chamber lacks the Peacock Throne, a stunning construction of gold and jewels surmounted by a golden arch and topped by two gilded peacocks, birds of allegedly incorruptible flesh which may have symbolised not only the splendour of the Mughals but their durability.

When Shahjahan held durbars for his subjects, dispensing justice and settling quarrels, he overlooked them from a high, canopied dais with a delicately painted ceiling. If he glanced upwards, he saw a panel which portrays Orpheus playing his lute before wild beasts who, bewitched by his music, are calmly seated around him. The scene was a reminder to the emperor and his successors that they were Solomonic kings. Like the Thracian musician they were bringers of harmony, spreading peace among subjects who, if left to their own devices, would live according to the laws of the jungle. It was a nice and revealing conceit, a key to the nature of Mughal kingship and, for that matter, its successor, the British Raj.

The structure of the empire was delicate and complex. At its apex was the Great Mogul in Delhi; beneath him were the Moslem (Turkish) nobility, who administered vast estates and princedoms; and beneath them were the occupied Hindu aristocracy who ran the bureaucracy and trade and also, in many cases, retained aristocratic privileges.

The arrangement was not a typically colonial one, because the Moslems had to make use of the upper caste of Hindus, and gave them prominent positions and privileges, permitting them to enjoy great wealth. Yet there was a tension between the thin layer of Moslem nobility and the large Hindu majority they presided over. The man who more than any laid the foundations of the East India Company, Sir Thomas Roe, observed once that the greatness of the emperor was 'not in itself, but in the weakness of his neighbours, who like an overgrown pike he feeds on in frenzy'.

James argues:

Appearances were misleading. Whatever its architecture announced to the contrary, the Mughal empire was never monolithic, nor did the emperor's will run freely throughout India. He was *shah-an-shah*, a king of kings, a monarch whose dominions were a political mosaic, whose tessera included provinces administered by imperial governors and semi-independent petty states. In the Deccan alone there were over a thousand fortified towns and villages, each under the thumb of its own samindar [landowner], who was both a subject of the emperor and his partner in government. The machinery of Mughal government needed the goodwill and cooperation of such men as well as the services of its salaried administrators who enforced the law and gathered imperial revenues.

The last of the great Mogul Emperors was Aurungzeb, who ruled India for nearly half a century, from 1659 to 1707. He first experienced the sudden, furious typhoon that was to shatter the peace of India in 1664. A huge tribe of low-caste Hindu dirt farmers, the Marathas, cultivating land on the west side of India around Bombay, combined to form one of the toughest and most vicious guerrilla armies in history, bent on undermining Mogul rule.

The Marathas were the second major ingredient of eighteenth-century India. Enormously powerful and destructive, they on the whole failed to provide an alternative administration over the parts they conquered and ruled; indeed, much of the time they were content to pillage and plunder, and then withdraw from their conquests. But they battered steadily away at the power of the throne at Delhi.

In 1664, the Marathas launched their first big attack, sacking the Mogul port of Surat. The emperor responded in traditional fashion by trying to buy them off and offering to employ them as a mercenary army – a role they were to fulfil regularly in Clive's day, selling themselves to the highest bidder. The Marathas refused, and in 1681 launched a frenzied assault on Mogul rule. They were badly beaten and their lands laid waste, but they retaliated with a vicious guerrilla campaign.

In 1707 Aurungzeb died, and only five years later his son followed him to the grave. A series of succession crises followed, as rival princes sought to install their nominees on the throne. Stability was restored under Muhammad Shah, who asserted himself over his overmighty subjects and ruled until 1748.

But the empire was already beginning to crumble. Asaf Jah, one of the mightiest Moslem noblemen, was appointed governor of the Deccan in 1713. When he was appointed chief minister to the emperor, the effective ruler of India, he was beset by conspiracies and returned to the Deccan in 1753, which he virtually ruled as an independent state.

This was not to spare him the attention of the Marathas, though. 'Let us strike at the trunk of the withering tree and the branches will fall by themselves,' asserted one of their leaders. A frontal assault was made upon Asaf Jah; as the fighting raged, the French and British settlements watched in anxiety from the Coromandel Coast, which was under the nominal control of the Deccan. The Maratha brushfire eventually subsided, leaving small pockets of the fighters available to local princes in their quarrels.

The great bulk of the Maratha army, however, swung north and staged an attack upon Delhi itself, in 1738 reaching and plundering its suburbs. Peace was bought by the emperor ceding the province of Malwa, a great slice across India, which cut off Delhi from the Deccan. The empire was now effectively cut into three: the north ruled by the emperor; the centre, ruled by the Marathas; and the south, ruled by Asaf Jah.

The weakness of the regime in Delhi was noticed by outsiders. The King of Persia, Nadir Shah, launched a sudden invasion of Northern India, razing Delhi, and had to be bought off at a huge cost, leaving a slaughterhouse behind him. 'The streets were strewn with corpses like a garden with weeds. The city was reduced to ashes and looked like a burnt plain,' according to an eyewitness. The Peacock Throne was carried off to Persia.

The Afghans soon invaded too, but were beaten back. In 1748 the Emperor Muhammad Shah died, and civil war broke out among the noble factions. Two emperors were slain, the Afghans attacked again, and the temporary dictator at Delhi called on the Marathas to fight them. To everyone's astonishment, in this war the fiercest of Indian fighters had met their match, and the Afghans plundered Delhi in 1756–58. The Afghan king, Ahmad Shah Abdali, had no wish to rule, though, and taking his spoils returned to his rugged kingdom, leaving Delhi and the old empire in a state of virtual anarchy.

These, then, were the five forces that now fought over the bloody corpse of the once mighty Mogul empire: what was left of imperial authority in Delhi; the Marathas; the fierce tribesmen of the North-West Frontier – Persians and Afghans; the semi-independent Moslem noble princes, ruling most parts of India including Bengal and the Deccan; and, last and least, the British, French and Dutch colonial settlers along the coast (the Portuguese had long been eclipsed), who exerted no real political power outside their enclaves up to that time.

All this was now to change; and Dupleix was the first to understand that in a continent where central authority had disintegrated, a small and determined group of well-disciplined troops could take advantage of the hatreds felt by Moslem prince against Moslem prince, Hindu aristocracy against Moslem overlord, Hindu merchant against Hindu prince and Moslem overlord, and Maratha soldier of fortune against anyone with authority, selling himself to those who would pay him most. In a continent already dominated by a foreign power and religion, albeit crumbling, where internal warfare was becoming endemic, the Europeans were no more than another mercantile player in the game, not colonial plunderers.

Indeed, at first the Hindu majority of India were to welcome the Europeans as less brutal than their Moslem masters. Ordinary people desperately desired order and peace of the kind the Mogul empire had imposed to warfare and insecurity. The Europeans, and in particular Dupleix, could see that what was required was not outright military victory, but an instinctive mind which could pick the winners and, through the judicious deployment of European troops, tilt the balance.

The Europeans might thus attach themselves to the huge armies of the challengers for power. Once established, their side would be beholden to them; and if the new incumbents tried to turn on the Europeans, the latter would switch their support to their opponents, bringing about their downfall. In this way a small number of Europeans could dominate a large empire. It was the trick that had been practised by the Moguls themselves, until they were blasted away by the Marathas. Even Cortés and Pizarro, founders of the Spanish empire in America, had done the same.

To many modern historians, the French and later British attitudes were simply 'colonialist': they were embarked upon the creation of a European empire over large and subject peoples which, in the event, was to last 200 years. Worse, the European powers were subjugating developed cultures beneath a rule that depended on superiority in weaponry alone; it was said that the degree of civilisation of the colonised people was equal, if not superior, to that of the invading power. Even in contemporary Britain, low-born colonial plunderers were to be sneered at as men who had despoiled ancient princes and nobles of their wealth through armed robbery.

At the time Clive was apprenticed at Fort St George, the motives of the French and the British would seem amply to lend themselves to such an analysis. The European settlements were there, first and foremost, out of commercial greed. Dupleix and Clive were soon to evoke ideals of honour and national interest, but the primary purpose of most of their followers in establishing the Indian empires was plunder. The colonists were usually men of moderate means in their own homelands and intent on enriching themselves as quickly as possible and, in many cases, getting out of the disease-ridden tropics as fast as they could.

It will be seen later how Clive first began to wrestle with the problem of institutionalising empire through good government and even a sense of moral purpose – something in which he was to be bitterly frustrated, and which was not to occur until several decades later. But there can be no romanticism about the motivation of the first European settlers in India.

Equally, however, there should be no illusion about the condition of India when the Europeans arrived. India was home to great civilisations, but it was not 'civilised' in the secondary meaning of the term. Its governance was based upon force, oppression, exploitation and superstition. While the formal rule of law existed, the concepts of impartial administration, of a contract between ruler and the ruled, of justice, of respect for the law, of non-violence – so vigorously debated in England for centuries, in particular during the previous one, and later to be the core of Gandhi's teachings – were entirely absent. The ruler was entitled to plunder as much as he could from the ruled who, in turn, were entitled to safeguard as much of their miserable lot as they could from the ruler.

Moreover, the rulers were themselves foreign colonial oppressors, Moslem overlords from central Asia throttling a Hindu middle class and, beneath that, a peasantry that counted for absolutely nothing at all. As the grip of the Mogul empire collapsed, the rulers were no longer capable of preserving even that minimalist justification for despotism – the protection of life, law and order. The life of ordinary Indians was not just nasty and brutish, but short, liable to be cut off by any of a host of invaders and warring factions. The Hindu middle class, and much of the Moslem aristocracy, yearned for some sort of order, even that imposed by an outside power – a factor Dupleix and Clive were to turn to their advantage by exploiting the very divisions of Moslem rulers.

It is hard to see the Hindus shrugging off the invasions from the north-east on their own – although the savage and anarchic Marathas were perhaps the nearest equivalent to native freedom-fighters in eighteenth-century India. It seems difficult to deny, though, that the main elements for stability in post-colonial India – democracy, respect for the constitutional order, an impartial judiciary, the settlement of disputes through adjudication, not force or corruption, an army and a civil service at the service of the people rather than its oppressors – were endowed by the Raj in its more mature phase.

A man may bitterly resent his schooling and, indeed, in many cases, it may have warped him. The Raj was in some ways enlightened, in others cruel and insensitive. But few would say that India would have been better off with no schooling at all. India in the eighteenth century was, in terms of governance, at an infant stage, where the law of the jungle prevailed. Its glittering scientific and architectural achievements, as well as its wealth, were under-pinned by the cruelties of the Pharaoh, imperial China and ancient Rome. The atrocities of the Moguls and their warring princes, the depredations of the Marathas, Persians and Afghans, and the avarice of the Hindu upper castes cannot be invoked as forebears by the modern followers of Gandhi.

Clive's Indian biographer, Chaudhury, points out that romantic European attitudes towards the Indians underwent a dramatic reappraisal once they had actually made contact with the subconti-nent:

As late as the eighteenth century, if there were any preconceptions regarding India they were all favourable. India was the country of spiritual wisdom, of material splendour, of gentleness of manners and benevolent dispositions. For so thoroughgoing a revolution of opinion to have taken place as soon as direct contact was established there must have been a great shock from the first direct contact.

Furthermore it should be kept in mind that the new attitude was shaped by empirical experience and the aims of the appraisal were severely practical. The men who formulated the opinions were neither moralists, not theorists, not idealists. They had come from eighteenth-century Europe, which had enough cynical immorality of its own, and they were cynical men. They had to deal with Indians in connection with political and commercial affairs. Dupleix and Bussy, more particularly, acquired a great reputation for their deep insight into the Indian character and their skill in dealing with those who mattered. The respect in which they were held was also due to this very clear-sightedness, for Indians do not admire those that they dupe.

Dupleix's view of a noble in Hyderabad is typical of the European attitude, and cannot have been without foundation: 'Sayyid Lashkar Khan is a very honest man, but an honest man among the Moors is only a rogue elsewhere. They are all possessed by avarice, and they have around them a band of rascals who always prompt a thousand chimeras and a thousand wicked calculations into them, so that one can never count on their constancy in being friendly.'

Clive's friend and biographer, Robert Orme, reflected a no more favourable British attitude when he wrote, 'The governments of Indostan have no idea of national honour in the conduct of their politics; and as soon as they think the party with whom they are engaged is reduced to great distress, they shift, without hesitation, their alliance to the opposite side, making immediate advantage the only rule of their action.'

Of the Moslem princes he wrote: 'A domineering insolence towards all who are in subjection to them, ungovernable wilfulness, inhumanity, cruelty, murders, and assassinations, deliberated with the same calmness and subtlety as the rest of their politics, an insensibility to remorse for these crimes, which are scarcely considered otherwise than as necessary accidents in the course of life, sensual excesses which revolt against nature, unbounded thirst for power, and an expaciousness of wealth equal to the extravagance of his propensities and vices – this is the character of the Indian Moor, who is of consequence sufficient to have any character at all.'

Orme acknowledged that the Moslem ruling class was scrupulously polite, yet:

the politeness of other nations may have risen from a natural ease and happiness of temper, a point of honour, the idea a man conveys of himself by the respect he shows to others; but the decorum with which the common ceremonies and occurrences of life are conducted in Indostan, is derived from the constant idea of subordination, joined to a constant habit of the deepest disguise and dissimulation of the heart. In Indostan every man may literally be said to be the maker of his own fortune. Great talents, unawed by scruples of conscience, seldom fail of success: from hence all persons of distinction are seen running in the same course. The perseverance necessary to attain his end teaches every man to bear and forbear contrary to the common instincts of human nature: hence arises their politeness . . . The general competition has put an end to mutual confidence; a sensibility capable of discerning everything, is soon taught a disguise capable of concealing everything. Where morality has no check upon ambition, it must form the blackest resolutions; and the dissimulation necessary to carry these into execution will, amongst a people circumstanced as I have described them, be carried into excess, which different manners and better mortals will scarcely imagine human nature to be capable of.

At least the Moslems were usually passive oppressors, as another English observer noted: 'As they sit for the most part (when they are not with their women) upon their sofas, smoking, and amusing themselves with their jewels, taking coffee or sweetmeats, seeing their quails fight, or such pastimes, nothing surprises them so much as to see a European walk about a room; and none but their very young people ever ride for amusement or exercise only.'

The Hindus instead were astute and energetic and could expiate guilt by paying the priests. Orme cited the example of the Rajah of Travancore, who was told by the brahmins that he must repent by being born out of the womb of a cow. A golden cow was made in which the rajah sat for several days before being 'born'; the cow was divided up among the priests.

Chaudhury emphasises that these faults were those of the ruling class, not the great majority of Indians, who were poor and oppressed, brutalised by crippling taxation and from time to time slaughtered in war or mutilated and raped by the Marathas. The defects were not racial but those of an indolent but tough-minded élite.

In 1748, Asaf Jah, the mighty and quasi-independent ruler of the Deccan (southern India) died, and a succession struggle began. Dupleix saw his chance to bring French support to install his candidate on the throne. This was Muzaffar Jang, who was backed by the powerful Chanda Sahib, the aspirant to the lesser throne of the Carnatic itself – the man who had infuriated Dupleix at one time by attacking his forces at Madras. Install these two, he believed, and he would become master of a third of India, the south, containing some 30 million people.

In August 1749, these two Indian princes and their French allies attacked and decisively defeated the Nawab of the Carnatic's forces, killing their ruler. His younger son, Muhammad Ali, who had led the force that supported the British at Fort St David, escaped, and with a small force galloped some 250 miles to the fort town of Trichinopoly. Chanda Sahib now controlled most of the Carnatic, and rewarded the French with generous grants of land around Pondicherry.

But while Muzaffar Jang was away in the Carnatic, another contender for the throne of the Deccan – the much bigger prize – had seized power in its capital, Hyderabad, a hundred miles inland: this was Nasir Jang. Dupleix spurred his Indian allies to attack him; but they were fearful; instead, in May 1750, Nasir Jang attacked them with a colossal army of 200,000–300,000 fighting men, and some 800,000 camp followers. The perimeter of his camp was 20 miles long.

As spectators, the British watched powerlessly and with alarm as this desperate battle for territory was fought out. The fleet had long since left, and the garrisons at Fort St George and Fort St David were, as usual, under strength. Once again, Dupleix bestrode the land. Feebly, Stringer Lawrence was despatched with a small force to support Nasir Jang, and a few soldiers were sent to assist Muhammad Ali at Trichinopoly. Nasir Jang inflicted a major defeat on his French-sponsored rivals, taking Muzaffar Jang prisoner, while Chanda Sahib was forced to take refuge at the French settlement at Pondicherry. Dupleix, it seemed, had suffered a serious setback and his intrigues had come to nothing.

However, during the autumn Dupleix, through Madame's friends, established contact with dissidents in Nasir Jang's camp; and in December the new ruler was assassinated. Muzaffar Jang was proclaimed the new Nawab of the Deccan. He rode to embrace his French friends at Pondicherry amidst great festivities, showering them with money and diamonds. Dupleix was appointed Muzaffar Jang's deputy in the south, and the new Indian ruler of southern

India rode to Hyderabad to take up his inheritance.

Remnants of forces loyal to the murdered Nasir Jang ambushed Muzaffar Jang's cavalcade, however, and he was killed. The commander of the French force accompanying him, Charles, Marquis de Bussy, realised the situation was desperate again, and set aside the claims of the slain prince's young sons in favour of his uncle, Salabat Jang, a French protégé. De Bussy personally stayed on at his court to ensure his loyalty. In effect the French now controlled all of southern India under a puppet ruler, and the British settlements along the Coromandel coast were desperately at risk again.

It is hard to defend the extraordinary shortsightedness of the men who ran the British enclaves up to that point. Committed only to commercial gain, incapable of doing more politically than to curl up in a ball and pretend that nothing was happening outside their settlements, parsimonious in cutting their defences to the bone, they had already managed to lose one settlement (only regained through a peace treaty with France in Europe), barely hung on to their other fort, failed to dislodge the French at Pondicherry with superior numbers, and were now, having learnt nothing, wholly unprepared to resist what was virtually a French occupation of all of southern India.

Inside Fort St David, life carried on in a strange spirit of panic and cheerful unreality. Governor Floyer, a portly, genial man addicted to cards, was thrown into confusion by the French encirclement, about which he could do nothing, having fewer than 1,000 troops, half Europeans, half sepoys. Fortunately Floyer was replaced by a much tougher governor, Thomas Saunders, in September 1750. Ironically, this occurred because the Reverend Fordyce, who had so incensed Clive, had, out of revenge, informed the East India Company of Floyer's addiction to gambling.

Taciturn, aloof and authoritarian, Saunders was to show coolness and good judgement – but not enough to ignore an edict from the East India Company in London (as usual a year behind developments in southern India) substantially cutting Stringer Lawrence's salary. The short-fused major stormed off in a huff, catching the next boat out and leaving the English garrison virtually devoid of good commanders. Lawrence's misfortune was to give Clive his opportunity.

Saunders from the first understood the threat posed by Dupleix. Most of the rest of the English community preferred to bury their heads in the sand: the endless round of balls, picnics, flirtation, scandal and affairs continued in the little settlement, as though it were possible to ignore the wars raging outside.

The few enclaves that were holding out against the French and their allies were in an increasingly desperate plight. They were concentrated around Muhammad Ali at Trichinopoly. Saunders appointed Captain Rudolph de Guingens, a Swiss mercenary, to command a force of British soldiers to go to the Indian prince's help before a huge army assembled by the French-sponsored Chanda Sahib attempted to crush this last holdout. Trichinopoly was the last bastion of opposition to the new French empire.

Robert Clive, now a civilian, was appointed Commissary, with the job of organising supplies to the forces. As Steward, he was a natural choice for the job, and showed in what high regard he was held for his commercial ability and organisational qualities. Far from being just the martial man sneered at by his enemies, he would probably have succeeded as well in business as in war.

His responsibility was to find provisions for a moving army. The job involved constant exhortation, negotiation with merchants, and, one suspects, an immense amount of bullying, both of his own subordinates and of Indian traders. Although Clive was to show humanity and moderation in later life, he had to be tough and hard-nosed in such an office, and his violent temper and impulsive decisiveness stood him in good stead, as did his energy.

Yet for a man of his martial inclinations, the job was hugely frustrating, as he could take no part in military decisions. De Guingens from the first proved to be sublimely incompetent. According to Dalton, he was 'a man of unfortunately jealous temper which made him mistrust the goodwill of any who affected to give him advice'.

Two months later, after a hard and arduous march, still 38 miles from Trichinopoly, the British first spied a huge French-led force outside the fort of Valikondapuram. De Guingens's small army was immediately joined by a detachment sent by Muhammad Ali, but he was still heavily outnumbered. For two weeks the rival armies glowered at each other, trying to persuade the fort's commander to take sides.

At length de Guingens's patience wore out, and he started to cannonade the old walls, to little effect. The following day, the French could be seen slowly advancing. Instead of moving forward, de Guingens held a council of war. The officers present recoiled at the prospect of taking on a much superior enemy, and many of the men refused to fight. A few officers, including Clive, urged de Guingens to fight, while Muhammad Ali ridiculed the British for cowardice.

The order to retreat was given, and British supplies were abandoned in a headlong retreat into the comparative safety of Trichinopoly. The British had faced the enemy, and run away. The message this sent was unequivocal: the British were not a force to be reckoned with in India. The French could frighten them away just by their approach. Any wavering Indian princes should make their peace with the superior power at once.

Clive watched the disorganised, humiliating rout from his horse. With a group of others, he sought permission to return to Fort St David, where his talents could be better employed. At the hot-headed age of 25 he was seething at this further humiliation for British arms; the military record of the past five years had been one of complete failure. He and his small party galloped for days back along the dusty roads that they had marched down so wearily weeks before.

In a state of high fury, dust-caked, sweating and sun-cooked, he went straight to the governor and offered to join the army, without pay, if he was given the rank of captain. For a rising star in the commercial world of Fort St David, this was an unprecedented sacrifice. Clive wanted a rank in which he would have a real command, and was ready to sacrifice his enormous commercial prospects. He understood something the bloated, partying burghers of the Company did not: that under the present military leadership, the British cause in India would be lost, and there would be no profits at all for anyone but the French.

Saunders had had a low opinion of Clive's mentor, Lawrence: the cold, calculating governor was the polar opposite of the strutting, self-important but highly competent military commander. He had distrusted Clive as Lawrence's protégé. But he was struck by Clive's extraordinary offer, and was so short of officer material that he agreed.

Clive was now ordered to accompany a small convoy of supplies to Trichinopoly, headed by George Pigot, a tough but friendly companion of Clive's. Some 40 miles out, the expedition came to the relief of a force being besieged by Chanda Sahib's forces. With this modest success of British arms accomplished, Clive and Pigot were ordered to return to Fort St David. After a few miles, their tiny force of twenty-six was attacked by a large body of horsemen. While their escorts fought bravely, Clive and Pigot, on fast horses, outran their pursuers.

Clive was promptly given new orders: to lead reinforcements that had arrived from England to swell the garrison at Trichinopoly. Once again, he embarked upon the long road, surviving a minor skirmish with French troops. He arrived to see the town clustered around its famous rock in an extensive plain littered with the vast spread of Chanda Sahib's besieging army.

It proved easy enough to find an undefended way through to reach the garrison. There the situation was serious, though not yet desperate. Muhammad Ali had some 60 English and 2,000 Indian troops. Chanda Sahib had some 800 French and 20,000 Indian troops. De Guingens combined prickliness with appalling leadership. The British were quarrelling among themselves. The treasury was nearly depleted and supplies were low.

CHAPTER 6

Arcot

C live now for the first time properly met the young Indian prince he had glimpsed on an elephant at Fort St George five years before. Pale, somewhat mannered and dandified, yet possessed of considerable intelligence and bravery, Muhammad Ali impressed Clive more than his fellow European officers. The young prince took the Englishman apart to suggest a desperate ruse to draw off his besiegers: an attack at the enemy's heart, the Carnatic's capital, Arcot, where Chanda Sahib had left very few forces. Muhammad Ali was obsessed with the idea. De Guingens had already refused to do this.

Clive, repelled by de Guingens and his strutting, quarrelling, idle officers holed up in the fort poormouthing Muhammad Ali and his officers, stayed only a few days before once again spurring his horse back along the two weeks' hard ride to Fort St David. He was entirely persuaded by the boldness of the plan and by the subtlety and intelligence of the prince.

It was the only hope the English had of escaping a desperate situation; for if Trichinopoly fell, Dupleix would next devour their coastal settlements. These had far too few troops to relieve Trichinopoly, or defend themselves. Only a fantastic propaganda coup or confidence trick, like the seizure of Arcot, the poorly defended enemy capital, could break the spell of Chanda Sahib and the French.

Clive sought an immediate audience with Saunders and the council. It was a plan that was irresponsible in the extreme, to reduce Fort St David of half its garrison on a wild adventure into the heartland of India. But the governor agreed, and appointed Clive to lead the expedition: he was very junior, but there were no other volunteers.

Saunders stripped his garrison to just 100 men, giving Clive command of 130 Europeans and around 100 sepoys. The little army was shipped to Madras, where it was reinforced by 80 men and 400 sepoys, leaving just 50 to guard Fort St George. The British settlements had been effectively denuded of their forces, and the tiny army set out on what must have seemed a hopeless, quixotic attempt to strike at the very heartland of the enemy while their overwhelming forces were away strangling the last redoubt of opposition at Trichinopoly.

There were to be few greater expeditions in the history of British arms. The 600 who rode down the Valley of Death in the Crimea a hundred years later went down in posterity as an example of bravery – and bungling. Clive's 700 – reduced to 300 in the actual defence of Arcot – are much less popularly celebrated, but their feat was achieved against far greater odds. It was an example of staggering boldness, resolution and, above all, endurance. Perhaps it was only their success that was to diminish their achievement in the eyes of their fellow countrymen. The British – like the Japanese – respect the nobility of failure.

Clive had just eight officers, all of them civilian volunteers from the Company, including his old friend John Pybus, as well as Bulkley, who like Clive had seen action, and a surgeon, Dr Wilson. Clive later described his own Englishmen as 'the scum and refuse of England', many of them ex-convicts or pressed into service; the Indian sepoys had received only the most rudimentary training. They had just three field-pieces between them.

The British soldiers wore colourful red uniforms, which must have been suffocating in the heat of southern India, while the Indians were more sensibly clad in shirts and shorts. Mark Bence-Jones has a fine description of their progress:

> They must have been a strange mixture of East and West, the European soldiers in red, the sepoys in ordinary Indian shirts with bare legs and marching to the beat of tom-toms. They marched through the dust of the Choultry Plain, a vast expanse of orange-coloured sand dotted with scrub and tall cactus, with distant grey hillocks to the left. Every now and then there was a village of straw huts, smelling of smoke, surrounded by scattered palm trees and inhabited not only by humans and cattle but also by grey monkeys with pink faces.

Peter Holt tells a delightful story about Clive's training methods: 'Clive was having difficulty teaching his Indian sepoys their left and their right. So he tied pieces of cloth to their left legs and palm leaves to their right legs. The Tamil for cloth is seelay and for palm leaves is wallay. Leg in Tamil is kal. Then Clive marched his soldiers up and down and they all shouted "Seelay kal, wallay kal, seelay kal, wallay kal."'

After a while the ground became paler and more like desert. They had 64 miles to go and the heat was intense. But they marched quickly. By the third day they had travelled 40 miles and were in sight of the great pagoda of Conjeveeram, which rose out of the plain, flanked by two smaller pagodas.

Clive himself looked at his most impressive. Just twenty-six, ruddied by the Indian sun, his face leathered by numerous hard cross-country rides, his features were set in a mixture of determination and strength, the jutting chin, sensitive yet resolute mouth and piercing eyes emanating purpose. Although he had put on a little weight, his frame was tall and strong, his bearing erect, that of a leader of men.

He was a man of few words (unless relaxing with friends), instant appreciation of a situation, and rapid decision-making. Completely unbending in enforcing discipline and in pushing his men to the limits of their endurance – as on this march, when he forced them along at a cracking pace (although the decision to move at night was less harsh than it seemed; it was better to rest in the intense heat of midday) – he was not unpopular with his men. He was not unapproachable or excessively severe. He was fair-minded, although he could be hot-tempered. When they rested, he would relax convivially with his friends, although never to the point of drunkenness or loss of self-control.

Merely to have such a man in charge was a remarkable change after the dismal litany of past commanders in India. He modelled himself on that other popular and able, but much vainer, commander, Stringer Lawrence. Impatient, tough and bold, Clive cannot have been overconfident, for he had never led a large body of men into action, and the enterprise before him – to carry the battle right into the heart of a vastly larger enemy camp – was extremely hazardous.

But he could do no worse than men like de Guingens; and, like

Saunders, he understood that the very future of British India depended on the success of the expedition. He did not consider it a rash undertaking, because there was no alternative.

Clive now put on a dazzling display of his abilities. He had learnt how to supply an army when he accompanied the force to Trichinopoly. He used the same organisational skill to chivvy, bully, cajole and encourage his men to move at astonishing speed through the summer heat. Using remarkably rapid horse couriers, Clive kept in constant touch both with Saunders at Fort St David and his deputy, Richard Prince, at Madras. The latter employed his own intelligence and organisational skills to keep Clive's forces supplied.

When Clive learnt that the garrison at Arcot was stronger than expected, he was undaunted: he requested that Prince send him two eighteen-pound guns. Clive's breakneck speed was essential for surprise; any delay, and reinforcements could be brought up to the garrison, which had undoubtedly heard of Clive's progress from its own scouts. Without waiting for the guns, he spurred his small army forward.

On 31 August, the searing tropical heat, which had turned from dust-dry to humid and menacing, suddenly ignited into a violent electrical storm. The rain poured all day, but to Clive it was a godsend: the garrison would not be expecting him to march on and, if he pushed through regardless, he would surprise Chanda Sahib's men.

He spurred his men on with unflinching resolve. As thunder and lightning raged about them, they trudged through dust turned to mud, soaked to the skin. By nightfall, when they made camp, they were already in the hills near Arcot and could see the peaks of the distant mountains of the interior. With only ten miles to go, they approached Arcot warily, sending forward an advance guard. There were no soldiers to intercept them.

Arcot was a walled city set in a spectacular location, a cluster of mud-brick dwellings, narrow streets and alleys huddled around the sprawling inner fort, with a backdrop of pleasant brown hills. They rode into it with great caution, expecting an attack at any moment. None came. The fort was overlooked by many houses, from which an ambush might occur. But the small party on horse – preparing for rapid retreat if necessary – reached the main gate unmolested, while the townspeople shouted a welcome.

Showing great courage, they entered – and found the citadel empty. The 1,000-strong garrison had fled during the night. Its commanders had heard of the march through the monsoon – unheard of in India, as it defied the very gods themselves – and concluded that the British must have supernatural powers. Clive was unopposed.

Clive exulted as the 100,000 inhabitants of Arcot took to the streets to cheer the arrival of the young commander and his little army. He had taken Chanda Sahib's capital without firing a shot. He raised Muhammad Ali's flag of white and green over the Nawab's palace while tom-toms proclaimed that the palace had been taken in the name of Muhammad Ali and the Great Mogul at Delhi. Wisely, he did not hoist the Union Jack.

Saunders sensibly sent a message to him 'not in any shape to molest or distress the inhabitants. If the merchants have a mind to make you a present, I say nothing to the contrary, but take care there be no compulsion.' The governor restored a sense of proportion to the young man. 'It is with pleasure I observe the reception you met with, but when you consider these people were entirely in your power, 'tis nothing extraordinary.' Clive had benefited from his leadership during the march and from an extraordinary piece of good luck. He had not yet won a single skirmish.

It took Clive little time to realise the precariousness of his position. The fort was in the middle of town, overlooked by densely packed housing, which made ideal cover for besiegers. One British sergeant commented that the townspeople's 'looks betrayed their traytours notwithstanding their pretended friendship and dirty presents'. At least 2,000 armed sympathisers of Chanda Sahib remained within the city 'willing to cut our throats had not that their dastardly spirits hindered them'. Its walls were a mile in length – far too extensive for 700 men to defend. The towers were crumbling, and none were strong enough to support a cannon; large parts of the moat had been filled in.

Clive doubted whether the fort could be defended at all, and considered moving to the smaller and more defensible one at Timiri nearby, dispersing his men among several forts, or even withdrawing to Madras. Prince advised him to pull out on hearing that Chanda Sahib was sending a force of 2,000 horsemen to Arcot. Pigot challengingly urged Clive to stand his ground. Saunders wrote advising him to hold the fort if at all possible. Clive set about trying to do up its defences and set fire to the nearby houses, without much success.

First, though, he resolved – in the first in a series of characteristically bold decisions – to take the offensive and attack the garrison that was now camped a few miles away from the town. As he led his men towards the enemy camp, however, the garrison's army moved away. A couple of days later a British advance party actually encountered the enemy and a handful of men were lost on both sides.

After this, Clive devoted himself to strengthening the fort, bringing in provisions and trying to secure the water supply. For about ten days, the enemy was unmolested, and assumed that they had driven the British off. Now swollen to around 3,000 men, the garrison marched up to the outskirts of the capital. On the night of 15 September, after the usual babble of the camp had died down, they posted their sentries and went to sleep.

At two o'clock in the morning, the camp was awoken by a fearful bedlam of noise: horse and men on foot rampaged through it, firing wildly in all directions. In the dark it was impossible to tell the size of the British force. Taken entirely by surprise, the men in the camp fled for their lives: most of Clive's small army had stolen out of the fort without attracting attention from enemy spies.

Wisely, Clive did not give chase. Screams and groans showed that many of the bullets had found their mark: when dawn came, it was apparent the camp had been abandoned. It had been a daring stroke, beautifully executed.

The following day, a new danger loomed. Clive learnt that the eighteen-pounders from Madras, with only a small escort of sepoys, were approaching Conjeeveram, and that a large contingent of Chanda Sahib's forces was on its way to intercept them. Clive promptly ordered most of the garrison out to bring the guns safely in; if they fell into enemy hands they could be used to destroy the walls of the fort. He stayed behind with only a handful of British soldiers and 70 sepoys.

It proved to be a disastrous miscalculation. Enemy scouts alerted the forces around Conjeeveram, which now hurriedly marched on

Arcot. Taking a leaf out of Clive's book, they attacked the main gates at two in the morning amid a great cacophony of shouts, blaring music and gunfire. Although Clive was unable to guard the whole length of the walls, the noise had given warning of the enemy's approach, and his men tossed grenades into the throng, causing great injury and confusion.

An hour later, there was another noisy attack on the back gate, which was similarly driven off. This time darkness had worked against the attackers. They had no way of knowing how many men were in the fort. Sniping now continued for several hours. When Bulkley returned with the main force, having secured around 300 cattle as well as the two guns, Chanda Sahib's men withdrew from the city.

For most of the next week, peace returned, and Clive was able to continue strengthening his defences and to build up his supplies, although some of his men were picked off as they walked the narrow streets of the town. Soon, however, news reached him that a force of 4,000, including French troops, commanded by Chanda Sahib's younger son, Raza Sahib, was approaching and that further reinforcements of some 3,000 men were on the way.

At this stage any normal commander would have cut and run. It seemed virtually impossible to defend the sprawling fort against a large army. Clive was forced to send some 250 of his men back to Madras, in case Raza Sahib's army changed direction and attacked the British settlement.

This left Clive, excluding casualties, with just 120 Europeans and 200 Indians. The whole enterprise, suggested by Muhammad Ali, passionately espoused by Clive and agreed to by the usually cautious Saunders, now began to look like the madcap gamble it undoubtedly was: the British forces were split and inadequate for the defence not just of Arcot but Madras and Fort St George. Far from diverting a large part of the army besieging Trichinopoly, Chanda Sahib had sent the bulk of his men from Pondicherry to Arcot. Muhammad Ali remained under as close a siege as before.

Dupleix was inclined to dismiss the whole affair as a joke and a feint, and believed the British posed no threat. Things seemed very different in Indian eyes: the seizure of Arcot, Chanda Sahib's capital, had immensely damaged his prestige, as Muhammad Ali had foreseen. Against such overwhelming odds, Clive's sole consolation was the thought that the Indian forces had so far proved less formidable than feared. Bolder than a more experienced commander might be, and encouraged by Saunders, who should have known better, he resolved to stay.

On the night of 23 September the siege turned serious. The enemy army arrived and entered the town of Arcot. Clive had withdrawn all his forces into the fort. Including the old garrison and local allies, Raza Sahib's army numbered at least 10,000 to Clive's 300 or so. Clive's response was characteristically bold – and desperately reckless. With his tiny band, he decided to mount a raid to seize the French guns being drawn up opposite the fortress walls.

The French had around 150 men under the control of du Saussay. Clive caught his opponents by surprise as most of his 300 men rushed out of the main gate, pushing his own artillery pieces and exchanging fire with the French guns, until they were abandoned and ceased fire. Clive and his men went forward to try and pull them into the fort.

Snipers suddenly opened up with a deadly rattle of musket fire from the Nawab's palace nearby and from several houses. Clive and his men desperately sought shelter, abandoning the attempt and seeking to haul their own guns back into the fort, using the windows of a nearby choultry – the ubiquitous shelter in Indian towns – from which to discharge a cannon shot, pulling the guns back a few yards on the recoil, and repeating the process through another window. As Clive urged his men back, Lieutenant Trenwith saw a sniper taking direct aim at him. The lieutenant pulled him aside, and was killed instead. The British finally reached the shelter of the fort.

Clive lost fifteen men and fifteen seriously wounded from this reckless escapade. From now on, he stayed inside the fort – although the sheer effrontery of his sortie had impressed the enemy, who were uncertain just how many there were inside the citadel.

It seemed only a matter of days before the fort would fall. Already the siege had lasted 23 days. Clive had three months' supplies inside, and no concerns on that score. But his only water came from a brackish reservoir inside the compound, which an ingenious Indian mason secured by blocking the channel from which it could be drained from outside.

Clive's worst shortage was manpower. Patrolling walls a mile long with only 300 men was an enormous undertaking. The fort consisted of a handful of buildings, a dusty compound and a small plantation behind the ill-repaired walls. Clive had to make sure there were enough sentries constantly watching to warn of any attack at the most vulnerable points – in particular where the moat could be forded.

The sentries had constantly to peer over the edge. From the nearby houses, a continuous musket fire was kept up to deter the sentries. 'A man could not show a nose over the parapet without being shot,' remarked Dr Wilson. So the siege settled into its fourth, and much more critical week. The steady crackle of sniper fire and the dangerous business of ensuring that no surprise attack was mounted took its toll on the men's morale and alertness.

Clive tirelessly walked the battlements exposing himself to danger, as much to encourage his troops as to check for himself that no attack was being prepared. Three men were shot down beside him on different days. He appeared to lead a charmed life. His unflagging determination gave heart to his men – both British and Indian – for whom the odds might otherwise have seemed entirely hopeless. Always he assured them that relief was at hand; always he spurred them to fight on.

One motivating factor was that Clive's men were under siege from the army of an Indian prince; the French were not in command. If he was defeated, there was no telling what the Indians would do: their frequent practice was to give no quarter. In the intense heat of the day, Clive's men, with their grimy, dusty, heavy red uniforms, racked by dysentery, soldiered on, patrolling the battlements, dodging musket fire, sharing out provisions, strengthening the defences, and, where they could, sleeping. The constant patrolling was wearing them down to breaking point.

The stalemate continued. The Indians made no attempt to storm the fort, fearing British firepower. Clive, emboldened, began to resort to minor morale-boosting sorties. He sent one of his lieutenants and a couple of others down the outer wall in a bid to blow up the house which contained the most merciless Indian marksmen. They could not get near, and Lieutenant Glass was injured when the rope pulling him back up the wall of the fort broke.

In mid-October Clive, after a formidable feat of military engineering, had a huge old cannon he had found in the fort hoisted on an earthwork built on top of the only solid tower in the fort. This blasted a 72-pound cannonball into the Nawab's palace, which Raza Sahib had made his headquarters, for three days running. On the fourth day the cannon exploded.

Raza Sahib countered by placing several cannon on top of a nearby house which had been filled with earth. This was ludicrously exposed, however, and once its crew was in place, the British blasted the earthwork with one of their eighteen-pounders, knocking it over and immobilising the guns and dispersing the 50-strong crew.

Clive's only hope lay in reinforcements, and that was a slender one indeed. Muhammad Ali and de Guingens at Trichinopoly refused to send support for fear it would prejudice their own chances of survival. The Regent of Mysore, supposedly hostile to Raza Sahib, was frightened of French retaliation and appeared to be waiting to join the winner.

Some of Raza Sahib's supporters went to Clive saying they were prepared to join him – but he did not trust them. There were rumours that the Marathas might come to his help, but they were no more than rumours. No faith could be placed in their loyalties, which were usually decided by the prospect of plunder.

Saunders meanwhile scratched together a tiny relief force of 130 Britons and 100 Indians, the most he could spare from the settlements. The report greatly heartened Clive and his men: relief was just days away. Bitter disappointment followed: the news soon reached him that this tiny column had been intercepted by an overwhelming enemy force and had had to return to Madras.

The siege went relentlessly on, day after day, Clive's men continually patrolling the parapets while musket fire crackled ceaselessly away. By 21 October Saunders, who still retained a channel of communication with Clive through intrepid Indian couriers, reported that Clive 'thinks himself able to defend a breach should the enemy make one; his only apprehensions therefore are his people's falling down through fatigue; that he thinks no less a force than 1,000 blacks and 200 Europeans can attempt to relieve him, as the enemy's situation is strong and their numbers increase daily'.

However, the position had deteriorated further. French heavy artillery had arrived from Pondicherry. One of Clive's two eighteen-pounders was disabled. For six days on end, the French guns blasted the north-west wall of the fort, reducing it to rubble, while Clive and his officers spurred and cursed their men into building up a new defence from the rubble, complete with a trench. Another French battery was set up on the south-west side, demolishing an even larger section of the wall. Again, improvised defences were thrown up.

Even Clive did not have much hope of holding out any longer. Disease, casualties and fatigue had taken their toll. According to one sergeant, only 80 of the Europeans and 120 Indians were fit for duty. If the fort was taken, Clive was conscious that whatever hope the British had of resisting the French domination of southern India would vanish. The French and their Indian allies, having won a victory of immense prestige, would be able to bring their full forces to bear on Trichinopoly. After that it would be an easy matter to mop up the undermanned garrisons at Madras and Fort St David.

Clive had been instrumental in persuading the council at Fort St David to adopt the reckless plan to seize Arcot. If it fell, he would be the man held responsible for having divided British forces and rendered Madras and Fort St David so vulnerable. Personal pride forced him to redouble his efforts. He was only 26 and desperate to see his gamble pay off.

Besides, he believed that, having lasted out so long, luck might just turn his way again. If he was wrong, the small British presence in southern India would be snuffed out. He did not waver in his outward determination; he could not afford to.

Early in November came the news that the Regent of Mysore had, at last, been able to bribe a force of Marathas under one of their most fearsome leaders, Morari Rao, to come to Clive's help. They had originally been engaged to assist Muhammad Ali at Trichinopoly, but the regent had been vastly impressed by Clive's seizure of Arcot and continued resistance there, and they were camped to the west of the city. However, Morari Rao refused to lead his 6,000 troops into battle until he had received payment from Muhammad Ali.

Still, the news was a psychological boost for Clive's desperate force – and a source of deep anxiety for the besiegers. In addition, a new relief force from Madras, under the command of Captain James

Kilpatrick, was said to be on its way. Clive, with the bright, fevered eyes of the exhausted and numbed by the continuous crackle of rifle fire around the fort for so many weeks, was astonished one afternoon to see an emissary of Raza Sahib under a white flag. He was there to offer terms. Clive could surrender and he personally would be well treated and his men spared. Otherwise he would be attacked at once and all his men killed.

Clive immediately rejected the offer, guessing correctly that it had been prompted by Raza Sahib's alarm at the prospect of reinforcements reaching the garrison. Clive insultingly told the emissary that Raza Sahib's father was a usurper, his army a rabble, and he should pause to think before sending his men into a gap defended by British soldiers. Now, nearly 70 days after the seizure of the fort, and after nearly 50 of close siege, the endgame was in sight. The huge army outside was about to attack. Clive and his shrunken band faced only slaughter if they lost.

On the evening of 13 November Clive learnt from a spy that the attack would be mounted next day. He hardly slept that night and was up before dawn. It was the last day of Muharram, the great Shia Moslem festival commemorating the martyrdom of the grandsons of the Prophet, Hassan and Hussein. The latter was butchered after all around him had been slain. His head was carried to the enemy leader, who struck at it with a stick, and, it was said, his lips were then seen pressed to the lips of the Prophet in a vision. If a Shia Moslem died on this holy day, he would go straight to heaven.

Shia is the most zealous branch of Islam, and Raza Sahib had no trouble working his men into the religious frenzy characteristic even when such a community is at peace. Clive and his soldiers could hear the wailing ululations and shrieking outside, the drum-banging and trumpet-blowing of an army drunk on liquor and high on drugs, as they worked themselves into a fever of vengeance.

Even for Clive, the terrifying sounds outside the fort that still late autumn evening must have been chilling. The fort had withstood two ham-handed attacks, a series of bombardments and relentless musket fire. But could just 200 battle-fit soldiers stand up to a whole religious-crazed army of more than 15,000?

Just before dawn a large number of men carrying ladders were seen running forward. Behind them elephants with huge protective iron plates on their foreheads charged forward to batter down the gates. Further behind, a huge torrent of enemy soldiers with muskets and spears surged as far as the eye could see.

Clive, entirely cool in a crisis and apparently fearless, promptly gave orders for his men to shoot at the unprotected flanks of the elephants. They stopped and reared up under the intense pain; and then turned and stampeded into the soldiers following them. The gates remained secure. However, simultaneous attacks were being mounted in the two major breaches caused by the French guns, the enemy spurred on by their religious frenzy 'with a mad kind of intrepidity'.

Clive had organised his tiny force to fire, and then hand back their muskets to loaders who would promptly pass on another gun, so as to make use of both his active and inactive soldiers. This concentrated fire at last caused the attackers to waver. Meanwhile grenades were being hurled from the ramparts at the second line of enemy troops.

At the north-west breach, the leader of the assailing forces, Abdul Kodah Khan, led his troops forward across the moat and to the first trench, waving his flag – before being struck by a bullet and knocked into the water below. Beside the other breach, the moat was still deep, and the attackers had launched a raft with some 70 men on it. This came under intense fire from two small English guns. Clive himself grabbed one of them and raked the vessel with the most accurate shots, causing the men on board to panic and capsize the raft. The moat was soon full of struggling figures under fire.

The French, meanwhile, were nowhere to be seen. The French commander, Goupil, had disapproved of Raza Sahib's decision to storm the fort, and had kept aloof. By now wave after wave of brave if undisciplined attacks had been driven off, and Raza Sahib decided to withdraw. His men tried to return to retrieve the bodies of the dead, a custom traditionally allowed by the enemy in India. But the British fired as they advanced, driving them back, either mistaking them for a new assault or as part of a deliberate tactic by Clive to terrify the enemy.

It was just before dawn, and the fierce fight, which had seemed interminable, had only lasted an hour. Robert Orme, Clive's first biographer, described how the British were 'left to gaze at each other in the first garish brilliance of the suddenly uplifted sun'.

The scene must have been eerie. The screams, battle chants and trumpets, the yells and groans of conflict had been replaced by the moans of the dying. Around 300 of the enemy lay strewn outside the wall; just four British soldiers had been killed and two Indians wounded. It had been a testament to the incredible difficulty of storming a well-defended fort, as well as to Clive's leadership.

Even so, the young captain, while triumphant and exhausted, could hardly afford to rest on his laurels. The enemy was almost certainly regrouping for another attack; they had a manpower reserve of some 15,000 fighters. The next attack could not be long in coming. If they kept up the pressure, Clive's exhausted men could hardly keep up the resistance indefinitely.

Two hours later a relentless barrage of musket and cannon fire began. This was presumably the softening up needed to deter his men from manning the ramparts again. Clive embarked on his rounds again, cheering up his men and cajoling them, checking on the defences. After more than four hours the relentless bombard-ment, which had set all of them on edge, ceased, and a small party arrived under a white flag requesting permission to carry off the dead, who were decomposing under the intense midday sun. The request was granted.

Two hours later the pounding began again. The exhausted garrison rested as best it could. The relentless bombardment continued for a full twelve hours; Clive imagined the enemy were seeking to exhaust the garrison mentally in preparation for the next assault. When it ceased at last at two in the morning, the jangled nerves of Clive and his men were tensed for the attack. All night they watched and waited for the next pre-dawn assault.

When the sun rose a second time, there was no sign of the enemy, although their guns and baggage were strewn before the fort. They had left the city, and the bombardment had been a cover to allow them to retire in good order, in case the formidable enemy within the fort sallied out to attack them.

They knew, too, what Clive did not: that Kilpatrick was on his way; he arrived the same afternoon. The Marathas, too, were nearby. 'You would never believe that four or five hundred beggarly Marathas would make M. Goupil decide to raise the siege,' railed Dupleix afterwards. But it was indeed all over. Clive's dusty, jaded, feverish, nerve-shattered forces were able to collapse in relief.

As one of them wrote, they experienced 'unbounded joy when we heard Captain Kilpatrick was within a few hours' march . . . Thus did providence disappoint our fears and relieve us from the dread necessity of starving or submitting to the terms of merciless barbarians. And Captain Kilpatrick's command joined us in the afternoon. We fully and unmolested enjoyed the fruits of the earth so long denied us . . . and solaced ourselves with the pleasing reflection of having maintained the character of Britons in a clime so remote from our own.'

CHAPTER 7

The Chase

Some 75 days after entering Arcot, more than 50 days of intensive siege were over. It had been one of the most astonishing feats of British arms and leadership ever undertaken: a 26-year-old with just 200 men defending a sprawling fortress with crumbling defences and two great breaches in the walls had prevailed against an army of 15,000 men. It was the first great triumph of British arms in the history of India, after a succession of lacklustre efforts seemed to have relegated Britain to the status of a second-class, even non-existent, power.

The repercussions in India of Arcot were far more significant than appeared at first. Both Clive and Kilpatrick, although blessing their good fortune in battle, realised that they still faced a far more numerous enemy, which had departed the city almost intact. Yet for Chanda Sahib, viceroy of the Carnatic, to have not just lost his capital by fluke, but then been unable to retake it, was a massive blow to his prestige among his fellow Indian princes.

Up to Arcot, the British in India had appeared to be the poor relations of the French, outshone by them in courage, fighting ability, commercial skill and magnificence. The British had staged one successful defence of Fort St David – or they would have been driven out of southern India – and suffered a string of disasters: the loss of Madras and Fort St George; the humiliating failure to capture Pondicherry with vastly superior forces; and their failure to break the siege of Trichinopoly.

Clive's victory at Arcot for the first time impressed upon the Indian princes that the British might be a match for the French after all. None had believed that he could possibly hold out against far superior forces backed by French troops and artillery.

It was a remarkable feat in itself, and doubly remarkable for a young man at the beginning of his military career.

The nature of Clive's ability as a commander was also revealed for the first time. He had shown remarkable proof of generalship. Constantly chivvying his men, inspiring them, determined and skilful in the deployment of his limited resources, keeping up their morale through prodding the enemy and reassuring his troops that help was on the way, he had demonstrated formidable ability.

He was now exhausted, physically and mentally; he had been drained by his responsibility. But he knew that he could not rest yet, he must consolidate his position. He had won only the first battle, not the war. After spending a fortnight recovering at Arcot, now plentifully supplied with food and drink, he marched to liaise with the Marathas.

One minor fort after another surrendered to his forces before he met up with 1,000 or so Maratha cavalry under the command of Morari Rao's brother, Buzangara, a swashbuckling rogue, the nearest equivalent to a pirate on land, even by the standards of his people. Buzangara's horse had split into small groups and were plundering and terrorising the countryside in the absence of central authority. However, Raza Sahib caught Buzangara himself in an ambush, and forced him to abandon his booty.

In fury, and also in the hope of further plunder, Buzangara joined up with Clive at last. Clive's objective was now to attack Raza Sahib's army while it was still demoralised, and before French reinforcements could be hurried up. The enemy army had retired to the large and imposingly sinister fortress of Vellore. Clive's chances of launching an attack with any prospect of success seemed hopeless. A prostitute employed as a spy by Clive was murdered in the temple of this forbidding grey buttress.

However, as Clive rode at the head of his force of 200 British soldiers, 300 sepoys and some 600 Marathas – the rest having gone off on a plundering expedition, the latter naked save for turbans and loincloths, and riding horses drugged with opium – he learnt that Raza Sahib had left Vellore to meet up with French reinforcements.

He urged his men forward to intercept the enemy now that they were beyond the security of the fortress; the Indian commander had made an appalling blunder in thus exposing his men. The British marched the whole night, and the two forces came into contact on 3 December near the town of Arni, some 20 miles south of Arcot. This time it was the enemy, stronger in numbers and self-confident under French generalship, that turned to give battle.

Clive drew his men up in a skilfully defensive position of his own choosing – on a small hill just behind flooded rice fields with only a narrow causeway for access. On the right he deployed his sepoys in the shelter of a small village, and on the left the Maratha cavalry in a palm grove.

The French and Indian forces advanced at midday. There were some 300 French troops, 2,500 Indian infantry and 2,000 cavalry. The enemy moved forward under cover from several cannon blasting at the British position: Clive's artillery fire, straight down the slope, proved more effective. The advance guard of the French had no option but to move along the causeway with their artillery. There they were easy targets for Clive's guns.

As the enemy approached the village they came under intense musket fire from the sepoys, and the infantry soon abandoned the causeway to take shelter in the lower rice fields, where they became bogged down, still under fire. Panic set in and they floundered about in disarray and retreated.

To the left, however, things were not going so well. A large contingent of Raza Sahib's troops had advanced towards the Maratha position. As the soldiers moved forward, the Marathas bravely launched one cavalry charge after another, being beaten back by the well-disciplined French-led troops five times.

Clive ordered Bulkley forward with two cannon to support them; in the rush, the ammunition was forgotten, and Clive had to order Bulkley and his men to retreat to fetch it – but to do so slowly, as though changing position, so as not to give the impression that the British were retreating. Puzzled by the manoeuvre, the French commanders assumed that Clive had ordered reinforcements to capture their guns which were now exposed on the causeway and undefended by artillery. Raza Sahib ordered part of his force away from the left flank to secure the guns.

This gave the Marathas the breakthrough they sought and, with Bulkley's help, they launched a successful attack on the French and Indian cavalry, driving them back. The sepoys now launched an attack upon the French reinforcements sent to protect the guns, who were already trapped in a hail of musket fire from the protected positions in the village. Clive ordered the remainder of his forces on the hill forward and battled the enemy down the causeway on which, because of the restricted width, their superiority in numbers was of no use. The French and Indians fought back furiously, trying to make a stand three times, but were relentlessly pushed back.

The Marathas meanwhile forced the enemy back on the left flank, and succeeded in capturing Raza Sahib's war chest of 100,000 rupees; the Maratha attacks continued during the night, when Clive's forces broke off the assault.

When the sun rose the enemy was gone, their baggage and their dead and wounded strewn about the battlefield. Clive had won a major field battle against superior forces, both French and Indian, through good judgement, flexibility, and the careful placing and repositioning of his troops. Arcot had been a triumph of endurance, courage to the point of recklessness and leadership. Arni was a classical military victory accomplished through good tactics, discipline and resourcefulness. Clive had shown himself to be an excellent and steady field commander.

Clive's military reputation was now rippling out among the Indians. Some 1,000 Indians sought to join his army, but he could only accept those that had weapons – around 600. Muhammad Ali labelled Clive Sabit Jang – 'Steady in War' – a great honour for a heathen. Some 200 British soldiers, 700 sepoys and 600 Maratha cavalry had put to flight 300 Frenchmen, 2,500 sepoys and 2,000 cavalry. No British or Marathas were killed; and there were just a dozen or so sepoy casualties. Around 200 of the enemy, 50 of them French, had been killed or seriously injured. In this battle both sides had been European-led and trained; this was no walkover against a cumbersome Indian army.

The enemy were now for the first time thrown on the defensive. Although still vastly superior numerically, they had twice been defeated by smaller though more effective British forces. It seemed likely that local Indian rulers would increasingly rally around Muhammad Ali and his British allies, still holding on to Trichinopoly. The French at Pondicherry arrogantly continued to assert that these setbacks were temporary, due to the failure of Raza Sahib's generalship; only Dupleix was uneasy.

Clive now considered that the greatest danger lay to Madras, which he feared that Raza Sahib's army would attack, knowing its garrison to be depleted; but Saunders told him not to be too hasty and instead ordered an assault on the enemy garrison at Conjeveeram. Clive seems to have been right in his view: Saunders at Fort St David had much less appreciation than Clive of the danger that Madras faced. But the governor feared Arcot would be exposed and isolated if the enemy controlled Conjeveeram along the main road to the coast.

Moreover, a party of British wounded who were being transferred to Madras had been attacked on the orders of the commander at Conjeveeram, a brutal, hunchbacked Portuguese mercenary called La Volonté. Most had been butchered. Two British officers had been captured, one being Lieutenant Glass, who had been injured falling from a rope during the attempt to silence the enemy guns at Arcot. They were threatened with death. This was probably the deciding factor with Saunders, and Clive agreed to go to their rescue.

The fate of the two officers, Glass and Revell, hung by a thread. The governor of Conjeveeram, Moden Sahib, had been corresponding secretly with Clive and had assured him he would seek to protect the Englishmen. La Volonté, meanwhile, strutted about the fort, threatening to hang the officers if Clive attacked. On 16 December Clive's batteries opened fire. It was a one-sided affair. The enemy had only muskets. But Clive, exposing himself fearlessly to the fire, suffered the tragedy of having his brave and capable friend John Bulkley, veteran of Arcot and Arni, cut down beside him: the carefree days of drinking and whoring at Fort St David had become altogether more serious.

After two days of bombardment, La Volonté had Revell brought on to the battlements to discourage English fire. But Moden Sahib appears to have convinced him to bring the hostage down again. La Volonté forced Revell to write to Clive to say that he and Glass would be hanged if the bombardment did not cease; but Moden Sahib intercepted the letter.

The same night La Volonté and his force fled, leaving behind the two English officers. Clive set about destroying the fortifications to the great temple, and then abandoned the town as strategically useless. The French soon returned, but also found it indefensible and valueless. Clive cannot but have been bitter about the episode: the two officers had been saved – if their lives were ever really endangered – but Bulkley had been killed. The place had been of no strategic value whatsoever.

Clive's forces were now depleted again: Buzangara and the Marathas wanted to return to Trichinopoly in an effort to secure further spoils for Muhammad Ali, and demanded an elephant as the prize for staying with Clive – something he could not deliver (although later he was to be overburdened with elephants). He sent half his force to Arcot and returned to Madras and Fort St David, where he was treated as a conquering hero. Clive delighted in his reception, but he was keen to move on to Trichinopoly, not to rest on his laurels.

Raza Sahib's scattered forces now began to pull themselves together. Fearing a British relief of Trichinopoly, he decided that the best form of defence was attack. In a move of astonishing boldness – which Clive had half feared, knowing Raza Sahib to be by no means beaten – he took a leaf out of Clive's book and marched to Madras to attack the British.

It was a daring gambit for a commander recently so badly mauled, and attested to his resilience. He had only thirty Frenchmen under his command, some 1,300 sepoys and 1,400 cavalry. This force appeared suddenly in the prosperous settlements to the west of the town, plundering the luxurious garden houses on the outskirts.

For the second time in six years, Madras seemed on the verge of enemy occupation and destruction. Its garrison was small and its defences as poor as ever. The British had miscalculated badly. Clive was promptly despatched from Fort St David to the rescue. He quickly put together an army of some 500 sepoys. Forces were despatched by Kilpatrick from Arcot; and, through luck, 100 British soldiers arrived from Bengal. By February 1752, Clive had around 400 Europeans and 1,300 sepoys under his command. Madras was saved. Raza Sahib did not dare attack. A major crisis had been defused whose cause had been the complacency of the British.

Saunders now ordered Clive to attack the Indian camp at Vendalore, some 25 miles away. This was well fortified, and Clive, although commanding a force almost equal in size, refused. He was showing the prudence of a great commander, although he was later criticised for lacking courage, a charge which rankled with him. Usually attacked for being reckless, he had made a fair assessment of the odds, and feared he would not win. Saunders was irked.

Finally Clive felt strong enough to stage an assault – only to find the camp abandoned – something Clive, with his excellent sources of Indian intelligence, may have already known. Raza Sahib had left for Arcot, to attack the poorly defended fort there.

What happened next is a matter of intense speculation and controversy. Raza Sahib has been so derided as a commander that it is often assumed that the near-disaster that befell the British happened almost by accident. But however poor his leadership in the past – and his detractors were chiefly the British, his enemies, and the French, accustomed to blaming their own mistakes on their Indian allies – his tactics and strategy on this occasion were equal to those of the British.

His raid on Madras had turned the tables on them, reviving the morale of his troops after the defeat of Arcot. Now he had surprised the British once again, showing flexibility and skill by suddenly making for poorly defended Arcot just as Clive's forces arrived to reinforce Madras. If Raza Sahib had indeed planned the trap and ambush that followed – and there is no reason to think he didn't – Clive certainly fell headlong into it.

The young captain's force hurried northwards at sunset on the night of 28 February, with the intention of resting at the village of Kaveripak. The roar of cannon suddenly engulfed them in the dark. Raza Sahib's army was all about them: they had been ambushed. It was Clive's worst misjudgement. One of the most extraordinary battles in the history of the British in India had begun.

As shells exploded about them and bodies were sent flying, Clive showed his legendary calm in a crisis. He ordered his men to shelter in a ditch by the side of the road on the left. The British cannon were dragged over to the opposite side along with the baggage, and began to fire back as Raza Sahib's force staged a frontal assault down the road. It was dark, but a nearly full moon provided some visibility. The flash of gunfire in the gloom was relentless.

Neither side gave an inch, but the British position was much the more precarious. They had no idea of the size of the enemy force, or their whereabouts, and could only hope that they would not be overcome by a major attack. Clive's most prudent course of action at this moment was to retreat, seeking to save his guns and baggage. But he had been stung by Saunders's criticism of his failure to attack the French camp outside Madras, and one of his major objectives in this war was to replace the myth of French with English invincibility.

If he were once defeated or forced to retreat, the concept of Clive as victor would be lost. His predicament was dire. No fewer than nine French cannon were firing upon him. The enemy cavalry were preparing to charge from a point further up the ditch.

Then luck and treachery intervened on his side. Clive had sent one of the commanders of his sepoys, a Portuguese half-caste called Shawlum, to scout out to the right, to find a possible avenue of escape in the darkness. Shawlum seems to have run into the commander of the Indian force behind the French guns and negotiated with him, through bribery or other means, to withdraw his men from the one flank behind the French position that was not defended by an embankment or a ditch.

When Shawlum returned, Clive at once grasped the opportunity and himself accompanied 200 British soldiers – the bulk of his force – and 700 sepoys across the flat but uneven ground and the mango grove. Almost certainly Clive went in order to give his personal seal of approval to the deal arranged between Shawlum and the local commander – a first example of the double-dealing essential to winning or avoiding battle in India, for which he was to be so unjustly pilloried later in life.

The scene, under a nearly full moon, with the French cannon blasting away in the darkness, the few British pieces attempting to fire back, and the two sides exchanging rapid rifle fire, can only be imagined. After Clive gave his agreement to the Indian commander, he returned. The defector led Shawlum and the British force around the back of the French position.

When Clive got back, the desperate soldiers in the ditch were already preparing to flee: the relentless French gunfire had unnerved them, and had found its range. Clive berated them furiously, forcing them to stand their ground; his very presence was enough to reassure them. Any normal commander forced to fight on the enemy's ground and terms by such an ambush would have called a retreat. Instead he had gambled desperately on a flank attack behind enemy lines at night.

The flanking party was commanded by a young ensign, William Keene. They stumbled over the rough ground in the dark, guided by their Indian deserter, until they came within 300 yards of the back of the French position.

Another young ensign, Symmonds, was sent forward to scout and fell into a trench of enemy sepoys. He pretended at once to be a French officer and strutted about. They behaved submissively: their French was not good enough to see through the deception. He was fortunate in that there was no actual French officer present. After checking that they were still pointing their weapons away from the ambushers, towards where the bulk of Clive's forces were pinned down in the darkness, guns flashing, he returned to Keene.

The British force then crept up on the French-led forces from behind, and let fire at them from a distance of just 50 yards with a volley. The effect was devastating. The French commander shouted immediately 'Sauve qui peut' and most of his soldiers surrendered. The French guns fell silent. Clive and his men were still under intense fire from the forces before them, although the ones to the side had fallen silent. But when news of the débâcle reached the enemy in front, the whole of Raza Sahib's force began to melt away. The moon had gone down, and Clive did not dare give chase.

As the sun rose the following morning, Clive was disconsolate: forty of his best European soldiers had been killed, as well as thirty of his Indian sepoys. Yet huge numbers of the enemy lay strewn about the field, including the commander of Raza Sahib's cavalry, which had been stationed nearby but not actually used in the fighting. Victory had been snatched from the jaws of defeat.

Through guile, quick thinking and sheer determination, Clive had turned the tables after, through foolhardiness, leading his men into a trap. It was one of the most brilliantly and daringly executed turnarounds in military history. But it had been a close thing, the nearest Clive had yet come to a serious defeat.

To the victor the spoils. Raza Shah now had been decisively beaten. The remainder of his army dispersed before Clive 'the invincible', who was able to win even when caught in a finely executed ambush. Dupleix's comments reveal the depth of bitterness he felt after Kaveripak. 'A few shots more and all would have been over with the English . . . Their commander, Mr Clive, hid throughout the combat,' he spat, presumably a reference to the mission away from the front.

Clive himself was in bitter mood. The nearly successful French ambush and the loss of so many of his men made him grim and determined. Moving southwards towards Fort St David, they reached an extraordinary folly constructed by Dupleix to mark the spot where Nasir Jang had been murdered a year and a half before. It was called Dupleixfatahabad – the City of the Victory of Dupleix. A great base had been laid on which a column was to be erected; around this a large native settlement had sprung up.

Clive destroyed 'this monument of villainy' and, in an uncharacteristic act of savagery, burnt the village to the ground. This act was to be laid against him in later life; he was to defend himself as having tried to break the French stranglehold over India, which was based as much on such displays of pomp and grandeur as anything else.

But the truth was that he was angry, aggressive and petty. He had been fighting too long, he had faced too many desperate situations, he had been coping with the stupidity of his military superiors again and again. He wanted now to march on Trichinopoly and chase the French from southern India. His biggest problem was that he was loathed by his nominal bosses, who were senior to him in the army and despised him as a non-soldier and a protégé of Saunders. For his part, Clive had nothing but contempt for the senior commander, de Guingens, who had never dared to venture out of Trichinopoly to attack his besiegers.

CHAPTER 8

The Siege of Trichinopoly

The command problem was resolved by the return of Stringer Lawrence to India, this time properly paid. He was placed in charge as the undisputed commander of the force to relieve Trichinopoly. Now the young 'invincible' could be given his head under the benevolent eye of the Old Cock.

The two set off at the head of their army along the by now familiar 150-mile road from Fort St David to Trichinopoly, the portly, diminutive, bluff old soldier alongside his tall, determined second-in-command. This time they went unmolested. When they reached Trichinopoly it was hard for them to comprehend how de Guingens could not have staged an attack against his besiegers. Muhammad Ali's forces had been joined by the forces of the Prince of Mysore and the Regent of Tanjori, convinced by Clive's victories that the British would now be the winning side; Morari Rao and his Marathas had also ridden in. Altogether the pro-British forces camped outside Trichinopoly amounted to some 40,000 men, outnumbering the besieging army of around 30,000.

The truth was that de Guingens still distrusted these princes and the Marathas, and feared that in any sally he would have to bear the brunt of the fighting while the Indians watched and waited to see which way the wind blew. Yet a show of bravery and leadership by the British commander would probably have rallied them. Instead, he compounded their uncertainty by skulking inside the fort, quarrelling bitterly with Muhammad Ali, who openly taunted the British with being cowards.

Dupleix at Pondicherry was well aware of the danger posed by Lawrence's and Clive's arrival and knew that the final great showdown between British and French in India was imminent. As soon as news of the approaching British army was relayed to him, he despatched reinforcements to the French commander, Jacques Law, a half-Scot, ordering him 'to neglect nothing in the effort to succeed'. Dupleix was now left with only a skeleton garrison at Pondicherry.

The great besieging armies of Law and Chanda Sahib, the colourful old warhorse who had so long been the French protégé, were camped to the east of Trichinopoly, which was protected to the north by two rivers, the Cauvery and Coleroon. To the south lay a great plain. It provided one of the most magnificent spectacles in southern India. On the riverside there were two striking pagodas. Behind, a rambling four-mile wall enclosed a bustling city at the heart of which was the rock fortress itself.

The rock was orange in colour: fortifications and battlements were built precipitously up its flanks, which divided to form two tiers. One, the lower, was a massive and ingeniously built fortress, clinging to the sheer rock; on the other were built two picturesque temples. Below lay the squalor and bustle of Indian urban life.

To comprehend the campaign at Trichinopoly, and indeed later in Bengal, it is necessary to understand the nature of the colourful, shambling circuses that were the Indian armies of the time. Those besieging the rock fortress-town were entirely typical. The forces of an Indian prince much more nearly resembled a travelling township than an army. Anything between 10,000 and 100,000 in strength, they consisted of a fighting force composed of four elements: commanders mounted on elephants; the élite cavalry; the artillery; and the infantry. The other three-quarters of the army were non-combatants.

The commanders on the elephants were deliberately conspicuous, so that they could provide rallying points for the men: if they were shot, Indian armies were usually demoralised and turned tail. But this made them an easy target for the enemy. As an English observer wrote, 'these enormous beasts (elephants) now seemed to be brought into the field for no other end but to be a mark for our artillery'. The commanders were accompanied by a train of wives, dancers, female family members, concubines and prostitutes, who in turn had their own maidservants, their male servants and *farashes*, who pitched their tents.

The élite, well-trained cavalrymen were also each accompanied by two servants – one paid to look after the horse, the other to forage for grass – as well as their families. The pride of Indian armies were the heavy artillery pieces, dragged by huge teams of bullocks; light English field-pieces were to enjoy manoeuvring around these and firing at the cattle, stampeding them. The Indians were eventually to retaliate by getting Europeans to man the artillery. Finally, the infantry were usually an ill-organised rabble without an internal command structure, armed with swords, lances and some matchlocks. As Chaudhury puts it, 'the fighting among the princes themselves is like rioting on a vast scale'.

The Indian armies were burdened by a number of disadvantages, apart from sheer size and unwieldiness: their men were press-ganged or induced to fight by the prospect of plunder (which was true, though to a lesser extent, of European armies of the time). Their tactics were often dictated by astrologers and omens – as happened in the siege of Trichinopoly. The men were usually induced to attack with a heavy dose of opium, intoxicating them to forget their terrors in a burst of courage and energy, but also muddling their judgements and reactions.

They also made easy targets for night attacks, as Clive was to show to devastating effect. As a contemporary English writer put it: 'At the close of the evening, every man eats an inconceivable quantity of rice, and many take after it some kind of soporific drugs; so that about midnight, the whole army is in a dead sleep: the consequence of these habits is obvious; and yet it would appear a strange proposition to an Eastern monarch, to endeavour to persuade him, that the security of his throne depended upon the regulation of the meals of a common soldier: much less would he be prevailed on to restrain him in the use of that opium, which is to warm his blood for action, and animate his soul with heroism. It must fill the mind of an European soldier at once with compassion and contempt, to see a heap of these poor creatures, solely animated by a momentary intoxication, crowded into a breach, and both in their garb and impotent fury, resembling a mob of frantic women.'

On the morning of 29 March Lawrence's and Clive's forces approached the city, seeking to make for the gap between it and the enemy camp. To Clive's delight, a force of 200 British soldiers and 400 Indians emerged from the fortress to meet them, and were not intercepted by the besiegers. They were commanded by Clive's swashbuckling old comrade, John Dalton.

The two friends embraced each other under the eyes of the tubby, self-important, genial Lawrence, and both forces were ordered to stop for breakfast under the intense sun. No doubt Dalton and Clive exchanged rude comments about the maddeningly cautious de Guingens: such an active man as Dalton could not but have been deeply frustrated at being cooped up in the fortress while the enemy went unmolested outside.

Scouts suddenly galloped into camp to warn that the enemy were approaching. A massive cannonade rang out. The British had been caught with their trousers down. As the British forces regrouped, a huge body of men approached in desperate flight: they were from the armies of Mysore and Tanjori as well as the Maratha forces.

Lawrence quickly rallied the Indian armies behind him, stopping their flight, and ordered his forces forward with drums beating, at a measured pace, to restore the battered confidence of the princely allies. As the army advanced, the whole horizon of that flat plain was suddenly blocked as far as the eye could see by an opposing force of elephants, camels, horsemen and infantry bearing pennants, flags, umbrellas, standards, pikes, spears and long trumpets in a riotous display of colour. The plain had become a great tournament ground, divided only by the narrow gulf between the two armies.

The British-led forces maintained their steady pace, under intense bombardment from Chanda Sahib's guns. Clive galloped off to reconnoitre, and found an ideal place to make a stand: a village with a choultry, providing plenty of cover. He returned and led a force, under heavy cannonade, to seize the choultry, positioning his guns behind it, returning the French fire and giving cover to the main British force, which now moved to the shelter of the village.

The two sides had almost matching firepower, and 'the hottest cannonade that was ever seen in the East Indies' now broke out. The French and Chanda Sahib's forces were unprotected and, after a spell of fierce artillery exchanges, withdrew their guns. Chanda Sahib's infantry stood their ground a long time, before retreating, leaving only his cavalry behind. When a cannonshot decapitated their commander, they too withdrew. Only around twenty of Lawrence's men had been killed, a third dying of the heat.

This first battle had been but a prelude, although the British had won on points: both armies were still virtually intact. Clive must be given the credit for finding his forces a defensible position. However, elephants and tributes were showered upon the three British commanders as they made their way into Trichinopoly.

At last all of the allies were united. These were: the formidable Muhammad Ali; the Prince of Mysore and the Regent of Tanjori; Morari Rao, the greatest Maratha commander; and on the English side, Lawrence, de Guingens, Clive and Dalton. The claustrophobia of Trichinopoly's siege had been lifted after nearly a year.

The feasting and celebrations that night were genuine, but the resentment that the relieving commanders felt towards the cautious and inert de Guingens was intense. Within a couple of days Lawrence was pressing for an attack to take the enemy off balance. The Indian commanders refused to move until their astrologers had chosen a suitable day.

Frustrated, Lawrence resorted to sending a raiding party at night to attack Chanda Sahib's army to the east, which was unprotected by fortified positions – Lawrence and Clive's favourite tactic in a siege. However the raiding party missed the enemy camp altogether in the dark, and was spotted by the French as it hastily returned to Trichinopoly at dawn.

Law now made what most consider to be his most disastrous mistake: he sought a place of shelter for his armies where they could not be attacked, as they nearly were that night. It is easy to be hard on Law. But he himself was in a cruel dilemma. He was outnumbered, by both European and Indian soldiers. He believed he could not win a set-piece battle.

At the same time, Dupleix had given him firm orders not to give up Trichinopoly. Later Law was to lament bitterly to Lawrence that 'Mr Dupleix is a good man, a generous man, and it is not to him that we owe our misfortunes but to his wife whose violent spirit leads him to do things against his nature and will always involve us in endless difficulties.'

But even Dupleix was in a genuine dilemma. Although often plagued by *folie de grandeur* and his constitutional optimism that things were better than they were, if he had ordered a French retreat, there was no guarantee that the huge army of Chanda Sahib would have stayed loyal. Almost certainly a French withdrawal would have led to the rapid disintegration of the French-led alliance in southern India. Dupleix may have believed he had no choice but to fight – even if it resulted in the defeat of his army. Not being on the spot, he may have overestimated the strength of the French-led forces.

In the event his decision was almost certainly the wrong one: had he ordered a retreat, he would have saved the bulk of the French forces, which could have been evacuated to Pondicherry and waited for events in southern India once again to present an opportunity. With no possibility of flight, and with no confidence in his ability to win a pitched battle, Law may have been right in believing he had no option but to look for a defensible redoubt behind stone walls. Thus, in a dramatic reversal of fortunes, the besiegers were now about to become the besieged.

Such a refuge lay nearby: the 'island' of Srirangam, in fact a long tongue of land several miles long and only a couple of miles in extent at its widest, resembling a serpent with, at its head, two of India's most important and beautiful pagodas towering over the great plain to the north of Trichinopoly. To the south side, opposite the city, it was defended by the Cauvery river; to the north, the Coleroon, both of which merged to the west.

Srirangam pagoda itself was protected by a defensive network of no fewer than seven walls, the outer ones some 25 feet high; to the east was another, smaller, equally well-defended pagoda. The fort of Muhammad Ali had held out for nearly a year. Law may have reckoned he could do the same until a relief force from Pondicherry, under the command of the venerable and aged General d'Auteuil, arrived.

When Dupleix heard of Law's withdrawal to the pagoda complex, he was livid. 'I am sure this decision will please your wife, who cannot wait for the opportunity to hold you in her arms again,' he wrote witheringly. The British reaction was more immediate still: a day later Lawrence ordered Clive across both rivers to try and intercept Law's lines of communication with Pondicherry and close the siege about the island.

Clive's force consisted of around half the allied army: 400 British soldiers, 1,200 sepoys, 700 Marathas and most of the Tanjori army. Lawrence remained in command of around 500 British soldiers, 1,000 sepoys, the remainder of the Marathas and the huge, if clumsy and ineffectual, army of Mysore.

The strategy entailed considerable risk: once Law learnt that the

British army had divided in two, he could concentrate all his forces against one side or other, leaving the other stranded across the rivers – reversing the odds. De Guingens and other senior commanders resented the young Clive's being given charge of so large a body of men; but the Indian contingent refused to join unless he was at their head.

On the night of 4 April, Clive's army forded the river and marched the short distance to the village of Samiaveram, where he found an ideal defensive position in two walled temples. Any supplies to Law from Pondicherry would have to pass his position, and Clive believed he could retreat across the river to Trichinopoly if Law staged an attack there.

Within days, news of the relief convoy led by d'Auteuil reached Clive. It was carrying substantial supplies and seven lakhs of rupees (700,000 rupees – a colossal amount) for buying food, part of it probably intended to buy over some of Muhammad Ali's Indian allies.

About 15 miles from Clive's position lay a narrow pass, Utatur, where Clive decided to ambush d'Auteuil's forces. He asked for reinforcements from Lawrence to hold Samiaveram, leaving him free to march against the French. Lawrence refused, disagreeing with his subordinate's high-risk tactic and fearing an attack by Law across the river against poorly defended Trichinopoly. ('It would be as full of bad consequences for me to divide my force as you yours.')

Clive took the hint about his own intention of leaving half his garrison behind – and decided on an even riskier strategy. He decided to move the whole garrison out by night to attack d'Auteuil, leaving Samiaveram virtually unguarded, in the hope that his men would be back by dawn, before Law noticed their departure.

What followed was a mixture of pure British Boys' Own adventure and French farce. No sooner had the young captain's forces departed the camp than Indian scouts reported the news back to Law. Hardly believing his luck, he sent 80 Frenchmen and 500 sepoys to seize the temples at Samiaveram. Meanwhile Clive force-marched his grumbling soldiers 14 miles up the Pondicherry road only to discover that d'Auteuil, instead of marching to relieve Law, had decided to seek refuge in the well-defended fort of Utatur. Clive promptly marched his men back down the road to arrive just four hours after they had left, at around eleven o'clock. It was the grand old Duke of York all over again.

Clive's exhausted men bedded down, while their commander retired grumpily to his quarters in a nightshirt. The French force was meanwhile on its way in the dark when it captured an Indian scout from Samiaveram, who told the commander, Calquier, that Clive had already returned. The French commander refused to believe the man, branded him a spy, and told him to lead the force to Clive's camp at the point of a pistol.

At Calquier's side was an English deserter, a former sergeant now turned French officer named Kelsey who, on arriving at the gates of the British camp – which the French still did not believe was occupied by Clive's returned army – told the sentry that he was commanding a relief force from Trichinopoly. Once inside, the sentry led the French column directly to Clive's headquarters, a choultry just outside the pagoda where Clive's bodyguard slept. The bulk of the British forces were sleeping inside the walls of the bigger pagoda.

The sentry at the entrance to Clive's quarters challenged the soldiers, and Kelsey again replied that he had been sent by Lawrence. When he failed to give the password, the suspicious sentry realised something was amiss and fired his rifle into the air. Enemy muskets immediately blazed out in return.

The French, on being discovered, battled their way into the smaller pagoda, fighting hand-to-hand to force Clive's astonished bodyguard out and gain possession. Clive himself was woken by a bullet which killed a servant sleeping on the ground beside his palanquin, and another that hit his small portable writing desk. Still in his nightshirt, he ran over to the main pagoda and assembled a force of 200 men.

Believing, wrongly, that the camp was under attack from outside, he rushed forward among the enemy sepoys in the smaller pagoda, thinking them to be his own men, firing randomly and in panic. He began furiously cuffing them and swearing at them in Indian, yelling at them to fire straight. A sepoy lashed out at him with a sword. Clive, at last realising he was in the middle of the enemy, grabbed the man, who cut him on his face and chest before being stabbed by a nearby English officer.

A moment later, Clive found himself surrounded by Frenchmen.

If a single one had moved with speed and courage, the British empire in India might never have been. But Clive, showing extraordinary coolness, told them they were surrounded and would be 'cut to pieces' if they did not surrender immediately. Three did so, while three others escaped. Clive returned to the large pagoda, and started to regroup his forces to mount an attack on the French position.

As they subjected the small pagoda to intense fire, the French fought furiously, blasting back through the gate and tossing grenades over the wall. Dawn approached. Clive feared an attack by the main French force, and ordered his men to storm the pagoda. A young lieutenant led the charge, calling for volunteers, but was cut down by French bayonets at the entrance. Calquier tried to break out with his men, and was impaled on a blade, while his men were driven back.

Clive himself presented a wretched spectacle. Weak with loss of blood, his nightdress coloured crimson, he leaned on the shoulders of two sergeants as, under a white flag, he stumbled forward to negotiate. Kelsey, now in charge of the remaining defenders, knew that as a deserter he would be executed. He fired a shot which, as Clive was stooping, passed though the bodies of both upright sergeants, sparing him. Clive may have exaggerated the story a little, as was his wont; but he was not one to indulge in pure invention. Neither Lawrence nor Dalton chronicles the incident, but they were not present and had no reason further to puff Clive's reputation. He had had another miraculous escape.

The standoff continued. After a couple more hours, the French surrendered; their Indian troops had slipped away in the night, only to be hacked down to the last man by a troop of Marathas on horseback. Muhammad Ali's envoy sought the execution of the English deserters. Clive refused, although he acceded to Lawrence's order to hang Kelsey and the unfortunate Indian sepoy who had led the French into the camp.

Through an incredible piece of luck, and the foolhardiness of the French, a significant victory had been achieved – although Clive had twice nearly been killed. By a hair's breadth, the British had avoided losing their camp and being trapped between two forces. Although Clive cannot be faulted for reacting swiftly and with enormous courage in adversity, showing exemplary leadership, he had only just reversed the situation with the help of extraordinary good fortune. Lawrence, who always seemed to turn a blind eye to Clive's mistakes, was cock-a-hoop. 'I rejoice at your success, your wounds are not dangerous, and if they spoil the beauty of your face they raise your fame,' he wrote glowingly. From then on, Dalton jovially nicknamed Clive 'beauty'.

Saunders was informed by Lawrence, with some exaggeration, that half the enemy had been beaten and the remainder 'so cooped up they cannot escape'. Certainly the British intent was now not just to win a victory, but to trap the entire French army.

Clive, sobered by his narrow escape, knew that the bulk of Law's forces were still intact, and discerned a new danger approaching: the waters of the wide, shallow rivers were rising, and he had heard reports that the armies of Law and Chanda Sahib were making rafts. It seemed likely that they were preparing to attack while Clive's forces were stranded on the north side of the Coleroon without hope of reinforcement. Indeed, if d'Auteuil moved out of the fort at Utatur, they would catch Clive between two pincers.

Once again he asked for reinforcements, and once again Lawrence refused. Clive now decided to cross the swollen river on horseback personally to argue the case before his commander. The discussion was heated. Lawrence feared that if his men crossed, the French would be able to slip out of the trap and down to the settlement of Karikal on the coast, where they could make a stand or be lifted off by ships and taken to Pondicherry. Clive's view was that at the very least he must not leave Samiaveram unprotected again, and he needed a strong force to deal with d'Auteuil, still cooped up at Utatur.

Lawrence at length gave way, sending Dalton across with a few hundred men to attack d'Auteuil. This he did with great difficulty; by the time he returned to Samiaveram, the river was unfordable, and so he joined Clive – something the latter had perhaps intended. Thus reinforced, Clive attacked Law's last bastion on the north side of the Coleroon, Pitchanda. As they moved their guns up to the pagoda there, they decided to blast Chanda Sahib's camp just across the water.

This they did early in the morning. The camp was less a military encampment than a large and colourful village, filled with servants, merchants (who provided the money to pay the soldiers), prostitutes, cooks, women, children, elephants, camels and oxen. As the shelling began, the civilians immediately panicked, removing their tents and baggage as fast as they could. Within two hours, and after just a few shots, all the tents had been removed. The refugees did not stop until they reached the second pagoda, where a new camp was set up out of range of the British guns.

Clive was later accused of deliberately targeting civilians, bombarding them from a position high above the river. In fact the river banks were flat and the waters at least half a mile wide, so he could have seen little of the camp itself. However, he would certainly have known that there was a large civilian presence, and of the terror likely to be caused by his bombardment.

As the soldiers dwelt among the civilians, he may have felt he had little choice. He had anyway indulged in the tactic of sowing terror in these huge camps before, notably during the night attack at Arcot. He is unlikely to have caused many casualties.

Clive's guns were now turned on Pitchanda, while army riflemen sniped away at the gunners in the pagoda. After only a few hours, the white flag was raised by the French commander and a drummer started up – which some of Clive's sepoys misinterpreted as a call to arms. They attacked through a breach in the wall, which caused a panic, and 15 Frenchmen trying to escape by water were drowned.

Clive disowned responsibility for the attack, saying he was not near the fort at the time, but three French officers insisted he had been and had personally violated the white flag of truce. It may be that Clive was getting his revenge for the French violation of the white flag at the pagoda in Samiaveram; or he may have been telling the truth. However, a shadow had been cast over his career for the second time – the first being the razing of Dupleixfatahabad.

Clive bombarded Chanda Sahib's army on the peninsula once again, which was no longer out of range or shelter. With no sign of an easing of the trap, under intense and demoralising artillery fire, and with no sign of a response from Law, ordinary people began to leave the enemy camp, while increasingly large numbers of soldiers deserted to Clive or simply walked away.

Chanda Sahib, like some old-fashioned knight of chivalry, warmly embraced his deserting officers, and hoped that they would return when his fortunes improved. He gave them most of the stores and animals, and kept some 2,000 cavalry and 3,000 infantry loyal to him in the security of the larger pagoda. Law and his Frenchmen repaired to the smaller one. Around 1,500 of his army and most of his Indians had deserted to Clive. The endgame was in sight.

Lawrence landed the bulk of his forces across the river on Srirangam, while Clive went to mop up the remaining resistance at Utatur fort. There d'Auteuil's half-starved forces surrendered, with only a fraction of the money they were supposed to be bearing – the rest presumably having been smuggled back to Pondicherry or looted by deserting soldiers. Clive returned with the prize of Raza Sahib's magnificent elephant, which was given to Lawrence.

On 30 May Clive reached Srirangam Island and the following day Lawrence tried to batter Law's force into submission with a massive cannonade. Law refused to surrender unless his troops were given safe passage to return to Pondicherry. The British replied by stating that Muhammad Ali wanted the garrison put to the sword. Law then agreed to meet Lawrence, Clive and Dalton.

The half-Frenchman, half-Scot, facing certain defeat, met the three victors in a tent outside the pagoda, and argued gamely that as France and Britain were not at war, he should be set free with his French troops. Equally bogusly, Lawrence insisted that he was merely a pawn of Muhammad Ali, and had to carry out his orders. Finally Law and his fellow officers were granted parole, while his men were marched off to prison. On 4 June the British entered the pagoda walls, and the French soldiers threw down their arms and were taken into custody.

CHAPTER 9

The Fall of Dupleix

C handa Sahib, although Muhammad Ali's sworn enemy and, as a defeated commander, qualifying for instant death, was under the protection of the French. Indeed, as pretender to the throne of the Carnatic, it was essential to their interests to keep him alive. The British had shown a good deal of humanity throughout the campaign, but it was certainly in their interests that Chanda Sahib should no longer pose a threat. On the other hand, they were usually prepared to pension off their opponents.

Nevertheless there is no evidence that any negotiations as to his fate were entered upon when the surrender terms were discussed with Law. Dupleix was later to argue that Lawrence had expressly ordered the Indian leader to meet his fate. This was transparently false.

Yet it is possible that a vigorous intervention by Lawrence and Clive, who had formidable bargaining cards, might have saved the deposed ruler. They left him to the wolves, as far as can be ascertained – just possibly because his removal would extinguish the main focus for French aspirations in India. The circumstances will always remain murky and discreditable.

Law attempted desperately to get Chanda Sahib spirited out of Srirangam. One possibility was to use the Marathas – but they would almost certainly use Chanda Sahib as a hostage and sell him to the highest bidder. The Regent of Mysore was intent on getting his part of the bargain for supporting Muhammad Ali: control of Trichinopoly itself. Already there were signs that Muhammad Ali was going to renege on the deal; Chanda Sahib would have provided a useful bargaining counter – and Law rightly decided against using the regent's bad offices.

That left only the commander of the Tanjori army, who promised to spirit Chanda Sahib to the coast. However, Tanjori had been repeatedly attacked and captured by Chanda Sahib in the past. Law sought a hostage in exchange for a guarantee that Chanda Sahib would be treated properly and accompanied to the coast. The Tanjori general refused, saying that 'if he had a mind to break his word, the hostage would signify nothing'. While this was probably true, it is a sign of Law's weakness that he quietly acquiesced.

As soon as Chanda Sahib was handed over, he was put in chains. The Tanjori general, who may actually have intended to spare Chanda Sahib's life, was now threatened with attack by both the Regent of Mysore and Muhammad Ali unless the old warrior was handed over.

Faced with these threats, the general coldly decided the fate of the former ruler of a third of India. A Pathan tribesman first strangled Chanda Sahib, then beheaded him. Thus ended the life of that formidable veteran and plunderer, broken in spirit but chivalrous to the end. He died in the place where he was supposed to have tried to rob the dowager Rani of Trichinopoly of her jewels; she had ground them into powder to forestall him.

Muhammad Ali was now undisputed ruler of the Carnatic. Thus ended the rule of France's chief protégé in India, and although Dupleix did not yet know it, all his vainglorious dreams. Butchery was a standard end for an Indian potentate, although this one was accompanied by strong suspicions of connivance by the British.

Although Dupleix is said to have burst into tears at the news of the death of Chanda Sahib, and been unable to eat, he soon showed his usual remarkable resilience and talent for self-deception. On the day of Law's surrender – which he presumably had authorised – he wrote ingratiatingly and with breathtaking cheek to Muhammad Ali saying that the ruler of the Deccan had authorised him to hand over Trichinopoly to its new ruler. It was an attempt both to woo the new ruler of the Carnatic and to treat the British with the contempt he felt they deserved.

It is hard not to conclude that by this time he really had lost touch with reality. His constant belittling of his opponents reflected this. Clive, said Dupleix, was a 'secondary figure reported dead or wounded times without number . . . a coward who had remained hidden behind a tree during one engagement . . . An arrogant fellow given to much boasting . . . indiscreet.' Saunders was 'a madman, an enragé. Lawrence was 'violent and corrupt'. All that was now needed to turn the tables once more, in Dupleix's opinion, was the arrival of reinforcements from France.

Dupleix seemed to believe that the loss of half of his army was merely a setback and that he could still bounce back. In fact the French were far from defeated and still had pockets of strength, but the tide had turned overwhelmingly against them after Trichinopoly. 'As Chanda Sahib is dead, I can see no reason why [peace] may not be easily accomplished,' Saunders wrote mildly to Dupleix. The latter's dreams of a French Indian empire were over for the time being, but they could be revived.

He moved into his magnificent new residence in Pondicherry. With its marble statues, colonnades, silver leaf and green velvet, it was a fitting palace for a French emperor that never was. He and Madame held a last couple of months of glittering social display there before news of the fall of Trichinopoly reached Paris and he was recalled in disgrace.

The first European who would be emperor of India had been knocked off his pedestal. Goliath had been slain by a David he would scarce acknowledge the existence of; hauteur and dreams by reality; the great schemer and armchair general – although he was not without courage, as his defence of Pondicherry showed – by the incompetence of such men as Law and d'Auteuil, and the ability in the field of men like Lawrence, Clive and Dalton.

Beneath his arrogance, Dupleix had been a man of extraordinary vision, daring, imagination and intelligence, and had almost pulled off his conquest. In so doing he had blazed a trail for Clive and the British. He was to die in poverty, recrimination and obscurity. First Chanda Sahib, then his backer, Dupleix: the first two of Clive's great opponents had been smitten down.

After Law's surrender, Lawrence was anxious to make for the coast, to protect the English settlements from any renewal of the French threat. However, Muhammad Ali's quarrel with the Regent of Mysore, who demanded the handover of Trichinopoly as promised, was intensifying. The British were committed to Muhammad Ali, and after a fortnight of fruitless argument, Lawrence left behind a small garrison and travelled to a position where he could intimidate Dupleix near Pondicherry.

Clive had already set out for Fort St David and then Madras to resume his position as Steward there. Lawrence felt he deserved a rest, and could always call upon his services if required. Shortly afterwards, a British force under an inexperienced commander was badly beaten off by the French at Gingee.

Lawrence, who had opposed the expedition in the first place, in turn attacked the pursuing French force, almost wiping it out. Dupleix was still refusing to negotiate until the British had released the French prisoners from Trichinopoly – which would have sharply increased his strength. Lawrence understandably turned him down. The French were now in no state to stage large-scale military operations – although they did capture a small convoy of boats in which Clive was believed to be travelling – a tribute to what they really thought of their adversary, whom Dupleix publicly regarded as insignificant.

Clive had been through a gruelling siege, a series of major battles which frequently hung in the balance, had narrowly escaped with his life on at least six occasions and had hardly enjoyed any rest for two years. He had experienced near-defeat twice and a succession of remarkable victories. In every crisis he had shown amazing calm and self-possession, although some vindictiveness.

The relentless, prolonged and concerted effort had eventually taken its toll, as with so many who give more than seems possible for a human constitution. Clive was no mere commander strutting about on a horse and risking the occasional lucky enemy shot. He took a major and dangerous part in virtually all of these engagements. He has been described as Britain's first guerrilla leader. Certainly rushing to and fro on horseback, rallying his troops under attack, improvising one plan after another, he had some claims to that title long before Wingate.

It was time for that highly strung, energetic and nervous frame to unwind. So he did, slightly. He had no compunction in enjoying the fruits of victory. His name was the toast of Madras society. He rented a large house in Charles Street, within Fort St George.

His business as Steward and Commissary would not have kept him seriously occupied; indeed in his absence, his subordinates had been amassing profits in his name. The Steward supervised the supply of the garrison and the settlement with stores: commissions were paid to Clive on the sale of every sack of rice, fodder for the horses, load of firewood or consignment of swordfish coming into the settlement. With a victualling allowance for every soldier, Clive as Commissary could also profit hugely from supplying their provisions cheaply. Madeira and high-quality tea had to be purchased for the officers.

One of Clive's lieutenants reports that his chief obtained his supplies at a low price from Indian suppliers because he was 'beloved' by them. This may or may not be true: a victorious commander like Clive would have inspired fear in Indian traders, who would have had good grounds for supplying him cheaply. As his earlier foraging showed, Clive was a tough, shrewd and intimidating bargainer and businessman. There is no evidence, though, that he was extortionate.

The money continued to roll in, as his office supervised the feeding of the armies still in the field and the tricky business of disposing of the many elephants the British had been given by grateful Indian princes throughout the campaign, which were eating their way through huge quantities of food. He had made an estimated £40,000 as Steward and Commissary – a fortune large enough to set him up as a substantial country landowner in England.

With this considerable shower of wealth upon one who had known only restricted circumstances, a new and controversial feature of Clive's personality emerged: his love of ostentation. His house was host to a round of parties; Clive himself bought fifteen pairs of silk breeches and three velvet ones, twenty ruffed shirts, forty pairs of stockings and magnificent silver lace, brown and blue coats – as well as the full costume of an Indian prince.

He was a young bachelor, just emerged from the slog and butchery of a long military campaign, wealthy beyond his wildest dreams. He was the star of the settlement that summer, regaling his hosts with tales of his exploits, dazzling the ladies and doing favours for his friends – one of his most attractive traits. Dalton, who was one of the prime beneficiaries, remarked, 'I hear that you keep one of the best houses in Madras,' and congratulated him on 'gallanting the ladies'.

He was perhaps naive as to the impact of all this display on other less gifted and successful contemporaries. Those jealous of him in the army and in civilian society began to sneer and attribute his victories to luck. Lawrence was quick to spring to his defence:

> Some people are pleased to term Captain Clive fortunate and lucky; but, in my opinion, from the knowledge I have of the gentleman, he deserved and might expect from his conduct everything as it fell out; – a man of undaunted resolution, of a cool temper, and of a presence of mind which never left him in the greatest danger – born a soldier; for without a military education of any sort or much conversing with any of the profession, from his judgment and good sense, he led on an army like an experienced officer and a brave soldier, with a prudence that certainly warranted success.

This was tribute indeed, from a superior officer, although Clive's detractors asserted that Lawrence was obsessed with his protégé Clive. Yet the Old Cock was a tough professional, and his confidence in Clive had rarely been misplaced so far. Lawrence added, in respect of the 'sneerers': 'let them sneer on, since they can't bite. You are right in making it a subject of mirth.' The brightness of Clive's candle was to arouse the flutterings of the envious for the rest of his life.

On his return, the glamorous captain was to indulge in one of his favourite pursuits: whoring. To today's generation, as to anyone brought up in the Christian ethic, this seems an ugly side to Clive's character – lacking morality, being exploitative and self-abasing in that he paid for sexual favours. In Clive's time it was but the customary practice of any man with the money to pay for it.

It must be remembered that no young lady of good reputation would even conceive of sex outside marriage – or she would forfeit her reputation. There was no available pool of young girls prepared to have premarital affairs with men, as there is today. For an energetic man with a high sexual drive in his twenties, the only available outlets were the local prostitutes.

This was not a matter of specifically 'colonial' exploitation either: every Indian ruler or nobleman had his own retinue of girls, or harem. Even a man of modest means went to prostitutes. They were just part of life and the local economy – a considerable one, judging by the number there were – of the time. The Victorian era – a colonial import – had not begun. While not flaunting this practice in the face of polite Madras society or the Church's prohibition, Clive, like any other young man, would hardly have bothered to conceal his habits from his contemporaries.

Female company of a higher order was also at hand. In June, soon after the fall of Trichinopoly, there had arrived to swell the small band of marriageable young ladies a party of eleven girls, among them Mun Maskelyne's sister, Margaret. Her brother had long seen her as a potential match for Clive, and had written home such glowing accounts of him even before she sailed for India that he must have seemed a figure of truly heroic stature for a pubescent girl in her mid-teens.

Just 17 years old when she reached India, she had been brought up by an aunt at Purton Stoke and an uncle at Purton Down, and educated at a good school near Cirencester. Both her aunt and uncle knew India well, and she must have been awed to reach the subcontinent at last after the usual cooped-up journey of eight months. She was put up at Mun's house, where he was in enforced idleness, having been released on parole by the French after being captured near Arcot.

From an early age she seems to have shown considerable intelligence and character. She was small and slim, with fine, delicate skin, large pretty eyes under attractive dark eyebrows, a gentle mouth, a slightly receding chin and a graceful neck. Her hair was dark and flowing, generally done up in a set on top of her head or cut fairly short.

Although not a conventional beauty – her nose was a little large and bulbous at the end and she could present a slightly mousy appearance – she displayed a keen intelligence in her eyes and was quick-witted and humorous as a talker. Mun at least considered her the equal of any man or woman in conversation, a suitable match for his now famous friend.

There is no record of her early courtship with Clive, but it is clear they must have met early that summer during the round of balls, picnics and dinners, although they did not begin to see each other frequently until the autumn. From the first this sweet, impressionable, but also shrewdly self-advancing girl was entirely bowled over by

Clive, the hero of the settlement, now worldly, self-confident and exuberant in place of his old shyness. The fact that he was not the best-looking man in Madras would have made no difference. He was certainly the most glamorous, most eligible and, for his age, the richest.

Margaret Maskelyne may also have considered him a little beneath her: coming as she did from more literate and sophisticated southern England, Clive may have seemed a little rough-hewn from backward Shropshire, although his gentry background was entirely respectable. But Mun had no objection to him socially, and that cannot have been much of a drawback in her eyes. She was in love with him from the first, if she was not already in love with his image from before.

Clive, who had long enjoyed the freedom of being a bachelor, although probably struck by her grace and intelligence, seems to have been a good deal less certain. He feared curtailment of his freedom to enjoy the company of his drinking friends and to go out on the town.

Dalton had teased him in a letter from Trichinopoly (which the former was longing to leave): 'I hear that you keep one of the best houses in Madras. By God, it would be a good joke if your countenance was to smite one of [the ladies] and you were to commit matrimony. I should however be concerned as it would put me out of all hopes of the pleasure I propose myself in ******* Covent Garden etc.'

The rumours were certainly flying fast from that autumn onwards, but Mun, at least, seems to have been far from certain of the match – or perhaps he was trying to scotch the gossip in case it put Clive off. Dalton wrote again to Clive in October, 'The swarthy world here had spread a report that you were on the point of committing matrimony. But Maskelyne has undeceived me on that particular, he says you fuck as usual.'

Before then, however, Clive was to interrupt his pleasant round of commerce, entertainment, courtship and womanising in Madras when he was called up again to do military service. The trouble this time was two French forts – Covelong, 30 miles south of Madras on the coast, and Chingleput, 20 miles inland from Covelong – which between them had the power to intercept traffic between Fort St George and Fort St David.

Clive was given command of the only troops then available – 200 men just arrived from England without any training at all – 'apparently the very refuse of London' – and 500 barely trained sepoys. The march to Covelong was short and easy, but when Clive's forces came under fire from the French, they panicked. Clive shamed them soon afterwards by exposing himself without hesitation to fire. As he positioned his guns for a bombardment, he heard reports that a strong French detachment was on its way from Chingleput. He speeded up his siege preparations and seems secretly to have made contact with the French commander at Covelong – who agreed to surrender without a fight.

Clive soon learnt that the relief force had turned back – it was said because they heard who was in command of the British – and he pursued them, successfully overtaking them and ambushing them, killing 100 men and taking 300 prisoner. He chased the remainder back into Chingleput.

This fort presented a potentially major challenge: it had formidable natural defences, being three-quarters surrounded by a lake, a swamp, and flooded rice fields. Only on the south side was it approachable, and that was well fortified. Clive settled down to a prolonged bombardment, while also secretly opening up negotiations with the commander.

On the fifth day of the siege, this functionary surrendered the fort – provided he was allowed to keep his flock of turkeys and his supply of snuff. Although no walkover – anyone other than Clive might have taken much longer to succeed – it was hardly the 'glorious campaign' described by Saunders. But it showed the almost effortless ease with which Clive could now conduct military campaigns, as well as the demoralisation of the French in southern India after the fall of Trichinopoly. For the local French commander, there hardly seemed any point in continued resistance.

Shortly afterwards Clive suffered the first of the painful attacks of fever and abdominal pain that were to dog him for the rest of his life. At first the attacks occurred every few hours, and then every few days, lasting much of October and November. It was widely assumed he was suffering from gallstones probably accentuated by malaria, which explained the fever – although he may have had a venereal disease as well.

The pain and fever were real enough to those around him, and could not be dismissed as psychosomatic, as some have claimed. However, modern research suggests that a man like Clive, prone to immense bouts of mental and physical activity over several months, may experience a sudden virtual collapse of his system as the toll on his body catches up with him during a period of inactivity.

This can produce quite strong physical symptoms, as well as leaving the victim much more vulnerable to conditions like gall-stones and malaria. The physical illness coincided with what seems to have been a manic-depressive mental breakdown of elation followed by deep depression, so unlike the usually cool-headed Clive. Again, such symptoms are typical in a man who has driven himself far beyond most people's endurance when finally his mind is allowed to rest and take stock.

Depression is, of course, also a symptom of malaria, which recurs throughout life, as in Clive's case, and which, if not the cause, would certainly have exacerbated the problem. To classify him as a manic-depressive, with a major mental illness, would be a mistake, however. Like Churchill and several other men of enormous physical and mental stamina who tax themselves virtually beyond endurance, black depression was the price to be paid at the end. Thus it may not have been a chronic condition for Clive, but an acute one brought on by exertion.

Certainly there was a sensitive and even morbidly self-critical side to Clive – as was demonstrated in his early youth. But then, unknown and unregarded, he had good reason for feeling un-loved. Now, wealthy beyond his wildest expectations and a hero to his fellow countrymen, he had no reason for his misery (although he may have been wounded by those jealous of him who, even then, had begun to belittle his achievements).

To relieve his physical pain, he was prescribed opium, which he was later to take also to relieve his depression. But there is no evidence that he took opium when well – that he became an addict. He may have been nursed by Margaret Maskelyne as he lay ill, which would have increased his feelings for her and satisfied her concern for him.

As the illness began to wane, Clive also experienced intense homesickness. He had not seen his father and family for fully ten years. His task in India seemed over for the time being and he wanted to enjoy the fruits of his achievement in a less claustrophobic small-town atmosphere than that of Fort St George.

As a poor boy made good, he undoubtedly wanted to demonstrate how the Clive family's steady drift downward in circumstances had been reversed. He may have felt, too, that his Indian ambitions had for the moment been satisfied: he had made a considerable fortune. As he later admitted, he was never lacking in ambition. He now wanted to go into British politics, perhaps believing he would one day become prime minister.

Returning to health, he still seems to have been uncertain about Miss Maskelyne. There can be no doubt that he was more attracted to her than to any suitable young lady of his acquaintance. But he was a man who hated to be tied down, and he feared that his days of womanising and jovial male company might be at an end. Although she was highly intelligent and acceptable, he may have felt she was slightly inferior to him in social terms: he the scion of a gentry family, she from the Home Counties' professional classes.

Who knew but that he might find a better match in Britain? He booked a single passage from India on 15 February aboard the *Admiral Vernon*. What then happened is not known. But Margaret may have got to hear of this. Her disappointment and sweetness may have touched a chord in his heart. Three days later, with Clive's customary impulsiveness, they were married; and ten days after that they set sail for England.

CHAPTER 10

Clive Superstar

I t would be hard to imagine a less auspicious start to Clive's sudden marriage than the seven-month journey back. Although the couple left amid the plaudits of the settlement at the fairytale wedding of its hero, there was a considerable amount of backbiting as well. Saunders and Lawrence had fallen out once again, and the haughty, reserved governor considered Clive primarily a protégé of Lawrence's.

This impression was confirmed by one of the least attractive personalities who had attached himself to Clive as a bosom companion for – as later events revealed – motives of pure self-interest. Robert Orme, now 24 years old, had first met Clive in Calcutta and moved to Madras a couple of years earlier. Orme appears to have tried to make mischief between Lawrence and Saunders, letting it be known that Clive sided with the former. Orme himself openly denigrated Saunders.

The latter unjustly assumed that Orme was Clive's mouthpiece, and took offence, whereas Clive had been trying to mediate between the two men, both of whose patronage he had enjoyed. Saunders refused even to send the traditional letter of thanks for Clive's services on his departure, and did not see him off.

Orme apologised to the governor for 'his slanders' just before boarding ship, mending his own fences, but not Clive's. Clive was deeply wounded: 'I think in justice to the military in general I cannot leave this coast without leaving a paper behind me representing the little notice taken of people of our profession,' he wrote to Lawrence. 'I hope the world will not accuse me of vanity or be of the opinion that I think too highly of my own successes as I seldom if ever open my lips upon this subject.' However, Saunders was too big a man to put down Clive, who had served him so well, in writing to the directors.

Under this slight shadow, the ship sailed. Macaulay's description of life aboard an Indiaman (during Warren Hastings's time, just twenty years later) has the ring of truth:

> No place is so propitious to the formation either of close friendships or of deadly enmities as an Indiaman. There are very few people who do not find a voyage which lasts several months unsupportably dull. Anything is welcome which may break that long monotony, a sail, a shark, an albatross, a man overboard. Most passengers find some resource in eating twice as many meals as on land. But the great devices for killing the time are quarrelling and flirting. The facilities for both these exciting pursuits are great. The inmates of the ship are thrown together far more than in any country seat or boarding house. None can escape from the rest except by imprisoning himself in a cell in which he can hardly turn. All food, all exercise, is taken in company. Ceremony is to a great extent banished. It is every day in the power of a mischievous person to inflict innumerable annoyances. It is every day in the power of an amiable person to confer little services.

Margaret's subsequent devotion suggests she would have been one of the latter, forever trying to please Clive. Still only 17, she was too besotted with, and hero-worshipping of, Clive to complain of the discomforts of the voyage. Ten years older than her, he was still a figure of awe.

From the first he loved her with, for him, real sensitivity and kindness; but his idea of marriage was not that of every girl, even in the eighteenth century. Much of the journey he spent discussing the recent military campaign with the ubiquitous Orme.

Orme, labelled Cicero by Clive, was at least a fine writer. Vain, bad-tempered, effeminate and snobbish, he was presumably resented intensely by Margaret as Clive spent much of the journey pacing the deck or closeted with him. Clive, for his part, later remarked that being cooped up in an East Indiaman was hardly conducive to romance. Few nights in the cramped bunks in their tiny cabin could have been given over to passion.

Provisions were low and had to be rationed, increasing the discomfort. Reaching Cape Town at last, they were transferred to a roomier, better-stocked ship and conditions improved, though

Clive and Orme spent innumerable hours discussing the recent campaigns while Margaret socialised with the other young ladies. Orme had already begun to write his *History of the Military Transactions of the British Nation in Indostan*.

When he arrived in England, he was to use the draft of the initial text to impress the Duke of Cumberland to appoint him a councillor in Madras – remarkably, as he had no record of achievement there. Clive remarked tolerantly at the way his friend unashamedly used him for his own advancement, 'You will allow that dear self gets the better of every other consideration.' Describing his friend as 'proud and overbearing', he continued to have a soft spot for him.

The *Pelham* docked on 18 October 1753. The Britain Clive returned to was not all that different from the one he had left. George II was still on the throne. In Clive's absence, the country had reeled from the earthquake of the 1745 rebellion by the 'Young Pretender', Bonnie Prince Charlie, which had plunged Scotland into civil war and proved strikingly more dangerous than anyone had expected. At one stage the 5,000-strong rebel army was approaching Derby, with virtually no government forces between them and London. But the failure of the Welsh, under Sir Watkin Williams Wynn, and of the English Tory squirearchy to rally to the Young Pretender forced him to retreat; and the last dynastic challenge to the Hanoverians was over in a shower of bloody revenge by 'Butcher' Cumberland.

The newly dominant Whig prime minister was Walpole's carefully groomed successor, Henry Pelham, skilful, statesmanlike and trusted by the king; and when Pelham died in 1754, shortly after Clive's return, he was succeeded by another of the political grandees of the eighteenth century, his brother the Duke of Newcastle. At first, Newcastle seemed something of a minor figure: seated in the Lords, he was an unimpressive orator, a small, nervous, excitable man, who was widely ridiculed. He made up for this by being a skilled manipulator of men and a dispenser of patronage on a grand scale. He was, in modern terms, a political survivor and a fixer.

At first he was overshadowed in the Lords by the formidable minister of war, the Duke of Cumberland, and in the Commons by the foremost speakers of the age, William Pitt and Henry Fox. It was natural that the headstrong young Clive should look to the patronage of these two larger-than-life figures as he sought to make his entrance on to the British political stage.

Pitt, a Ciceronian orator with a hawk-like profile and a streak of cold ruthlessness, displayed an almost uncanny prescience and clarity of thought, and was deeply distrusted by the new king. 'The Great Commoner', from a middle-class background, was already spellbinding the nation. Fox, a former Tory, was regarded as the corrupt and devious Machiavelli of modern British politics, a man of dazzling, raffish charm, insincerity and great wealth. The strutting victor of Trichinopoly was sucked into the struggles between the three men and tossed aside a couple of years later like a discarded plaything.

Clive, the prosperous young hero, epitomised the cocky, wealthy nouveaux riches now asserting themselves throughout the land. London was for the first time becoming a middle-class city: the division between the palaces of the great and the crowded slums and hovels of the poor was being cut through by a proliferation of neat, purpose-built housing for men of considerable, though not excessive, prosperity. One observer, Arthur Young, rejoiced of another city that 'each side of the whole street forms but one front, and in a very neat taste. How much is it to be lamented, that it is not the method in all the towns of England.'

In Clive's London, the relentless expansion of middle-class housing westwards, away from the centre where people worked by day, was already under way. The villages around the capital were being gently clasped into the capital's embrace: in 1744, John Armstrong, in his popular *Art of Preserving Health*, had celebrated the salubrity of London's half-developed country villages: 'Umbrageous Ham', 'sun-burnt Epsom', 'Chelsea low', 'high Blackheath, with wintry woods assailed', Hampstead 'courted by the western wind', Greenwich 'waving over the water', Dulwich 'yet by barbarous arts unspoiled'. Only Richmond was expanding rapidly. Thirty years later all these villages were growing fast, mainly to accommodate middle-class housing.

Clive's own house in Queen Square, Ormond Street, was not far from the expanding mecca of cheap middle-class housing, St Marylebone, and just north of the recently constructed elegance of Berkeley Square, Grosvenor Square, Cavendish Square and Hanover Square. Nearby Regent Street was an insalubrious dive of prostitutes and footpads. Clive, in his well-appointed, modern, terraced surroundings, was worldly and full of himself, every bit the representative of a new class, and the young military hero of his times. With his high-powered wife and a comfortable household which included two Indian servants and a carriage, he was glad to cock a snook at the fusty aristocratic former ruling class. He was new money, and proud of it; he was set to conquer England.

Within two years, he had fallen flat on his face.

Clive's reception from family friends, the East India Company and the populace was an ecstatic one. England was badly in need of heroes after so long a period of internecine strife; and Clive had youth, vigour and a spectacular succession of victories on his side.

One verse addressed to Clive perhaps overstated it:

> The proof is now beyond all doubt
> Since about Clive they keep such rout
> Where'er he goes 'tis holiday
> The Tradesmen throw their work away,
> All run in crowds unto the windows
> To see the Conqu'ror of the Indies.

But it gives a flavour of his reception. In the Company he was widely viewed as the man who had frustrated the designs of Dupleix and saved the settlements in southern India. The directors nicknamed him 'General Clive'. His string of victories – Arcot, Arni, Kaveripak, Trichinopoly, Covelong and Chingleput – had been followed breathlessly, if with a time-lapse of several months, by much of London society.

He was summoned by the directors and offered a gold-lined sword set with diamonds worth around £500. He refused to accept it unless Lawrence was offered one: the Old Cock was then awarded a sword worth £750 to reflect his rank in relation to Clive. Wherever Clive was received he was treated as a national hero.

He was not yet the superstar he was to become, but the dashing and successful young man of 27 provided a focus for popular pride and patriotism in a country only recently reunited after a succession of civil wars and rebellions, the last of which had ended just eight years before. He was Hanoverian Britain's first real popular hero.

His parents, now lodged in a large house in London, possibly rented on the expectation of Clive's financial support, and his sisters and brothers gave him a warm welcome. Richard Clive doted on the successes of his son, and as an advocate pushed him assiduously in order to obtain the young man's preferment in whatever exalted circles he could.

Clive himself pressed hard in the Company for promotion, endlessly recounting his exploits to the directors. He was offered a senior post and the chance to succeed George Pigot, now designated Saunders's successor as Governor of Madras. Although Pigot had been a friend, Clive was disappointed not to be offered the governorship himself. An inkling of this might have been the cause of the quarrel with Saunders. Clive refused to return immediately to India – at the same time not burning his boats by offering to come out a year later.

He and his father were keener on a more ambitious route to the top, this time in England: that of becoming a Member of Parliament. Thomas Herring, Archbishop of Canterbury, was an acquaintance of his father; as was the Lord Chancellor, the Earl of Hardwicke, a friend of Clive's one distinguished cousin, Sir Edward Clive, a judge of the Court of Common Pleas. The latter had been MP for the Cornish rotten borough of Mitchell for four years.

The borough contained 55 votes. Sir Edward pointed his young cousin in that direction. Backing Clive in the contest was Thomas Scawen, the major local landlord, and the Earl of Sandwich, who between them controlled just under half the votes. It was necessary to secure others to get elected, and in those days patronage and bribery were the standard methods.

Clive spent around £5,000, and when the votes came in his investment had paid off – he won 30 out of the 55 votes cast. He had now taken the first step up the ladder of power in Britain itself.

Although still occasionally laid low by bouts of fever – he had to go to Bath to recover – life must have seemed very rosy to Clive. An MP at just 28, an acknowledged hero, he gave his father £6,000 to reduce the mortgage on Styche, the country's family estate, to just £2,500. He was also generous to his friends.

The Clives do not appear to have entertained much at their London house. Margaret herself, self-reliant and withdrawn, was occupied with bearing their first child, Edward, in March 1754, and

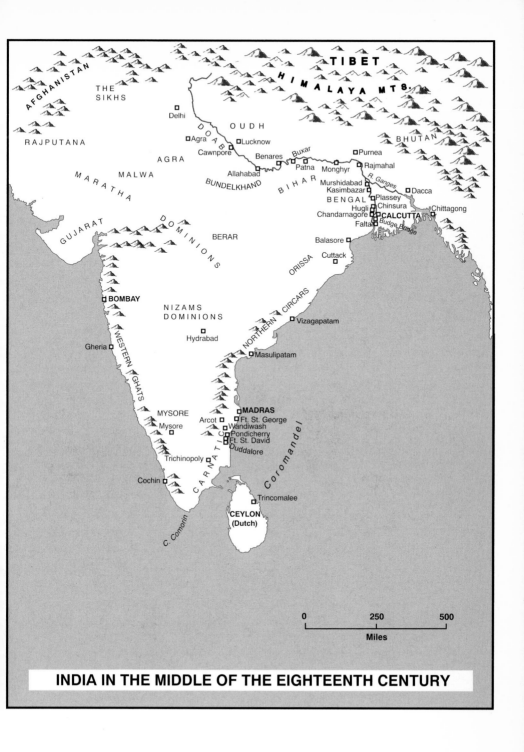

INDIA IN THE MIDDLE OF THE EIGHTEENTH CENTURY

1. The Churchill look: Robert Clive. Engraving after Thomas Gainsborough by J. McArdell.

2. Clive's first posting: Fort St. George, Madras, showing St. Mary's Church.

3. Scene of the siege: The Fort at Trichinopoly, by F. S. Ward.

4. The pirate fortress at Gheria, under attack by Clive and Watson.

5. Imperial Britain: Major-General
Stringer Lawrence in Roman dress, by
Peter Scheemakers.

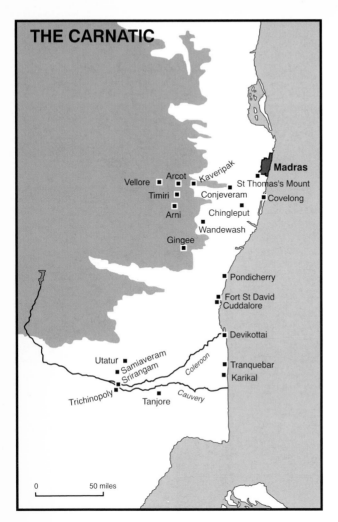

THE CARNATIC

Madras

Vellore ■ Arcot ■ Kaveripak
St Thomas's Mount
Timiri ■ Conjeveram ■ Covelong
Arni ■ Chingleput ■
Wandewash ■
Gingee ■

Pondicherry ■

Fort St David ■
Cuddalore

Devikottai ■

Utatur ■ Samiaveram
Srirangam ■ Coleroon
Tranquebar ■
Karikal ■

Trichinopoly ■ Tanjore ■ Cauvery

0   50 miles

6. Pondicherry after its sacking by the British, by John McClean.

7. Before the sacking: Fort William, Calcutta, showing St. Anne's Church.

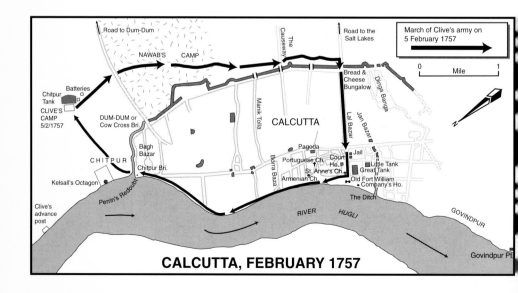

CALCUTTA, FEBRUARY 1757

seems to have led a reclusive life, not uncommon for a young mother. A second child was born a year later, but was sickly from the first.

Clive was soon in financial difficulty: part of his fortune was being repatriated in the form of diamonds, and local customs officials did not permit them to go forward from Holland, where they had been disembarked; he had to sell them for well below their value. This rude shock coincided with a sudden decline in his political fortunes.

The two candidates he and his colleague had defeated were supporters of the Duke of Newcastle, the prime minister, who was a shrewd and underhand political survivor. Clive had been backed not just by Sandwich but by Henry Fox, the most gifted politician of his day, and one with a reputation for reckless intrigue. Fox had gone into opposition against Newcastle within the ruling party, the Whigs (the Tories were outcasts after the failure of the 1745 'Bonnie Prince Charlie' rebellion, in which many of their supporters were implicated) and was challenging him for the job of prime minister.

Newcastle was a vicious and implacable opponent. Clive was suddenly made aware that, fearless as he might be against large armies in India, he was out of his depth in the political intrigues of eighteenth-century Britain. The young man was a pawn in a ferocious power struggle.

The election was adjudicated by a Committee of the Whole House. Fox made speech after speech on Clive's behalf, tearing to shreds the arguments put across by the lawyers from the opposite side. The committee decided in Clive's favour, and their recommendation was then reported to the House for a final vote. The fate of the government depended upon it: if Clive's party had won, Newcastle would have been ousted and Fox become prime minister.

The small Tory opposition was appalled at the prospect: Fox was a far abler man than Newcastle. The Tories preferred a weak Whig prime minister to a strong one and joined Newcastle. They turned the scales against Clive's election. This was narrowly defeated after a year of wrangling. The same day as the defeat – which he had anticipated – he signed up at last for the East India Company's offer. He was starting all over again. India had always been the alternative: and he was now fast running out of money, having wasted a great deal of it on trying to get into parliament.

Clive found his spell in London deeply frustrating. He had been disappointed on his first attempt to get into parliament, after an intense battle, and had lost a lot of money as a result. After his warm initial reception as a returning hero had worn off, he could sense that his Indian successes cut little ice in the real centres of power in England. The great noble houses, which still controlled many seats in parliament through their placemen, made no effort to receive him. His sponsors, Fox and Sandwich, had been slightly raffish characters, outside the social mainstream.

Just eleven days after signing the contract, Clive and Margaret set sail again on the *Stretham* for India, along with two young cousins to keep Margaret company and make their own fortunes. The two were Jenny Kelsall, a good-looking, flirtatious and precocious 16-year-old daughter of Margaret's uncle; and George Clive, a cousin of Robert's. Jenny was very close to Margaret, and helped to make up for her sorrow in having to leave her two infant children behind.

Richard Clive and Jenny's father rushed down to the dockside to say goodbye to their children, but the ship had already sailed. At the age of 29, Clive's second great adventure in India was about to begin. Few – least of all Clive himself – dreamt that it would far eclipse even his first.

This time he was in active pursuit of a military career. Later historians have often portrayed his career as a succession of accidents and suggested that he was destined for obscurity as deputy governor in Madras. In fact, there was a hidden agenda in the Company's directives to Clive. As a highly effective military commander, he was embarked for Bombay, where he was to launch a daring new stage in the British campaign to root the French out of India and conquer their territories – particularly as war between Britain and France in Europe was judged to be imminent.

Dupleix had been defeated. But the target this time was to be Dupleix's old ally, the Marquis de Bussy, who controlled central India through a reluctant puppet, the Nizam of Hyderabad, Nawab of the Deccan, Salabat Jang. De Bussy also all but controlled the huge swathe of territory, the Northern Circars, between the Carnatic and Bengal. Clive's mission was to threaten an attack from Bombay in the west into Salabat Jang's possessions in the centre, and force him to break with the French.

The plan involved an alliance with the Marathas and the despatch of a large naval convoy from Britain, including 300 royal troops and three companies of artillery. The aim was to expand the area of India under British control from around a fifth, in the south, to nearly half – although at the expense of the French, rather than the native princes.

Clive himself had been promoted to lieutenant-colonel, and was greeted when he went aboard ship with a nine-gun salute. The journey this time was comfortable and uneventful, and they reached Bombay after only six months. This time Margaret was spared the disagreeable presence of Orme, and had her young cousins to keep her amused.

Bombay was something of a backwater compared to Fort St George and Fort William. It consisted of a fortress surrounded by a large town, the prosperous merchant houses close to the citadel, the less so further away. It was positioned on 'the island', a peninsula, and there was no distinction between 'black town' and 'white town': unusually, the races were largely integrated in the Moorish-style settlement.

The magnificent British architecture of the east-coast settlements was absent. Bombay was occupied by only the less ambitious and successful British traders; in addition, it had a reputation for disease. Clive, however, found Bombay 'in a very flourishing condition'. But if he liked Bombay – and he seems to have been in an extraordinarily outgoing mood, no doubt at the prospect of returning to a continent where he was so famous – the locals didn't like him.

He threw a ball to liven things up within a month of his arrival. But the down-to-earth British settlers disapproved of him and his wife and young cousins 'running about the town from morning to night, laughing immoderately at just nothing, affecting to be very noisy and loud and making a great rout and bustle about nothing, witty chits flying about like wildfire', as they appeared to the crabby wife of a local doctor.

She later commented with provincial primness, 'Madam Jane rules that family entirely and both the Colonel and Mrs Clive cannot do anything without first asking Miss Jenny. Don't you think their economy must cut a pretty figure to be governed and directed by a child, for I reckon Jenny very little better . . . The Colonel . . . [appears] to me very weak and ridiculous, not in this affair alone but in many other respects . . . The Madrassers don't like Bombay, we are all too reserved and grave for them,' she griped. Hardly weak, but insouciant, Clive appears to have behaved with the exultation of a young man promoted fast with two pretty girls in tow.

He was to be disappointed in his military venture. In January 1755 an agreement had been signed by Governor Pigot of Madras and Dupleix's successor at Pondicherry, M. Godeheu, which provided that neither side would now interfere in the internal affairs of Indian princes. Britain thus accepted the status quo, leaving de Bussy in charge of Hyderabad.

Empire-building for the time being was over. The prosaic down-to-earth burghers of Bombay firmly argued that Clive's proposed attack on Salabat Jang would violate the spirit of the agreement. Clive and Pigot both argued that the agreement applied only to the Carnatic, but the council at Bombay would not discuss the matter further and refused to approve the venture. It seemed that Clive would have little to do at Bombay except socialise, and then take up his appointment as deputy governor in Madras.

However, a month after Clive's arrival, the British naval squadron arrived in Bombay on its way to reinforce Madras in the expected war against the French. It was under the command of Vice-Admiral Charles Watson and Rear-Admiral George Pocock. The flighty, pretty Jenny soon fell in love with Captain Thomas Latham, commander of the *Tiger*. The council at Bombay decided to take advantage of this sudden increase in its military punch to deal with a matter of intense parochial concern: to rid the Indian Ocean of its worst pirate chieftain, Tulaji Angria.

Clive's next adventure might have been scripted by the classic Italian adventure writer Emilio Salgari. Tulaji was the bastard son of Kanoje Angria, a descendant of the Maratha leader Sivajo in the late sixteenth century. Kanoje had set himself up as an autonomous chieftain on land, robbing shipping routes along the coast and building up a huge fortune. He died in 1728 having repeatedly beaten off European attacks. Tulaji was, if anything, even more ferocious. The British garrison had to maintain an expensive naval presence to protect its shipping, and other craft were regularly raided by the small fast-moving sailboats – grabs – and 40-oared galleys – gallivats – operating out of Gheria.

Gheria was a rocky fastness with a fort, believed to be as impregnable as Gibraltar. In December a ship under Commodore James was sent to reconnoitre it but was attacked by the small fleet in the harbour. He reported that the fortress was sited on a large rock connected to the mainland by a spur of sand about a mile long and a quarter of a mile wide.

On the isthmus itself there were shipyards where the grabs and gallivats were built, while the harbour was by the entrance to a small river. The rock itself was a sheer cliff, but no more than 50 feet high. Two sets of walls and a series of towers housing Angria's garrison were perched on top. James reported that the fortress was not as impregnable as widely believed.

The British had been negotiating with the leader of the local Marathas, Balaji Rao, to obtain his co-operation in attacking the fort. He was offered some of the land around Gheria, as well as the pirate stronghold – a promise the British had no intention of keeping unless they actually needed his help.

As to the huge spoils believed to be within the stronghold, the British quarrelled bitterly about their shares: Clive was to command the land forces, and demanded an equal amount to Watson and Pocock together. Being only a lieutenant-colonel – the equivalent to a captain in the navy – he was entitled to much less. At length Watson sensibly settled by offering to make up Clive's share from his own. Pocock refused to budge. The Marathas were completely excluded from these considerations.

Early in February 1756, no fewer than 14 ships set out for Gheria with 800 European troops and 1,000 sepoys on board. As soon as this large force was sighted off the rock, Tulaji Angria knew he was in serious trouble, and left the fort in a hurry to negotiate with the Marathas, now about 100 miles away, in an attempt to secure their support.

The day after the ships' arrival, some of Angria's men came out in a boat to visit Watson's flagship, where he showed them the size of his guns and advised them to surrender peacefully. Hours later, however, the guns of the fort opened fire on the British fleet. This was now drawn up in two lines, and responded with a barrage from no fewer than 150 guns. Soon the entire pirate fleet was ablaze, and the fire reached the magazine, which exploded with a tremendous roar, and then spread to part of the fort.

Clive's land force went ashore largely to prevent the Maratha army, whose intentions were uncertain, from reaching the fort. Even if they only joined in the fighting, it was feared that they would demand a large share of the spoils. Meanwhile, the relentless naval bombardment continued.

On 13 February, after just two days, Gheria surrendered and Angria was seized by the Marathas. Clive feared that if it had held out, he would have had to storm the fortress from land, which would have cost him many men. As it was, only 20 were killed or seriously wounded. The Marathas, who by now had reached the landward side of the fort, offered an English officer, Captain Andrew Buchanan, a large amount of money to let them through. Buchanan – unusually for the time, when such considerations were routinely accepted – threatened to cut off the Maratha commander's head by way of reply. 'A very easy conquest,' commented Clive truthfully – and, for once, modestly.

Disappointingly, the pirates' treasure trove turned out to be worth about £140,000, of which Clive took £5,000. When Watson offered to contribute £1,000 to bring him up to Pocock's share, Clive refused, saying he had been arguing about principle, not money. Ten English and three Dutch slaves, who had been badly abused, were released. Angria's family, weeping, surrounded Watson when he landed, saying they had lost their father and their fortune. Moved, Watson offered to be 'their father and their friend' and even wept himself.

After a heated argument, the Marathas were allowed to take possession of the fortress – stripped of its wealth. The British force left. The battle had been a walkover, but could have proven tricky if the Marathas has joined Tulaji, or if the fortress had held out. The most impregnable pirate stronghold in India had been crushed, albeit by a vastly superior force.

On 17 April, after six months in Bombay, during which he quarrelled bitterly with the burghers over their court-martial of one of his officers, Clive and Margaret, who was pregnant again, set sail in

Admiral Watson's convoy for Fort St David to take up his appointment as deputy governor, arriving a fortnight later. The welcome in Madras was a warm one: Clive was greeted by the governor, his old friend Pigot, and by the military commander, his old boss, Lawrence, with warm affection. Margaret's brother Mun was on hand to embrace her, as was her cousin John Walsh and Jane's brother Thomas.

A less sincere welcome came from the scheming Orme, who had been zealously attempting to supplant Clive as the putative next governor, and who had been openly engaged in doing down Clive's reputation, which, as his biographer, he was to some extent creating – and benefiting – from. Orme indulged in further mischief-making by suggesting that the former governor, Saunders, had objected to Clive's promotion. In fact, Saunders had been turned against Clive in the first place by Orme's malice.

On 22 June 1756, at the age of only 30 (not that unusual for Indian appointments), Clive arrived as commander of Fort St David, the guns barking a salute, the first lady of the settlement a girl of just 20. He was attended by a retinue of servants, was carried around on formal occasions in a palanquin, and his official residence was the Garden House, in whose grounds he had fought a skirmish. He was deferred to by everyone.

Margaret revelled in her new-found importance and, accompanied by Jenny and an old friend, Philadelphia Austen (Jane Austen's aunt), felt among friends, refreshingly refusing to become spoilt or pompous. The peace of the settlement must have been some consolation when tragedy struck unexpectedly: she was informed that her second son had died in England. Clive, always impatient, rushed about, enforcing justice, penalising black marketeers who had been levying an unofficial tariff against goods coming over the Bounds Hedge, demanding more troops from Madras for his garrison against the possibility of French attack, auditing the settlement accounts.

But it looked as though he was in for a long five years as pronconsul of this colonial enclave – a far cry from the excitements of Arcot, Arni, Kaveripak and Trichinopoly, and his frustrated political ambitions. Clive, the shooting star of his generation, had settled down by 30 into the job of stodgy provincial governor.

BOOK TWO

EMPEROR,
1756–1764

CHAPTER 11

Bengal

S ome 36 hours before Clive embarked on his new and dull
duties, a number of British soldiers and civilians suffocated
and were trampled to death in their own vomit, excrement
and blood in a tiny cell in the once elegant Fort William in Calcutta,
now a smouldering ruin.

Certain events in history acquire an importance entirely disproportionate to their innate significance. They start a chain-reaction.
Such an event was the Bengali seizure of Calcutta from the British,
which was followed the same night by the massacre known as the
Black Hole of Calcutta. As many as 123, or as few as 18, may have
died during that terrible night. Far worse and larger massacres have
occurred before and since. Yet somehow this particular incident
became the focus for the indignation of an entire nation, midwife to
the birth of the British empire in India.

Macaulay, one of the most judicious of historians in regard to the
faults of his countrymen, as his famous essay on Warren Hastings
shows, conveys the sensation of pure outrage evoked by the crime.
His spellbinding prose, written over 60 years after the event,
captures the emotions aroused by the Black Hole, the single event
upon which the morality for establishing the British Raj in India is
based.

The English captives were left at the mercy of the guards, and the
guards determined to secure them for the night in the prison of the
garrison, a chamber known by the fearful name of the Black Hole.
Even for a single European malefactor, that dungeon would, in such
a climate, have been too close and narrow. The space was only
twenty feet square. The air holes were small and obstructed. It was
the summer solstice, the season when the fierce heat of Bengal can
scarcely be rendered tolerable to natives of England by lofty halls

and the constant waving of fans. The number of prisoners was one hundred and forty-six. When they were ordered to enter the cell, they imagined that the soldiers were joking; and, being in high spirits on account of the promise of the Nabob to spare their lives, they laughed and jested at the absurdity of the notion. They soon discovered their mistake. They expostulated; they entreated, but in vain. The guards threatened to cut down all who hesitated. The captives were driven into the cell at the point of the sword, and the door was instantly shut and locked upon them.

Nothing in the history of fiction, not even the story which Ugolino told in the sea of everlasting ice, after he had wiped his bloody lips on the scalp of his murderer, approaches the horrors which were recounted by the few survivors of that night. They cried for mercy. They strove to burst the door. Holwell who, even in that extremity, retained some presence of mind, offered large bribes to the gaolers. But the answer was that nothing could be done without the Nabob's orders, that the Nabob was asleep, and that he would be angry if anybody woke him.

Then the prisoners went mad with despair. They trampled each other down, fought for the places at the windows, fought for the pittance of water with which the cruel mercy of the murderers mocked their agonies, raved, prayed, blasphemed, implored the guards to fire among them. The gaolers in the meantime held lights to the bars, and shouted with laughter at the frantic struggles of their victims. At length the tumult died away in low gaspings and moanings.

The day broke. The Nabob had slept off his debauch, and permitted the door to be opened. But it was some time before the soldiers could make a lane for the survivors, by piling up on each side the heaps of corpses on which the burning climate had already begun to do its loathsome work. When at length a passage was made, twenty-three ghastly figures, such as their own mothers would not have known, staggered one by one out of the charnel house. A pit was instantly dug. The dead bodies, a hundred and twenty-three in number, were flung into it promiscuously, and covered up.

Lust for money and territory have never been enough for empire builders. Even for the British in the eighteenth century, moral justification and indignation were still more important. Terrible as it was, the Black Hole provided the pretext for the events that created the Raj.

The Black Hole was also to propel Robert Clive, a prematurely successful young man enjoying a premature retirement, to his destiny as the first and only British emperor by conquest, enticing him inexorably up the Hugli, one of the tributaries of the Ganges, India's greatest river, into the heart of a continent whose fate he was to transform. There he confronted the darkness that lay within himself – later, as with Warren Hastings, his successor but one, to be exposed to the pitiless glare of public scrutiny. The Bengali occupation of Calcutta and the Black Hole sucked Clive and the British in India into a vortex of power and temptation such as few men have been exposed to before or since.

The fall of Calcutta, much more than the fall of Madras to the French years before, was an almost entirely self-inflicted wound for the British. Represented as a naked and ignoble act of aggression by an oriental despot, in fact it was the logical outcome of a series of increasingly stupid, high-handed and arrogant actions against a prince insecure on his newly acquired throne.

To understand the débâcle represented by the fall of Calcutta – one which in turn could only be expunged by accusing the Indians of a monstrous atrocity – it is necessary to understand the nature of the settlement. Of the three main British enclaves in India – Bombay, Madras and Calcutta – the last was undoubtedly the most thriving and cosmopolitan. This was because it controlled the bulk of the trade of India's richest province, Bengal, to the outside world. To the Bengalis it was not just a pimple on their periphery, as Bombay and Madras were to the Indian princes of the interior: it was the tap through which passed most of the commerce of the province.

The fertile lower Ganges basin provided the basis of an economy second to none in India. More so than in other parts of India – perhaps also because of the oppressively hot and humid climate – the Bengali temperament was suited to commerce and making money, rather than war. Bengal suffered from this unmartial spirit in that its riches were immensely attractive to the more warlike tribes to the north and the west. Again, Macaulay's description, while exaggerated, has not been bettered:

Of the provinces which had been subject to the house of Tamerlane, the wealthiest was Bengal. No part of India possessed such natural advantages, both for agriculture and for commerce. The Ganges, rushing through a hundred channels to the sea, has formed a vast plain of rich mould which, even under the tropical sky, rivals the verdure of an English April. The rice-fields yield an increase such as is elsewhere unknown. Spices, sugar, vegetable oil, are produced with marvellous exuberance. The rivers afford an inexhaustible supply of fish.

The desolate islands along the sea-coast, overgrown by noxious vegetation, and swarming with deer and tigers, supply the culti-vated districts with abundance of salt. The great stream which fertilises the soil is, at the same time, the chief highway of Eastern commerce. On its banks, and on those of most of its tributary waters, are the wealthiest marts, the most splendid capitals, and the most sacred shrines of India.

The tyranny of man had for ages struggled in vain against the overflowing bounty of nature. In spite of the Mussulman despot, and of the Mahratta freebooter, Bengal was known throughout the East as the garden of Eden, as the rich kingdom. Its population multiplied exceedingly. Distant provinces were nourished from the overflowing of its granaries; and the noble ladies of London and Paris were clothed in the delicate produce of its looms. The race by whom this rich tract was peopled, enervated by a soft climate and accustomed to peaceful employments, bore the same relation to other Asiatics which the Asiatics generally bear to the bold and energetic children of Europe.

The Castilians have a proverb, that in Valencia the earth is water and the men women; and the description is at least equally applic-able to the vast plain of the Lower Ganges. Whatever the Bangalee does he does languidly. His favourite pursuits are sedentary. He shrinks from bodily exertion; and, though voluble in dispute, and singularly pertinacious in the ways of chicane, he seldom engages in a personal conflict, and scarcely ever enlists as a soldier. We doubt whether there be a hundred genuine Bengalees in the whole army of the East India Company. There never, perhaps, existed a people as thoroughly fitted by nature and habit for a foreign yoke.

When Bengal was at peace, the spoils were immensely lucrative for the British and smaller French and Dutch settlements up the Hugli river. The British had for some time enjoyed an uneasy, if pragmatic relationship with the rulers of Bengal. They had obtained a *firman* – a grant of trading privileges – from the Mogul Emperor himself at the court in Delhi in 1717. The East India Company had spent a staggering £100,000 in bribes on the cost of the mission so that 'the Lord of the World and of the Present Age' should grant 'the smallest particle of sand' – the governor of Fort William – the firman.

However, the wording of the text was vague on several key issues, and friction abounded between the British and Bengali government, usually about money. The Bengali authorities, for example, insisted that the agents of the Company could not trade as private individuals and thus exploit its monopoly in the outside world. The Company merely pretended that their private trade was its own. The Bengali authorities insisted on inspecting cargoes to check that these were not private transactions, and had to be bribed to desist.

As the settlement expanded from the original three villages granted to the Company, it had to buy land through its local employees, purchasing 38 villages in all. The enclave was prohibited from coining its own currency, which meant it was dependent on the good offices of the immensely powerful Bengali banking community. The settlement's leaders and a succession of Bengali rulers continued to squabble over these and other issues throughout the early part of the eighteenth century.

In April 1740 a coup that was to have immense repercussions was staged at the Bengali capital of Murshidabad, some 50 miles upriver from Calcutta. The Nawab Sarfaraz was murdered by a tough and shrewd low-born new ruler, Aliverdi Khan, and the countdown began towards the events that led to the ignominious British loss of Calcutta 16 years later. Aliverdi Khan's ascent to power was fortunate for the Bengalis, who were suddenly attacked by wave after wave of Maratha invaders.

The first wave came in 1742, and the Marathas got as far as plundering the capital Murshidabad, before being beaten off; a second invasion followed in 1743, and a third the following year. This time Aliverdi Khan held a peace conference – at which, Borgia-style, Baskar Pandit and twenty Maratha commanders were murdered by soldiers hidden behind the curtains of the conference room.

Enraged, the Marathas returned in 1745, and nearly drove the Nawab from his throne. After several more attacks, Aliverdi Khan in 1751 bought them off with the province of Orissa. Almost certainly, had Bengal been governed by a less tough-minded ruler, India's richest province would have fallen to the Marathas.

During this period the European trading settlements understandably began to improve their defences, with the Nawab's blessing. The British started to build a moat around northern Calcutta, the Maratha Ditch. After the peace of 1751, however, the Nawab told them to stop building. 'You are merchants. What need have you of a fortress? Being under my protection, you have no enemies to fear.'

However – as Aliverdi was well aware – the Europeans were now building defences against the possibility that they might have to go to war with one another. Already France and Britain were at war in the Carnatic. Dupleix, at his most ambitious, encouraged de Bussy to march from Hyderabad to Bengal to carve out a French Bengali empire: 'Nothing can be easier than to humble the pride of that man [Aliverdi Khan] whose troops are as worthless as you already know. By sending to Bengal, Balasore or Masulipatam four to five hundred men . . . [and] some light artillery – that is all you would need in Bengal, where there isn't a single fort and the whole country lies open to the first glance. By taking a few precautions we could make ourselves masters of Hugli.'

Later he wrote, 'The Nawab is hated there because of his vexations. The English and the Dutch are not in a position to give him any help . . . You are alone strong enough to become the master of the country which is ripe for invasion because of the tyranny of the present government.' Unsurprisingly, in view of these threats, the East India Company instructed Fort William to form a garrison, and nearly sixty pieces of artillery were shipped in.

Aliverdi was too wily an old bird, however, to do more than occasionally threaten the Europeans. On one occasion he compared them prophetically to bees 'of whose honey you might reap the benefit', but which, if attacked in their hives, 'would sting you to death'. On another, he warned his advisers, 'What have the English done against me that I should use them ill? It is not difficult to extinguish fire on land; but should the sea be in flames, who can put them out?' Aliverdi sometimes made a show of force: he blockaded trade with the English factories when they seized the goods of an Armenian merchant in 1749. After the murder of the French-sponsored Nasir Jang in 1750, he tried unsuccessfully to seize the French factories.

In 1756 a new crisis arose when the authorities in Calcutta refused to hand over the estates of two Indians who had died without heirs. Under Bengali law, the land belonged to the state and these lands should revert to the Nawab. The British council at Fort William was indignant: 'We cannot think of subjecting our flag and protection to so much contempt as to abandon our tenants and inhabitants and permit our estates and properties to be seized and plundered . . . in case this demand is not laid aside we shall be under necessity to withdraw our factory and take proper measures to secure our employees from these impositions . . . we have taken to submit rather to a stoppage of our business than suffer this protection of our flag to grow contemptible.'

Aliverdi did nothing. At around the same time asylum in Calcutta was granted to one Krishna Das, son of a wealthy Indian civil servant who had been deeply involved in court intrigue over the succession to Aliverdi Khan. This was abruptly to become of key importance: for the man described by Orme as 'always extremely temperate, with no pleasures, with no seraglio and always lived the husband of one wife', who had shown such remarkable firmness, statesmanship and flexibility in office, died soon after on 10 April 1756 at the remarkable old age – for the times – of 82.

Four years earlier, by another irony of fate, Fort William had acquired the most stupid, stubborn and incompetent young governor in its history. With Aliverdi's death, power in Bengal was to pass to a more intelligent, but no less rash and feckless young man. The scene was set for the tragedy that ensued with astonishing rapidity.

Aliverdi Khan's chosen successor was his favourite grandson, Mirza Muhammad, known by the adopted name of Siraj-ud-Daula – 'Lamp of the State', who was aged 27 or 29 when he ascended the throne. Macaulay's description of him was memorable, although as usual over the top:

Oriental despots are perhaps the worst class of human beings; and this unhappy boy was one of the worst specimens of his class. His understanding was naturally feeble, and his temper naturally unamiable. His education had been such as would have enervated even a vigorous intellect and perverted even a generous disposition. He was unreasonable, because no one ever had to reason with him, and selfish, because he had never been made to feel dependent on the good will of others. Early debauchery had unnerved his body and his mind. He indulged immoderately in the use of ardent spirits, which inflamed his weak brain almost to madness.

His chosen companions were flatterers sprung from the dregs of the people, and recommended by nothing but buffoonery and servility. It is said that he had arrived at that last stage of human depravity, when cruelty becomes pleasing for its own sake, when the sight of pain, as pain, where no advantage is to be gained, no offence punished, no danger averted, is an agreeable excitement. It had early been his amusement to torture beasts and birds; and, when he grew up, he enjoyed with still keener relish the misery of his fellow creatures.

There is more reliable evidence to suggest he was one of history's less savoury rulers. The contemporary historian – and cousin of the Nawab – Ghulam Husain Tabatabai, paints a vivid picture:

Patrolling every street and every lane with a cohort composed of Aliverdi Khan's children and grandchildren, he fell into an abominable way of life, that respected neither age, nor sex, but was calculated to prepare from afar the ruin and desolation of that sublime building of fortune and sovereignty which its founder had been rearing with so much toil and danger . . .

He had a sport of sacrificing to his lust almost every person of either sex, to which he took a fancy; or else, he converted them without scruples into as many objects of the malignity of his temper, or the frolics of his inconsiderate youth. And having by this time provided himself with a number of like-minded followers, he commenced a course of insolencies, infamies and profligacies; and either out of that ignorance incident to that age, or because of an ardour natural to his constitution (although it was because of his perfect reliance on his uncle's forbearance), such a course of life became in him his real character. This is so far true that he was observed to be low spirited and melancholy, when he fell short of opportunities to commit his usual excesses and enormities; and they became so customary to him that he acted all along without a grain of remorse, or a spark of recollection.

Making no distinction between vice and virtue . . . he carried defilement wherever he went, and, like a man alienated in his mind, he made the houses of men and women of distinction the scenes of his profligacy, without minding either rank or station. In a little time he became as detested as Pharaoh, and people on meeting him by chance used to say, 'God save us from him'.

Another historian of the time, Ghulam Husain Salim, wrote:

Owing to Siraj-ud-Daula's harshness of temper and indulgence in violent language, fear and terror had settled on the hearts of everyone to such an extent that no one among his generals of the army or the noblemen of the city was free from anxiety. Amongst his officers, whoever went to wait on Siraj-ud-Daula despaired of life and honour, and whoever returned without being disgraced and ill-treated offered thanks to God.

Siraj-ud-Daula treated all the noblemen and generals of Mahabat Jang [Aliverdi Khan] with ridicule and drollery, and bestowed on each some contemptuous nickname that ill-suited any of them. And whatever harsh expressions and abusive epithet came to his lips, Siraj-ud-Daula uttered them unhesitatingly in the face of everyone, and no one had the boldness to breathe freely in his presence.

Siraj-ud-Daula was the son of Aliverdi's favourite son-in-law and best commander, Zain-ud-Din, who had been tortured to death by Afghan mercenaries. In his teens, he had been tainted by the corruption of the Bengali court: his domineering aunt, Ghasita Begum, had a supremely capable army commander, Husain Ali Khan, who threatened the youth's right of succession. Dark and good-looking, the commander became the lover of the Begum's bisexual husband; this she was prepared to tolerate. But when the commander also took as his lover Siraj-ud-Daula's mother, Amina, the infuriated Begum asked for the young prince to send his soldiers to murder him, which he did with relish.

Siraj-ud-Daula differed sharply from the conventional dissolute prince of India, as described in the classic *Raghuvamsa* by the Sanskrit poet Kalidasa, who is manipulated by a senior minister who 'accustoms him to the pleasures of a life of luxury and gives him every possible opportunity to indulge in them . . . he accustoms [the young ruler] to believe that the ruler's share in royal authority consists merely in sitting on the throne, shaking hands, being addressed as Sire, and sitting with women in the seclusion of the harem'.

Siraj-ud-Daula was dissipated, but he was also ambitious, hyperactive, and showed considerable cunning, if not statecraft. Apart from his pathological contempt for his own nobility, three other traits stand out: an insatiable sexual appetite; a penchant for frivolous cruelty; and a loathing of the British.

It was normal for Indian princes to have liaisons with willing girls from noble families; to buy slaves and dancing girls; to take women as spoils of war; to buy women from fathers, husbands and brothers; and to seduce willing partners. The only rule was compliance, or payment of a just price.

This huge pool of potential partners was not enough for Siraj-ud-Daula. According to his ally, Jean Law, head of the French settlement at Kasimbazar: 'Hindu women are accustomed to bathe on the banks of the Ganges. 'Siraj-ud-Daula, who was informed by his spies which of them were beautiful, sent his satellites in disguise in little boats to carry them off.' Siraj-ud-Daula further outraged convention by violating girls from noble families and insisting that the new bride of his banker, the Jagat Seth, be brought to him so that he could view her – although she escaped with her honour intact. According to Law, Siraj-ud-Daula was also sexually profligate with young men – which did not greatly offend his nobles, although it was looked upon with a certain contempt.

Siraj-ud-Daula's cruelty was legendary. He would rip open the stomachs of pregnant women to satisfy his curiosity as to how the child lay in the womb. According to Law, 'he was often seen, in the season when the river overflows, causing ferry boats to be upset or sunk, in order to have the cruel pleasure of seeing the confusion of a hundred people at a time, men, women and children, of whom many, not being able to swim, were sure to perish'. To the British trader William Watts, Siraj-ud-Daula was 'that imbecile murderer who breaks birds' wings and cuts off men's privities'.

A contemporary British comment was that he was 'violent, passionate, of great ambition tinctured with avarice'. He also indulged excessively in alcohol, although Aliverdi made him swear on the Koran to give up this unIslamic pursuit. Apparently considered 'famous for beauty', his portraits suggest a weak and delicate face with pursed lips, a large nose and wide, vague eyes. He was prone to high-pitched giggling, fits of violent temper, and alternated hyperactivity with indolence. Perhaps this made the British, in particular, underestimate his toughness and guile.

Law remarked, 'the violent character of Siraj-ud-Daula and the general hatred for him had given many people the idea that he could never become *subadar* (ruler). Among others the English thought so. They never addressed themselves to Siraj-ud-Daula for their business in the *durbar* (court) but on the contrary avoided all communications with him. On certain occasions they refused him admission into their factory at Kasimbazar and their country houses because, in fact, this excessively blustering and impertinent young man used to break the furniture or, if it pleased him, take it away' – an echo of Ghulam Husain Tabatabai's remarks.

Law also pointed out that Siraj-ud-Daula was:

One of the richest Nawabs that ever lived. Without mentioning his revenues, of which he gave no account to the court at Delhi, he possessed immense wealth both in gold and silver coin and in jewels and precious stones which had been left by the preceding three nawabs. Nevertheless he thought only of increasing his wealth. If any extraordinary expense had to be met he ordered contributions, and levied them with extreme rigour.

Having never known himself of what it was to be in want of money he supposed that, in due proportion, money was as common with other people as with himself, and that the resources of the Europeans especially were inexhaustible. His violence towards them was partly due to this. In fact from his behaviour it appeared as if his object was to ruin everybody. He spared no-one, not even his relations, from whom he took all the pensions and all the offices which they had held at the time of Aliverdi Khan.

However, Aliverdi had been determined that his spoilt, disagreeable grandson should succeed, and arranged for his chief minister,

Rai Durlabh, and army commander and brother-in-law, a bluff, straightforward man, Mir Jafar, to act as his protectors. Protectors he certainly needed: for his aunt, Ghasita Begum, was determined to frustrate him, backing one, then another, pretender to the throne. The most formidable was Siraj-ud-Daula's cousin, Shaukut Jang.

Most people in Calcutta believed that she would inevitably triumph: and the young Nawab had a shock when it became evident that Mir Jafar had changed sides and also supported Shaukut Jang. However, most of the court at the capital of Murshidabad stood by Aliverdi Khan's chosen successor.

Siraj-ud-Daula sent his dead uncle's widow, the Begum's sister, along with the chief banker in Bengal and head of its most influential Hindu family, the Jagat Seth – 'Banker of the World' – to persuade his aunt to submit in the exotic moated palace – the Moti Jhil – where she had retired with her lover. She submitted, but only after Siraj-ud-Daula had agreed to spare her lover's life. He was banished, she was bundled off to the Nawab's harem, and her fortune was seized.

Siraj-ud-Daula then set off with his army to Shaukut Jang's base. His cousin hastily acknowledged his right to the throne before the Nawab reached him. Having bribed the Nawab of Oudh, Bengal's most powerful neighbour, not to attack, the young prince quickly established a decisive ascendancy. So far there was little to justify the view that Siraj-ud-Daula was an incompetent or a coward, however capricious and cruel he might be.

CHAPTER 12

The Black Hole

O ne of the Begum's chief advisers – by some accounts the real power behind her – was Raj Ballabh, a high government official. It was his son, Krishna Das, who had sought asylum in Calcutta, as his father was being investigated for embezzlement. He brought his family and a large fortune with him, and almost certainly bribed British officials to let him in.

The Calcutta authorities showed an extraordinary insensitivity and ignorance of local politics. Siraj-ud-Daula, always suspicious of the British after the contemptuous way they had treated him, now became convinced that they had been behind the Begum's plot all along (there is no evidence for this, although they certainly preferred her).

The Nawab now turned his attention to the British. His principal courtiers, including Mir Jafar, too strong a man to strike against, in spite of his earlier disloyalty, advocated a show of force, backed by strength, but also urged flexibility.

Siraj-ud-Daula had three principal arguments against the British: first, that they continued to occupy Bengali territory and engage in illegal private trade; second, that they had taken in a wanted opponent of his; and, third, that, like the French and the Dutch, they were trying to strengthen their defences. He resolved to get tough.

Whatever the new Nawab's personal failings, his policy towards the British at least had the virtue of coherence and was even reasonable under the circumstances. The British response had neither of those things to be said for it: it was foolish, arrogant, complacent, provocative, insulting and conducted from a position of acute weakness.

With exquisite ineptness, the Calcutta council proceeded to drive Siraj-ud-Daula into a corner from which an attack on the settlement was the only way he could save face, and possibly his throne. The only conceivable defence of the British action is that they supposed he was anyway resolved to attack, and that to have made concessions would have displayed weakness. Unfortunately, all the evidence suggests that they thought he would never attack, that they believed they were acting from a position of strength, and that they could treat him with contempt. In this they were totally and tragically mistaken.

The four senior members of the council in Calcutta were the governor, Roger Drake, two traders, William Frankland and Charles Manningham, and James Holwell, the magistrate. The two traders were united in placing commercial considerations above all others. Holwell showed some vestiges of common sense, but was also vain and self-seeking, a chubby, self-important little man.

The nominal leader of the council, Drake, was widely despised among his own people. Appointed acting governor at the age of only 30, he had still not been confirmed in the job after four years and was treated by many of the local merchants with ribaldry and contempt. This increased when his wife died and he married her sister.

As one contemporary observer recalled, this could 'never be forgiven him, for the crime was not only itself bad but after that every man of character and sense shunned and avoided him, and this was the means of his running after and keeping very indifferent company, and of committing a thousand little meannesses and low actions, far unbecoming any man, much more a governor'. This brash, arrogant young man, singularly ill-suited for negotiation during a period of extreme danger, now had the task of dealing with an even younger and more unstable potential adversary – although undoubtedly a cleverer one.

Drake's first mistake was his response to a plea by the best-informed and most intelligent of the British merchants in Bengal, William Watts, who ran the trading post just outside the Bengali capital of Murshidabad, that Krishna Das should be handed over to the authorities. Drake overrode his fellow council members and refused. Siraj-ud-Daula sent an emissary to ask for the fugitive. Drake is said to have torn the emissary's letter up before his face. He was thrown out of town on the allegation that he was a spy.

Watts was appalled. 'The moment I was acquainted with the affair I dreaded the consequences of affronting so considerable a servant of a young man intoxicated with power and wealth, and who expected an implicit obedience to his will. I therefore immediately applied to all the great men about the nabob to prevent [the envoy] complaining, and the affair was seemingly hushed up.'

Meanwhile, Siraj-ud-Daula received replies from the three European settlements to his order that they should stop building up their fortifications. The Dutch denied they were doing so, the French answered that they were merely repairing existing defences. The official British reply was on similar lines to that of the French. The Nawab knew that the British had in fact been repositioning their guns along the river in front of Fort William, had built a new redoubt, and were clearing parts of the Maratha Ditch – all fairly minor activities.

But Drake was said to have been personally rude to the Nawab's emissary, even telling him that if the Nawab wanted the Ditch filled up, it could be with the heads of his own subjects. The envoy insulted by Drake is said to have asked Siraj-ud-Daula, 'What honour is left to us when a few traitors who have not yet learned to wash their backsides reply to the ruler's orders by expelling his envoys?'

The young king was furious at the direct insult. He expostulated: 'I swear by the Great God and the prophets that unless the English consent to fill up their ditch, raze their fortifications, and trade upon the same terms they did . . . I will totally expel them from the country.' But he added to his envoy that 'if [the British] are willing to comply . . . they may remain'.

Yet his attitude towards the British was straighforward. As he put it:

I have three substantial motives for extirpating the English out of my country; one is that they have built strong fortifications and dug a large ditch in the King's dominions contrary to the established laws of the country; the second is that they have abused the privileges of their *dustucks* [duty-free passes] by granting them to such as were in no ways entitled to them, from which practice the King has suffered greatly in the revenue of his customs; the third motive is that they give protection to such of the King's subjects as have by their behaviour in the employs they were entrusted with made themselves liable to be called to an account and instead of giving them up on demand they allow such persons to shelter themselves within their bounds from the hands of justice. For these reasons it is become requisite to drive them out.

His demands were an end to the fortification programme, an end to abuses of the trading concession, and a withdrawal of political asylum for the Nawab's enemies. These were not unreasonable. However, the same envoy he had sent to Calcutta three times already was 'threatened to be ill used if he came again on the same errand'.

The Nawab now began to resort to tougher tactics. Watts's fort at Kasimbazar was surrounded by armed men, while measures were taken to intercept British craft along the Hugli and at the entrance to the Bay of Bengal. By 2 June Watts was begging for reinforcements of at least 100 men because he feared attack. He urged the council at Calcutta either to send the men or yield to the Nawab's demands. It refused to do either.

Watts, who had only 50 men and a handful of old guns to defend the fort against the Nawab's 30,000-strong army, was summoned to Siraj-ud-Daula's presence. Suddenly he was seized, his hands were bound behind his back and he was forced to order his men to surrender. The colonel of the garrison committed suicide in protest at the decision.

Watts was later much criticised for his weakness. But the council's refusal to reinforce him made any attempt at resistance by the garrison pointless, and a fight there would have brought Fort William only a short breathing space. Watts's pregnant wife was allowed to take refuge in the French settlement where Jean Law, its senior trader, treated her courteously. Watts and his second-in-command were treated with respect by the Nawab. His chief minister, Rai Durlabh, suggested that matters would be settled if the British paid a ransom of 2 million rupees – but he was willing to haggle. Not only would Drake not consider paying the ransom, but the seizure of Kasimbazar convinced him that the Bengalis did indeed intend to attack Calcutta – and he was almost mystically certain of his ability to defeat them.

The Nawab's army confirmed his worst suspicions by moving southwards towards Calcutta. By now it had been swollen to 50,000 men, accompanied by 500 elephants and 50 guns. The British were unimpressed; the guns, it was said, had only clay projectiles. Drake decided to take the offensive, sending 15 soldiers in a boat upstream with instructions to make as much noise as possible, and also sending three boats to a fort near Calcutta, which landed a force to spike the guns there. These actions achieved little, but enraged Siraj-ud-Daula.

Only after this display of bravado did Drake summon a council of war to prepare for the defence of Fort William on 7 June. The state of readiness was pitiable, even a criminal dereliction of duty. The commander of the garrison, Captain Minchin, was so abysmal a soldier that Holwell later remarked, 'touching the military capacity of our commandant, I am a stranger. I can only say we are unhappy in him keeping it to himself, if he had any; as neither I, nor I believe anyone else, was witness to any part of his conduct that spoke or bore the appearance of his being the commanding military officer in the garrison.'

Worse still was the state of the ordnance and ammunition. The adjutant-general wrote afterwards that there were 'no cartridges of any kind ready. The small quantity of grape in store had lain by so long that it was destroyed by worms; no shells fitted nor fuses prepared for small or great. The few that were thrown at the siege burst half way. There were two iron mortars, one of 13 and the other of 10 inches, sent out about three years ago. The 10-inch mortar we had just finished the bed for it, but the 13-inch one lay but useless for want of one; tho' there was upwards of three hundred shells sent out for both, all that could be prepared was not above twenty, and such as was thrown of them burst, some after quitting the mortar, others half way. We had but a small quantity of powder, and the greatest part of that damp.'

There were hardly any men, either, to wield this pitiable arsenal. Nominally the garrison contained 500 men, but was down to half strength. Some 70 were sick, and 25 had been deployed outside Calcutta, leaving just 165, mainly of Portuguese-Indian descent. As for the defences, these consisted of a line of guns along the waterfront of Fort William itself, pointed out over the river as a deterrent to attack from that side.

To protect these, a wall had been erected at either end of the fort which, Orme was later to remark, 'would resist one shot of a six-pounder, but be forced by the second'. The bastions on the landward side of the fort were overlooked just 30 or 40 yards away by substantial merchants' houses.

The principal British houses of the settlement stretched away on either side of the fort along the river bank for about a mile altogether, and extended a quarter mile or so inland. To the north of these were prosperous Indian merchant houses; to the south the 'black town' of the poorer Indians began. The 'Maratha Ditch', which was supposed to protect the whole city, was only four miles long on the north side and petered out further down.

Still wildly optimistic about the superiority of British arms and their chances of survival, and doubtful whether an Indian attack would ever take place – although Drake himself showed rare insight in now believing it would – the council decided to defend a circle around the European houses. In practice such a line was indefensible except against very feeble opposition, and the British would have done best to concentrate all their inadequate firepower inside the fort itself, which might then have been capable of withstanding a prolonged siege.

Manningham, a pompous trader with no military experience, was solemnly proclaimed a colonel by the council, and Frankland a lieutenant-colonel, to earn the honours of fighting off the Indian assault. Drake meanwhile 'by beat of drum caused all the inhabitants fit to bear arms to be assembled'.

In the humid central square of Fort William, some 250 English, Portuguese and Armenian settlers in a motley variety of civilian clothing were organised in lines to reinforce the red-coated garrison up to 365 men. They made a shambolic army. According to Holwell, 'when we came to action there was hardly any among the Armenian and Portuguese inhabitants, and but a few among the European militia, who knew the right from the wrong end of their pieces [matchlocks]'.

This tiny force was split into four. Some 100 men trooped to the east to take up a position near the courthouse, to face the threat from the landward side of Calcutta, under the command of the second-ranking soldier, Captain Clayton, and Holwell. Another 100 or so were sent to protect the southern approach. Some 70 went north under the command of the fort's chaplain. A further 25 under Ensign Piccard were sent to man Perrin's Redoubt to the north, while some 20 were held in reserve to reinforce any of these four positions that needed it.

The remaining 200 or so, under the command of Governor Drake, 'Colonel' Manningham and 'Lieutenant-Colonel' Frankland, and Captain Minchin, remained to man the fort – uselessly, unless the outlying positions fell. These, in turn were all the more indefensible and likely to fall because nearly half the garrison was well behind their lines.

On 16 June the English citizens of Calcutta retired into Fort William, along with several hundred men, women and children of mixed Portuguese-Indian ancestry. Intimidated by the Nawab's approaching armies, local landowners withheld food from the town; the siege had begun.

Three sloops – the *Prince George, Fortune* and *Chance* – were sent to reinforce Perrin's Redoubt upriver in an attempt to block an attack from the seaward side. The scene was now fully set for one of the worst and most disgraceful fiascos in British military history, mitigated only by the appalling tragedy that was to befall some of the defenders.

That same day the Nawab's forces, a gigantic army of tens of thousands supported by retainers, elephants, camels, concubines and looters, began to pour into the outlying areas of Calcutta. The inhabitants of the 'black town' had already fled. In a great cacophony of noise and colour, looting began.

The first real engagement of the battle was a Bengali cannonade against Perrin's Redoubt and the three sloops nearby. With just three dozen men, the commander at the redoubt, Ensign Piccard, kept up such intense fire that the Nawab's 4,000 men could not mount a successful attack. The six cannon of the Indians also surprisingly failed to make much impact on the walls of the outpost.

At six o'clock, as equatorial darkness without dusk blanketed the scene, the Nawab's guns abruptly ceased firing. At midnight, Piccard led a raid into the thicket from which most of the firing had come, caught the enemy sleeping and unawares, killed about 80 men and drove the rest from the cover of the trees, successfully spiking four cannon.

The Nawab's army withdrew from its positions and moved

eastward and southward to try and find another way across the Ditch into the central part of Calcutta. The complacent council of war could be forgiven for going to bed that night with little to ruffle their mood: the British had driven off the first attack of the enemy.

The sheer size of Siraj-ud-Daula's army had not yet sunk in, and the British had gravely underestimated his determination. His commanders soon found that the Maratha Ditch could be crossed by men, though not by cannon. The Nawab himself, with his guard of honour, moved over it at Dum Dum (Cow Cross Bridge), establishing his headquarters in the garden of one of the wealthiest Indian merchants in Calcutta, Omichand, a name to recur throughout the rest of Clive's life, and to be fatally intertwined with his own.

There could now be no doubt that Siraj-ud-Daula was in deadly earnest about seizing Calcutta, and that one setback would not send the Bengali army scurrying. In this, due credit should be given him. All too frequently a determined show of European force could cause panic in an Indian army; no significant victory had ever yet been won by an Indian prince against a major European force. Although the British were woefully unprepared, Siraj-ud-Daula could not be sure of this.

That same night, the council – wisely for once – gave orders to burn down the merchants' houses overlooking the fort. To the 3,000 or so encamped inside Fort William in conditions of varying squalor, the loss of the peace and security of that beautiful and prosperous settlement with its elegant façades must have seemed sudden and bewildering.

As the houses dissolved into flames, crimson against the darkness, the sound of looting and revelry could be heard beyond; some 7,000 Bengali camp followers had gone on a plundering spree in the 'black town'. For most of the inhabitants of the fort, the women and children in particular, the situation must have been fraught with horror and terror. But Drake and his men, consoled by Piccard's success, were still confident even as the noose closed about them.

On the next day, 17 June, to British satisfaction, the Bengali attack appeared to falter. Firing was sporadic. In fact the Nawab's forces were merely regrouping. They set fire to the 'black town'; as darkness fell and flames raged through the town again, the blackened remains of a large part of Calcutta were 'too horrible to contemplate'.

The Indian servants and camp followers of the British now deserted in droves. 'We had not a black fellow to draw or work a gun, not even to carry a cotton bale or sandbag on the ramparts; and what work of that kind had been done was by the military and militia. This want of workmen at last and scarcity at the beginning harassed us prodigiously, and prevented our doing several works that would have been necessary.'

The following day was the nineteenth of Moslem Ramadam. The Nawab's siege now began in earnest. It then became apparent that, on top of their incompetence and stupidity, the British had also been betrayed. The figure who looms largest in the body of circumstantial evidence on this score was the Bengali merchant Omichand.

Omichand was perhaps the richest Indian trader in Calcutta, a position he had acquired through acting as an agent for the British. However, some years earlier he had lost this superiority to English traders, and certainly bore them a major grudge. Omichand had been in direct contact with Siraj-ud-Daula's ambassador to Calcutta, introducing him to the British, only to see him snubbed by Drake.

It seems certain that around this time Omichand decided to throw in his lot with Siraj-ud-Daula, while retaining close British links. Whether he did so out of resentment of the British or because he genuinely believed that their absurdly arrogant attitude to the Nawab portended only disaster and the certainty of a Bengali occupation of the city cannot be properly guessed at. It was probably a mixture of both.

When two letters were found in Omichand's handwriting to the Nawab's principal spy in Calcutta, Drake not unreasonably ordered his arrest. The merchant surrendered quietly enough, but at his brother-in-law's house there was a fight, and a loyal servant killed thirteen women in the house, to save them from the dishonour of being exposed to the eyes of strangers, before attempting to kill himself.

On 17 June, during a lull in the fighting, the same servant, together with another bearing a letter from Omichand, went to the Nawab – who almost certainly by prior arrangement now occupied Omichand's house – and offered to lead the Bengali forces and their guns across the Maratha Ditch. Thousands of men now began to infiltrate Calcutta proper around and behind the two exposed British positions to the east and the south, occupying the few houses still left standing.

At 8 a.m. the fighting began, as Siraj-ud-Daula's men, now in control of several of the buildings around the southern British position, opened fire with muskets. The British cannon there fired back but could make little impression on the buildings. An hour later the Nawab's forces started another attack on Perrin's Redoubt, and again were driven off by a volley of grapeshot. Two hours later, an attack began on the east battery. Considering that the British positions were indefensible and all but surrounded, the defenders fought bravely and well.

Finally Clayton and Holwell on the eastern flank decided they could no longer hold out, and the latter left to seek authority from the council to evacuate his men to the fort. When he returned he found that most of the guns had been spiked – although 'with so little art that they were easily drilled and turned against us' and that the little force was close to panic. They retreated 'giving the appearance of a confused rout, managing to carry back only one cannon'.

The southern position was evacuated in more orderly fashion under fire from the nearby houses. Ensign Piccard and his valiant men were evacuated from their redoubt that evening by boat. The council now decided to make a further stand along a line consisting of the burnt-out shells of the houses around the fort. The noose was tightening. Siraj-ud-Daula's offensive had proved successful so far. He had driven the British from the town itself and into their second last bastion.

Drake, astonishingly, remained optimistic. He 'imagined from the number of men slain that evening, a terror might seize [the enemy] and that they would decamp'. Even he, though, had the common sense to realise that the English women and children should now be evacuated to the ships. 'Colonel' Manningham and 'Lieutenant-Colonel' Frankland escorted them aboard – where they decided to remain themselves, the first of an appalling string of acts of cowardice by the senior merchants supposedly entrusted with the defence of Calcutta.

Inside the fort some 3,000 people were jammed in chaotic conditions, as an attack was expected at any moment. As Drake later reported, 'Three different times did ye drums beat to arms, but in vain, not a man could be got to stand to their arms, tho' we had frequent alarms of ye enemy preparing under our walls to scale them.'

Much of the garrison was drunk; the wounded lay strewn around the fort; the civilians were in panic. Fortunately no attack came. But conditions inside the fort continued to deteriorate, forcing Drake to call a council of war at one o'clock in the morning. The despair of the half-dozen men present could be seen on every face except Drake's.

The officers reported that the men were virtually out of control. The artillery officers reported that they had 'not enough powder and shot for three days; our bombs and grenades were of no use, the fuses being spoiled by the dampness of the climate owing to their being filled some years ago and never looked into afterwards.' Even in this extremity, Drake was playing his own variety of bowls, showing an almost comical refusal to be flustered.

It was agreed that a retreat should take place and the fort be evacuated, although not until the following night. The day should be given over to evacuating the Portuguese women and children and the garrison's valuables so as to avoid 'confusion and tumult' – as if this was not the case already. It was as though the captain of a sinking ship had decided to postpone manning the lifeboats until the following day.

The council was under the illusion that the timing still rested with themselves, not Siraj-ud-Daula; and they had no time left. If the fort had been evacuated that night – admittedly probably under con-ditions of panic – most of the garrison might have got away. But the Bengali forces, although unwilling to attack by night, were not going to give Drake and his men a day's respite to prepare their withdrawal. The council resolved that Manningham and Frankland must return to shore – which they refused to do – and the meeting ended when a cannonball crashed into the room.

The following morning dawned to reveal a dismal spectacle. Siraj-ud-Daula's army now not only controlled all the houses in the town outside the fort: they were on the river bank, firing upon the small fleet of British vessels and sending burning arrows into the air in an attempt to set fire to them. It seemed only a matter of time before they broke through the thin wall to the north that protected the

British guns to seaward and so also cut off the escape route from the fort to the sea.

The 'orderly' evacuation of the Portuguese women turned into a pathetic rout as they crowded, screaming, into every available boat, swamping them. Only a handful of boats made it to the British ships offshore. Several sank and the women drowned. Others were carried by the tide to Bengali-held positions, and the women on them were either captured or massacred.

By 10 a.m. Drake was told that the garrison was about to run out of ammunition because the little gunpowder left was damp and unusable. The remaining Portuguese women heard this, stampeded to the remaining boats with their children, swamped them, and some 200 were drowned. The ships, meanwhile, began to pull away out to sea out of range of the fire arrows and Siraj-ud-Daula's guns.

This increased the state of panic in the garrison. The sole hero remained Ensign Piccard who, with twenty men, occupied Company House, just outside the fort, driving out its nest of snipers. After two hours of intense fire from nearby houses, he was forced to retreat. Drake was still desperately trying to get men and guns to protect the flimsy north wall that commanded the escape route to the river. No one obeyed him.

Captain Minchin and the other senior members of the settlement remaining had commandeered boats. Drake, who had ordered the ships to return, also now embarked, in one of the most shameful actions of a British commander in history.

As soon as these illustrious figures had boarded, the ships moved downriver, leaving the rest of the garrison to its fate. The captains of the ships, which were private merchantmen, felt no obligation to rescue those on shore and had no wish to come under fire again. Only Captain Nicholson of the *Hunter* attempted to return to evacuate the garrison; but his Indian crew threatened to jump overboard if he did so. The ships slipped anchor, and watched as evening fell and the receding flames of the burning houses and the fort illuminated the night sky.

There were still around 300 people inside, more than half of them British. The only two senior figures remaining were Holwell, the magistrate, and Richard Pearkes, a junior officer. Holwell appointed himself governor after Drake's desertion, and Pearkes was ordered to escape from the fort to reach their last remaining hope of rescue – the *Prince George*, still guarding the northern redoubt.

When Pearkes and his small party reached the shore opposite the ship, however, they found it had been run aground, and fled to the nearby Dutch settlement. The Dutch promptly returned them to the Nawab's forces – who, however, did not ill-treat them.

Holwell, expecting the ship at any moment to evacuate the remainder of the garrison, tried desperately to rally his exhausted men, promising them treasure in return for continuing to defend the settlement and sending desperate signals to the ships down the river; but 'there was never a single effort made to send a boat or vessel to bring off the garrison'.

Surprisingly, the fort withstood relentless attacks throughout the day. The defenders proved remarkably resilient. They 'got up a quantity of broadcloth in bales, with which we made traverses along the curtains and bastions; we fixed up likewise some bales of cotton against the parapets (which were very thin and of brickwork only) to resist the cannonballs, and did everything in our power to baffle their attempts'. At last, as night fell, the attacks ceased.

Much of the garrison now turned to the liquor stores. 'The Company's House, Mr Cruttenden's, Mr Nixon's, Dr Knox's and the marine yard were now in flames and exhibited a spectacle of unspeakable horror. We were surrounded on all sides by the Nabob's forces, which made a retreat by land impracticable.' Around a third of the garrison now deserted. It had managed to hold out more than 36 hours after the flight of Drake.

On Sunday, 20 June the Bengalis renewed their attack. Again, the garrison resisted bitterly, the sole redeeming act throughout this sorry tale. But by midday 25 soldiers had been killed, and some 70 of the artillerymen wounded, so that only 14 men remained to man the guns, whose ammunition would last no more than two hours. Holwell had no option but to call a truce, asking Omichand, still a prisoner in the fort, to write to Raja Manik Chand, Siraj-ud-Daula's confidant.

Two hours later an emissary from the Nawab arrived, saying that he was prepared to talk if the British stopped firing. This they did. The scene in the fortress was now one of utter desolation: exhausted, battle-weary men abandoned by their leaders rested after four days of intense siege. The wounded were screaming and groaning, the dead putrefying in the heat.

Shortly afterwards another emissary appeared to tell the British that they would be spared if they surrendered. Holwell sought a personal reassurance that this was the Nawab's own promise, writing a letter to his commander on the spot, Rai Durlabh, which was thrown over the ramparts.

> The letter was taken up by the person who advanced with the flag, who returned with it. Soon after multitudes of the enemy came out of their hiding places round us and flocked under the walls; a short parley ensued. I demanded a truce to hostilities until the Suba's [Nawab's] pleasure could be known. To which I was answered by one of his officers from below that the Suba was there, and his pleasure was that we should have quarter. I was going to reply when at that instant Mr William Baillie, standing near me, was slightly wounded by a musket ball from the enemy on the side of the head, and word was brought to me that they were attempting to force the south-west barrier and were cutting at the eastern gate.

The Nawab's patience had in fact run out. His men had finally climbed the north-west bastion and killed the occupants, while the western gate had been opened by a deserter, and the Bengali army flooded in. Holwell hastily gave his sword up to the nearest officer 'who had scaled the walls and seemed to act with some authority'. It was perhaps the first ever instance of a European fort being taken by an Indian army.

This humiliation had been brought on by the impetuousness and arrogance of the British settlers themselves: the bulk of the evidence suggests that Siraj-ud-Daula could, at the very least, have been bought off until the British garrison was adequately strengthened. His attack was brought on by needless provocation as well as the wretchedness of the commanders in defending Fort William. The only mitigating factor was that Drake and his council were essentially merchants, absolutely unprepared for war, and that most of the British community were accustomed to lifestyles of considerable comfort. They had been traumatised by the threat of attack.

Holwell himself was put in irons, and his men rounded up. There now followed the event that has passed into myth, and it is hard to separate fact from polemic. Certainly the myth was to be extra-ordinarily convenient for the British, both in obscuring indignation about the inadequacy and cowardice of the principal defenders of Calcutta, and in providing the justification for what was later to be the conquest of Bengal.

Holwell was soon released on the Nawab's orders, and taken to see him three times in his temporary encampment in one of the more luxurious European houses. The portly little magistrate must have been deeply apprehensive as he approached the effete young man with his high-pitched laugh known for his extreme cruelty and hatred of the British.

But Siraj-ud-Daula was in an excellent mood, savouring his great victory, which he was later to claim rivalled the exploits of Tamer-lane. Some 7,000 of his men, it was estimated, had been killed. Not the least of his feats had been in spurring his men to fight on in the face of such huge losses. He could not have known the state of unpreparedness of the British in advance; and his gamble in taking on the invincible strength of a European army had paid off.

He had achieved what no Indian prince had before, and he was in a high good humour. He promised Holwell that no harm would befall the prisoners. His army in fact was busy looting the English houses and many of the Armenians and Portuguese managed to escape the fort in the confusion. Holwell himself claimed he could have escaped but decided to stay to share the fate of the garrison. Clive later was to observe caustically that 'nothing but the want of a boat prevented his escape and flight with the rest'.

As dusk fell, some of the garrison's soldiers began drunkenly to attack the Bengali soldiers. News of this, and of the escape of the Europeans, was brought to the Nawab with the suggestion that the prisoners should be locked up. Siraj-ud-Daula asked whether there was a suitable prison in the fort, and was told of the Black Hole – the common name of the punishment cell in British garrisons where soldiers who had caused some offence were held. It was decided to put the prisoners there for the night.

Did the Nawab know that the cell was only 18 feet by 14 feet wide, with just two barred windows? It is commonly assumed today that he did not, and that he merely made an error. It is nevertheless strange that he did not enquire whether the cell was large enough to accommodate all the prisoners, or that his aides did not inform him.

They at least cannot have been ignorant as to the consequences of forcing so many into this tiny space.

The implications of such an act were bound to be considerable. Taking a British fort was one thing; massacring its inhabitants in so sadistic a way quite another – virtually demanding a massive response from the European power involved. Any subordinate of Siraj-ud-Daula must have known he would be in desperate trouble if he carried out such a massacre against the Nawab's wishes.

The bulk of probability suggests that the Nawab knew exactly what he was doing when he ordered the prisoners into the lockup – whether to teach them a lesson for insubordination against the occupying power or whether out of some reflex sadism in his character can only be surmised. Macaulay gave the classic account of what then ensued, which at least captures the horror of the event as it seared itself into the minds of eighteenth-century Englishmen.

Macaulay's account was based on Holwell's, and the latter, although founded on truth, was almost certainly exaggerated. The magistrate claimed that 146 people were locked up; but his own account suggested that the garrison by that time had been reduced to no more than 70 men (and two heroic women who refused to abandon their husbands). Modern Indian studies suggest that the number of people who could have been in the Black Hole was 69, while others put the figure as low as 39. During that appalling night, the sufferings of the sweating, panicking, fighting, defecating, vomiting, screaming, expiring bodies must have made it seem far more.

Holwell's figure for the number of survivors – 23 – is much more likely to have been accurate, and even Indian historians have stuck to it. On the highest revised figure, 43 would have been killed; on the lowest, 16. Holwell claims that he pleaded from inside the jail for the Nawab to be informed of their plight, but was told that he could not be awoken. Victorian sources embellished the account with tales that the guards taunted the prisoners by holding water to the windows and urinating on them. Holwell survived by drinking from a handkerchief made sodden by his own sweat.

It is not necessary to believe the exaggerations to see that a major atrocity had occurred. To the jailers and officers involved, the effect of crowding so many Europeans into so small a chamber on a night of high summer in Bengal must have seemed obvious; and the yells and the groans of the dying must have made it more obvious still. To suggest that the Nawab gave the wrong order, that he was not aware of the size of the cell, and that the guards were too fearful to awake him stretches credulity.

More likely the Nawab had decided to punish the British as a further retaliation to the snubs they had inflicted upon him, and his officers had instructions to do what they did. True, the Indians may have underestimated the effects of holding the Europeans under such conditions.

When morning came and dawn trickled its thin light through the bars on to the grisly scene, the door was opened. Holwell was again shackled and brought before the Nawab, who showed no sign of remorse or apology. Nor were any of his officers disciplined for the 'mistake'. With the other survivors, the magistrate was taken to Murshidabad, the Nawab's capital. The two women survivors were pressed into harems. The men were paraded naked through the city, humiliated and sexually abused. The remainder of the garrison, and any other Europeans still there, were told to leave Calcutta under threat of having their noses and ears cut off.

Siraj-ud-Daula appointed Manik Chand, one of his favourites, as his viceroy over the city, now renamed Alinagar, and ordered a mosque to be built there. The Nawab retired slowly up the river bank and threatened to occupy the Dutch settlement at Chinsurah unless he was paid a ransom of 2 million rupees.

The Dutch, lacking such sums, threatened to withdraw from Bengal altogether; eventually the Nawab settled for 450,000 rupees, which the Dutch had to borrow from the Jagat Seth, the Nawab's banker, at a hefty rate of interest. The French at Chandernagore were the next to attract the Nawab's attentions, but they bought him off for 350,000 rupees, paid for from a shipment of gold bullion from France. The British were convinced the French had got off lightly because they had provided artillery for the attack on Calcutta.

On his return to Murshidabad, Siraj-ud-Daula wrote triumphantly to his nominal superior, the Mogul Emperor, claiming that his victory had been on a par with the conquests of Tamerlane. Holwell, who had been brought to the capital, pleaded for his freedom, offering to pay 'a considerable amount of money'. The monarch replied, in one of his rare displays of magnanimity, that 'his sufferings have been great; let him have his liberty'. Holwell and his three companions were taken in by the Dutch, and were then brought down the Hugli to join the main body of English refugees.

The plight of the English in the ships was pitiable beyond measure. The flotilla of around 15 vessels was crowded out with men, women and children. They barely had a week's supplies to support them. As it made its way downriver from Govindpur Point, fearing attack from the land and river at the same time, it came under the guns of Thana Fort; two of the ships anchored, and were promptly seized by the Bengalis. The rest of the flotilla again ran the gauntlet of fire from the fort, and this time succeeded in getting through with minimal damage.

On 24 June the ships reached Budge Budge, where all the Indians were put ashore in order to conserve supplies. Two days later, they reached Fulta, a comparatively safe point, but no more than a primitive village, where they dropped anchor. Their supplies were now almost exhausted. The ships were in the most inhospitable part of the Ganges basin, yet they stayed there for almost three weeks before the Dutch at last agreed to send them food and water secretly via the small settlement there.

It was astonishing that Drake had not taken his chance of breaking out into the open sea – for Madras. His hopes of obtaining food were better the further down the coast and away from Siraj-ud-Daula – who had ordered an embargo on supplies locally – they travelled. Almost certainly Drake and his now reduced council refused to move because of their embarrassment at the rout. If they fled now, they would also lose their chance to influence events if Calcutta were to be retaken.

Once again, vain political considerations took precedence in Drake's mind over the fate of his starving compatriots. It was not the least display of self-centredness by this most inept of British leaders. He preferred to reopen talks with Siraj-ud-Daula in the hope of saving what little remained of his own face.

Those aboard the ships paid the price. 'The want of convenient shelter, as well as the dread of being surprised, obliged them all to sleep on board the vessels, which were so crowded that all lay promiscuously on the decks, without shelter from the rains of the season, and for some time without a change of raiment, for none had brought any store away, and these hardships, inconsiderable as they may seem, were grievous to persons of whom the greatest part had lived many years in the gentle ease of India. Sickness likewise increased their sufferings, for the lower part of Bengal between the two arms of the Ganges is the most unhealthy country in the world, and many died of a malignant fever which infected all the vessels.'

Drake and the council wrote to William Watts, who had been released at the end of the previous month after being carried around as a captive with the Nawab's army for nearly four weeks and had taken refuge at the French settlement at Chandernagore. Drake asked Watts to mediate with the Nawab.

Watts was shocked at the idea and refused disdainfully, saying he would not recognise the authority of the 'governor'. The Nawab, he said, would settle only 'on such shameful terms that Englishmen we hope would never consent to'. Watts himself, on being released, had been given a letter from the Nawab to George Pigot, Governor of Madras, to explain his motives in seizing Calcutta. He sought negotiations which would allow the British to re-establish themselves in Bengal, though humbled and respectful of the power of the Nawab:

Director Pigot, of high and great rank, and greatest of the merchants, may you be possessor of the Patcha's [Emperor's] favour. It was not my intention to remove the mercantile business of the Company belonging to you from out of Bengal, but Roger Drake, your *gomasta* [agent] was a very wicked and unruly man and began to give protection to persons who had accounts with the Emperor in the factor.

Notwithstanding all my admonitions, yet he did not desist from his shameless actions. Why should these people who come to transact the mercantile affairs of the Company do such things? However, that shameless man has met with the desert of his actions and was expelled from this subah [province]. I gave leave to Mr Watts who is a helpless, poor and innocent man, to go to you. As I esteem you to be a substantial person belonging to the Company, I have written these circumstances of [Drake's] shameless and wicked proceeding.

Watts forwarded the note to Madras, as well as a copy of Drake's letter, and advised the British instead to bring sufficient 'military force – to attack the Nawab in his metropolis'. Meanwhile Drake himself despatched 'Colonel' Manningham – the first of the senior officials to flee Calcutta – along with a French officer who had rallied to the British cause to give the council at Madras their version of events.

Towards the end of July, both Watts and Holwell arrived at Fulta where, with an adequate food supply now established, Drake and his 'council', now again labelling themselves Company agents, were beginning to regain their confidence. Holwell quarrelled bitterly with the deserter Drake, but the latter was confirmed by his equally fleet-footed peers as governor and pompously insisted on being saluted as he travelled from his 'flagship', the *Dodalay*, to dine on one of the other ships in that stinking backwater.

At about the same time the English refugees took heart at being joined by a small flotilla containing 200 soldiers commanded by Major Kilpatrick, which had been despatched as soon as Pigot heard of the outbreak of war in Bengal. There was great rejoicing when the tiny squadron bearing the English flag reached that dismal settlement: at last it seemed to Drake that he might get his chance of revenge against the Nawab.

A 'council of war' was set up comprising Drake, Kilpatrick, Holwell and Watts. Omichand too reappeared as an intermediary between the British and the Bengalis, to advise that conciliatory letters should be sent to the Nawab and his chief advisers. The British were happy to do this to buy time, for there were unsubstantiated rumours that Manik Chand was preparing to launch fireboats down the river and attack them at Fulta.

The British took further heart when they learnt that the Nawab, who believed himself to be secure on his throne after the defeat of the British at Calcutta, was once again being challenged by his cousin, Shaukut Jang. On 17 September the remaining British agent at Kasimbazar after Watts's departure, the young Warren Hastings, reported that war between the two cousins was imminent.

The Jagat Seth and other Hindu nobles, heavily disapproving of the recklessness with which Siraj-ud-Daula had attacked the British and thereby removed Bengal's main source of revenue, had intrigued against the giggling, sadistic ruler, even asking for the Emperor's *firman* – seal of approval – to be bestowed on his rival for the throne, Shaukut Jang. Another covert supporter of Shaukut Jang was, as ever, Mir Jafir, the Nawab's chief army commander and head of the Moslem military aristocracy, who complained of 'the growing and daily cruelties of Siraj-ud-Daula'.

As the pretender to the throne assembled a large army of 15,000 infantry and 6,000 cavalry, the Nawab accused the Jagat Seth of betraying him, hysterically slapping him across the face, threatening him with circumcision and confining him to his house – although he did not dare to execute so powerful a man. The Nawab's army commanders refused to support him unless the Jagat Seth was set free, which the Nawab did with ill grace at the beginning of October.

Siraj-ud-Daula, facing mutiny from his own senior officers and retainers, was saved by one thing. Although not so cruel, Shaukut Jang was erratic, heavily drugged much of the time and, according to one of his closest supporters, actually mad. He announced that after deposing Siraj-ud-Daula he would seize the throne in Delhi – near-blasphemy to Indian princes who regarded the powerless Emperor as their underlying source of legitimacy.

The pretender fired several of his senior generals, threatening to flay one alive, and told the Nawab that he would spare his life only if he at once left the throne. In mid-October, the armies of the two cousins at last met near Rajmahal. Of the two, Siraj-ud-Daula possessed by far the most cunning. Fearing he would be slain by his own officers, who hated him, he sent several decoys dressed up in his robes at the head of his troops, while he stayed behind his forces. His own officers made no attempt against these, however.

But Shaukut Jang believed he saw Siraj-ud-Daula among the enemy, led a charge against him and was shot; his leaderless army surrendered. Siraj-ud-Daula was once again undisputed ruler of Bengal – but only for a moment. Within weeks three new challenges were to press in to him in his capital of Murshidabad: from Afghan invaders in the north; from the French in the south; and from the British.

After the defeat of his rival, the Nawab was faced by a demand from Manik Chand, his commander in Calcutta, for a frontal attack on the ragged British forces at Fulta. The Nawab was uncertain. 'A pair of slippers is all that is needed to get them,' he remarked. In fact he was probably right: the British were in no shape to withstand a concerted assault. He prevaricated, probably believing himself to be in so strong a position that he could spare them; and his policy was now to bring them back, humbled, as traders.

At Fulta, as the weeks dragged by and the sickness continued to rage among the ships, while food supplies began to falter again because the British lacked the ready money to pay for them, Drake and his ludicrous council of war became increasingly restless. Rumours that Manik Chand was assembling an army at Budge Budge did nothing to reassure them. On 23 October a sloop, the *Kingfisher*, arrived: it brought the news that a large expedition was on its way from Madras. There was rejoicing on all the ships, and the flag was hoisted for the first time on Drake's 'flagship'.

CHAPTER 13

To the Hugli

R obert Clive is commonly described as having settled down to the routine of serving as deputy governor to what was now, once again, just a colonial backwater, when news of the 'catastrophe' – as he described the attack on Calcutta – reached Fort St David. In fact Clive had been sent to Madras as the potential military commander in the event of hostilities breaking out with the French. And those, to all in Madras, seemed imminent.

The Nizam of Hyderabad, who ruled the Deccan with the Marquis de Bussy perched on his shoulder, had called on the British to help him against the French overlords. Governor Pigot and his council decided to send him 400 men equipped with artillery. It was said that a French fleet of 19 ships and 3,000 men was sailing to Pondicherry. In Europe, war between the British and the French again appeared imminent. Clive was preparing the settlement in readiness for the outbreak of hostilities.

When news of the war in Bengal first arrived, it must have appeared an unwelcome distraction from the more serious task in hand: a single sloop, the *Bridgwater*, was despatched under the competent Major Kilpatrick with 200 men; tiresomely, this meant postponing the proposed offensive against de Bussy. But on 16 August Pigot heard the incredible news of the fall of Calcutta.

Pigot, Clive, and the council, as well as Admiral Watson, commander of the British fleet, were immediately thrown into a major strategic dilemma. The humiliation of British arms involved in the fall of Calcutta was without precedent. Moreover, there were rumours that the French had been helping the Nawab's forces. Throughout the continent, the news that a British garrison had been humiliated and taken by a native army would stir up revolt and contempt against them, setting them back to where they had been fifteen years before.

The Company in London, when the news finally reached it, would be beside itself with anxiety and anger; it would scarcely understand if no attempt was immediately made to retake Calcutta. Yet there were tremendous risks involved: the British would have to abandon the attempt to dislodge de Bussy and the French from central India.

Watson angrily protested that if a French fleet did arrive on the east coast of India, it could bottle him up the Hugli river. 'Is it not very probable, if the French squadron should arrive here, which you have reason to expect, that they, having intelligence where I am gone to, will under the presumption of the largest ships not being able to get higher [up the Hugli river] than Balasore Road, come there in search of me? How then should I be able to defend His Majesty's ships without men? Would they not become an easy capture to the French and thereby contribute to the ruin of your affairs instead of being of any service?'

The council prevaricated, deciding to see if hostilities did indeed break out between Britain and France in Europe. On 19 September two ships from England brought no news of war. Meanwhile the rainy season in Bengal was coming to an end, and as the floodwaters in that sodden delta subsided, a land campaign would be possible there.

Pigot decided that they could wait no longer: an expedition would have to be sent of sufficient size as to ensure their chances of success. If war should break out between Britain and France, the expedition would be recalled. This meant that the expedition would have to be ultimately responsible not to the disgraced council in Calcutta, but to the council in Madras, which in practice meant the commanders of the expedition on the ground – a decision not entirely unwelcome to Pigot and his colleagues.

It was without precedent to set the military over the civil authority in this way. Manningham, who arrived on 29 September, was indignant. The next row concerned the command of the expedition. Stringer Lawrence was the obvious choice; but he was now beginning to show his age and was asthmatic – a fatal combination in the damp climate of the lower Ganges.

Pigot himself possessed the necessary authority, but lacked the military experience and wisely declined. The third obvious choice was Colonel John Adlercron, commander of the king's regiment of several hundred troops in Madras assigned to help with the Deccan expedition. Small and pompous, Adlercron insisted that the king's troops, which looked upon Company troops as little more than half-caste rabble, would not accompany the expedition unless he was given command of land forces.

He expostulated: 'Surely, gentlemen, you are not so unreasonable as to expect that I will send away any part of His Majesty's train or regiment (who are so immediately under my direction) and to leave to you the nomination [of its commander].'

But he refused to guarantee the Company any share of the booty he might win, and even suggested that, once despatched, the troops might not return to Madras – thus possibly placing the town at the mercy of French attack. The council was horrified – and the prestigious plum of leading this massive expedition now fell to Robert Clive – 'the capablest person in India for an undertaking of this nature', as Orme described him.

Adlercron was beside himself with fury and insisted that his artillery be taken off the fleet. The Company had hastily to embark its own artillery for the expedition. Only at the last moment did the pompous colonel permit just three companies of his men to go aboard as 'marines' – thus placing them under the command of the King's admiral, Watson, not of the upstart Company man, Clive. The most impressive officer among them was Captain Eyre Coote. But it was a recipe for friction and conflict.

From the first, Clive understood the full significance of the hand destiny had once again dealt him. He wrote to his father in high excitement, 'This expedition, if attended with success, may enable me to do great things. It is by far the grandest of my undertakings. I go with great forces and great authority.'

To the East India Company he showed clear awareness of the long-term possibilities of the expedition: 'I flatter myself that this expedition will not end with the retaking of Calcutta only: and that the Company's estate in these parts will be settled in a better and more lasting condition than ever. There is less reason to apprehend a check from the Nabob's forces than from the nature of the climate and country. The news of a war [with France] may likewise interfere with the success of this expedition; however, should that happen, and hostilities be committed in India, I hope we shall be able to dispossess the French of

Chandernagore and leave Calcutta in a state of defence.'

Although it is possible to read from this letter that even at this early stage Clive had formulated a hidden agenda of imperial conquest in Bengal, he was only stating the obvious: that after the Nawab's attack on Calcutta restoration of the *status quo ante* was not an option. Any settlement with the Bengalis would have to ensure that no such attack could be repeated.

As for a plan to attack the French, this would be only in the event of war breaking out between Britain and France in Europe. The goals of the expedition were to change and grow as Clive and his forces were sucked inexorably up that river of ambition and delusion. Significantly, Clive was given the vaguest of remits – which suggested that the directors in London, at least, did not wish to limit his ambitions: he was to 'pursue such measures as you shall judge most conducive to the Company's benefit'.

On 16 October one of the mightiest expeditionary forces ever assembled in the eighteenth century set sail. The people of Madras turned out in their hundreds to wave goodbye to this formidable and magnificent spectacle. There were four major ships of the line – the *Kent*, Watt's flagship, with 64 guns; the *Cumberland*, under Admiral Pocock, with 70 guns; the *Tyger*, with 60 guns; and the *Salisbury*, with 50. In addition, there was a smaller ship, the *Bridgwater*, with 20 guns, and a fireship named, without imagination, the *Blaze*. They were escorting three company warships (also equipped with some guns), the *Protector*, *Walpole* and *Marlborough*, and three ketches. There were more than 500 British Company soldiers, 150 marines, 100 artillerymen, nearly 1,000 Indian troops and 160 support troops. Including the crews, over 2,500 sailed with six weeks' worth of provisions.

Pigot had tried to tie Clive's hands with the admonition that 'the sword shall go hand in hand with the pen'. He now sent Siraj-ud-Daula a threatening letter which also held out the hope of avoiding hostilities: 'The great commander of the King of England's ships has not slept in peace since this news and is come down with many ships, and I have sent a great *sardar* who will govern after me, by name Colonel Clive, with troops and land forces . . . You are wise: consider whether it is better to engage in a war that will never end or to do what is just and right in the sight of God.'

But Clive was not to be inhibited by Pigot, who would soon be several hundred miles away in Madras. He had been bewitched by Calcutta on his only visit there, as by the river leading away into a kingdom of vast wealth and extent. Siraj-ud-Daula had furnished him with the pretext for going after it.

As the prows of the ships steered proudly north-west, and the cheers from the quayside grew more distant, Clive, who had been so scarred by the humiliation of the British surrender at Fort St George years earlier, felt pride surge in his breast. He had been picked to command the restoration of British rule to another scene of national shame and humiliation. He knew that he was at another turning point in his life. Once again, fate had thrown him the dice and he must seize the initiative.

His exploits in the Carnatic, while remembered, had propelled him only to the status of a minor British hero: his personal ambitions in Britain had been frustrated and his fortune diminished. His immense abilities and energies were now in their prime, leavened by experience.

He understood that a defeat would never be acceptable to a restless tyrant like Siraj-ud-Daula. Nothing less than the removal of the Nawab from his throne would secure British rule in Calcutta again. But if the Nawab were to be removed, why should the British make terms with another oriental despot? They would be mad to relinquish any authority they acquired. A new law was to apply to Clive's gains in Bengal: the law of accelerating ambitions. To secure a gain it is always necessary to annex more land, and then secure that, and so on.

Clive felt he had been placed in a position of unprecedented authority for a British commander (although he was to under-estimate the resistance to him from his peers). The bulk of the forces – the Company troops and the sepoys – were under his sole command. The council in Madras, much less the directors in England, were too far away to restrain him. The council in Calcutta was discredited. He had the power to enforce his own settlement on Bengal; he had been given, in effect, the authority and discretion of a dictator.

In the Carnatic he had always been subordinate not just to the military commander, Lawrence, but to the civilian power as well. Now he possessed both. His hour of destiny had arrived. The once obscure, diffident clerk was in charge of the greatest British force that had ever sailed the seas off India.

His one pang of regret was leaving the pregnant Margaret in Madras. Her brother, Mun, sailed with him as a captain of Company troops, and her cousin Walsh as paymaster of the forces – Clive's lucrative old job – with Clive's own cousin George in a junior post. Those twelve ships headed by the seven magnificent warships steering into the wind made the greatest spectacle Fort St George had seen in years.

It was not to last: few expeditions can have got off to a less auspicious start. As though all the Hindu gods had decided to try and block its passage to Bengal, the post-monsoon winds were ferocious, the seas extremely rough. Those elegant eighteenth-century craft, with their three masts, billowing sails, defiant prows, buoyant, stately, tub-like hulls and erect, duck's-bottom sterns were buffeted and dispersed all the way down to Ceylon in the first fortnight of sailing, the wretched soldiers on board, who had departed in such high spirits, cramped, battered and sickly in the tumultuous seas.

As the winds veered round, the fleet made its way slowly back up towards the Bay of Bengal, only to be blown again by typhoon-like winds across to the other side, the coast of Tenasserim (Burma). It was remarkable, indeed, that none were lost; the near-helplessness of the vessels before the storm must have given Clive and his men pause for thought.

But those sturdy ships fought their way back again across the heavy seas, although two – Pocock's *Cumberland* and the *Marlborough*, further south than the others and encountering fierce winds, were forced to turn back to Madras. This reduced Clive's force by more than a third; he lost 243 infantry and 430 sepoys; the *Cumberland*'s 70 guns were also sorely to be missed. A third ship, the *Salisbury*, sprang a leak early in November and threatened to go under, but carpenters worked night and day to repair the damage, and the ship managed to limp along with the rest of them.

The delay caused by atrocious weather forced the ships to cut down to half rations, and supplies of rice ran out, so that the sepoys had to be persuaded to feed off beef and pork. 'Some did submit to this defilement, yet many preferred a languishing death by famine to life polluted beyond recovery.' Water was rationed, and scurvy broke out.

After this dreadful voyage, and in a much sorrier state than when they had set out, on 5 December the ships at last reached the mouth of the Hugli, with the troop carrier the *Protector* proudly in the vanguard. The fleet was now approaching hostile territory, controlled by Siraj-ud-Daula. There were no local pilots available, and the waters at the mouth of the river were boiling with currents and impregnated with reefs and shifting mudflats.

Only on 8 December did a high tide arrive to buoy them, permitting them to start the long journey upriver. For Clive, striding impatiently up and down his ship, despairing for land and for action, deeply frustrated by the ferocious sea passage, the spectacle of the endless rainforest that lined the banks of that huge waterway seemed an enormous relief, but also a challenge beyond anything yet undertaken, luring him into the very heart of northern India.

He at least sensed that an empire was at his feet. He would be enticed slowly up into the silent jungle, he was being offered the chance of true greatness. The recapture of Calcutta was but the first step. He would have to go on and on, ever greater ambitions and dangers unravelling before him, as well as temptation beyond most people's endurance.

It is hard to accept, as some biographers have, that he blundered slowly upriver and won an empire by accident. All the evidence suggests he was quite conscious of the opportunities when others about him were not, and he was determined to make the most of them. He was both hugely ambitious and clear-sighted about his goals: those two qualities were to transform him into an emperor.

As the mudflats and green foliage slipped past on that dismal and eternal river, the question was whether, like many of his fellow countrymen, he would become suborned and destroyed by the riches of the civilisation he now sought to subdue and by power over the huge territories he now sought to control. He had the authority, he believed, to behave like a despot and fulfil his wildest dreams: the foundation of a British Indian empire no longer seemed impossible.

But could even a character as strong as Clive's resist the corruption of personality that absolute authority over a huge area of the world's surface would ultimately bring? Over the next few months, treachery, power and money were each to clasp him to their bosom; he was to be pursued to the end of his life by the accusation that they had blackened the very depths of his soul. The truth, as we shall see, was somewhat different.

Those with him were occupied with more prosaic matters than dreaming of empire: that of restoring the morale of the seasick, hungry, discontented men aboard, to whom the even waters of the Hugli were a massive relief after the buffeting at sea. When they reached the settlement at Fulta, which was no more than a scruffy makeshift village on a malarial swamp, they found the remnants of the British colony at Calcutta in a wretched, ragged state, but joyous in their welcome for the avenging force whose several large ships seemed hugely impressive to them.

Drake pompously received Clive and Watson, announcing that a new 'select secret committee', consisting of himself, Holwell, Watts and a newcomer, Becker, had been set up to steer the affairs of the British in Bengal. Clive and Watson merely ignored them. With food now at last plentifully available, after three weeks' resupply, the fleet was at last ready to move on.

Clive sent a letter to the Nawab's governor of Calcutta, Manik Chand, couched in courteous terms, and then asked him to pass on a veiled ultimatum to Siraj-ud-Daula. The British force, said Clive, 'was one never before seen in your province'. Manik Chand insisted that the letter be addressed to his master as 'sacred and godlike prince'. Clive brushed the request contemptuously aside. 'I cannot consistently with my duty to the Company or their honour, accept of your advice in writing to the Nabob a letter couched in such a style, which, however proper it might have been before the taking of Calcutta, would but ill suit with the present time, when we are come to demand satisfaction for the injuries done us by the Nabob, not entreat his favour and with a force which we think sufficient to vindicate our claims.'

Without waiting for an answer, the fleet made its first strike upriver on 29 December. Clive and a force of 500 and two cannon were landed to lead an attack on the fort at Budge Budge. Clive had wanted to go by ship, but was prevailed upon by Watson to land downriver. Manik Chand, warned of the enemy's approach, sensibly evacuated and camped outside.

Unaware of this, Clive spurred his forces across appalling terrain on one of his characteristic night marches. 'In order to prevent discovery', the guides 'led the troops at a distance from the river, through a part of the country which was uninhabited indeed, but full of swamps and continually intersected by deep rivulets, which rendered the draught and transportation of the [gun] carriages so tedious and laborious that the troops did not arrive until an hour after sunrise at the place of ambuscade'.

On arrival, Clive sent half of his men forward in thick bush country towards the fort – which he could not see – believing Manik Chand to be still there, and remained with a force of some 250. He was exhausted and, unusually for him when in the field, in low spirits. Suddenly, a force of around 3,000 cavalry from Manik Chand's camp launched a surprise attack. The British were very nearly overwhelmed but, instead of fleeing, stood firm against the swords and pikes slashing at them, and launched flanking attacks. After Manik Chand's turban was grazed by a shot, the Indian force retreated with the loss of around 150 men.

Meanwhile, the ships had arrived opposite the fort, where they came under fire. Hearing that Clive was under attack, a company of marines was landed to help him. Clive himself, still exhausted, now made for the river bank and embarked for Watson's flagship.

There he met with the seasoned, commonsense, if occasionally prickly admiral and Captain Eyre Coote, the king's officer, commander of the marines, who despised Clive as a 'Company' soldier – in his eyes not an officer at all. The spectacle of Clive worn out after his first engagement, leaving his men behind, made Coote more contemptuous still.

The two commanders of the expedition, Clive and Watson, decided to postpone the attack on the fort until the following morning. Coote, who was to have led it, was furious. Good-looking, haughty, arrogant, hot-tempered, quarrelsome, vain, lacking Clive's intelligence and coolness, Coote was nevertheless a brave soldier and an able commander.

He lived under a shadow. He had been court-martialled for cowardice at the Battle of Falkirk, acquitted though cashiered, then pardoned, probably through the intervention of the Duke of

Cumberland. He was deeply anxious to regain his reputation and self-respect.

To Coote, as was the case to a lesser extent with Watson, Clive's reputation in the Carnatic meant little. Neither had seen any evidence of this self-assured visionary's military prowess; and this first example was hardly inspiring. Coote fumed on board ship, his chance for glory postponed, late that afternoon. Worse was to follow. He recorded:

> One Strahan, a common sailor belonging to the *Kent*, having just been served with a quantity of grog (arrack mixed with water) had his spirits too much elated to think of taking any rest; he therefore strayed by himself towards the fort, and imperceptibly got under the walls; being advanced thus far without interruption, he took it into his head to scale it at a breach that had been made by the cannon of the ships; and having luckily gotten upon the bastion, he there discovered several Moor-men sitting on the platform, at whom he flourished his cutlass, and fired his pistol, and then, after having given three loud huzzas, cried out, 'the place is mine'.

Others rushed to join him, and only four were wounded altogether in the seizure of the virtually abandoned fort. 'Thus the place was taken without the least honour to anyone!' The unfortunate Strahan was summoned before Watson for indiscipline and threatened with punishment. He was said to have muttered the immortal lines, immediately after his dressing down for what was largely a case of wounded vanity on the part of his superiors, 'If I am flogged for this here action, I will never take another fort by myself for as long as I live, by God.'

The first engagement was thus a colossal anti-climax. Budge Budge had been seized without a fight. Manik Chand had sensibly chosen to make his stand elsewhere. Clive's own first engagement had been only narrowly won against a well-prepared Indian ambush. A day later the fort was demolished.

By now it was beginning to become apparent in the oppressive heat of the lower Ganges basin that the main enemies of the British – as indeed was the case with the Bengalis – were not their opponents but their own internal hatreds, jealousies and rivalries. Clive had been nearly seven weeks cooped up on board the rolling flagship at close quarters with Admiral Watson. Impatient, overbearing, fuming, at the length of the journey, casting aspersions on the navy's navigational ability to make it to the Hugli river at all, Clive made an impossible guest particularly as, when at sea, he was subject to Watson's authority.

Moreover, Colonel Adlercron, by having his soldiers designated 'marines', had placed them under Watson's authority, thus sidestepping the 'upstart Indian' Clive. Watson, while a more eventempered man than Clive, himself resented the dual command and, as a king's officer, looked down on the amateur soldier. By the time they had reached the mouth of the Hugli, tempers were already at boiling point.

These internal jealousies were further exacerbated by the loathing of the ludicrous Drake and his council for Clive, whom they saw as the creature of the Governor of Madras, unanswerable to them, and usurping their authority. When the clammy heat of the jungle and the invisibility of their opponents was added to the brew, the mixture was explosive; a madness had taken hold of the British, and in particular of these three men.

Clive had hoped that a spectacular action at Budge Budge – the seizure of the fort after one of his daring night marches – would assert his authority. Both the other two men were themselves intent on seeking credit for the victory. In the event it had proved a risible fiasco.

The following day – New Year's Day – the fleet reached Thana, while the sepoys marched by land. The town had been hastily abandoned by the Bengalis, who left some forty guns – most of them seized from Calcutta. Once again the enemy, unseen, was melting before them, leaving them uncertain when it would turn to make a stand, or of the size and disposition of its forces. The territory was hostile, reports from spies few and probably misleading. The British ships crept slowly forward through the overcast gloom. That same night, advance boats from the fleet discovered several vessels laden with wood to be used as fireships, and burned them.

The progress so far had been unsettling and eerie. With the exception of Clive's first accidental firefight, the enemy was moving before them beyond the trees and bushes, unseen. They could be all around them or, more probably, some way off, luring them into a trap, or genuinely retreating. Calcutta itself was now just upriver. As the elegant ships glided through the slow-moving waters, the silence was nerve-racking.

At 5 a.m. on the morning of 22 January, Clive and his Company troops landed to liaise with the sepoys, still moving by land. Watson moved upstream with his two main ships, the 64-gun *Kent* and the 60-gun *Tyger*. Now random shooting at last started from the shore; but soon the ships spotted the great green-damp walls of Fort William and the skyline of half-burnt buildings. Cannon opened up on them from within; but the spectacle of the immense ships and their firepower soon caused the Bengali artillerymen to panic.

As the ships came opposite Fort William, volleys of cannon exploded at them from the fort – dangerously, as the ships were now caught in a swirl of tidal eddies and swung around helplessly until anchored. Then they responded with a few massive broadsides that quickly put the shore gunners to flight, along with the rest of the small garrison left by Manik Chand, which escaped through the Eastern Gate. There had only been nine deaths on board the ships. Once again, the Indian commander had preferred to withdraw – out of fear, or in preparation for an ambush later?

Coote, along with a naval officer, was put ashore to take Fort William: the spectacle he encountered there was dismal indeed. The magnificent factory that had towered over the battlements had been gutted. Anything wooden had been torn down and used for firewood. Window fronts, doors and furniture were all ripped apart. Many of the houses within the fort had been burnt. Outside, the once magnificent merchants' houses had been burnt down and the 'black town' was a wreck, plundered from end to end. The place was deserted, desolate, and stank of destruction and decay.

Farce now intruded into this pitiable scene. Coote, so infuriated by being denied the 'honour' of taking Budge Budge, was delighted in his historic – if not particularly hard-fought (in his case not fought at all) – prize of Calcutta, all the more so when Clive's troops approached through the desolate remnants of the 'black town' and the ruins of one of the walls of the fort, destroyed to make way for the mosque that Siraj-ud-Daula decreed should be built there.

Coote took pleasure in having the commander of Clive's sepoys arrested and pushing out his soldiers. He said he had received instructions from Watson to let no one into the fort. When the matter was reported back to Clive, he was incensed. 'This I own enraged me to such degree that I was resolved to enter if possible, which I did.'

He walked forward in front of his troops, confronting Coote and declaring that the latter would be put under arrest unless he handed over control of the fort to Clive himself. While Coote had been absurdly heavy-handed in denying Clive's men entry – and it is possible to detect the hand of Watson behind him – it was true that the honour of possessing Calcutta really belonged to the navy, which had done what little fighting was necessary. Clive's land forces had played no part.

Coote stalled for time, signalling Admiral Watson what was happening. Now it was Watson's turn to behave as though the fever had reached him. The admiral threatened that if Clive's men did not leave the fort immediately, 'he shall be fired out', as the captain of Watson's flagship, Henry Speke, put it. 'If you still persist in continuing in the fort, you will force me to such measures as will be disagreeable to me, as they possibly can be to you.'

Clive stood firm. He 'could not answer for the consequences but he would not give up his command'. It looked as though the first real battle of the Bengal campaign was about to be fought – between Clive's Company troops and the British navy, backed by the King's soldiers in this burnt-out shell of a once elegant eighteenth-century town on a tropical waterway, between three angry Englishmen bitterly quarrelling their way upriver watched by an unseen, stealthy, always retreating enemy.

An intermediary was despatched by Watson in the shape of Thomas Latham who, although a naval captain, was a friend of Clive's and married to Margaret's cousin, Jenny. An agreement was reached by which Clive was to take over the fort, being the senior officer on land, and hand over the keys to Admiral Watson next day, in recognition of the fact that the navy had actually taken over the garrison. In turn Watson would hand them over to the civil authority – the strutting, self-important and cowardly Drake and his council. Thus was Clive's face saved: he was the commander of the land forces, and recognised as such; but the honour of victory – such as it was – went to Admiral Watson.

This astonishing episode was no more than one example of how the madness of the jungle could affect three men in a boat, each possessed with a mighty ego. It represented the beginning of a conflict that was to be etched deep into the history of the British in India. The contempt of the King's men – both army and navy – for the Indian regiments and their sepoys was to run like a constant thread throughout the Raj. So was the tension between the civil and military authority, represented by the council at Calcutta and Clive and Watson.

Yet the potential conflict between motherland and colonists that was to erupt so explosively in America 20 years later was never allowed to reach a similar breaking point through much abler British policy in India. Also present was the jealousy between Madras and Calcutta (and to a lesser extent Bombay) that was eventually to result in the creation of a single authority – Governor-General of India, a position Clive was effectively to fashion, in large part, for himself. Finally, there was also the perennial inter-service rivalry between army and navy. Every subsequent snobbery and struggle for hierarchy in British India was present, in microcosm, on that first expedition up the Hugli.

The near-firefight between Clive, Watson and Coote also said much about Clive's state of mind. He had been given full authority over the expedition, particularly now that it had reached land. Yet the admiral, with his massive firepower along the river, was still trying to retain control.

So far the expedition had proved a complete fiasco: all three forts had been taken virtually unopposed. In the one serious engagement, Clive's forces had been taken by surprise and only narrowly survived an attack by a relatively small enemy force. Clive's tactics of a night attack by stealth had been held up to ridicule by the abandonment of the enemy fort.

The hero of the Carnatic, so given to boisterousness and loud behaviour, so self-confident in Madras, so boastful of his exploits, the dreamer of an Indian empire, had done nothing to impress Watson – who reasoned that he had taken both Gheria and Calcutta through the navy's efforts – or Coote. Apart from Gheria, Clive had not seen active service for nearly four and a half years; he was now 31. He must have wondered if his magic touch was failing, if his youthful successes had been merely a sudden flash of early exuberance.

Both Watson and Coote relished the humbling of a man of great reputation. There was no evidence on this expedition to justify his swollen-headedness. Clive's own prickliness reflected his concern that his reputation was diminishing by the moment to that of a braggart who had been put to the test and was failing. Arcot and Trichinopoly meant nothing to Watson and Coote, who had seen only the dismal evidence of Budge Budge and Calcutta.

But both Watson's and Coote's behaviour did them even less credit than Clive's. Coote was an arrogant, impetuous young man with a chip on his shoulder, later to show himself a fine soldier, but of no major intellect. Watson, certainly an able seaman, showed no great depth either.

After the occupation of Calcutta, it gradually became apparent that the appalling Drake had suborned Watson at Fulta, playing on his pretensions and resentments against Clive after the long sea voyage. The former governor and his council had both insisted that Watson ensure that authority in Calcutta was handed to them, rather than to Clive with his mandate from distant Madras. Despite Clive's stand – justified by Coote's effrontery – this in fact happened.

The men who had deserted Calcutta so shamefully thus regained their wrecked capital. Clive recognised this: he commented bitterly in a letter to Pigot at Madras that he had been the victim of a 'dirty underhand contrivance'. In respect of Drake and his council, 'I would have you guard against everything these gentlemen can say, for believe me they are bad subjects and rotten at heart and will stick at nothing to prejudice you. The riches of Peru and Mexico would not induce me to dwell among them.'

He was deeply depressed by Fort William. 'It is not possible to describe the distresses of the inhabitants of this once opulent and populous town. The private losses amount to upward of two million sterling,' he wrote to his father. To Pigot he confessed, 'Between friends, I cannot help regretting that ever I undertook this mission.' The dreamer of empire was back on earth, amid the petty jealousies and intrigues of lesser men.

Once in occupation of Fort William, Clive could hardly wait to get out and away from Drake and his crew. The next target was Hugli, which Clive said should 'fall a sacrifice' for the invasion of Calcutta. Thus the first fateful step was taken: the restoration of Calcutta was not enough for the British commander: his further designs were coming into view. He could defend himself on the grounds that Calcutta was indefensible unless the British occupied Hugli, but with Bengali territory outside Calcutta now being attacked for the first time, it was impossible for Siraj-ud-Daula not to respond without losing face. His conquests were being reversed. Now his nose was being tweaked.

This time, both Watson and Clive were keen to move on to the offensive. On 4 July Kilpatrick, Clive's second-in-command, was sent upstream at the head of a substantial force of more than 500 men on three ships, one of which promptly ran aground but was floated again after a Dutch pilot was press-ganged in to help. The river was deeply treacherous, constantly changing course. When the tide was ebbing it was hard to fight the current. More dangerous still was the tidal bore, a huge wave, when it thundered upstream. A few days later troops were landed at Hugli, while the familiar boom of cannon rolled out again from the ships opposite the town. Manik Chand, with a force of around 2,000, was based there. As the bombardment got under way, he withdrew yet again.

Clive's troops set about looting the town – presumably in retaliation for the rape of Calcutta. Eyre Coote, with a small party, was then despatched to burn down the Nawab's granaries upriver. Hugli itself was burnt down. The British were taunting the Nawab to attack; they could hardly have been more provocative. At last, news came that he had assembled a huge army north of Hugli.

Clive, meanwhile, had not been slow in improving the defences of Fort William. 'Fort William can never be taken by the Moors except by cowardice,' he remarked, in a stinging rebuke to what had happened under Drake. However, there was no cause for complacency: bad news had just reached Clive. War had broken out between Britain and France at last, and he had to reckon with the possibility that the French would attach their 300-strong European garrison at Chandernagore to the Nawab's forces.

Chapter 14

The Battle of Calcutta

A real battle was now approaching. With furious energy, Clive formed 300 or so irregulars into the First Regiment of Bengal Native Infantry. He also set about the more difficult task of persuading Watson to lend his own forces to the defence of Calcutta. He complained bitterly that as for the King's soldiers, 'it had been better for the service they had never come and I had the like number of Company's in their room'.

He begged Watson for assistance in terms the latter found impossible to refuse, as he said when later justifying himself to his superiors. 'You are very sensible sir, that with sickness and other accidents how far this force falls short of what was intended to act offensively against the Nabob of Bengal; indeed at present nothing but our strong situation can enable us to act against him at all. I must therefore request a favour of you, Sir, to land the King's forces and to lay your commands on the officer [Coote] who commands them to put himself under my orders; assuring you at the same time that whenever you think it good for the service to recall them, upon signification thereof to me by letter, they shall be returned.'

Watson had no choice but to agree. Drake and the select committee pompously announced to Clive that he would have to carry out their orders – to which he replied that he would if they happened to coincide with his. Drake said he should attack forthwith and defeat the Nawab. Clive ignored them. He now proceeded to set out his terms for an agreement with the Nawab, clearly designed to be unacceptable: reparations, the restoration of the British to their privileges, permission for the settlement to be fully fortified and for a mint to be set up at Calcutta – the last two openly insulting in that they had been refused by the Bengalis before the seizure of Calcutta.

Clive seems to have been anxious to provoke the Nawab to strike before the French could come to his aid. The Nawab, in return, sent flowers and fruit to Calcutta, while his army moved closer. Clive responded to this deceit by sending him an embassy consisting of his old confidant Walsh and Luke Scrafton. Whether either believed he was fooling the other was not clear.

It was evident that the Nawab was preparing to attack and Clive to defend; indeed, it was clear that Clive favoured a Bengali attack on Calcutta as being on his chosen ground, rather than that of the Nawab. Clive positioned his troops at Bernagul, north-east of Calcutta, enclosed by the river to the south, the Maratha Ditch to the west, and salt lakes to the north.

The Bengali army moved steadily closer. Clive anxiously waited for reinforcements from the Carnatic or Bombay to enable him 'to finish everything by a decisive strike'. Reports were reaching him of the huge size of the Nawab's army, which helps to explain why the usually quarrelsome Watson and Coote were being so quiet and accommodating, ready at last to put their trust in a single commander, Clive, who knew India well and was reacting to the crisis with vigour and coolness.

The Nawab, meanwhile, was bent on securing French support. He wrote to Pierre Renault, Governor of Chandernagore, that he would 'abolish for ever the annual imposts on your commerce and give you the right to establish a mint at Chandernagore. I will demand a *firman* for this from the Light of the Presence, the greatest and purest, the Emperor of Delhi, and will send it to you. Until the arrival of the *firman* I will you a *parwana*, with my seal, so that you may exercise these two privileges with perfect tranquillity of mind.'

But the French were still resentful at the Nawab's exaction of a ransom after the fall of Calcutta, and rightly distrusted him. If he defeated the British, they believed he would then pick them off; if, on the other hand, the British won, they would instantly turn their fire on the French. In the circumstances they tried to use the threat of intervention on the Nawab's side to obtain a neutrality agreement from the British. They refused to help either side – which must have come as an immense relief to Clive, as well-trained European troops supporting the Nawab's immense army might decisively have tipped the scales against him.

On the morning of 3 February the advance guard of the Nawab's army reached Calcutta, and Clive despatched first a small force, then a large one, to meet them. The two sides exchanged cannonades for about an hour before the Nawab's outriders returned to camp at nightfall.

The British commander had already witnessed the arrival of the Nawab's army on the flat land to the north of the city; and a fearsome sight it made. There were around 22,000 infantry and camp followers, 18,000 cavalry, 50 elephants and 40 guns, besides camels and oxen. Some reports put the enemy strength around 100,000, although half of these at least were servants and prostitutes. Clive had seen nothing like it since the spectacle of Chanda Sahib's huge army at Trichinopoly years before.

He has been criticised for failing to attack the Bengalis on their arrival. But his caution was justified by the sheer size of the force; he watched as it made camp north of the Maratha Ditch. Absurdly, the Nawab informed Clive that he had marched upon Calcutta merely to find a better camping ground.

Clive's two emissaries meanwhile found that the Nawab had departed his camp, and hurried back to catch up with him. On 4 February, at seven in the morning, they reached Siraj-ud-Daula at his headquarters: he had crossed the Ditch and taken up residence once again in Omichand's country house.

The Nawab was surrounded by an impressive phalanx of well-armed senior officers. Walsh and Scrafton were not allowed to address him, because he believed 'they had private arms about them and waited to assassinate him', but his ministers refused the English request to withdraw the Bengali army. Walsh and Scrafton were then advised to see the Seths' agent as 'he had something to communicate to them that would be very agreeable to their colonel'.

The two Englishmen, suspecting this was a trick and that they would be arrested, turned in for the night, pleading exhaustion, and slipped away across the lines to tell of their encounter. Clive immediately decided to launch a daring attack straight at the Nawab himself in his refuge in Omichand's garden. 'I went immediately on board Admiral Watson's ship and represented to him the necessity for attacking the Nawab without delay; and desired the assistance of four or five hundred sailors, to carry the ammunition and draw the artillery; which he assented to. The sailors were landed about one o'clock in the morning. About two, the troops were under arms, and by four, they marched to the attack of the Nawab's camp.'

It was Arcot all over again: a surprise attack in the early hours of the morning at the very heart of the enemy, ignoring the massive odds against him, with just 470 soldiers, 600 sailors, 800 sepoys and 70 artillerymen equipped with a howitzer and six guns. It nearly went disastrously wrong, and was to require all Clive's skill at last-minute improvisation to save the day.

The fog of the early morning provided cover for Clive's men, as his force crossed the road to Dum Dum, intending to bypass the Nawab's main camp to the south and reach another road, the Causeway, which crossed the Maratha Ditch; just beyond was Omichand's house, the Nawab's headquarters. However, the guides got lost in the mist and led Clive's force straight into the heart of the enemy camp.

Suddenly aware of the vast concourse of people about them, they loosed off shots in all directions, causing panic. The enemy were able to assemble a force of some 300 cavalry, which charged. The British stood their ground, and fired volley after volley until the attacks ceased.

They then blundered on by this roundabout route to the road leading to the Causeway; but the Nawab's forces, alerted to the danger to their leader, had assembled there and put up such resistance that a crossing of the Ditch proved impossible. Clive's men were now in a desperate state: with the huge enemy army behind them, they had also been cut off from returning over the Ditch to the garrison. His only hope was to press on and reach the next crossing, across some paddy fields.

As his men frantically pushed their guns across the boggy terrain, the fog suddenly lifted, exposing the British force to the Nawab's formidable cavalry and artillery. The guns opened up, while hordes of horsemen swirled past them. Clive's men, deprived of any cover, abandoned two of the cannon and, with great difficulty, made it to the next road, beside the picturesquely named Bread and Cheese Bungalow.

However, this crossing too was solidly defended. The British position was now critical: with their escape cut off, the Nawab would have time to bring up reinforcements and pick them off at will. At last a single cannon brought up by Ensign Yorke blasted away with such ferocity at the enemy position defending the crossing that they were forced out, and Clive and his men escaped across.

He was now presented with a choice: to go back along the south side of the Ditch to attack the Nawab's headquarters would have been fraught with risk. Omichand's house had been heavily rein-forced as soon as the Nawab had become aware of the danger to his personal safety, and there was a huge force of Bengalis now concentrated along the north side of the Ditch. With his tail between his legs, Clive decided to abandon his goal and retire to Fort William; his daring raid had utterly failed, and he had been extremely lucky to extricate his small army from being surrounded and annihilated.

It had been, said Clive later, 'the warmest service I ever yet was engaged in'. Clive's aide-de-camp had been killed by his side in yet another of the near-misses that dogged the young man's career. Some 40 of his British troops had been killed, along with 18 sepoys, and 137 wounded – a heavy toll for a small force. Clive's strategic objective had been frustrated and he had been compelled to retreat. This was one exploit that had turned out to be too bold, and only through bravery and quick thinking had he been rescued from humiliating disaster.

Yet, to Clive's astonishment, the Nawab did not see what had happened as a victory at all. In the course of the blundering British rampage across his main camp, some 1,300 of his men had been killed or wounded and 500 horses and elephants lost. Once again, the sheer suicidal boldness of Clive's attack into the heart of the enemy camp (which had been accidental) had inspired, if not terror, at least serious concern about the capabilities of the British under their fearsome commander.

To British surprise, the Nawab's army now began to retreat several miles north of Calcutta, out of the range of Clive's forces, amid indignant reproaches that the British had acted treacherously in attacking an army that had arrived at the outskirts of Calcutta merely to find a suitable camping ground.

The Nawab's emissary, Ranjit Rai, wrote indignantly, 'I thought that the English were always faithful to their words. The Nawab agrees to give you back Calcutta with all the privileges of your *firman* and whatever goods you lost at Kasimbazar or elsewhere, and will grant you permission to coin currency in your mint at Calcutta . . . and that you may make whatever fortifications you please at Calcutta. Your conduct yesterday morning greatly amazed me and put me to shame before the Nawab . . . If you think war necessary acquaint me seriously with your intentions, and I will acquit myself of any further trouble in this affair.'

The British could hardly believe their luck: in blundering into the camp they had inspired just as much fear among the enemy as if they had succeeded in their original objective – kidnapping the Nawab. Clive, never one to show diffidence, or fail to take advantage of a reversal of fortunes, wrote a blistering ultimatum in return. 'I am surprised that the Nabob and you trifle. I observe that you are not inclinable to agree to our proposals. God is my witness that my actions have been open and generous, and that my inclinations have been peaceful. I now send you the articles wrote fair. Let the Nabob sign "agreed" to each separate article in the manner that I have upon the copy. If this is done, there shall be peace. If not, do not concern yourself further in this affair. War must take its course.'

Watson urged Clive to attack the Nawab's army again, while it was off balance. But Clive feared it would turn to the French for support, and believed he could obtain the terms he needed – which were in fact the sum of British demands before the sack of Calcutta, and thus wholly humiliating to Siraj-ud-Daula.

At around this time, the Nawab learnt that the Afghan commander, Ahmad Shah Abdali, was moving across northern India towards Bengal; this thoroughly alarmed him, and after accepting the British proposals with some haggling and ill grace, he withdrew his army to defend his capital of Murshidabad.

After his extraordinary stroke of luck in seeing the attackers off from Calcutta, Clive's position as the main commander of the expedition was reinforced – although Watson still pressed his claims. A touch of the legendary guerrilla leader of the south had been glimpsed, and his efforts had been unexpectedly crowned by success. The squabbling on the journey upriver began to fade into the past.

Characteristically, as he secured victory, he fell into a mood of despondency, wondering whether he should now return south to

Madras to take a 'slap at Bussy'. He soon recovered, and was writing to his father of his ambition to create and hold a new post, Governor-General of India, 'if such an appointment should be necessary'. This was an astounding ambition, an aspiration towards absolute power over the three quarrelsome governors and their councils in Madras, Bombay and Calcutta.

His more immediate objective was a further turn of the screw in securing British predominance in India: to seize the settlement of Chandernagore from the French. Once again, this was a defensible objective. The French and the British were at war in Europe and had been so, on and off, for the best part of a decade in India. To dispossess their European rivals was an entirely understandable aim, and not an act of colonialism as such.

Clive had come to believe that the French had conspired with the Nawab in the attack on Calcutta. He was possessed of a considerable armed force on the Hugli river; the opportunity might not recur. Also, while the settlement remained, there was always the danger that the French would conspire with the Nawab in another attack on the British. It seemed too good a chance to miss. The expedition, prevented by low waters from proceeding upstream, was now buoyed up by the spring tides and resolved to move on to its final objective, ever deeper into northern India.

The French at Chandernagore were commanded by Pierre Renault, an able if unambitious commander, heavily advised by Jean Law, the factory chief at Kasimbazar, who by coincidence was the elder and more intelligent brother of Clive's defeated foe at Trichinopoly. Although irritated by the predatory excesses of Siraj-ud-Daula, the French had been anxious to appease him, and had sent emissaries to Calcutta on 4 January – only to discover that the British had retaken the city.

Watson promptly offered them an alliance against the Nawab – which they refused. Their inclination was to join the Nawab against the British. Law argued that 'we should not hesitate to ally ourselves with the Nawab, whose friendship may procure us great advantages in the augmentation of our privileges and several other matters, not to mention the special enemy of our nation in obliging her to retire perhaps with loss and to abandon an enterprise for the accomplishment of which she has stripped her principal establishments in India'.

However, both he and Renault were overruled from Pondicherry. As the Nawab's huge army drew close on its way from Calcutta to Murshidabad, the French became alarmed lest he should attack them. Instead Siraj-ud-Daula offered them presents and an alliance. Renault agreed to oppose the passage of the English past Chandernagore if their ships moved further upstream.

This gave the British the pretext they needed to attack their European rivals. Siraj-ud-Daula now slyly tried to give the impression that he was on neither side – merely opposed to the principle of aggression by one European settlement against another. As the French themselves posed no threat to the British except through their alliance with the Nawab, this seemed a specious argument, and made no impression on Clive and Watson.

Clive's next moves were to be crucial in establishing British dominance over north-east India – and were to return to haunt him in later life.

The two men principally involved were William Watts, the straightforward, highly intelligent and likeable former factory manager at Kasimbazar outside Murshidabad, who more than any other Englishman knew the inner workings of the Nawab's court and was an early example of an English spy; and Omichand, who had performed exactly the reverse role for the Nawab in Calcutta.

Omichand, probably the richest merchant in Calcutta because of initial British patronage, had, after slights and then outright snubs, turned into an *agent provocateur* and Trojan horse for the Nawab's occupation of the city – if he was not its actual instigator. Each time the Nawab had advanced on Calcutta, he had stayed at one of Omichand's properties, where he was assured a warm welcome.

Omichand had bitterly resented his imprisonment by the British before the fall of Calcutta, justified though this was. His fortune derived from his value as a go-between for the British and the Bengali government, and neither could be sure of his loyalty. He had taken the Nawab's side against the British latterly and almost certainly abetted the Nawab in his failed attempt to occupy Calcutta a second time. But after what was seen on the Bengali side as a convincing display of British strength in the battle of the Maratha Ditch, he now offered his services to both sides as a mediator.

The Nawab regarded him – with good reason – as his conduit to the British; but it is clear that Omichand at this stage decided to offer his services to the British partly because he viewed them as the likely winners, in order to re-establish his old trading privileges. The Hindu merchant soon showed his usefulness by bribing the deputy governor of the Nawab's garrison at Hugli, an even wilier brahmin, Nundcomar – who was to exercise a similarly baleful effect upon Clive's successor, Warren Hastings, three decades later.

Nundcomar agreed not to support the French in exchange for 12,000 rupees. He revealed that there was a secret alliance between them and the Nawab, who had no intention of sticking to the agreement signed with the British, but was merely waiting for his chance to attack again with superior forces. Watts argued that it was necessary to oppose 'corruption with corruption making friends out of the mammon of unrighteousness, and getting upon even ground with those whom we are obliged to contend'.

At this stage a fresh row broke out between Clive and Watson who, taking advantage of the hatred of the select committee for the commander on the ground, had secured the upper hand in policy-making. Watson argued that no attack could be made on the French without the approval of the Nawab. Clive, who knew of the secret agreement between the French and the Bengalis, said he had been put to 'great shame' by the Nawab's refusal to countenance an attack on the French and claimed he could have taken Chanderna-gore in two days.

Watson, writing to the Nawab, insisted that, 'had I imagined it would have given you umbrage, I should never have entertained the least thoughts of disturbing the tranquillity of your country, by acting against that nation within the Ganges; and am now ready to desist from attacking . . . if they will consent to a solid treaty of neutrality and if you . . . will under your hand guarantee to this treaty'. Clive reluctantly agreed to this letter.

As the admiral continued to prevaricate, Clive threatened to return to Madras; he was determined to spur the British further on in Bengal. Prophetically, he wrote, 'You can be assured the instant the French find these offers of neutrality refused, they will immediately assist the Nabob in all his designs against us.' Within a few days, ships had arrived from Bombay with some 400 reinforce-ments, and from Madras with 300. The British force was now formidable: some 800 European soldiers and 1,800 sepoys.

Even Watson now found fire in his belly, and threatened the Nawab that, if he should come to the aid of the French, 'I will kindle such a flame in your country as all the water in the Ganges shall not be able to extinguish' (the phrase is more redolent of the grandiose Clive than the prosaic Watson). At this the Nawab gave in, promising not to interfere in the event of a British attack on Chandernagore.

By this time, 12 March, Clive was only two miles from Chandernagore, and despatched a curt ultimatum to Renault: 'Sir – the King of Great Britain having declared war against France, I summons you in his name to surrender the fort of Chandernagore. In case of refusal you are to answer the consequences and expect to be treated according to the usage of war in such case. I have the honour to be, sir, your most obedient and humble servant, R Clive.'

For once Clive's force was superior: some 2,600 men were ranged against 600 European troops and 200 sepoys. In addition, though, Renault had the support of some 2,000 men from the Nawab's army. The fort of the settlement had a delightful baroque façade fronting the river. Many of the buildings immediately surrounding it had been burnt down in preparation for a siege. Within a few days of Clive's beginning a rather slow artillery attack, the native garrison had abandoned Renault under the orders of the suborned Nundcomar, who also falsely informed the Nawab that the town had fallen.

The Nawab, who had learned that the Afghans had decided not to press forward and attack Bengal after all, and had been preparing to send help to the French, hesitated. After first despatching a force of 5,000 troops to go to the aid of the French, he ordered them to stand down. Meanwhile the desultory siege went on: Clive was shy of attacking until the fleet could be moved upstream to bombard the fort.

Several ships had been sunk in the river by the French to block the passage of the British ships. A boom had also been erected across it, and three fireships prepared – which, however, a British shore party cut loose before they could be set alight; they drifted uselessly on to a sandbank. The British ships – the *Kent*, the *Tyger* and, later, the *Salisbury* – had to navigate their way with great difficulty past the sunken French ships, using sightings of their masts above the water at low tide to reckon their position. They came under intense French fire, which Clive's small force of artillery did its best to divert.

In the early hours of 23 March Clive's men, who were now occupying most of the town surrounding the fort, managed to seize the French battery below it, permitting the British ships to move upriver. This was the turning point: the three ships were in a position to open fire – but the *Kent* was dragged downriver by currents and blocked the passage of the *Salisbury*. Reduced to two, the *Kent* and *Tyger* opened fire in what was to be the most vicious cannonade of the Bengali war.

There was something surreal about the spectacle of two of the most important eighteenth-century ships of the line, with their towering masts, proud prows, curved hulls and stolid sterns blasting away in a ferocious battery of flame and smoke against the cannonade from the fort opposite. Each seemed too elegant to be indulging in such brutal demolition and carnage. All this was set against the peaceful slow-flowing backdrop of the Hugli river, not so wide as further down, and the lush tropical foliage on both banks. It was like a theatrical set piece, a game in a tranquil ornamental lake.

Yet there was nothing theatrical about the carnage inflicted. Inside the fort, as the British guns found their range, huge gaps in the walls soon showed, and bodies were slumped behind them as the brutal thundering of cannon striking home and explosions from the outgoing guns were punctuated by the screams of the dying and wounded. On the ships, the pounding from the French guns took a terrible toll.

On the *Kent*, only Admiral Watson and one other officer escaped unscathed; all the others were killed or injured. One shot narrowly missed the admiral, after he had rashly declared that the French 'shall have a fair shot' when the ship had been about to take evasive action. Captain Speke and his son, a 16-year-old midshipman, were hit by the same bullet: 'One shot took off Captain Speke's calf of his left leg, and struck off Billy Speke's thigh; as soon as one got up he saw the other and a shocking sight it was. Billy bore it very courageously, and the other was no more concerned for himself but said, "father and son at one time and with one shot is hard indeed".' Billy died of the injury. On the *Tyger* Admiral Pocock was wounded by splinters; thirteen of his men were killed and eighty wounded.

After three hours, with Clive waiting to attack from land, Renault had had enough. Lieutenant Brereton, the uninjured officer aboard the *Kent*, and Eyre Coote went to ask for terms: the French officers were granted parole, while the soldiers were taken prisoner. Clive's men took the fort. Watson was critical of Clive for taking so little part in the attack; and the British rank-and-file, especially those aboard the ships, fumed at the lenient terms offered the French after so vicious a fight. They went on a rampage through the town, sacking the church and the treasury. Clive promptly had three men hanged and withdrew his troops from the town.

Meanwhile, around 140 members of the captured garrison broke loose from the town, taking advantage of an explosion in the gunpowder arsenal. Two-thirds of these were either killed or captured outside, while 40 or so made their way to join Jean Law at Kasimbazar. In more orderly fashion, Renault and his senior officers on parole were allowed to take refuge in the Dutch settlement at Chinsurah – where, however, they immediately began to help the opposition to the British.

Clive's forces moved on to their houses and, with the Dutch wisely offering no protection, seized them, sending them off under escort to Calcutta. After three months they were allowed to return to Chandernagore. The French civilians were allowed to go as they pleased. Some fifty of the captured soldiers held in jail escaped, but most were later killed or captured. The British had meanwhile captured a large store of military and naval equipment, offsetting their losses from the Nawab's plundering at Calcutta.

The French influence had been decisively crushed in Bengal. Throughout India, there was now much greater fear of the English than of the French. Moreover, Calcutta was secured and the British controlled a large swathe of the Hugli river. The issue for the British was, once again, whether to be content with their gains or to embark further upstream into the Indian continent. For Clive at least, much as he protested that he expected to return to Madras at any time, the answer was clearcut.

Yet for the moment his rivals – Watson, Coote and the council –

had regained the initiative through a battle in which Clive's forces had made little of the running. Although by now fully confident that he had regained his old abilities as a commander on the swampy marshland of that diseased tropical riverside, he was still only one of a number of chiefs among the British forces.

CHAPTER 15

The Deceivers

Later public opinion in Britain was to rage about the morality of what now happened: full-scale British complicity in a conspiracy to rid a huge Indian kingdom of its ruler. Macaulay's judgement is typical. Clive,

in other parts of his life an honourable English gentleman and soldier, was no sooner matched against an Indian intriguer, than he himself became an Indian intriguer, and descended, without scruple, to falsehood, to hypocritical caresses, to the substitution of documents, and to the counterfeiting of hands . . .

We are convinced that Clive was altogether in the wrong, and that he committed, not merely a crime but a blunder. That honesty is the best policy is a maxim which we firmly believe to be generally correct, even with respect to the temporal interest of individuals; but, with respect to societies, the rule is subject to still fewer exceptions, and that for this reason, that the life of societies is longer than the life of individuals . . .

The entire history of the British in India is an illustration of the great truth, that it is not prudent to oppose perfidy to perfidy, and that the most efficient weapon with which men can encounter falsehood is truth. During a long course of years, the English rulers of India, surrounded by allies and enemies whom no engagement could bind, have generally acted with sincerity and uprightness; and the event has proved that sincerity and uprightness are wisdom. English valour and English intelligence have done less to extend and to preserve our Oriental empire than English veracity. All that we could have gained by imitating the doublings, the evasions, the fictions, the perjuries which have been employed against us, is as nothing, when compared with what we have gained by being the one power in India on whose word reliance can be placed.

No oath which superstition can devise, no hostage however precious, inspires a hundredth part of the confidence which is produced by the 'yea, yea', and 'nay, nay' of a British envoy. No fastness, however strong by art or nature, gives to its inmates a security like that enjoyed by the chief who, passing through the territories of powerful and deadly enemies, is armed with a British guarantee.

The mightiest princes of the East can scarcely, by the offer of enormous usury, draw forth any portion of the wealth which is concealed under the hearths of their subjects. The British government offers little more than four per cent; and avarice hastens to bring forth tens of millions of rupees from its most secret repositories . . . The greatest advantage which a government can possess is to be the one trustworthy government in the midst of governments which nobody can trust.

In fact, *pace* Macaulay, the deciding factor in the British ability to redeem its promises was British power. Without power – and this hung in the balance in Bengal – no promise could have been kept. Any blow-by-blow account of the actual course of events, while far from clearing Clive of duplicity (in fact he deserves enormous credit for his skill in deceit, which was essential to victory), must adjudge this claim as a ludicrous example of Victorian moral hypocrisy – heartily approving of the conquest of Bengal, but denouncing the means by which it was brought about. Without employment of such means, the end would never have been achieved.

As we shall see, Clive's policy was a masterpiece of tactical manoeuvring against an extremely devious and not unintelligent ruler, surrounded by untrustworthy middlemen bent on betraying both sides. In that Clive's intrigues avoided serious bloodshed, a colossal defeat for British arms and the probable end of the British presence in India, they must be considered an unqualified success, far exceeding that of other, less-skilled generals whose more conventional and prosaic victories were achieved at a huge cost in lives.

Clive's failing, to most conventional historians, was not that he displayed the qualities of a master diplomat, politician and statesman, showing formidable cunning and skill; but that victory was achieved – although to the last Clive could not be sure of it – largely before the battle was ever fought, disappointing those who like their battles to be straightforward confrontations of arms, leaving piles of corpses.

The true criticism of Clive is altogether different: once again, he showed a guerrilla's almost reckless courage. He staked everything on one throw, against enormous odds. He was gambling beyond measure. That he knew the exact size of the risk he was taking is clear. Yet for any man to have placed not just the survival of his men in battle, but the very future of the British in India, into one colossal throw of the dice, is open to question. But the justification of any gamble is success, and he succeeded. That fact alone exonerated and justified him. He had that greatest asset of the most accomplished of statesmen and generals, luck.

There were not one, but two, conspiracies. The one supported by Omichand involving Yar Latuf Khan, one of the Nawab's senior generals, which was backed also by the Seths and the Hindu aristocracy. And the one backed by Clive, in which most of the Moslem aristocracy was rallying around Mir Jafar, the chief general of Siraj-ud-Daula's army.

Scrafton, Clive's young, reckless and unscrupulous agent, was informed of the first by Omichand, who was in his sickroom. Scrafton then called on the Nawab – whom he had last seen on the eve of the battle for Calcutta in all his martial magnificence. Siraj-ud-Daula 'fell a'laughing and shaking his head', exclaiming 'give him a horse and a dress, no let it be an elephant'. In the event it was just a horse.

Watts, much better informed than Scrafton, favoured the second conspiracy surrounding Mir Jafar, which was backed by Manik Chand and the Nawab's best general, Rai Durlabh, who had had enough of being ordered around by Siraj-ud-Daula's effete young favourites. Mir Jafar was son-in-law to Aliverdi Khan, his most trusted general, and uncle to Siraj-ud-Daula, who had repeatedly humiliated him in public and dismissed him. Moreover, Mir Jafar effectively sent Clive a blank cheque to set out his demands in a treaty in exchange for British support.

Watts wrote on 23 April 1757 that Mir Jafar was 'ready and willing to join their forces, seize the Nabob and put up another person approved of. If you approve of this scheme, which is more feasible than the other [Omichand's] I wrote about, he [Mir Jafar] requests that you will write your proposals of what money, what land you want, or what treaties you will engage in.'

The select committee, acting sensibly for almost the first time, decided to act on the recommendation of the agent in Murshidabad with the best knowledge and judgement – Watts. They even proposed recalling Scrafton, although eventually they decided to leave him there after Clive protested vigorously.

However, all sides now gave Mir Jafar their seal of approval. On 1 May the committee fatefully decreed that Siraj-ud-Daula's 'dishonesty and insolence show that the recently made treaty was concluded by him only to gain time; the absolute certainty of his intention to break the peace, as shown by his intrigues with the French; the hatred felt for the Nabob by everybody makes it probable that there will be a revolution whether we interfere or not, and it would be a mistake not to assist a probable successor and so obtain the exclusion of the French'.

Omichand, however, was furious at what he saw as the discarding of his own plot. The Seths now switched their own support to the more powerful Mir Jafar, and the merchant's role as an intermediary was reduced to almost nothing. Indignant and devious, he now sought to switch sides, offering himself to the Nawab as his agent.

The pressure on Watts became intense. The Seths had warned him that the Nawab had twice threatened to impale him or cut off his head. Now the Englishman believed Omichand was about to betray him and Mir Jafar. The other conspirators would have nothing to do with Omichand. But Watts attempted desperately to appease him and prevent news of the plot leaking out.

The merchant now astonishingly insisted that, as the price of his not revealing all, he must be awarded 5 per cent of the Nawab's treasury, reckoned at £40 million, under the terms of the treaty with Mir Jafar. On 16 May Watts, in a panic, fearing for his life as well as the success of the conspiracy, told Clive of Omichand's terms, and also sent a signed and sealed blank piece of paper from Mir Jafar on which the British were to set out their terms for supporting the conspiracy.

It was evident at this stage that Mir Jafar and his associates were desperate to be rid of Siraj-ud-Daula, and that they believed they could not do so without British support. The Bengalis needed the

British as much as vice versa to be rid of an unpopular, dissolute, frivolous and often vicious tyrant.

A major crisis had arrived in the form of Omichand's potential betrayal, which threatened to unravel the whole conspiracy. Clive came up with a simple and entirely dishonest solution. He could not bow to Omichand's demands without infuriating the other conspirators; but he could not take the risk that the Calcutta merchant would betray the plot. So he came up with an astonishing contrivance.

The select committee was by now almost entirely under the spell of this energetic, frantic, decisive personality, so changed from the morose figure of the earlier part of the campaign. It debated 'how we might deceive Omichand and prevent a discovery of the whole project, which we run the risk of, should we refuse to insist on the unreasonable gratification he expects and demands; and on the one hand it would be entirely improper to stipulate, much more to demand with any obstinacy, such extravagant terms from Mir Jafar for a person who can be of no service in the intended revolution. So on the other it would be dangerous to provoke a man of Omichand's character by seeming to take no care at all of his interests, and slighting his weight and influence, which might prompt him to make a sacrifice of us and ruin our affairs entirely.'

Thus a 'double treaty' must be drafted, 'both to be signed by Mir Jafar and by us; in one of which the article in favour of Omichand is to be inserted, in the other to be left out, and Mir Jafar is to be informed of that which we design to abide by and esteem authentic with our reasons for taking such a step'.

The real treaty was drafted on white paper, the fake one on red. The payment Omichand sought was reduced through haggling by a third, so as not to make him suspicious. For good measure, with unblinking insincerity, Clive told Watts to 'flatter Omichand greatly, tell him the Admiral, Committee and self are infinitely obliged to him for the pains he has taken to aggrandise the Company's affairs, and that his name will be greater in England than it ever was in India'.

A further obstacle suddenly raised its head. Watson refused to sign the red treaty on 'a strict principle of delicacy' – presumably that to do so would be to compromise the good name of His

Majesty's navy – as opposed to the agents of the Company, who were on a lower and more venal plane. Omichand, who knew that Watson's authority was equal to Clive's, would have suspected treachery without his signature; and in the immortal words of Macaulay: 'Clive was not a man to do anything by halves. We almost blush to write it. He forged Admiral Watson's name.'

In fact, Watson almost certainly authorised the forgery. The secretary of the Bengal select committee at the time wrote that 'he shrugged up his shoulders and said laughingly that he had not signed it but that he had left it to them to do as they pleased'. One of Watson's officers was later to claim that he objected not just to the forgery – which he certainly knew of – but to the whole conspiracy. In fact, he consistently lent Clive his support, and even that of his sailors, over the next few weeks, although he expressed doubts about the chances of success.

According to Clive, the admiral 'gave the gentleman who carried it [the treaty to his flagship] leave to sign his name upon it'. The gentleman was called Mr Lushington. Watson had no hesitation in claiming his share of the prize money after the conspiracy had proved successful; unfortunately he died just two months later, so the exact truth was never established. It was to be the most controversial episode in Clive's career, and one which returned to haunt him in later life.

The historian Sir Henry Cotton's comment seems appropriate:

In war, fraud is no more dishonorable than killing is murder. The Duke of Wellington might have thought the sham treaty a needless finesse; but he would have hanged the Hindu banker without scruple on the morrow of Plassey. He would certainly not have paid him the quarter-of-a-million sterling which was his price, as Colonel Malleson thinks Clive should have done.

This is echoed by the Indian historian Fazl Rubee:

If Mir Jafar and Clive used any deceit at the time of the revolution such things were always done on such occasions. Whenever any revolution took place at the time of the Hindu Raj or Mohammedan government such plottings were carried on to a far greater extent. We know, for instance, what Rajah Khan did and how Aliverdi Khan plotted against Serferaz Khan. These things have always occurred, and politicians have justified them when they have been done in the service of their country. But such things were not carried on against Siraj-ud-Daula to the extent that had been common in former times.

It is hard to escape the conclusion that the controversy of the Omichand deal was a storm got up purely by Clive's enemies as a means of pulling him down, and later resurrected by Victorian moralists.

Clive resorted to a flurry of deception, perhaps counting on the fact that Drake and the council by their obtuseness and arrogance before his arrival had given the impression to the Bengalis that they were incapable of either intrigue or intelligence. The Nawab had by now decided to take on the British, ordering Mir Jafar to Plassey, where the bulk of his forces under Rai Durlabh, some 15,000 men, were still concentrated.

Nundcomar, another treacherous go-between, was suddenly summoned at midnight. He refused to come. He was then invited at dawn by Clive to watch the British army exercising outside Chandernagore, where he was lectured about the Nawab's behaviour. This was the beginning of an extraordinary softness on the part of Clive towards Nundcomar, a brahmin whose duplicity was later far to exceed even that of Omichand.

In a panic, Nundcomar informed Siraj-ud-Daula that Clive was planning to march that very day – which sent the Nawab into one of his characteristic rages. He heard a rumour simultaneously that the British were sending ammunition to Kasimbazar in a small flotilla of barges. They were searched and found to be empty. The Nawab was by now in a state bordering on hysteria.

These signs of hostility were succeeded by a small flurry of acts of appeasement. Clive announced that he was sending half his army down from Chandernagore, as well as his cannon. He said he was keeping the rest there only because, since the Nawab's army had destroyed Calcutta, 'there is not much room for more soldiers without endangering their lives by sickness'. But he suggested the Nawab should also withdraw his troops from Plassey.

Even more subtle was Clive's reaction to a letter that arrived on 12 May purporting to come from the chief of the Marathas, promising him the support of 120,000 cavalry against the Nawab. This said, among other things, that 'whatever goods and riches you have lost in Bengal, the double of its value shall be restored by me. Do not on any account make peace with the Nabob. In a few days my forces shall enter Bengal, and the trade of that province shall be entirely yours. The French shall not remain in Bengal. Your forces shall keep them out by sea, mine, by land.'

It was too good an offer to be true. Clive assumed at once it was a forgery of the Nawab's. He wrote back with fine calculation that while he still got on well with the Nawab, there was a possibility of war after the rainy season had ended – when in fact he was determined to overthrow him well before then. He instructed Watts and Scrafton to show a copy to the Nawab, to demonstrate that the British would have none of these conspiracies, and that they would 'stand by him to the last'. Siraj-ud-Daula was so pleased that he recalled half of his forces, and all his three commanders – Mir Jafar, Rai Durlabh and Manik Chand. He told their troops to stand easy, but failed to pay them off promptly.

The climax was now approaching. On the one hand Clive seemed fully to have regained his old furious energy, self-confidence and extraordinary ability to persuade others to get things done. The relationship between him and the select committee had completely changed: he was in charge, and they did his bidding. Watson, while retaining his prickliness and sense of professional superiority, was no match for his intellect or energy, and his ships anyway could proceed no further upriver, thus being unable to contribute further.

On the other hand the stress upon this brilliant, vigorous man in assuming responsibility for the whole expedition was exacting. He was, as he preferred, once again ensconced in luxury: he had commandeered the colonnaded house of Renault at Ghyretty, near Chandernagore. A magnificent rococo French building, embellished with columns and frescoes, it stood in an extensive park by the river, like something transplanted from Versailles to the disease-infected tropics.

The gloom of ruined Calcutta must have seemed behind him; he even confidently invited Margaret to join him. He was encircled again by colonial magnificence. In this splendid house he seems to have recovered his sense of proportion and self-confidence. It was the first real comfort he had enjoyed since leaving the peace and luxury of Fort St George nearly a year earlier.

Clive always showed a remarkable ability to combine the endurance of extraordinary hardship and squalor in the field with his men with a love of wealth and luxury when he was off it. It must have seemed quite surreal to dwell in this baroque palace by the banks of the sluggish Hugli while a great battle that would decide the fate of India seemed imminent and plots raged through the Nawab's capital upriver. His only melancholy was to observe the bodies of children swathed in garlands of flowers and left to float downstream by Hindu custom.

Clive was being driven relentlessly forward, weaving the most complex webs of deceit. This once straightforward – if able and extraordinarily vigorous and talented – military hero was now to show himself on a level with anything out of Renaissance Italy or contemporary France. He conspired like a Medici or a Talleyrand, and, like them, was quite clear in his goals.

Clive brooded on the intrigue that would seal his fate and that of the British in India during the dark nights in that astonishing palace dripping with humidity and infested by insects and lizards. He was making a bid for absolute power. Yet he was close to losing the very rules that are necessary to regulate any man, beyond which there is only the limitless horizon of madness.

Some 100 miles upriver at Murshidabad, madness seemed already to be gnawing at the soul of his principal adversary, Siraj-ud-Daula, as, immersed in idleness and pleasure, he awaited the slow approach of the man dubbed in southern India 'the Invincible'. In place of the decisive arrogance which he had shown as he marched at the head of the armies that had taken Calcutta, he faced his nemesis with a giggling insouciance.

His advisers warned him that Mir Jafar 'is treacherously bent on ruining this royal house . . . we ought to put them [the conspirators] down first, so that the English, on hearing the news, will take themselves to flight. The presence of these two will be the cause of distraction and anxiety to us as they are sure to practise treachery.' But Siraj-ud-Daula, in his splendid palace across the river from the teeming immensity of Murshidabad took no notice, fearing that to move would precipitate the crisis; Mir Jafar was too strong.

The atmosphere in the Nawab's capital was pregnant with intrigue. Watts, who was in fear for his life, was desperate to get the agreement with Mir Jafar concluded, and also to spirit Omichand, who might at any moment betray the plot to the Nawab, out of Murshidabad. At last he succeeded in arranging for Scrafton and the Calcutta merchant to leave in palanquins.

However, on the journey, Omichand managed to give Scrafton the slip and go and visit Rai Durlabh, the commander of the Nawab's standing forces at Plassey and one of the conspirators. Whether he suspected or not that he was being double-crossed by the British, he made mischief, and caused Rai Durlabh to raise further objections to the British terms – in particular the huge payments demanded from the Bengalis, as he was also the Nawab's treasurer. These were transmitted to Mir Jafar, causing further delay.

The terms included, as well as the restoration of British privileges, the total expulsion of the French from Bengal, 177 lakhs in reparations for damage to Calcutta, a large increase in Company land around Calcutta, and a ban on building Bengali fortifications anywhere between Hugli and Calcutta. In addition, the fake treaty provided for the payment of 20 lakhs to Omichand.

After Rai Durlabh's intervention, the bargaining was suddenly resumed, with Watts growing ever more desperate. There were rumours that his head had been exhibited on a pike. He wrote to Clive in exasperation, 'If you think you are strong enough, I am of the opinion we had better depend on ourselves and enter into no contract or have any connection with such a set of shuffling, lying, spiritless wretches.'

At last Watts was summoned to Mir Jafar: he was taken to his palace in a closed dooley usually used to transport women to the harem, to deceive the Nawab's spies. In the exotic surroundings of the women's quarters, Mir Jafar solemnly signed the treaty, swearing both on the Koran and on the head of his beloved 17-year-old son, Miran.

Watts was spirited away again. But, as the fevered atmosphere in Murshidabad continued to grow, he had to wait in an agony of frustration until the treaty reached Clive safely, taken by one of the few couriers trusted by both sides, Omar Beg. With every day that passed, Watts's position grew more dangerous.

At last the Nawab decided to move against Mir Jafar, and sent a party of soldiers to arrest him. They were beaten up by the general's retainers and sent back to the Nawab. Mir Jafar was promptly dismissed as paymaster-general; but Siraj-ud-Daula lacked the nerve to send a larger force against him, for fear of igniting civil war in the capital.

Watts, fearing for his life, left Murshidabad along with the two remaining members of the British mission on the evening of 12 June, ostensibly to join a hunting party near Kasimbazar. This turned into a desperate and dangerous flight. According to Sykes, who accompanied them initially:

> They set out from the country seat, attended by a Mughal servant, a few peons, and their greyhounds, having previously left directions with their servants to provide a supper, telling them they would return and entertain the Dutch that evening.
>
> It was dark before they arrived at Daudpur, although they travelled at speed. On the nearby plain was encamped Rai Durlabh, an officer of the Nabob's with a very large force. Here they were exposed to imminent danger, falling unawares of the outposted guards, but the darkness of the night favoured their escape.
>
> By striking off into the plain and taking a circuit of the whole camp they regained the road and arrived about one o'clock in the morning at Augurdip, where a second misfortune threatened their destruction. They unexpectedly found themselves in the midst of a body of horse, which had been stationed there to prevent the passing or repassing down or up the country of any Europeans.
>
> The first notice they had of this danger was the neighing and kicking of the horses about; their riders luckily were asleep. At this place they quitted their horses, and embarking on two open boats which they had the good fortune to seize, proceeded down the river.

They reached Clive himself two days later. With their flight, Murshidabad was thrown into further turmoil. The Nawab had previously assembled an armed force to attack and seize Mir Jafar, and mobs ran wildly through the streets in preparation. Not knowing the specifics of the conspiracy, Siraj-ud-Daula was thrown into a panic by Watts's flight. He feared that the British were about to make their move; with much of his army ready to desert on account of non-payment, he suddenly reversed himself again, deciding he needed Mir Jafar on his side to ensure the loyalty of his troops.

He went personally to his rival to beg his services. As Mir Jafar wrote, 'The guns and arrows were all ready against me, and the people were in arms day and night. Mr Watts's news was known early on Monday. This startled the Nabob; he thought it absolutely necessary I should be soothed; he came to me himself. On Thursday Eve the Hugli letter arrived that they [the British] were marched. I was to be with him.

'On three conditions I consented to it. One, that I would not enter into his service; secondly, I would not visit him; lastly I would not take a post in the army. I sent him word that if he agreed to these terms I was ready. As he wanted me, he consented. But I took this writing from all the commanders of the army and artillery: that when they had conquered the English they should be bound to see me and my family safe wherever I chose to go.'

Clive's plot now seemed in serious danger of unravelling altogether. It looked as though Mir Jafar had switched sides again and joined up, albeit with ill-grace, with the Nawab. The latter, thus strengthened, ordered his forces out of Murshidabad to join his standing army at Plassey.

Clive decided to strike before the onset of the rainy season made movement impossible. The countryside would soon be treacherously swampy, and he could not expect the conspiracy, such as it was, to survive until after the rains. He ordered reinforcements up from Calcutta: some 150 soldiers and sailors were sent up, leaving the town totally undefended.

On 11 June Clive's forces moved, leaving 100 or so to defend Chandernagore. Altogether, he controlled some 3,000 men – 600 British and European soldiers, 100 Eurasians, 170 artillerymen, and around 2,100 Indian troops. The sepoys, along with ten cannon and two howitzers, travelled by land, the Europeans by boat. The main British ships with their cannon could travel no further upstream.

The reckoning was now drawing close. Clive had been sucked further and further into the continent, up the Hugli river, calculating always that boldness was its own reward. Yet beyond the treacherous river and the oppressive jungle there lay an unseen enemy of tens of thousands. Clive now sent a disguised ultimatum to the

Nawab, listing the wrongs done to the British and the way he had broken the previous treaty. He offered to accept mediation by the Nawab's principal generals, headed by Mir Jafar.

By 17 June Clive had reached Patna and ordered Eyre Coote, now promoted to major, to advance to the front at Kutwa, some 14 miles away, with a force of 700 and two cannon. It was an impressive obstacle, a fort whose walls were about a mile long altogether and which commanded the approach to Murshidabad and contained a lot of grain.

Coote's force came under fire as it approached the fort, and he promptly threatened to storm it, giving no quarter. As his forces attacked, the defenders fled. Clive's small army moved forward and had to shelter in the squalid native town from a sudden torrent of tropical rain.

Chapter 16

Plassey

I n this dismal encampment, far removed from the decadent baroque palace of Chandernagore, Clive had to make the most agonising decision of his life. Before him lay a branch of the Hugli river which he needed to cross if he was to attack the Nawab's force at Plassey, halfway to Murshidabad, some 40 miles away. Ferrying his army in boats presented no problem; but retreating across it after a defeat would be to invite appalling carnage among his men, particularly if the river had been further swollen in the interval by the monsoon rains.

If the British were beaten, Clive faced the danger not just of a lost battle and orderly retreat, but a rout with his army caught like rats in a trap by the rising waters. The stakes were immense. It was rumoured that de Bussy was approaching Bengal with a considerable French force, and that Law was despatching men to help the Nawab.

A defeat for Clive would leave Calcutta virtually defenceless, except for the guns of Watson's ships, and at the mercy of a second occupation by the Nawab. The French might join with the Nawab as his partners in Bengal while also attacking Madras, now so depleted of its forces.

Against that, there was only a colossal gamble: that Clive's conspiracy would come off. In effect he depended upon the word of Indian princes, which Clive's long experience in India had shown to be entirely untrustworthy – and nowhere more so than in Bengal.

Desperately, he sought to pin down Mir Jafar, now riding alongside the Nawab once again.

It gives me great concern that in an affair of so great consequence to yourself in particular that you do not exert yourself more. So long as I have been on my march you have not yet given me the least information what measures it is necessary for me to take, nor do I know what is going forward at Murshidabad.

Surely it is in your power to send me news daily; it must be more difficult for me to procure trusty messengers than you; however the bearer of this is a sensible, intelligent man, in whom I have great confidence. Let me know your sentiments freely by him. I shall wait here till I have proper intelligence to proceed. I think it absolutely necessary that you should join my army as soon as possible.

Consider the Nabob will increase in strength daily. Come over to me at Plassey or any other place you judge proper, with what force you have. Even a thousand horse will be sufficient, and I will engage to march immediately with you to Murshidabad. I prefer conquering by open force.

He heard nothing in reply. He was growing frantic, sending emissaries to any of the Nawab's enemies he could think of – the Marathas, the Nawab of Oudh, the powerful prince on Bengal's northern borders – in a desperate search for allies. Reports from scouts reckoned that Law and 300 or so Frenchmen were only three days' march away. Clive was being lured into a trap; all his time-consuming manipulations were coming to nought. Mir Jafar had double-crossed him and was with the Nawab.

He wrote desperately and uncharacteristically for advice from the select committee in Calcutta, so that he would not be entirely left out on a limb whatever decision he might take. 'I am really at a loss how to act over the present situation of our opponents' – but he received no reply. None indeed was to come until after the Battle of Plassey, and its views were 'so indefinite and contradictory that I can put no other construction on it than an attempt to clear yourselves at my expense had this expedition miscarried'. The general in his tent, agonising and unhappy, could find no helpful advice from the quarrelsome, grasping pygmies of Calcutta.

The decision would have to be his alone. The mind of this usually impulsive, decisive man was a turmoil, a battleground between his instincts, which were to advance, and his formidable intelligence, which told him that to do so would be suicidal folly. Nothing seemed to be coming right. The signs were universally inauspicious. In a state of agitation and grim pessimism he did something he had never done before an engagement – summoned a council of war to seek the advice of his commanders.

Just in advance of the meeting a letter, sewn in a slipper, arrived from Mir Jafar at last. It was a sign; but it could scarcely have been less committal. 'Tomorrow, the day of the Eade [a Moslem festival], by the blessing of God I shall march. I shall have my tent fixed to the right or left of the army. I have hitherto been afraid to send you intelligence. After I am arrived in the army mutual intelligence will be easier, but here the Nabob has fixed guards on all the roads. Your letters come too open to me; I hope that till our affairs are publicly declared you will be very careful.'

The missive could hardly have said less: although friendly in tone, it carefully avoided any commitment – whether through fear it might be intercepted, or because Mir Jafar had reached a deal with the Nawab, and the letter was intended as a feint, Clive could not know. He felt less than reassured. Meanwhile a letter had reached him from Watts describing how Mir Jafar had denounced him as a spy to impress the Nawab's emissary, who had arrived during a talk between the army commander and the Englishman.

The once all-certain, all-powerful Clive summoned his council of war. There were nine senior officers present and seven junior ones. The first group divided seven–two against fighting, among the noes Clive and his second-in-command, Kilpatrick. Of the junior officers, four were in favour of fighting, three against.

Coote was one of those who argued passionately that they should move forward. 'We should come to an immediate action; or, if that was thought entirely impracticable, we should return to Calcutta; the consequence of which must be our own disgrace, and the inevitable destruction of the Company's affairs.'

Clive intensely disliked the overbearing Coote, who had little understanding of the conspiracy. The British commander himself was not considering a return to Calcutta; but if Mir Jafar failed to come forward with any specific promise, he felt the British should wait in force on the other side of the river, possibly until the end of the monsoon. The conspiracy would have been proved worthless, and would unravel; but equally the Nawab would prove incapable of striking across the river until the autumn.

To cross a river which might soon become unfordable, and to face a vastly superior force, must be folly. The battle was off after the decision of the council of war, which confirmed Clive in his pessimism. A famous scene was now played out.

In Orme's description, Clive retired 'into an adjoining grove, where he remained near an hour in meditation which convinced him of the absurdity of stopping where he was; and acting now entirely from himself, he gave orders, on his return to his quarters, that the army cross the river next morning'. Clive was later to deny this version of events, because it shows him to have been both unheroically hesitant and dangerously impulsive. But it seems certainly to have been the truth. Coote confirmed that Clive told him only an hour after the council had met that he intended to move next day.

It was the key decision. The more robust attitude of his junior officers had impressed him. Also, if he missed his chance, Coote would forever be able to castigate him with lacking boldness. Finally, and most importantly, he decided that if he failed to cross he would lose the initiative for the first time against Siraj-ud-Daula.

The Clive myth was based on his fearlessness, which he had hitherto displayed throughout the Bengal campaign; to hesitate now would allow the enemy to gain new heart. Clive's old maxim of attack being the best form of defence reasserted itself; but it was a gamble on an altogether different scale from anything he had tried before. He was engaged in a huge game of bluff, a poker game where upstaging his opponents was all. If he lacked the confidence to move forward, it was quite certain that the conspirators would be quick to mend their fences with the Nawab; a gigantic opportunity would have been lost. If he did move forward boldly, Mir Jafar and the others might just yet be prevailed upon to keep to their side of the bargain.

All of Clive's successes had been based on a judicious decision to take the offensive, suddenly and against seemingly impossible odds, which every time had thrown his Indian enemies into confusion. The only difference this time was the stakes involved – the very survival of the British in Bengal and, possibly, India.

Many men have been rendered over-cautious by the size of the responsibility involved. Clive, at the age of 32, decided to turn against the caution of seniority and resort to youthful type. He was composed and decisive when he returned from the grove, although it is believed he agonised most of the night. The following day, as the first of his troops crossed over, he wrote to Mir Jafar: 'If you cannot go even this length to assist us, I call God to witness the fault is not mine, and I must desire your consent for concluding a peace with the Nawab.'

In reply to this threat he received at last what seemed like a definite commitment: 'The sooner you march to fall upon him the better, before his design can take place. As yet you are now only designing, but it is not now proper to be indolent. When you come near I shall then be able to join you. If you could send two or three hundred good fighting men [along] the upper road towards Kasimbazar, the Nabob's army would of themselves retreat. Then the battle will have no difficulty. When I am arrived near the army I will send you privately all the intelligence. Let me have previous notice of the time you intend to fight.'

Again, it could all be a trick. Clive had no way of knowing. But he replied without hesitation.

I am determined to risk everything on your account, though you will not exert yourself. I shall be on the other side of the river this evening. If you will join me at Plassey, I will march halfway to meet you, then the whole Nabob's army will I know fight for you. Give me to call to your mind how much your own glory and safety depends upon it.

Be assured if you do this you will be Subah of these provinces, but if you cannot go even this length to assist us I call God to witness the fault is not mine, and I must desire your consent for concluding a peace with the Nabob, and what has passed between us will never be known. What can I say more than that I am as desirous of your success and welfare as my own.

That same evening, Clive crossed over himself with the last of his troops. It must have been a painfully lonely journey. This was his Rubicon, his burning of the boats. Like Caesar and Cortés, he had made his decision and there would be no going back. In the sultry evening, he gazed upon the slow-moving waters of the tributary of the Upper Hugli as he committed his small force to the chance that a Bengali general might be telling the truth.

Typically, once the decision was made, furious energy replaced hesitation; he pushed his troops forward in a precipitate night march. The rain was torrential as darkness fell, and the progress was slow and dismal through rapidly flooding fields. Drenched and determined, he spurred his men on through the sodden gloom, sparing none, until they reached a substantial building, the Nawab's hunting lodge at Plassey, an elegant country house which Clive immediately chose as his headquarters.

The British labelled this Plassey House: it overlooked the river from behind a fine Moorish colonnade. The place was a delightful country estate. Steps led down to the water where the Nawab's royal barge would take him downstream for his parties; around it was a large garden within a substantial wall. To the south, behind it, was a splendid mango grove for the Nawab's delectation, nearly half a mile long and 300 yards wide. It was laid out in carefully symmetrical lines and was surrounded by a mudbank and ditch.

The hunting lodge had been well chosen. As a British visitor, James Forbes, was later to comment in 1781:

The country surrounding Plassey abounds with best of prey, and game of every description. A gentleman lately engaged on a shooting party gave us an account of their success in one month . . . in which space they killed one royal tiger, six wild buffaloes, 186 hog deer, 25 wild hogs, 11 antelopes, 3 foxes, 35 hares, 15 brace of partridges and floricans, with quails, ducks, snipes and smaller birds in abundance.

Clive instantly appreciated the use of the Nawab's shangri-la as a defensive position. His scouts informed him they were only three miles from the Nawab's approaching army and one mile from the camp of the standing army, under Rai Durlabh. The grove was known, poetically, as the Orchard of the Hundred Thousand Trees, and the name Plassey itself was taken from the palas trees present – the Flame of the Forest. It was a name that was to resonate throughout history.

Clive dried out and quartered comfortably in the Nawab's small country house. Macaulay sets the scene:

Clive was unable to sleep; he heard, through the whole night, the sound of drums and cymbals from the vast camp of the Nabob. It is not strange that even his stout heart should now and then have sunk, when he reflected against what odds, and for what a prize, he was in a few hours to contend.

Nor was the rest of Surajah Dowlah more peaceful. His mind, at once weak and stormy, was distracted by wild and horrible apprehensions. Appalled by the greatness and nearness of the crisis, distrusting his captains, dreading every one who approached him, dreading to be left alone, he sat gloomily in his tent, haunted, a Greek poet would have said, by the furies of those who had cursed him with their last breath in the Black Hole.

Clive had seized a defensible position. But his small force was desperately isolated and any determined show of resistance by the enemy the following day would overwhelm or surround the British.

When dawn broke, Clive was on the roof of the lodge, telescope in hand. What he saw must have shaken him. He had heard reports that the Nawab's army was only 8,000 strong, because his treasury had failed to pay the rest of his men. Others believed the number to be much greater; but the evidence suggests Clive was reasonably confident the numbers were on the low side.

Instead, in the clear light of the morning, while the sun cast its early cold light as the monsoon clouds began to gather, there lay before him an extensive green plain as far as the river. A rolling sea of enemy troops – the standing army of Rai Durlabh reinforced by the whole might of Murshidabad, including Mir Jafar – was fanning out towards and around the British position.

Scrafton, for one, was in awe. 'What with the number of elephants, all covered with scarlet cloth and embroidery; their horse, with their drawn swords glittering in the sun; their heavy cannon drawn by vast trains of oxen; and their standards flying, they made a most pompous and formidable appearance.' Pennants were aloft, bands with trumpets and cymbals were playing. Elephants with exotically tailored, clanking, suffocating armour bore the major commanders.

A large and well-trained cavalry was among them, their swords at the ready. A large number of cannon were in their midst, heavily outnumbering the English; they were on mobile wooden platforms, each pulled by some 50 oxen; behind, elephants pushed them forward. The odds were the worst that Clive had ever faced. The forces against him were relatively well disciplined. He had fewer than a tenth of their cannon and no cavalry; he had no native supporting armies as he had had at Trichinopoly.

His position, although a good defensive one, was hardly a fort. He had only 3,000 men. Against him was an army of at least 50,000 – 35,000 disciplined infantry, admittedly often mutinous, but just sweetened by large sums of back pay; there were 15,000 of the best cavalry available – Pathans from the north-west border, fine fighters and riders. The Nawab also had more than 50 cannon; the most advanced of these had sophisticated screw devices to raise and lower their barrels and, more threatening still, were maintained and fired by 50 Frenchmen under the control of M. de St Frais, bent on avenging the defeat at Chandernagore.

There had been no reply, in the night or early morning, from Mir Jafar. As the forces before Clive began to outflank the British to the south, he wondered whether he would soon be entirely surrounded and cut off with his back to the river. He had never been in such dire straits; he feared that he had lost his gamble. He remarked grimly, 'We must make the best fight we can during the day and at night sling our muskets over our shoulders and march back to Calcutta.'

The night before, the youthful adventurer, the boy who had climbed the church steeple, the guerrilla leader who had outfoxed such huge armies, had prevailed at the last minute over the general. The dreamer who believed in founding a great Bengali empire had triumphed over a man beginning to grow mature and cautious as the stakes had escalated dizzyingly. Clive had invested everything in the belief that Siraj-ud-Daula was on his last legs – and now it seemed certain that the British commander had guessed wrong. The force before him was not the ramshackle army of a tottering despot, symbolic and demoralised. It was a huge and well-equipped military machine that made his own tiny army look ludicrous.

Although he comforted himself with hopes of retreat at nightfall, there was every prospect of his tiny force being cut off, surrounded, and left to the mercies of the butcher of Calcutta; he had stumbled into a trap. There is no doubt he was bitterly dismayed. Yet, with no hope of orderly retreat, he now had no alternative to pursuing his bluff.

Clive was a man who had reached the zenith of his career. If he failed now, with the council at Calcutta having disowned him,

Watson having urged him to show caution and his own council of war having insisted that he should not cross the river, the responsibility would be his alone. The defeat of his men would be accompanied by the wholesale destruction of his reputation. His every youthful triumph would be annulled. He would have little choice but to die on the battlefield amid the cries and carnage of his own misjudgement.

As the Bengali campaign had proceeded, from its shambolic and quarrelsome beginnings, he had recovered his old verve, and had earned the respect even of the naval officers surrounding Watson, if not of the prickly Coote – who, however, had at last submitted to his authority. But Clive seemed to have overreached himself once again; his self-confidence had got the better of his sound military judgement. He was finished, unless one of two improbabilities occurred: either that the conspiracy should succeed and Mir Jafar at last join him; or that the Nawab's forces after all should prove to be merely a paper threat.

He feared that neither was likely as he watched the well-disciplined armies moving to outflank him; and in this he would have been right. For contrary to what some historians, notably the usually perspicacious Bence-Jones, argue, Plassey was to be no 'walkover' nor, *pace* Macaulay, was it 'over in an hour'. It was to be a close-run thing, lasting a whole day of shifting fortunes in spite of the remarkably low British casualties suffered. Clive, for one, believed he stood little chance that chilly early morning as the first of the monsoon clouds scudded over and the swarms of men below moved to encircle his small force. The pistol was loaded at his head once more, the trigger about to be pulled.

His adversary, Siraj-ud-Daula, was also facing his moment of destiny. He had been in a desperate political corner, and he knew it. His treasury was almost exhausted as a result of his unwise decision to take on the British and throttle his main source of revenue, the trade through Calcutta. He had lost the support of both his Moslem aristocracy and his Hindu bankers and middle class. His soldiers had been verging on rebellion but had been brought together for one last fight.

Giggling, indecisive, sadistic, sexually self-indulgent, yet quick-witted and intelligent, he had done what no Indian prince had before or since – attacked a major European power and won a great victory. He was now rallying his forces for a magnificent fight against the revenge expedition on his own ground. He had seen off a succession of domestic opponents. Like Clive, his main enemy had been his own rashness and overambition. His enemies would close in on him, if he failed, just as those of Clive would.

In spite of all his weaknesses and failings, he had lured Clive into battle on his own terms. If he defeated the English at Plassey, he was set to rule for decades, and become the foremost prince in India. If he was beaten, he would lose everything. Watching from his headquarters a mile away, he cannot have been able to guess the precise English strength violating his hunting lodge; but he must have regarded what he could see with satisfied contempt as his great army encircled it. This tiny force was being led into a slaughterhouse.

Clive watched as St Frais, his Frenchmen and their guns entrenched themselves behind earthworks near a pond only 200 yards from the British, deliberately provoking them. Between the Frenchmen and the river two more guns were set up to give cover to 5,000 cavalry and 7,000 infantry. This force was commanded by Mir Madan, the loyal favourite of the Nawab.

In response, Clive ordered his men well beyond the shelter of the grove, to a position directly in front of the enemy line. He placed three of his small guns on either side, and hundreds of his soldiers in between. Sepoys guarded his flanks. A little further back he placed his two remaining six-pound guns and howitzers protected by brick kilns. Not until Gordon's stand at Khartoum a hundred years later can a more hopeless position have been defended by the British, and so few have faced such overwhelming odds to so little apparent purpose. They faced a wipeout; it looked like the last stand of a defeated army. To the south the Nawab's huge armies continued relentlessly to encircle him.

At 8 a.m. the first cannonade from the French guns began, and the British replied. The British fire ripped through Mir Madan's men; but the French had killed 10 British soldiers and 20 Indians within half an hour. Clive's boldness in venturing beyond the mango grove had been an absurd mistake in the face of overwhelming enemy firepower, directed by the accurate French.

He was quick-witted enough to realise the consequences and gave his men the order to pull the guns back to the grove; the cannon were moved behind the mudbank, where they could fire through holes while being protected. Only the howitzers remained in a forward position. One, by an incredibly lucky shot, seriously wounded Mir Madan.

Not knowing this, the position appeared quite desperate to Clive. The enemy cavalry were moving forward to attack, and he decided to pull back his remaining guns. The enemy cannon were blasting huge holes in the Nawab's beloved mango trees, but inflicting few casualties as the British were sheltering beneath the mudbank. The two sides continued exchanging relentless fire in this way for three hours.

Clive summoned his commanders to suggest that they concentrate on holding out until midnight, and then resort to his old tactic of a surprise night attack as a last desperate measure. Clive believed he could hold his position to the front, provided the forces moving to encircle him did not attack from the flank or the rear.

Significantly these, although he did not know it, were commanded by the three main conspirators – Mir Jafar, Yar Latuf Khan and Rai Durlabh. They were waiting and circling like vultures to see which side would prevail. While they would not attack until the battle moved decisively to one side or another, as soon as it did they would join the victors. All the intense plotting and negotiating of the past month had at least entombed a large part of the Nawab's army in a kind of neutrality – but no more than that. The rebels would not go over to Clive, but they would stay aloof from the battle.

Clive knew nothing of this. The cannonade continued on both sides. In the shelter of the mango grove, his hope was that a direct frontal attack could be repulsed. Then, suddenly, the monsoon clouds, which had been building up for hours, broke; the rain, although lasting only half an hour, was torrential, soaking all, including Clive, to the skin. The British had hastily pulled tarpaulins over the ammunition as soon as the downpour started; the Bengali ammunition was soaked. Throughout the downpour the British guns continued to fire, while the enemy ones fell silent.

The sound of thunder mixed with that of cannon. As one of Clive's officers wrote, 'We had some apprehension that the enemy would take advantage of this opportunity and make a push with their horse, but our guns continuing to play very briskly prevented any such motion. The enemy's guns during the rain, which lasted half an hour, did not fire a shot.'

Unknown to Clive, Mir Madan, the Nawab's best commander, was taken to the latter's camp, where he died of his wounds. Another loyal commander, Bahadur Ali Khan, was also killed in the British cannonade. This left only his favourite, the foppish Mohan Lal, who fought with remarkable bravery at the head of the troops attacking the English line.

Siraj-ud-Daula was now beginning to panic: Mir Jafar and the other senior commanders had so far taken no part in the fighting, although their flanking move had continued and they were now in a position to attack from the side, and very nearly from the back, cutting Clive off. The Nawab sent repeatedly for Mir Jafar, who came at last on horseback with a huge and magnificent escort, in case there was an attempt to assassinate him.

The contemporary Indian historian Ghulam Husain describes what followed:

> Siraj-ud-Daula spoke to him [Mir Jafar] in the humblest terms, and at last descended to the lowest supplication; he even took his turban from off his head (at least this was the report) and placed it before the general; to whom he addressed these very words, 'I now repent of what I have done; and availing myself of those ties of consanguinity which subsist between us, as well as of those rights which my grandfather, Aliverdi Khan, has doubtless acquired upon your gratitude I look up to you, as the only representative of that venerable personage; and hope therefore, that, forgetting my past trespasses, you shall henceforth behave as becomes a Seyd, a man united in blood to me, and a man of sentiments, who conserves a grateful remembrance of all the benefits he has received from my family; I recommend myself to you; take care of the conservation of my honour and life.' Siraj-ud-Daula was pleading for his throne and his life before his unsupportive senior general.
>
> Mir Jafar coldly replied that the day was now drawing to its end; and that there remained no time for an attack; 'send a counter order to the troops that are advancing,' said he; 'recall those engaged; and

tomorrow, with the blessing of God, I will join all the troops together, and provide for the engagement.' Siraj-ud-Daula observed, that they might be attacked by the enemy in the night; this also the general took upon himself to provide against, and he surmised that the enemy would not form a night attack.

Siraj-ud-Daula promptly called for Rai Durlabh to give his opinion; this second of the Nawab's generals also in on the conspiracy advised just as Mir Jafar had. The turning point had been reached. The conspirators, it seemed, had decided that the Nawab would not prevail and were now prepared to tilt the scales against him.

There remains a possibility that the advice was given in good faith, and that Mir Jafar and Rai Durlabh were indeed preparing to join forces with the Nawab the following morning. But events were to overtake them all – and the probability is that Mir Jafar, who hated his vicious young nephew, intended this, and was going in for the kill.

Reluctantly, Siraj-ud-Daula ordered Mohan Lal, in charge of the Bengali front line, to order a retreat. He angrily refused to do this, and only under equally furious orders was he prevailed to withdraw in an orderly fashion from a position where he had the British on the defensive. Meanwhile Mir Jafar at last played his hand, sending a message to Clive advising him to attack; but the letter failed to get through until much later.

Instead, chance once again intervened. When Clive, depressed and soaked to the skin, saw to his astonishment that the enemy front line was beginning to pull back, he assumed this was a temporary lull in the fighting and went to change his clothes; as he was pulling them off, he was informed that some of his forward troops under Kilpatrick were going after the retreating enemy – and preparing to attack the French gunners' strategic position on a piece of high ground.

This was madness. Clive had no men to spare for a chase that could over-extend his forces and lead them into a trap. He was beside himself with rage, and went off in pursuit; he needed every man to defend the British position. He caught up with Kilpatrick just as the troops reached the now abandoned French position. The

French had retreated, with their guns, to a nearby redoubt. Furious, he ordered Kilpatrick put under arrest, but the latter apologised, and was ordered back to the mango grove to take charge there, while Clive took command of the forward troops.

He resolved that having once advanced, the British could not retreat, and ordered Coote to bring up reinforcements. Although Mohan Lal's men poured musket fire into the exposed British position, it held with some difficulty. Then the Bengalis turned and advanced again, and were met with withering British fire. But the British were in trouble, under the fire of French guns, and potentially faced by a third of the Nawab's forces.

The Bengali cavalry now prepared to charge the British on open ground. Clive asked desperately for more reinforcements, only to be told that another cavalry attack was being prepared against the mango grove itself. Clive countermanded the order for reinforcements. The few British cannon blazed away at the oxen dragging the Indian cannon and forced them back. Although Bengali infantrymen attacked bravely and in waves, they were not reinforced. Under intense British fire, their elephants were rearing up and getting out of control.

When Mohan Lal's forces began to pull away, Clive ordered his soldiers forward to take the forward Bengali positions. Simultaneously, one of the enemy ammunition dumps blew up. Coote captured the little hill in front of Plassey House, while St Frais's men fled the redoubt from which their guns had kept the British pinned down for so long.

Siraj-ud-Daula, hearing that the British were attacking, had jumped aboard a camel and fled back with 2,000 horsemen towards the capital. The Bengalis, after fighting so furiously, were faced with the flight of the Nawab, the death of two senior commanders and the near-desertion of three others. The huge army now also fled, their panic becoming a rout. As the English moved forward, hardly believing their luck, they found the stores and baggage of the encampment abandoned. Around 500 of the enemy had been killed compared to just 20 dead and 50 wounded on the British side.

Clive urged his men forward in hot pursuit of the fleeing enemy for about six miles, capturing four more cannon before calling a halt in exhaustion. Kilpatrick eventually caught him up at Daudpur. It was around five o'clock, and only an hour of daylight remained.

Clive sent a laconic, succinct despatch to Watson and the select committee:

> Gentlemen – this morning at one o'clock we arrived at Plassey grove and early in the morning the Nabob's whole army appeared in sight and cannonaded us for several hours, and about noon returned to a very strong camp in sight, lately Rai Durlabh's, upon which we advanced and stormed the Nabob's camp, which we have taken with all his cannon, and pursued him six miles, being now at Daudpur and shall proceed to Murshidabad tomorrow. Mir Jafar, Rai Durlabh and Yar Latuf Khan gave us no other assistance than standing neutral. They are with me with a large force. Mir Madan and five hundred horse are killed and three elephants. Our loss is trifling, not above 20 Europeans killed and wounded.

There were also some 16 sepoys killed and 36 wounded. The Battle of Plassey was over.

It had been an astonishing victory, in its nature, achievement and consequences. The battle had been decided by a number of factors. Clive's choice of ground had been masterful, in that it was to provide an almost impenetrable cover for his small force, not just against well-directed French artillery but – because of the thickness of the trees – against cavalry attack. His worst mistake early on in the fight was nearly to throw this advantage away by exposing his men and cannon on the ground in front during the first fighting; but he had shown the courage and quickness of mind to reverse himself. What the Nawab had needed was a speedy victory, and this was unforthcoming.

Clive had been absolutely correct in his caution in sticking to the hunting lodge and the grove thereafter. When Kilpatrick staged his pursuit, he very nearly caused his men to be cut off and lose the battle. Clive's superb leadership skills and rapid reinforcement held the position. Had the Nawab not demoralised his forces by ordering a retreat and fleeing from the scene of battle, Clive might have been beaten back.

It was not Kilpatrick's reckless attack that caused the Bengalis to withdraw; it was the collapse of confidence within the enemy camp. But the sortie may have had the effect of turning an orderly retreat into a rout; and for this Kilpatrick deserves some credit against the more cautious instincts of Clive – even if the assault could have led to disaster.

Clive's and Watson's scheming was in the end vindicated. Three-quarters of the Nawab's forces – about 38,000 out of the 50,000 present – failed to attack. Mir Jafar and his colleagues certainly behaved treacherously in keeping their options open and waiting to join the winning side; but at least they failed to join the Nawab. Had they done so, Clive would certainly have been overwhelmed.

The rains helped to even the overwhelming superiority of the French-manned guns against the British at a crucial moment. In addition, the Nawab made singularly poor use of his cavalry, which was well trained and bold. In spite of the difficulty of attacking well-entrenched soldiers behind a mudbank in a thick plantation of trees, a major attack on the British position by an overwhelming cavalry force might have stood a chance of success.

Finally, Clive had luck on his side, in the death of two of the enemy's best commanders at an early stage, and in the Nawab's premature decision that, without the support of Mir Jafar, he had to flee to Murshidabad, thus demoralising his forces. Clive had won through good choice of ground, boldness tempered by caution, relentless intriguing, steadiness under fire and, when required, excellent and cool-headed leadership of men in battle. Above all, his courage in ordering the march across the river to a position where the British would have no choice but to fight and the Bengalis, impressed, had none but to oppose him, was a colossal military gamble of the highest order – and one borne out by success.

Almost as soon as the dust had died down, his detractors were at work. Clive, it was said, had opposed the march across the river. This was demonstrably untrue: after the initial hesitation he had changed his mind and ordered the march. Clive had slept through the battle; even if it were remotely in character for this brilliant, nervous man to have done so, this was exposed later as a falsehood spread by a personal enemy, William Belchier, who was not present at the battle.

It was said that the 'skirmish' had been a 'walkover'. The battle had in fact lasted ten hours, from just after dawn to nearly dusk; the British position initially seemed hopeless, and was very nearly lost by Kilpatrick's sortie. It was alleged that the real bravery and leadership had been displayed by Kilpatrick in his attack, which routed the Bengali forces. In fact their withdrawal began before Kilpatrick's attack, and his move in response, while certainly brave, very nearly lost the British advantage by exposing them to a withering counterattack which was only just rescued by Clive's cool command. Certainly, though, Kilpatrick's attack contributed to the panic in the Nawab's camp and to the Nawab's flight.

It was said that Clive had won because of the divisions of his enemies and the Nawab's escape. In fact, Clive had worked tirelessly in the preceding weeks to promote those divisions, and the Nawab's flight was at least partly the direct result of the conspiracy. It was said that, with so few casualties, Plassey was not a real battle. Yet a general who achieves victory at very little cost through cunning and statecraft is surely greater than one who triumphs amidst massive carnage.

Conventional military tactics played little part in Plassey, although Clive was unusually cautious during the battle; but then Clive throughout his career achieved extraordinary results by flouting conventional tactics through his remarkable and almost unerring judgement of acceptable risk. At Plassey he took breathtaking risks. His 3,000 men without cavalry support and only a handful of light field guns put to flight an army fifteen or sixteen times greater, furnished with around 15,000 cavalry and four times as much artillery manned by Europeans and a relatively disciplined native army.

True, Clive had luck on his side: the downpour, the death of the Nawab's generals, and the Nawab's own panic. But Plassey must stand as a triumph of British arms, generalship, statecraft and intelligence second to none, alongside Agincourt, Blenheim and, later, Trafalgar and Waterloo.

The consequences both for the British in India and Clive personally were momentous. The East India Company and Britain had acquired, at a stroke, effective control of the largest and wealthiest part of the subcontinent. Taken together with their superiority in the south, they now held nearly a third of its land area. Only the central belt, divided between the Marathas and the French, the north, controlled by the Nawab of Oudh, and the wild north-west eluded them. Clive had effectively doubled the British area of occupation. The Company was now indisputably the major power in India. The foundations had been laid for a British rule that was to endure for two centuries.

Clive himself was in a position of unparalleled power for any British national in history, before or since. He had a kingdom of 40 million people at his feet, more than six times the subjects of the British monarch. There was no effective control over his personal rule from the civilian authorities in Madras or Calcutta. His rivals – Watson, Coote – although acquitting themselves well in the campaign, had shrunk to insignificance.

The gamble he had taken in crossing the Kasimbazar river had been his, and his alone, supported only by Coote, disavowed by Watson and the Calcutta councillors. Just as he would have had to face the consequences if he had failed and his force been surrounded and defeated, now he took the credit, fully vindicated. He had reached his finest hour, his crowning moment of glory. Drake and Raleigh had achieved extraordinary feats, but had never ruled over an empire. His was larger than those of Cortés or Pizarro.

He was the new Nawab of Bengal – king, emperor and effective dictator rolled into one. In Macaulay's words, 'great provinces [were] dependent on his pleasure, an opulent city afraid of being given up to plunder; wealthy bankers bidding against each other for his smile; vaults piled with gold and jewels thrown open to him alone'. He also now faced ultimate temptation, the possession of absolute power over a country much more populous than Britain, unchecked by the rule of constitutional law.

Yet it would be wrong to say that Clive ruled as a conqueror through force of arms alone. The Emperor of Delhi, the nominal source of authority, had refused to recognise Siraj-ud-Daula as Nawab of Bengal, preferring his cousin, Shaukut Jang. The Nawab's other senior courtiers had turned against him, also making use of the argument that he lacked imperial recognition. Clive from the first ruled through Mir Jafar as the legitimate Nawab; and Clive was not to assume legal responsibility for governing Bengal until he was granted the *diwani* (management of the revenue) in perpetuity by the emperor in 1765. Clive was always scrupulous to observe the legal proprieties, whatever the realities of power might be; and in deposing the Nawab he had a strong case for arguing he was acting with legal sanction in the interests of the Bengalis themselves.

He had been adventurer, soldier, governor of a small province, expeditionary commander. Now he was absolute ruler. Could even his strong, though neurotic, character cope with the awesome temptations of oriental despotism that so often corrupted their wielder, and had turned his immediate predecessor in Bengal into a sadistic, giggling, pleasure-seeking predator against his neighbours' lands? The first signs were not encouraging.

CHAPTER 17

The Nawab's Baubles

E vents now unfolded as in some fairy tale, some fabulous yarn out of the *Arabian Nights* or, to a later generation, a story out of Rudyard Kipling or Rider Haggard. At 5 p.m., with the battle over, Mir Jafar, who had played so ambivalent a role, arrived, seeking to apologise to Clive for not coming to his help because to do so would have been to violate an oath he had given on the Koran to the Nawab. After resting, Clive said he would welcome Mir Jafar and his son Miran.

As the two reached his headquarters, a troop of guards turned out to salute the Bengali general; Mir Jafar was visibly alarmed, fearing they would arrest him. Instead, to his astonishment, Clive came out and embraced the new Nawab of the three provinces of Bengal. To this day, a person who betrays a promise in India is decried as a Mir Jafar. This was unfair: the Bengali commander had served Aliverdi Khan loyally. Only mistreatment had driven Mir Jafar against the Nawab; and the young king had made it clear that, if given the chance, he would have killed his uncle.

They went inside Clive's tent for talks. A tough old soldier with a shrewd, cunning expression and a tidy white beard, Mir Jafar was advised by Clive to take up his throne at Murshidabad at once for fear that the city might degenerate into chaos or Siraj-ud-Daula would yet rally his forces. Watts and Walsh were despatched to ensure that British interests were protected and the treasury was not plundered before Clive got there. When Mir Jafar arrived, he found that the deposed Nawab had indeed been plundering the treasury and trying to raise a new army to fight his opponents.

Mir Jafar cautiously took up residence in his own palace. In the Mansurgans, the enormous and splendid Nawab's palace across the river, Siraj-ud-Daula realised that he could muster little support. He put his favourite wife, Luft un-Nisa, his three-year-old daughter, a loyal eunuch and several of his concubines 'into covered coaches and covered chairs, loaded them with as much gold and as many jewels as they could contain, and taking with him a number of elephants, with his best baggage and furniture he quitted his palace about three in the morning and fled'.

Clive himself moved slowly to Mandipur. He had rested there a couple of days when the Seths informed him that there was a plot to assassinate him as he rode into Murshidabad. At last, on 29 June, the 32-year-old ruler of Bengal, the man who would be emperor, arrived to take up his capital.

The scene of his entry into Murshidabad was at once exotic and dangerous. The city was an immense one, stretching four miles along the riverside and half again as wide, teeming with people, a massive area of impoverished shacks and slums cheek-by-jowl with prosperous merchants' houses and a fabulous central waterfront of palaces and mosques.

Tens of thousands turned out to greet Clive as he passed. He was accompanied by a formidable force of 200 British soldiers, resplendent in their red uniforms, and a disciplined posse of 300 sepoys, as well as two cannon, a band, and streaming colours. He rode impressively towards the front of his retinue, still an astonishingly young man with a gravitas and command well beyond his years, tall, imposing, slightly portly already.

Murshidabad impressed Clive: 'The city of Murshidabad is as extensive, populous and rich as the city of London with this difference, that there are individuals in the first possessing infinitely greater property than any in the last city.' He was taken across by boat to a splendid palace on the opposite bank, close to the Nawab's palace, the Morad-Bagh. He was taking no chances: his large escort camped on the grounds, as much to protect him against surprise attack as to impress.

There, in the spacious coolness of an Indian prince's palace, after a long rest he went to the state quarters to receive the great men of the city. 'Jagat Seth and several of the great men, anxious for their fate, sent their submission, with offers of large presents . . . the Indian millionaires, as well as other men of property, made me the greatest offers (which nevertheless are usual upon such occasions, and what they expected would have been required), and had I accepted these offers I might have been in possession of millions . . . but preferring the reputation of the English nation, the interest of the Nawab and the advantage of the Company to all pecuniary considerations, I refused all offers that were made to me.'

The same afternoon, Clive went to the Nawab's palace, the real ruler of Bengal paying acknowledgement to the nominal one. The teenage Miran, who had allegedly been in on the plot to assassinate Clive, accompanied him. A huge throng of rajahs and other rulers, bearing a dazzling display of swords and jewels, were assembled to greet him in the great hall of the palace.

At the other end was Mir Jafar, gravely standing by the carpet of state, the Masnud, upon which he refused to take his place in submission to Clive. Graciously, Clive led him up to it and bowed in submission to the new Nawab, offering him a few token pieces of gold as tribute. All the other princes then gave him their own offerings.

The real business began the following day: Mir Jafar called on Clive in his palace, and the two of them rode in state to the house of the Seths, the 'bankers to the world'. Clive was informed that the treasury had been found to contain only 140 lakhs (£2.1 million), not enough even to pay the obligations under Mir Jafar's treaty to the British, and only around a tenth of previous estimates. Although much had been plundered by Siraj-ud-Daula, almost certainly there existed a secret strongroom elsewhere in the city to which the new ruler had had much of the money transferred.

After lengthy haggling, it was agreed that the new Nawab should pay half of what he owed the British immediately, two-thirds in bullion and one-third in jewels, plate and gold, and the rest in equal instalments over the next three years. Clive visited the treasury himself to satisfy his curiosity. From this was to derive his most famous remark before an inquiry of the House of Commons: 'When I entered the Nawab's treasury at Murshidabad, with heaps of gold and silver to the right and left, and these crowned with jewels . . . by God . . . at this moment I stand astonished at my own moderation.'

He was led into the large chamber, where fabulous wealth glittered all around him: King Solomon's mines could not have been more resplendent. In addition to his two lakhs under the treaty, Clive was given a personal gift by the new Nawab of 16 lakhs: altogether he took some £230,000 (at today's values, a colossal fortune worthy of an English duke). It was true he could have taken more, and that he turned down the gifts of the Hindu nobility. But by any standards his victory had made him fabulously wealthy.

Within a couple of days, the first half-payment to the British was loaded on to 75 boats, each carrying a lakh (around £15,000). This procession, bearing around £1 million altogether, perhaps the largest shipment of booty in history, set off in a large and colourful regatta of music, drums and flags, and was joined at Hugli by an impressive British naval escort. To those who watched, it must have seemed that the very wealth of Bengal was being taken downriver.

At Calcutta, salutes were fired, balls were held and partying went on into the night in celebration of Clive's victory and the astonishing quantity of plunder. Each member of the council received around £27,000 and each subaltern in the army some £3,000. The navy and army received around £400,000 altogether. There was a near-mutiny in the army at the proposal to give the navy, which had done so little, a share. Clive, always a stickler for military discipline, promptly issued an edict declaring that he had been treated by some of his officers with 'the greatest disrespect and ingratitude', and threatening to withdraw their share of the money. It was one of the greatest treasure hauls in history. Altogether, by the end of his rule, Mir Jafar was to pay the British some £3 million or so, of which five-sixths went directly back to England.

What of Omichand? According to Orme's account of Clive's conversation with the Seths, Scrafton is said to have taken the merchant, who had been standing outside the conference room, aside and told him, 'Omichand, the red paper is a trick; you are to have nothing.' Orme went on, 'These words overpowered him like a blast of sulphur, he sank back fainting, and would have fallen to the ground had not one of his attendants caught him in his arms.' Omichand thereupon 'lapsed into a state of imbecility'.

Clive was later to remark that 'when the real treaty came to be read, the indignation and resentment on that man's countenance bars all description'. According to Macaulay:

Omichand revived; but his mind was irreparably ruined. Clive, who, although little troubled by scruples of conscience in dealing with Indian potentates, was not inhuman, seems to have been touched.

He saw Omichand a few days later, spoke to him kindly, advised him to make a pilgrimage to one of the great temples of India, in the hope that a change of scene might restore his health, and was even disposed, notwithstanding all that had passed, again to employ him in the public service. But, from the moment of that sudden shock, the unhappy man sank gradually into idiocy. He, who had formerly been distinguished by the strength of his understanding and the simplicity of his habits, now squandered the remains of his fortune on childish trinkets, and loved to exhibit himself in rich garments, and hung with precious stones, and then died.

Parts of this account seem to have been untrue. 'Omichand shams sick and swears he has lost faith in man,' Scrafton wrote. Clive even suggested the merchant could be useful again: 'he is a person capable of rendering . . . great services while properly restrained, therefore not to be wholly discarded'. Omichand in fact continued to conspire, and Clive offered to restore his saltpetre contract, but eventually grew sufficiently irritated with him to suggest he go on a pilgrimage to get him out of the way. The merchant died 18 months later, certainly deeply embittered, but not out of his mind.

Clive's revolution now moved inexorably on to devour its next victim. Siraj-ud-Daula had fled for the region of Patna, which was said to be still loyal. After nearly a week of travelling upstream the deposed Nawab's party reached Rajmahal. There, dirty and disguised as peasants, they arrived at the cell of a Moslem fakir, Dana Shah. He took pity on them, and prepared a meal of rice cooked with butter and dhal and shredded onion. The holy man noticed that his chief guest was wearing very rich slippers, and slipped out to question the boatman. When he learned the truth, the holy man, whom the Nawab had either oppressed or, on some accounts, mutilated in the days of his full power, 'rejoiced at this first fair opportunity of glutting his resentment and enjoyed his revenge'.

Meanwhile Jean Law, with his party of itinerant Frenchmen, had reached Rajmahal, where he had secretly learnt of Siraj-ud-Daula's approach and intended to join him and set him up against the British. Tipped off by the fakir, the governor of Rajmahal, Mir Kasim – Mir Jafar's brother-in-law – and Mir Daud, the new Nawab's brother, arrived with a large armed guard and seized Siraj-ud-Daula. Law, hearing what had happened, quickly retreated. Mir

Kasim, a powerful and ruthless personality soon to feature large in the history of Bengal, threatened and bullied Luft un-Nisa to reveal the whereabouts of her treasure, worth tens of thousands of pounds, while Mir Daud helped himself to the pleasures and treasures of the other women.

By 2 July the former Nawab was back in Murshidabad, and paraded mockingly through the streets as crowds jeered and spat on him. 'He was in so wretched a condition, that the people of God, who saw him in that wretchedness, and remembered the delicacy, the glory, and the care and pomp in which he had been bred from his very infancy, forgot at once the ferocity of his temper, and the shameful actions of his life, and gave themselves up to every sentiment of pity and compassion, on beholding him pass by.'

According to Scrafton, Mir Jafar and his son Miran now decided to put him to death immediately lest 'Clive's clemency and moderation should plead for his preservation'. This may have been special pleading; there is no other evidence that Clive sought to intercede. It was Trichinopoly all over again. Mir Jafar entrusted his predecessor to the care of Miran, who at just 17 years old had a personality such that 'pity and compassion answered no other purpose than that of spoiling business', according to Ghulam Husain Khan. He was 'more expeditious and quick-minded in slaughtering people' than his father.

A retainer, Muhammad Beg, stabbed Siraj-ud-Daula viciously to death, and the body was then paraded on the back of an elephant through the streets of the city. Mir Jafar came to Clive next morning to apologise for the murder, saying that the captive was trying to organise an insurrection in the city – something clearly impossible in his wretched and imprisoned state. Clive later disingenuously asserted that the Nawab had been killed by a disgruntled retainer. As with Chanda Sahib at Trichinopoly, Clive's second great opponent had met his death at the hands of his traditional enemies without the English commander's intercession. Ghasita Begum, the former Nawab's hostile aunt, and his mother Amina, were put in a boat, rowed out into the Buriganga river and drowned.

The morality of these events later caused Clive to be dogged by a storm of controversy never experienced by a British commander. It is worth noting, though, that at the time in India they aroused no controversy whatever. Clive's treatment of Omichand has already been touched on: the merchant, who had twice betrayed the British, was bent on doing so a third time out of greed, and was deceived by a trick on his own level – which probably saved hundreds of British lives as well as their interests in India.

Clive's acceptance of his huge prize was seen in contemporary India as simply taking possession of the spoils of war; any Indian conqueror would have done the same, and taken more. Clive's Bengali biographer Chaudhury has a fine passage on the subject:

> With respect to all methods of money-making, fair or foul, England and India stood at opposite poles. To consider corruption alone, there was in England a recognised and accepted form of it – which was to use money to gain or keep political power and position; in India, on the contrary, it lay in using political power for personal monetary gain. Far from being regarded as corruption, monetary gain from personal position was universally regarded in India as the main use of political power. Statecraft had evolved in such a manner that for a long time politics, strictly so-called, had been thought of in terms of wars against other kings or one's own king for the purpose of personal aggrandisement; and administration was the means of making money. To have political power and not to use it for making money was inconceivable in India.

Hence the total incomprehension between the two systems.

Should Clive have abided by a higher European morality? No such standard existed at the time in Britain. To the winner his booty – the recognised principle abroad. The king's commanders – Watson and Coote – saw no reason not to help themselves to their fair share, as did the council in Calcutta.

The directors of the Company in London congratulated him on his good fortune. He formally reported these transactions. They were entirely public and above board. The Indian conspirators, Mir Jafar and Rai Durlabh, his chief minister, helped themselves to their own share of the treasury. Only as the British later began to accept a measure of responsibility for the good government of Bengal – and in this Clive ironically was to be the catalyst – did they begin to show scruples about such behaviour. For the moment, Clive had captured the biggest privateer's hoard in history, and good luck to him.

It is harder to absolve Clive for some degree of responsibility in the murder of the Nawab. Undoubtedly the British commander had the power to stop it, particularly as the wretched parade through the city must have alerted him to what was about to happen. Certainly the ex-king had been responsible for terrible sufferings among his own people and the British at Calcutta. At the same time, Clive answered to British law and, as the effective ruler of Murshidabad, had a responsibility to see it applied to so illustrious a figure, even if the outcome might have been the same.

Instead he made no move to take charge of the prisoner or to make his concerns known. He must have expected the murder, yet did not attempt to stop it. It can be assumed he saw Siraj-ud-Daula, if he had lived, as a possible threat to Mir Jafar, and had few scruples about seeing him done away with. The Nawab had been a particularly cruel and nasty piece of work, and his murder was extremely popular among the British community in Calcutta, who had suffered so much. Clive was an accomplice through his inaction; although his behaviour was entirely understandable, it besmirched a man who showed remarkably little spirit of revenge against his military enemies throughout his career.

Clive's first instinct after his triumph had been, in a characteristic fit of sadness after exertion, to return to Britain – which hardly suggested that his role as the new monarch of Bengal had gone to his head. Within a couple of months, tropical diseases had carried off his two chief lieutenants, Watson and Kilpatrick, before they had the chance to enjoy their new fortunes. Just before he died, Watson learnt that Admiral Byng had been shot for hesitating to fight at Minorca. Watson's surgeon observed: 'He reflected and reasoned much on the uncertain basis on which an officer's character stands, and concluded with observing how much more hazardous it is for him to err on the cautious than the desperate side' – a judgement no doubt influenced by Clive's success. Clive himself fell ill in the aftermath of the great stress and exhaustion of the campaign up the Hugli.

Many of his friends returned home. He wanted to enjoy his new and colossal wealth in England. He aspired to build a new and grand country seat at Styche Hall; his ambition was to get into parliament, this time on the king's side. He was suffering from post-battle depression.

But he shrugged it off more quickly than usual: as the magnitude of his power sunk in, so did a proper perception of his responsibilities. He had won only a battle; he needed now to consolidate victory and place British control of Bengal on a permanent footing. It was threatened on all sides: from the French, by princes along the border, from the outlying rulers of Bengal, by intrigues against Mir Jafar and through the schemes of the new Nawab himself, who had no intention of subordinating himself to the British for longer than absolutely necessary.

Clive's first priority was to deal with the French. He had been incensed by Law's attempts to rescue Siraj-ud-Daula, and advised him to surrender. As Law and his small party set off to escape, Clive sent Coote in hot pursuit. The king's officer embarked on an intensive chase in the heat of the summer of no fewer than 450 miles, before giving up his quarry when Law reached the territory of the powerful Nawab of Oudh. On the way Coote's men were accused of mistreating the women of Rajmahal – a charge he vehemently denied. Clive bitterly – and, it seems, unjustifiably – criticised the failure of Coote's expedition.

On 12 July Margaret Clive and her tiny daughter had reached Calcutta from Madras, along with Jenny Latham. There Clive joined her in late summer, having decided after all to postpone his departure because of the 'superior considerations' of leaving 'this country in peace' and ensuring 'the settlement of the province'.

Clive's first priority was to ensure that Mir Jafar knew in no uncertain terms who was boss. He wrote a series of letters to the princes of India explaining how he had won his wars and given the throne to the new Nawab. He informed the Nawab of the Carnatic, Muhammad Ali, that he had defeated an army of 100,000 men.

Cheekily he himself wrote to the Great Mogul asking him to confer his seal of approval – the *subah* – upon Mir Jafar while the hapless ruler of Bengal was ordered to put up the funds for the necessary bribe to the emperor. This was no mere boastfulness on Clive's part: he had to ensure that all of India knew that the British were paramount in Bengal.

The Mogul Emperor nominally appointed Clive commander of 5,000 horse and 6,000 foot, with the title of Flower of the Empire, Defender of the Country, the Brave First in War – which raised him to the status of the great Indian nobility. While this secured an official seal of approval for British rule, Clive set out to force the peppery Mir Jafar to stick to his treaty obligations and pay his monies on time.

It soon became apparent that while the new Nawab was not so capricious and cruel as his predecessor, he could make himself almost as unpopular by quarrelling with everyone. Heavily influenced by the vicious, psychopathic and increasingly powerful Miran, he began to fall out with his much wiser and more effective chief minister, Rai Durlabh, and then with the Seths and the Hindu merchant aristocracy as well.

High on drink and bhang – a drug made from a hemp-like plant – for most of the day, Mir Jafar also indulged heavily in his harem. Luke Scrafton, whom Clive left behind as his proconsul in Murshidabad, described him as 'a sour old chap and must be sweetened by applications of well-timed presents, though I believe nothing would be so acceptable as some fine liqueurs'. Clive, who saw little enough to be grateful for in Mir Jafar's actions at Plassey, was soon describing him as 'the old fool' and Miran as a 'worthless young dog'.

Clive's problems were hugely exacerbated by the shortage of good men with which to administer his new empire. Scrafton himself, although immensely able, was unscrupulous. He engaged in raising illicit taxes. The Company's servants were paid only modestly, and encouraged to make their fortunes through their own self-aggrandisement; they had no duty to administer good government.

Naturally, this caused intense local resentment. Clive, who believed that British rule would endure only through good government, begged the Company for 'capable young men from the civil service' to be sent out to him, as well as keen professional soldiers. Owing to sickness, a staggering three quarters of the men who had embarked with Clive from Madras were dead a year later.

In November the first crisis in Clive's dominion broke out. The crotchety old man in Murshidabad announced his intention to go into the Indian hinterland to Patna, in order to tame the governor of the border state of Bihar, Ramnarayan, who had been a supporter of Siraj-ud-Daula and was now said to be intriguing with the powerful Nawab of Oudh – and possibly the French – in the next-door state.

Mir Jafar also wanted to make a show of strength in the outlying areas of the country. The Nawab's plan was to murder Ramnarayan and install his own brother-in-law, the feared Mir Kasim, as governor.

Clive instantly resolved that he must send an expedition to accompany the Nawab: it was essential that Mir Jafar remain under British restraint. Moreover, Bengal itself would be threatened if his forces were defeated by the Nawab of Oudh. However, he had no wish to leave Calcutta undefended, as there were reports that the French were again gathering in strength in southern India. A French fleet was also said to be on the way, and Clive was about to lose his naval support, which was returning home. In addition, Kilpatrick and many of the garrison had been struck down by cholera and died.

Clive was forced to march on 17 November. He found Murshidabad in a state bordering on civil war. Rai Durlabh and the Hindu notables had been intriguing against Mir Jafar in the outlying areas of Bengal. The chief minister was allegedly conspiring to oust the old warrior and install a new Nawab; two possible candidates had emerged – and Mir Jafar had retaliated by having one assassinated. The Nawab was himself said to be plotting to murder the chief minister, who stayed behind in the capital, protected by his personal bodyguard, while Mir Jafar travelled to Patna.

Clive skilfully saw his chance to reduce Mir Jafar's power still further by lending his protection to the conspirators, while at the same time continuing to support the Nawab's rule. For the British, a weakened Mir Jafar was the best option of all. From Murshidabad, Clive travelled upriver to join the Nawab at Rajmahal, where he summoned Rai Durlabh to a reconciliation in his tent on 30 December.

Having sorted out the matter, he turned to the question of the Nawab's late payment of the treaty revenues to the British. The Nawab protested that he had no money. Clive proposed that he raise special taxes – tuncas – on four provinces. Under threat of British military intervention, Mir Jafar had no choice but to obey. These taxes were particularly harsh on the peasants and resented by all classes. Mir Jafar now resolved to set off on his expedition to Patna, although Clive urged reconciliation with Ramnarayan.

The British commander appears to have been in much better

health away from the disease-ridden lower Ganges and travelled like the emperor he in effect was in a budgerow, a long barge with a windowed cabin, followed by a colourful retinue of lesser boats. In this leisurely and luxurious fashion, he was sucked much further into the Indian interior than he had ever been before, to the very boundaries of his new empire.

When he arrived, he was unexpectedly struck down with a painful attack of gout. A few miles from Patna, he met the astute and dignified Ramnarayan, and engaged in vigorous horsetrading. Ramnarayan had indeed been engaged in a plot with Rai Durlabh to overthrow the Nawab, and had nearly already attempted to stage a coup. Clive discouraged this, promised him his protection, but equally insisted that the Nawab be reconciled to Ramnarayan.

At last Mir Jafar, fearful of concerted action by all his enemies – the Nawab of Oudh across the border, the Marathas, Ramnarayan and Rai Durlabh – agreed to recognise the government of Patna on 23 February. However, he then stubbornly refused to return to Murshidabad, no doubt hoping to launch an attack on his northern enemy as soon as Clive had departed. Clive saw through his bluff and stayed until April. Eventually Mir Jafar relented, sending back most of his army.

Clive and Rai Durlabh returned together, the English dictator well satisfied. He had frustrated Mir Jafar's attempt to subdue his northern dominion. He had lent his protection to Rai Durlabh, the Nawab's chief rival, and Ramnarayan, governor of his biggest outlying province, so that they owed their survival to Clive.

Mir Jafar in turn was weakened and unable to use his armies against the British. It was as fine and subtle a use of the divide-and-rule principle as any, and showed how natural and consummate an administrator Clive could be. The humiliated Nawab saved face by returning in a magnificent convoy from his futile expedition, bearing tigers and other animals he had caught, entertained by a large company of the most beautiful women in Patna, whom he had carried off on elephants as a consolation prize.

Clive might have been forgiven for complacency after he had put down Mir Jafar's attempt to escape the British yoke. He returned to find the capital in an appalling mess, and dressed down Miran, who had been largely responsible. From there he travelled back to

Calcutta – to hear the astonishing news that the very foundations on which British India had been built were under threat.

On 20 June 1758, he learnt in Calcutta that Fort St David, in whose defence he had played such a part ten long years before, had fallen to the French virtually without a fight. The walls had not been breached, the British fleet had been nearby. Once again, the impotence of British colonial settlements without military leadership of the kind provided by Clive, Lawrence and Coote was exposed. He raged, 'were our enemies supplied with wings to fly into the place? . . . I would wish for the honour and welfare of our nation, that court martial would make the severest example of the guilty in these cases.'

He had immediate and sound advice for Pigot: 'remember all is at stake in India and that necessity has no law'. He suggested that Pigot ravage the countryside so that the French would be unable to find food or money to buy it with. 'Their great want of money is well known, and every method which can be thought of to increase their want of it, must greatly conduce to overset all their offensive schemes: can't a body of Maratha or other horse be taken into pay to burn, ravage and destroy the whole country, in such manner that no revenue can be drawn from thence?' The British, in contrast, could be supplied from Bengal.

The French attack represented a completely new kind of challenge in India. Equipped with a large fleet and a force of some 4,000 European soldiers, they had decided to attack the British and win through what would now be called conventional military tactics. The Comte de Lally, one of the foremost military commanders schooled in the new tactics, was their commander. He was a fine soldier, with no experience of India, unlike Dupleix or de Bussy, and all the contempt of a professional soldier for the French settlers in India.

Triumphant at Fort St David, Lally's force now marched on Madras itself: its only setback was that the French fleet, under Admiral d'Ache, had fought two indecisive naval engagements with Admiral Pocock's ships, and then decided to withdraw from the coast of India. As Clive had predicted, Lally was short of money and set off on a series of expeditions to bully local rulers into paying for his army. Lally got as far as Tanjore, and was forced to pull back without a fight or a siege of the city because of the state of his men.

In his own words, his troops were without 'victuals, money or munitions, barefoot and half-naked, worn out with fatigue and in despair at having engaged in so wild an adventure'. He returned to lay siege to Madras again; but as there was no French fleet to blockade it, it could be supplied from the sea. In June he ordered de Bussy, so long the ruler by proxy of the Deccan, to his side. Once again, the British conquests in India seemed precarious – at the mercy of the largest and most formidable European army ever seen on the continent.

Word of the French successes soon reached Mir Jafar, who silently began to conspire against the British and his domestic enemies. Rai Durlabh found his position increasingly precarious: he attempted to flee to Calcutta, but his palace was surrounded by Miran's supporters, intent on murdering the chief minister, until Scrafton came to his rescue with a British contingent. Under British protection, Rai Durlabh and his family fled to Calcutta.

Clive, always quick to react to a change in circumstances, became supplicant again to the Nawab, inviting him to Calcutta on a formal visit, which turned into a mixture of carnival and orgy. As Scrafton lamented afterwards, 'Thank God his excellency has at last gone. He has led me a hell of a life here by the constant attendance I have been obliged to pay to him and his wenches, for he never went twenty yards from his house but they were with him.' The Nawab was presented with, among other copious gifts, 'twelve standing venusses to pull off behind; one lying ditto'. Mir Jafar may have felt that at last the British hold on Bengal was weakening.

In fact, Clive as usual was far from idle. With his genius for sniffing out the weakness of his opponents, and his propensity to gamble, he had hit on the most efficient way of striking back at the French in southern India. He decided to send his ablest officer, Lieutenant-Colonel Francis Forde, to take charge of an expedition to wrest control of de Bussy's mini-empire now that its leader had at last been forced to leave by Lally, along with most of the French forces there.

Forde was an extrovert, loud personality, and a natural leader of men, to whom Clive had immediately taken a shine. On the first anniversary of Plassey, he had held a wild party at Kasimbazar with dancing girls provided for his officers. As one witness recounts,

' "By God this is mine, I know her by the ring in her nose," shouted one officer, but when he went to call his servant to take her to his room, one of his comrades whips the ring out of her nose, and carries her off before his face.' Forde, however, was forced to entertain the formidable Mrs Warren Hastings at the party, and while doing so, sadly, 'the Adjutant had the assurance to carry off the lady he had fixed to sing him to sleep after the fatigues of the day'.

This soldier's soldier was despatched in September 1758, with 500 of Clive's best European troops and 2,000 sepoys, to go to the help of the local rajah who had grabbed hold of Vizagapatnam from the departing French forces. Clive's action deeply alarmed the burghers of Calcutta, who saw their garrison reduced by two-thirds at a time when Mir Jafar and Miran were showing signs of increasing cockiness. It was another apparently reckless decision.

But Clive accurately understood that Mir Jafar's bark was worse than his bite, and that if the French advances went unchecked, the British position in Bengal would be endangered much more than by a temporary withdrawal of forces. Local princes began to conclude that the British were, after all, a paper tiger. Forde's expedition was delayed by storms, and did not reach Vizagapatnam until after late October.

After a month in which Forde established himself, trying to control restless and ill-paid troops, he met a French force under de Bussy's deputy, Conflans, at the Battle of Condore, and inflicted a decisive defeat. After nearly ten years, the private French kingdom of the Deccan was under threat. Winning a series of further clashes, Forde captured the main French garrison at Masulipatam four months later. French reinforcements did not arrive, but fled to Ganjam.

Salabat Jang, so long the French puppet ruler in the Northern Circars, assembled a large army against Forde, but entered into negotiations with him when the British threatened to install his brother on the throne. Eventually he agreed to help the British drive the French out. Forde's expedition had been a complete, though hard-fought, success.

Meanwhile the leaden-footed Lally was laying siege to Madras, while de Bussy fumed not just at his decision to abandon the

Deccan, but at his ham-handed tactics. De Bussy was regarded by Lally as intrinsically corrupt and gone native; whereas the former, for all his love of ostentation and vainglory, was by far the most skilful and adept servant of the French in India, outstripping even Dupleix, who was less realistic.

De Bussy advocated alliances with the local nawabs centred on the remaining French influence at the court of Hyderabad. He was an intriguer by nature. 'Among a people as doublefaced as are those with whom we have to deal, to show only straightforwardness and probity is, to my thinking, only to be their dupe, and we shall inevitably be that if we do not conform to the usages of the country.' He was probably right, but Lally replied brusquely, 'The King and the Company have sent me to India to chase the English Company out of it . . . It does not concern me that such and such rajahs dispute for such and such a nawabship.'

Lally's large army marched on Madras, taking one small settlement after another and consuming their supplies. On 14 December the French attacked the city itself, entering the 'black town' and laying waste to much of it. The French cannon now laid siege to Fort St George, doing immense damage to it, and opening a large breach.

The British forces, headed by Pigot and Stringer Lawrence, fought back with ferocity. The fort continued to be well supplied from the sea. Lally's forces were large and well disciplined, but the British resistance was equally formidable. At last, on 16 February, Pocock's fleet reappeared, and the French realised the fight was over as they came within the range of British naval guns.

The capture of Fort St David had not been followed by a further triumph in Fort St George. Although the pride of the British in southern India had been savaged for the second time in a decade, Madras had held out. The ghastly fiasco of the fall of Madras, which had launched Clive's military career, had not been repeated.

Clive wrote with relief, warmth and admiration to one of his younger protégés in Madras, Henry Vansittart, 'I would gladly have given some of my riches to have shared some of your reputation. I know it has been a conceived opinion among the old soldiers in England that our exploits in India have been much of the same nature as those of Hernando Cortés; but your foiling such a man as M. Lally, and two of the oldest regiments in France, will induce another way of thinking.'

Clive's old friend, Orme, who fled Madras before it came under siege, came under suspicion of cowardice, and was to return to Britain a relatively poor man. The French failure to capture Madras represented the end of their last really major push in India. Huge forces had been committed, exceeding those available to Dupleix; and under Lally's less subtle hand they had failed. It was a turning point.

Clive had not been directly involved. His own achievement in Bengal had now been matched by two other spectacular feats of British arms – Forde's in the Carnatic and Northern Circars and Lawrence's in Madras. The British ascendancy was no longer so dependent on one man. Meanwhile Clive's gamble in despoiling Calcutta of most of its forces had paid off: the Nawab had made no move, although Clive had been careful to take no major initiative in Bengal.

Instead, the longstanding threat to British rule in Bengal, an attack by de Bussy from the Northern Circars, had been removed. Forde's expedition had been a masterstroke. Forde himself had taken over de Bussy's mantle at Masulipatam, peering over the shoulder of Salabat Jang. In effect, a large slice of India had been seized from the French and appended to British rule.

While the British appeared to be on the run in southern India, this achievement did not appear to be especially impressive. But, after the lifting of the siege of Madras, the French were in retreat. Lally's army was openly mutinous, owing to the lack of pay and supplies after the departure of the French fleet.

The latter, deprived of its usual source of supplies from Chandernagore, had had to sail as far as South Africa to stock up. When it returned in September 1759, the British fleet attacked; Admiral d'Ache was wounded and half his ships destroyed. He limped to Pondicherry, deposited the stores and money he had picked up, and departed at speed, so as not to be caught by the British ships again. Lally was furious; in fact, unknown to d'Ache, the British ships had suffered such serious damage to their masts that they could not have taken on the French again. The endgame for the French was now in sight.

Forde confidently expected to be appointed commander-in-chief of British forces in Bengal after his successes, on Clive's recommendation. In 1759, to the fury of both men, the directors in London, disapproving Forde's original appointment, made Eyre Coote commander of the Company's forces in Bengal. Clive had always loathed Coote. 'I tremble when I think of the fatal consequences of such a man as Coote commanding here. For God's sake keep him on the coast, where he can only get a little drubbing, but here he may ruin the Company's affairs for ever.' Forde, in a blind fury, immediately resolved to return to England by way of Bengal.

Coote indeed seems to have had a talent for upsetting people. But his military abilities were not in doubt. In January 1760, he won a tremendous victory against the French at the Battle of Wandewash, in which Lally was wounded and de Bussy taken prisoner. A year later, Coote finally mopped up the last major enclave of the French in India by capturing Pondicherry, nearly twenty years after Dupleix had become its governor and had set about the seemingly impossible and mad dream of creating the first European empire in India. Four years later, 'the city was like another Jerusalem, razed to the ground, its walls overthrown, its houses destroyed and its inhabitants led to captivity'. French power was eliminated from India for ever, the last French stronghold captured, and the baton had passed to the English.

With two-thirds of the garrison at Calcutta absent, Mir Jafar was growing more troublesome, and a new danger suddenly materialised. Indeed, Clive, ever since he had become effective Nawab of Bengal, had faced a fresh challenge whenever one was fended off. This was nothing new. Siraj-ud-Daula had also had to deal with repeated threats while establishing his ascendancy.

The latest came from no less than the occupant of the nominal throne of India, the Mogul Emperor in Delhi – or rather his son. Accurately diagnosing the depletion of British forces in Bengal, and overestimating the size of the threat the French posed to their interests, the heir to the Mogul throne, the Shahzada, had cast his eyes eastwards towards Bengal. A tough fighter and a far-sighted young man, he was determined not to become a puppet like his father, Alamgir, and had fled Delhi when the vizier, Ghazi-ud-Din, had seized power.

The Shahzada was no decadent like Siraj-ud-Daula or Miran; moreover, he possessed the immense mystical prestige of the imperial court. Loathing Mir Jafar, the Seths decided to conspire with the Shahzada. It has subsequently been argued that they were doing no more than currying favour with the emperor's heir. Yet the evidence suggests that they, representing the Hindu upper classes, saw the Shahzada as a replacement for the Nawab.

The Seths left on a pilgrimage with a force of some 3,000 soldiers and four pieces of artillery to protect them from attack by the deeply suspicious Mir Jafar. In the north, Ramnarayan, Governor of Bihar and the Nawab's old enemy, was said to be considering supporting the Shahzada, presumably as a way of deposing the Nawab. But instead he sent an urgent appeal both to Clive and to Mir Jafar for help as the Shahzada's army approached.

Mir Jafar and Miran also appealed to Clive frantically. Their recent cockiness had evaporated: they were terrified of the combination of the Governor of Bihar, the Seths and, possibly, the Mogul Emperor's heir. The Shahzada's army consisted of nearly 10,000 Rohillas – the formidable Afghan fighters with their own kingdom in northern India and a reputation even more fearsome than the Marathas – as well as some 400 mercenaries under the command of the ever peripatetic Jean Law, and an Indian army of 30,000 men. The Shahzada wrote to Clive in tones of imperial hauteur, telling the British to obey him 'like a faithful servant'.

Clive's reply was blunt. 'I am under the strictest engagements with the present Nawab of these provinces to assist him at all times; and it is not the custom of the English nation to be guilty of insincerity.' Clive told Mir Jafar: 'It is the custom of the English to treat the persons of ambassadors as sacred, and I told the Shahzada's agents as much; but at the same time warned them never to come near me again, for, if they did, I would take their heads for their pains.'

Within days he had set off with what was left of the garrison in Calcutta – around 450 men – leaving it defenceless. The council was frantic. Once again the Bengali empire seemed threatened, with Clive at the head of a tiny force and Calcutta wholly unprotected should Mir Jafar and Miran suddenly turn on it.

When Clive arrived at Kasimbazar, the British base outside Murshidabad, he found Mir Jafar yet again presiding over a shambles of plots and counter-plots. The Nawab had also run out of money to pay the British or his own troops. Omar Beg, now his chief minister after Rai Durlabh's removal, a man trusted by both sides, joined Clive and the Nawab on an elephant for lengthy discussions. Immediately afterwards, Clive set off for Patna with a large force commanded by Miran; wisely, for once, Mir Jafar had decided to stay at home to hold the capital while his scheming son was out of harm's way.

As Clive and Miran travelled north at great speed, the urgency of the crisis became apparent. Ramnarayan was said to have visited the Shahzada's camp to make his peace; the latter had meanwhile crossed the Karamnassa river from Oudh into Bihar. Clive, who had backed Ramnarayan in the past against Mir Jafar, was incensed: 'What power has the Shahzada to resist the united forces of the Nawab and the English? Think then, what will be your fate,' he told Ramnarayan by messenger.

Once again Clive mercilessly pushed his forces forwards to the very limits of their endurance: they covered some 400 miles in just three weeks. As they approached Patna, he learned that Ramnarayan was after all preparing to fight the Shahzada. The governor had been apparently prevaricating only because there was no sign of reinforcement.

With Clive approaching, Ramnarayan escaped from the Shahzada's camp, sent him an offensive letter and provoked an attack. Heavy casualties were inflicted on Ramnarayan's forces, although the besieging army was kept outside the walled city. When the Shahzada heard of Clive's approach – he was still ten miles away from the city – the siege was lifted and his army retreated.

Clive went in hot pursuit, and the Shahzada's men were soon wholly dispersed, the young heir crossing back over the river with just 300 men and asking the British commander for his protection. Clive replied with contempt and warned the Nawab of Oudh, who had backed him but cunningly refrained from direct intervention, that he would fight him after the monsoon if he tried anything.

Two of the rajahs in the hill country of Boadgerore, who had sided with the Shahzada, promptly made their peace. Uncharacteristically, Clive went in pursuit of the third, the rajah of Pulwansing, deep in rocky and wooded hills. In intense heat he methodically laid waste to the country, destroying some 300 villages and the main town of Nookah before the rajah made his peace. It was a remarkable act of savagery by Clive, prompted by a legitimate desire to secure Bengal's borders, but more reminiscent of his Indian and British opponents than the normally clement commander.

His savagery suggests that his always fragile psychological façade had cracked at last, perhaps under the pressure of the march, perhaps under that of his over-extended position – at the head of a small force, surrounded by treachery on all sides, his capital of Calcutta far away and undefended. It was to be the blackest mark against Clive's humanity. Clive returned in cruel triumph to Murshidabad at the end of June. He had arrived at his heart of darkness at last.

CHAPTER 18

Emperor of Bengal

Patna was not to be the farthest he was to travel into the subcontinent, but Clive now seemed corrupted beyond repair by power. In the past eighteen months he had followed up his triumph at Plassey with the seizure of a colossal portion of Bengal's wealth, much of it for himself; with a series of brilliant manoeuvres aimed at reducing the power of the new Nawab and keeping him dependent on British goodwill; and with a masterful tactical stroke against the French, followed by a frenzied campaign in northern India that had ended in an orgy of destruction entirely untypical of the man.

He was all-powerful, his tactical genius overwhelming. Indian princes quailed before him. He was carried everywhere in palanquins, on elephants, by magnificent barges, enjoying the best house in Calcutta. There was no Englishman on the continent to challenge his authority. Having cowed Bihar and repulsed the very Emperor of India's scion, he was returning to the ever-treacherous Mir Jafar, whom he had protected, to exact his reward. The ruler of Bengal was deeply in his debt. But for the Englishman, the country might have been invaded by the army of the Shahzada and the Nawab's throne in Murshidabad toppled by the conspirators around him.

Some credit for the defeat of the Shahzada must go to Ramnarayan – although his sudden escape from the imperial camp probably owed much to his guess that Clive would scatter all before him. But for Clive's approach, Ramnarayan might well have made his peace with the Shahzada. Only the ferocity and speed of the British advance changed his mind and persuaded him to give serious resistance to the invader.

But Clive was now confirmed as the all-powerful 'Invincible', a man whose very presence could put his enemies to flight. Mir Jafar, always scheming and yearning to throw off the British yoke, must have viewed the proconsul's return with deep apprehension. In fact Clive thought the Nawab might have to be replaced in the fullness of time – but not immediately – in order to prevent any attempt at the succession by the cruel and scheming Miran.

Meanwhile, Mir Jafar was what Clive wanted: an extremely weak Nawab, beset by enemies. Now, high on challenge, sated by power, apparently omnipotent and feared by all, Clive was to commit the single most controversial and indefensible act of his career.

Clive had already asked for the customary payment for his imperial rank, a jagir – the tax take of a particular area – from the Seths as early as January 1759. As the Englishman's honour from the Mogul Emperor was an entirely honorary one, Clive was pressing his hand a little far – particularly in view of the immense payments to him after Plassey.

Mir Jafar parried by saying he would grant Clive the revenues from an area of Orissa then under threat of external invasion and impossible to extract taxes from – unless Clive in person was prepared to do so. In June, however, the Seths went to him to tell him the Nawab was now willing to award him the jagir from land in Bengal.

When Clive returned to Murshidabad after the Patna expedition, Mir Jafar turned out to meet him in all his splendour, with a full retinue and accompanied by the Jagat Seth – who, it will be remembered, was believed to have been conspiring with the Shahzada and must certainly have had a hand in the return of Ramnarayan to the Bengali fold, earning Mir Jafar's gratitude. The Jagat Seth bore a silk bag containing a document.

Clive did not open it – presumably because he knew the contents, although the aim was to demonstrate his public indifference towards this offering. It was a gift 'unasked, or indeed unthought of' – an annual income of 300,000 rupees, befitting his imperial rank, around £27,000 a year, which would give him an income to equal that of the largest magnates in England. But – the gift was nothing other than the rent the East India Company paid to the Nawab for its lands around Calcutta. As the rent had already been stopped because of the Nawab's slow payment of monies due under the treaty before Plassey, it barely affected him.

It was, in fact, a poisoned chalice. The Company's landlord would now be its own employee: Clive, its servant, would receive its rent.

Moreover, as would not have been the case if Clive had been awarded a jagir from Bengali-controlled lands, Clive could be certain of being paid – both under English law and honour. Perhaps this was its attraction for him. It was an entirely reliable source of income.

Whether the idea was a fantastically misconceived one of Clive's in the first place, or whether, unusually, he had been taken in by his adversaries, he proved staggeringly inept and ill-judged in accepting the jagir rather than pressing for a major payment directly from the treasury at Murshidabad. Greed – the lure of a truly colossal income on top of his already staggering capital gains in Bengal – had got the better of him. For him to become collector of rents from the East India Company showed an astounding lack of judgement, and one which was to haunt him and destroy his political career in England.

Clive was later to defend himself on the grounds that he made a full report to the East India Company at the time; and the directors had approved. But they had no choice in view of Clive's virtuous defence of their interests in Bengal. Others, such as Dupleix, had received jagirs, or at least been promised them.

But this was no defence: Clive was laying claim to his own Company's monies – which at the time were not being paid, for good reason, to the Nawab – but would have to be paid to Clive under English law. That he failed to foresee the intense fury that his decision to award himself a payment from his own employers would arouse in Britain shows that he was losing his grip on reality after two and a half years as dictator of Bengal. The seeds of his political failure in Britain were being sown.

Moreover, Clive was clearly being excessive in seeking an income which would virtually double the one he could expect from his existing capital. He could not possibly argue that his achievement in driving off the Shahzada justified it. From a 'colonial' point of view, there could be less objection; as a result of the Seths and Mir Jafar's contrivance, the money was to come from London, not Bengal. But for Clive not to see through the ruse or, as one must suppose, to welcome the fact that the income was cast-iron precisely because it would have to be paid by the East India Company exposed a giant hole at the heart of his previously robustly healthy commonsense.

To a man whose word was god, at whose approach armies fled,

who was courted by every nobleman and deferred to by his British peers, who was high on the intoxication and corruption of absolute power, it seemed defensible. Yet it was not to appear so to anyone else. For the first time in his career, Clive had been outwitted by his Indian opponents.

On his return to Calcutta in July 1759, Clive found that Mir Jafar and Miran had duped him on another score – compelling him once again to respond to a sudden crisis. This time the problem lay with the smallest of the foreign communities – the Dutch, whom Clive had been relentlessly squeezing out. The saltpetre monopoly had already been taken away from them and given to the British. The latter also now had the right to search Dutch ships passing up the Hugli.

Vernet, head of the Dutch factory at Kasimbazar, had approached first Miran, then the Nawab, to prepare a strategy of resistance to the British. Mir Jafar readily agreed, indicating he was ready to abandon them. Thus encouraged, the Dutch sent a large force from Batavia, their headquarters in the Dutch East Indies; they knew the British strength at Calcutta had been reduced to one-third owing to the despatch of Forde's force to the Northern Circars. The British agent in Batavia advised the council in Calcutta of the despatch of the Dutch ships.

Forde himself had arrived in Bengal in a fury after Coote was preferred as British commander, and agreed to work with Clive against the Dutch. According to reports reaching Calcutta, the Dutch force was around twice the size of the English army of some 500. Clive advised the Nawab to punish the Dutch for exceeding their powers in Bengal, and sent troops downstream from Calcutta to search boats coming upriver.

The Nawab, meanwhile, had been invited to another massive jamboree in Calcutta, including bands, a theatre performance and a shower of gifts. But the Dutch had by now reached Fulta. Mir Jafar promised the British he would threaten the Dutch ships.

Instead, when he returned, he spoke to the Dutch 'very graciously' – although he did not offer them help against the British. He was playing his old double game, as at Plassey, of waiting to see which side would prevail. The Dutch themselves hesitated, wondering if they could succeed without the Nawab's open support.

Adrian Bisdom, head of the Chinsurah command, argued for restraint; Vernet for war.

Clive showed no such hesitation. Three ships were sent downriver while guns were positioned along the shore and a company of sepoys was moved up to Chinsurah. On 7 November, with Bisdom struck down by illness, Vernet acted, threatening retaliation if Dutch ships continued to be searched (one had been found to contain troops). Clive replied tongue-in-cheek that he was acting under the Nawab's orders, but that he would use 'his friendly offices' to mitigate the former's temper.

Angrily, the Dutch burnt down East India Company houses near Fulta and searched seven English vessels, tearing down their colours. Clive, who had been careful about taking aggressive action against ships from a country with which Britain was not at war, now had his pretext for acting. He at least was not guilty of firing the first shot. He ordered the British ships to outflank the Dutch, trapping them in the river. The Dutch threatened to open fire but did not do so.

On the night of 21 November the Dutch, who lacked pilots to navigate further upriver, landed 700 European and 800 Malay troops downstream from Calcutta. When Forde informed Clive, the British commander was said to have been playing cards, and sent him the laconic note, 'Dear Forde, fight 'em immediately, I will send an order of council tomorrow.'

Three small British ships now moved forward to intercept the Dutch squadron of seven men-of-war: within two hours of furious fighting and brilliant British manoeuvring, six were captured or sunk, and the seventh was seized shortly afterwards. The Dutch troops were now cut off on land. An attempt was made by the Dutch in Chinsurah to send a force to rendezvous with the main expedition; this was intercepted on 24 November by Forde and routed. The following day, with 370 Europeans and 800 sepoys, he encircled the much larger, but by now demoralised and apprehensive Dutch force on the plains of Badara, near the river, and, in just half an hour of 'short, bloody and decisive action', the Dutch were defeated and surrendered for the loss of no more than 10 British dead, against 320 of the enemy.

The council in Chinsurah was in consternation. Miran had suddenly appeared with a large army and, instead of attacking the British, as arranged, was threatening to sack the Dutch garrison.

Clive turned up in person to warn the psychopathic youth off. The Dutch surrendered, paying the British a ransom of ten lakhs, and agreeing not to strengthen the garrison.

A merchant viewed as 'the prime instigator of these troubles', Khwaja Wajid, was arrested and a few days later died of a fever. Some alleged he was murdered by the British, but this seems highly improbable. They were not vengeful, and permitted the settlement to continue. The British triumph was now complete: the last major European presence in Bengal had been humbled beyond recovery, the French expelled from India.

Clive now faced a more formidable enemy: his own masters in Britain. Seen from at least six months' travelling and 5,000 miles away, news in India came back as though through the wrong end of a telescope. Both the directors and public opinion in England had been appalled by the news of the fall of Calcutta – which reached them fully a year after the event.

Just a month later the good news came of its recapture. The man who had brought them up to date with events was Josiah Holwell, the self-important and energetic little magistrate who had survived the Black Hole and had styled himself the sole hero of the darkest days of the siege of Calcutta. With eminent political sense he had immediately travelled to England to give his version of events and to insist that he be made governor of Fort William.

Even the directors saw through his unsuitability for the post, and instead decided to appoint a rotating chairmanship, changing every three months, which would include Holwell, as well as the mediocre Becker, the cowardly Manningham and the heroic Watts. The wretched and ludicrous Drake was at last to be dispensed with – although in fact Clive had long been de facto Governor of Calcutta and the whole of Bengal. The directors had not yet learnt of the success at Plassey.

When news of the new leadership reached Clive on 20 June, he was incensed; his name was not even mentioned, the directors assuming he had returned to Madras (although Holwell, at least, must have known he would stay on). The three local rotating governors promptly handed their mandate on to Clive, which he accepted, although he remained furious with his superiors. The first really bad blood had been sown between them.

Clive's authority now grew increasingly absolute: the deaths of Watson and Kilpatrick had been followed by the departure from India of Watts early in 1759 and Scrafton from Murshidabad the following August. Warren Hastings, then aged just 25, another protégé of Clive's, was appointed to the post of resident at the palace – Clive's man at the Nawab's court.

Clive showed no hesitation in advising the young man: 'It is a nature of these people though to do nothing through inclination, a few sepoys or chokeys now and then will greatly expedite the payment . . . [avoid] extremities and [show] as much spirit and resolution as will convince [the Nawab] that we will always have it in our power to make ourselves respected. [Because of British weakness] instil into the Nawab high notions of the great force which is coming out . . . assure him Pondicherry will soon be in our possession.'

He added, in an unconscious echo of Macaulay's later strictures that was entirely at variance with his past actions, 'I would leave all trickery to the Hindus and Muslims to whom it is natural, being well convinced that the reputation we have in this country is owing among other causes to the ingenuity and plain dealing for which we are distinguished.'

Hastings seems to have accepted his directions, although he thought Clive was a poor judge of character in admiring the qualities of Nundcomar, now appointed tax collector for the British of a large region. The young resident intensely distrusted the brahmin. Scrafton had written, 'It is really amazing to see how Nundcomar dupes the colonel.' Hastings labelled Nundcomar 'the Necromancer'. It was an uncharacteristic error of Clive's judgement that was to haunt the British in India, and Hastings in particular. Hastings himself, however, was to make a fortune at Murshidabad trading in salt, opium, tobacco, timber and boat-building.

When news of Plassey finally filtered across, the directors in London awarded Clive the post of governor. His family lavished praise on him – his father exclaimed, 'may heaven preserve you safe to Old England, where not only your friends and relations but strangers who never saw you will congratulate you for the glorious actions you have done for your country. With what joy shall I embrace you! Oh, may I live to see that day! Your mother and sisters are sitting with me round the fire, drinking to your health a safe voyage.'

His five-year-old son Ned drank his health every day. His other relatives were persuaded that they would be spared the need to travel to India because their fortunes had already been made. Clive promised his cousin an eastern prince. She replied, 'I have a taste to be a princess. Pray, is he a black in the Othello taste and I to be his Desdemona?' There seems little doubt that Clive's success had struck a genuine chord among ordinary people and the gentry. 'Every person is your friend,' remarked Clive's cousin, the judge.

George II was reported to have said to a young nobleman, 'If he wants to learn the art of war, let him go to Clive.' William Pitt, secretary for war and foreign affairs, and England's greatest statesman at the time, elevated Clive to new oratorical heights in the House of Commons, particularly after a succession of setbacks for Britain in other parts of the world.

'We had lost our glory, honour and reputation everywhere, but in India. There the country had a heaven-born general who had never learned the art of war, nor was his name enrolled among the great officers who had for many years received their country's pay. Yet he was not afraid to attack a numerous army with a handful of men, and overcame them . . . Everyone knows that I mean Colonel Clive.' He went on to compare him with Alexander the Great. This was the highest possible accolade from a government of the time. If Clive had been in England, he would have basked in popularity and glory and perhaps been elevated to the House of Lords.

But, out of public spirit, Clive had remained in India to consolidate his success instead of returning home to capitalise upon it. It was a fatal decision. Even at this stage his enemies in England were beginning to gather. John Pym, chairman of the East India Company, proposed no reward and actively dissuaded the prime minister, the Duke of Newcastle, from giving him an honour. The directors were alarmed by his successes, jealous of his popular appeal, and determined not to let him become a rival to their constitutional authority: the example of the American colonists was before them. Clive had to be kept in his place.

As the months of his rule in Bengal passed by, the directors affected to grow alarmed by what they saw. True, Clive had secured a massive new province for the Company. But instead of revenues, bills came flooding in: the expeditions to Patna were paid by Mir

Jafar, but Forde's expeditions to the Northern Circars had been expensive, and so had the cost of local troops employed throughout the campaigns. Meanwhile the merchants of Calcutta continued to borrow money at extraordinary rates from Bengal, issuing promissory notes – 'drafts' – in abundance. The directors in London became increasingly concerned and wrote to Calcutta.

Holwell, now Clive's deputy, drafted a rude reply: 'The diction of your letter is most unworthy of ourselves and us in whatever relation considered, either as masters to servants or gentlemen to gentlemen . . . Groundless information have without further scrutiny borne with you the stamp of truth.' Clive signed the letter: it was evident that after the directors' decision to appoint Coote as commander of the Company's forces in Bengal he now regarded them with contempt.

Part of this was *folie de grandeur* – the visible corruption of Clive after two years as conqueror and emperor of Bengal. Yet Clive understood that Britain's power in India depended upon territorial acquisition. If this proved expensive in the short term, so be it: large revenues would accrue in the long term. The directors instead were concerned with the immediate cash flow.

In Bengal, Clive's word was law; he was looked upon with awe and fear by the native population, and with uncritical respect by the cowed and subdued council. He had no time for those men seeking to make money out of his exertions from the comfort of their offices in London. His ambitions were altogether greater: to establish the foundations of an empire that would belong not to the East India Company but the Crown itself. In this he was ahead of his time, and was to be found guilty of unpardonable treason by the East India Company.

He wrote to the Company shortly before he left, 'a glorious opportunity now presents itself of making us considerable indeed in India and perhaps of giving a King to Hindostan'. To Pitt, his admirer, one of the most powerful men in England, he wrote advocating the incorporation of Bengal under the Crown: 'I leave you to judge whether an income of upwards of two millions sterling, with the possession of three provinces abounding in the most valuable productions of nature and of art be an object deserving the public attention . . . an acquisition which, under the management of so able and disinterested a Minister, would prove a source of immense wealth to the kingdom and might in time be appropriate in part as a fund towards diminishing the heavy load of debt under which we at present labour . . . this project may be brought about without draining the mother country, as has been too much the case with our possessions in America.'

He undoubtedly saw this as a stepping stone towards the establishment of a unified British empire in India of which he would be Governor-General – an idea already discussed in letters to his father. To Pitt, Clive's ideas may have had some attraction, both on the revenue side and in offsetting the disastrous losses elsewhere in America and Europe. However, the state had limited resources. Preventing the loss of the American colonies had priority, as had the struggles against the French in Canada and North America.

Clive's ideas were to be shelved, but not before the directors of the East India Company had heard of their nominal servant's intention to bypass their authority in the Crown's favour. The directors admired, distrusted and feared Clive all at the same time. Their chief ambition was now to contain him, to cut him down to size. A new and formidable chairman was appointed to head them: Laurence Sulivan.

Of Irish origins, a successful trader in Bombay, Sulivan spent six years in England as a director of the Company before being elected chairman in 1758. He was what today would be called a 'company man', more concerned with the interests of his organisation even than with his own. He was fussy, methodical and puritanical (although he claims to have led a wild life in his youth). As he wrote to his son: 'I call upon my son in the space of twenty-five years if he remembers me ten times in a tavern, eight times in a coffee house, rarely ever from my family.'

He was devious, vicious, implacable towards his foes, a good judge of character, an autocrat who controlled the Company through his friends even when he was not its chairman, and relentlessly devoted to its interests. He was an early example of the authoritarian corporate bureaucrat, skilful at managing his company and at maintaining his authority within it. Dame Lucy Sutherland, chronicler of the East India Company, wrote that he was 'one of the greatest of the company's rulers, fertile and expedient, quick to recognise merit'.

A contemporary view is less kind: Richard Atkinson wrote that he had 'great experience and some talents, great cunning, will go through thick and thin with his party while he remains attached to it, but not to be trusted for a moment when his own views lead him to be faithless'. He was devoted to his wife, to whose judgement he deferred.

He was the polar opposite of Clive, who was generous, boastful, adventurous, brave, larger than life, direct, an outdoor figure who despised the directors in their chairs in London, loved to indulge in the pleasures of life, and was none too shy of leaving his wife for months at a time. Their only common points were tactical cunning, a penchant for unremitting hard work, a furious and vindictive temper, and a tendency to be petty. Sulivan's sensitivity was that of the pedagogue; Clive's that of the creator, the artist.

Sulivan was to become perhaps the most effective and implacable enemy Clive had ever faced, with the bureaucratic skills and intelligence to match him. In place of the bravery of Chanda Sahib and the cunning of Siraj-ud-Daula, Clive now had an opponent much more like his old foe, Dupleix – clever, devious and ruthless, and also possessed of the formidable power of the Company.

Clive was deeply concerned as he realised in 1759 the extent of the opposition to him within the Company. As ruler of his empire, he could afford to treat his fussy superiors, at six months' minimum sailing distance, with contempt; but in London, their power would be far greater. For its part the Company was deeply apprehensive that Clive would seek to bypass its authority or even destroy it.

The scene was set for Clive's next battle, to be waged by word, pen and slanders, not swords, guns and manoeuvres in the night. To his roles as soldier, diplomat and administrator was now to be added that of businessman – in an environment every bit as hostile as that which he had first encountered in Bengal.

CHAPTER 19

The First Couple

E xactly why Clive decided to return from Bengal after two and a half years as its absolute ruler cannot be known for sure. His depression and the concern that matters were getting out of hand among the directors certainly contributed. Sulivan's general letter of March 1759 had furiously censured Clive's administration. He may also have felt that his reputation in England was being undermined; his wave of successes, reaching its crest at Plassey, had subsided.

He still nursed huge political ambitions in England, where he believed the real power to lie. Had he returned immediately after Plassey, as so many others did, he would have been a popular hero and politically powerful. Instead, in an entirely worthy attempt to secure the conquests he had made, he may have feared he had missed his moment to capitalise on his success in his own country. He may simply have been worn out by a succession of exhausting and nerve-racking crises to preserve his Indian dominion.

Now possessed of immense wealth, he could enjoy the elevation of status it would grant him back home, having discharged his duty to Bengal and been fortunate enough to avoid the early deaths by disease suffered by so many of his contemporaries – a run of luck that might not endure forever. In the course of the last thirty months he had approached the very brink of madness – the megalomania of the all-powerful, where all reality is distorted by men's apparent obeisance and backhand plotting.

Clive the merciful had displayed fierce vengeance – admittedly for the first time in his career, and in a small area. Clive the judicious had squeezed a colossal and controversial exaction from his own countrymen, tipping his privateering into naked greed. Clive the statesman was now behaving with needless arrogance and contempt towards his superiors. Clive the de facto emperor now wished to become Governor-General of the continent, as previously evinced in his letter to his father. Although not unhinged, he had become unbalanced; darkness was gnawing at a mind which had so far resisted corruption. It was time to go home.

Margaret certainly thought so. She had viewed her life in India over these past four years with deeply mixed feelings, although these are never apparent in her letters to Robert, which were full of loyalty and affection. She had arrived expecting to lead the comfortable, if staid, life of a wife of a deputy governor in a colonial backwater. Instead she was to face much greater challenges, although her husband was absent for much of the time.

She had pined for Clive during the first ten months of his expedition to Bengal; when she reached Calcutta at last, she experienced a settlement in the throes of rebuilding after the devastation inflicted upon it by the Nawab the previous year. She was housed in the finest luxury in the heart of Fort William, in a spacious mansion with an extensive, colonnaded verandah. It was furnished with huge mirrors, wardrobes and marble-topped tables. The impression, typical of its time in India, was one of space, air, high ceilings and proportion, elegance rather than an excess of furniture or decorations.

Margaret had an extensive library and a harpsichord, which she enjoyed playing. By any standards her life was idyllic, particularly so for India in the eighteenth century. She had all the servants she could possibly want – from Chowry, the butler, to Black Robin, their attendant, the nurse Maria, and Mercury, a boy-servant, as well as parlour-maids, cooks and manservants. She possessed a small menagerie of pets – a tame mynah bird, 'a young tiger, a bear, two porcupines, three of these new-fashioned birds and an owl almost as big as myself'.

Busying herself with ordering the household, entertaining, writing letters, reading, or playing the harpsichord, she led a life of agreeable leisure. Her letters convey its flavour: 'It is just turned of eleven o'clock and the sun's so fierce that our umbrellas and a gentle southerly wind which comes charging at my windows are not sufficient to keep me from almost fainting . . . my genius is, I cannot say chilled or frozen, but quite (to use a country expression) expended, and myself in danger of expiring. Thank you, good

Chowry, you have quite restored me to health by your seasonable supply of toasted bread scrubbed with nutmeg, and the glass of Madeira wine. Having drunk half thereof, without any ceremony, as life and death were in the case, I tope of the remainder to the health of my friends in Camp . . . Mrs Hancock is squeezing mangoes down her throat to your health and safe return, and, if she be not sincere, she wishes that they may choke her. Amen, say I.'

After her afternoon siesta in the heat, she often went for a ride with respectable male friends, and then had dinner. Only 'squalls and hurricanes' which raged through the house, blowing out candles, as well as 'swarms of flies, mosquitoes, cockroaches and doubledores' interrupted this heady existence. 'We have all the plagues of Egypt together, for some of my visitors have boils.'

Tragically, the suppurating heat of Calcutta was soon to claim another tiny victim: her infant daughter Jenny, to whom she had devoted herself the previous two years, died in the autumn. Following the loss of her second child in England, the tragedy affected her deeply; but to her joy she was soon pregnant again.

Clive shows no sign of having been a thoughtless husband and father. He was devoted to her and her letters show she revered him. The trouble was he had so little time to spend with her. For much of the thirty months or so she was in Calcutta, he was absent from the city, on expeditions to secure control of his vast domain. When he was in Calcutta, he was the first citizen of the town and on official business much of the time, presiding over a household of guests and huge dinner parties, at which bread rolls were thrown high-spiritedly about.

He seems to have spent little time in conversation with her, his interests being public affairs, soldiering and good living, hers astronomy, pets and gossip. He preferred the company of his cronies, playing cards for sizeable stakes, and smoking his hookah, which was inlaid with precious stones and beautifully wrought. He did not regard it as part of the duty of a husband to spend much time alone with her; others were present with them both virtually throughout the day.

Today she would be described as lonely. But she was very rarely alone, and she showed no signs of minding this lack of intimacy, except when he was up-country and she pined for him. Married to the most famous man in India and ten years older than her, she could not but accept *force majeure*. She protected herself by having her own circle of intimates – most rather bluestocking, like her: a matronly woman friend, Philadelphia Hancock; a Swedish missionary; a minor English clergyman; her doctor, William Fullerton. Jane Latham, Margaret's cousin and intimate, had left with her husband and the fleet. She had her own small court to make up for Clive's absence, and he happily tolerated this state of affairs. Endless conversations took place between these earnest, somewhat sycophantic intellectuals and the first citizen's wife while Clive rushed about on affairs of state or was away altogether.

She pined for Clive, complaining of his absence in the most enchanting terms. 'May the heroes return shortly to receive the wreath of laurel their ladies are preparing them! Alas! I think of mine too often for my repose, but on such an account who would not wish to be in my case? . . . Every one of my past melancholy ideas is far overbalanced by the most pleasing hope of seeing again the comfort of my life.'

Her greatest consolation in those years was Major John Carnac, Clive's aide-de-camp, older than his superior at nearly 40, a slightly fussy and effeminate man, whose 'blooming cheeks are dyed with colours all their own, excelling far the pride of roses newly blown'. He seems to have cut a faintly comical figure, which he may have played up to, although he was also a formidable soldier. It is not known how close this relationship was, save that Carnac made up for Clive's absences. He found her intelligent, attractive in her petite, sweet way and, at 23, still extremely young; she found him a mixture of father figure and attentive courtier – which Clive assuredly was not.

Carnac was Margaret's closest male friend since her marriage to Clive. Clive seems to have borne no resentment – indeed appears to have favoured the relationship, perhaps because he felt guilty at his own absence and may have believed his subordinate incapable of indiscretion – which may indeed have been the case. Carnac, still unmarried, was much more of a retainer than a potential lover.

She wrote to the aide at great length when he accompanied Clive on his expeditions, but probably more to find out what her husband was doing than from affection. She complained, 'I frequently accuse him [Clive] of writing less than any other husband, and so great is my impudence that I mention these neglects before company.' She may have been trying to provoke a pang of jealousy in Clive through her attentiveness towards Carnac.

There is no evidence that the relationship with the older man was romantic or sexual. Clive, still dashing, remote, usually absent, uncommunicative to his young wife, was the stuff of which romantic heroes were made. Yet Carnac was certainly the second love of her life.

She had long pressed Robert to return to England; they had been abroad for more than three troubled years, during which Clive's energies were exerted to the full. She had lost her third child, and must have been desperately anxious for the health of the one she was bearing. Although pampered beyond most people's wildest dreams, the tranquillity, good health and luxury of life in eighteenth-century England for the very wealthy beckoned – as did the prospect of seeing more of her husband. It was time to go home.

Parting was not without its sorrow. The grandees of Calcutta, so contemptuous of Clive when he arrived, were thrown into a panic: 'There is so strong an appearance of intestine wars, foreign invasions, or irruptions from the inland country powers, and which is only prevented by the eminent character you deservedly bear throughout the Mogul's dominions.' As one observer wrote, 'It appeared as though the soul were departing from the government of Bengal.' There were threats again that the Shahzada would return in alliance with the Nawab of Oudh.

When Clive went to Murshidabad to take his leave of that old rogue, Mir Jafar, the latter for once appeared sincere in wishing him to stay. Intrigue against him as they might, the Indians regarded Clive as a kind of god-figure, invincible and also, by comparison with their own rulers, merciful. Clive believed the threats were much exaggerated. Bengal, he said, was 'out of all danger but that of venality and corruption'. In any case, it was for others now to show their worth. British dominion in India could not depend upon the reputation of one man alone, or it would surely perish.

The real threat, as he saw it, came from the board of directors in London. 'I may perhaps be able to serve you more effectually [in England] than my continuing here.' He had left the fortunes of Bengal in good order, the Nawab dependent on the British, the Hindu merchant class their close allies, Fort William immensely strengthened, the borders of Bengal and Bihar settled and secured. He could not stay for ever.

Substantial reinforcements were on their way to the garrison at Calcutta under Major Caillaud, a soldier with a distinguished record. Clive's successor as governor, Henry Vansittart, was a friend with a solid reputation in the Carnatic. The French had been crushed in India, the Dutch swatted aside from Bengal. Clive left his empire in as good order as seemed possible.

He had no doubt he was departing his empire for ever, that he would never see that sluggish, languid, muddy river again as the ship set out on 21 February 1760; he was now to make his political fortunes in his own land. The only Englishman who had ever been an emperor gazed back at the land of his absolute power for more than two years. He and Margaret were accompanied by his young cousin, George Clive, and Carnac, along with many servants and animals. However, Margaret's new baby, Bob – their fourth, and only the second surviving – was not well, and had to be left behind at the last moment with Dr Fullerton.

When the ship reached St Helena a couple of months later, Carnac learnt he had been appointed to a senior command in Bengal, and returned on the next ship back. He wrote with passionate disappointment at being parted from Margaret, but consoled her with the thought that he had bought 'a coral with bells' for tiny Bob to play with. The baby was dead by the time he reached Calcutta, the third of Clive's four children to die in infancy.

Clive arrived at Spithead on 9 July 1760, after a lightning voyage for those days of only four and a half months. He must have viewed his return with a mixture of anticipation and apprehension. Even just twenty weeks of enforced idleness aboard the *Royal George*, while allowing him to get over his ailments and depression, had him like a caged lion, striding about the ship.

Now at last he believed he had enough money to acquire real political power in Britain. He was returning as the hero of Plassey, conqueror of Bengal. He was Pitt's 'heaven-born general'. He had prestige and fame. He would acquire a clutch of parliamentary seats and would attach them to the prevailing interest. He would not repeat his old mistake of siding with the opposition. He now had a real prospect of becoming a senior minister, perhaps one day he would even become prime minister. At just 34, his ambitions were as great as ever. The man who had ruled over an empire much more populous than Britain in his early thirties was now coming home to conquer his own land politically.

He was a striking figure: 'To a countenance which was saved from vulgarity only by the expression of decision and natural intelligence which pervaded it, he added a figure without symmetry or grace,' according to his biographer Grieg, 'which he rendered doubly conspicuous by the elaborate care with which it was his custom to adorn it.'

He returned to a fine official welcome and an astonishing broadside of sniping and animosity from the sneering classes that must have left him gasping. He was greeted by his elderly father, Richard, who in spite of his years had been exasperating his contemporaries by promoting Clive's interests at home; and by the six-year-old Ned, the couple's only surviving child of four.

Clive was invited to Leadenhall Street by Sulivan and the directors of the East India Company a couple of days later. They proposed that a statue be erected in his honour at East India House. Sulivan later invited Clive to his sumptuous house at Mile End, a village east of London. Less than a week after his return, Clive, along with his adoring father, was invited to an audience with the doddering 77-year-old George II at Buckingham Palace. It was clear that the king, at least, was one of Clive's warm admirers. Unfortunately, the monarch was not to live long. In September Clive was given an honorary degree by the University of Oxford and accorded a unanimous vote of thanks by the East India Company. He was a popular hero, although eclipsed a little by the dramatic death of Wolfe at Quebec.

The Britain in which Clive had disembarked in 1760 at the height of his riches, success and power, was itself on the threshold of national glory. With his non-aristocratic origins and fabulous wealth he embodied a new age for a country which, for the next century and a half, was to blaze a glorious trail as the foremost nation on earth. Its system of freedoms and government, so painfully forged on the anvil of civil war over the previous century, was to give it the resilience to weather revolutionary pressures and the advent of a mass society for generations to come.

The country's colossal overseas empire, created in part by accident, in part by design, was just coming into being, dwarfing any the world had ever seen. Britain's artistic achievement, so long the poor relation of Europe, was now about to flower in a dazzling display of innovation and taste. Catalysed by the capital and labour freed from the land by enclosure, as well as by the proceeds of empire, the country's economy was about to embark on the world's first industrial revolution, leaving other nations standing.

Clive straddled the end of a previous age for Britain and the birth of a new one. He was the last of the old military adventurers – a romantic hero in the mould of Drake or Raleigh, in contrast to the mechanical 'professional' generalship of Wellington and his successors; he was also the first of the new breed of self-made men. To have lived in Britain in 1760 was an uplifting experience: even those at the very bottom enjoyed domestic peace, rising living standards and an era of social concern as yet spared the terrible conditions of deprivation and urban squalor that were to sully the age of industrialisation in the next century. To be fabulously wealthy, after having been born into gentrified poverty, must have been a heady experience indeed.

It was an age of greatness for Britain's constitution and government. To some modern historians, the eighteenth century reeked of faction, corruption and squalid backroom dealing. Yet it is possible to identify in mid-eighteenth-century Britain every key ingredient of the system of liberties which was eventually to become a model for democracy around the world.

First, the British monarchy had become constitutional, a valuable and sometimes powerful underpinning to national continuity, but no longer the foremost power in the land. The attempts by George III to restore the Crown's influence were to underline that only through intrigue and prestige could it become first among equals again – not as of right. It took the king the best part of his reign to acquire influence on a level with his prime ministers, and even then he was far from unchallenged.

In other countries, such as France, the monarchy had in practice become a figurehead too. But there its power had been usurped by the state, which was largely unchecked. In Britain the power of the state was subordinated to that of parliament, and a host of written and unwritten rules also restrained it, guaranteeing the individual –

in practice the propertied and professional classes – against its encroachments. This was no mere matter of form: it was almost certainly the reason why Britain, almost alone, survived the revolutionary turmoil that periodically engulfed continental Europe over the next couple of centuries.

Disaffection in Britain, from about the middle of the century, had its place, enshrined at the very top. On one major issue after another debate raged in parliament between different factions, first one side gaining the upper hand, then the other. Certainly much of the infighting was squalid enough. The instability this generated might have seemed a serious weakness for the nation: in fact, though, it was a massive strength. All strands of opinion within the propertied classes were represented, and even the uneducated, who were not, took sides. With the competing claims of all viewpoints wrangled over in public, there was little opportunity for dissent to build up outside parliament.

In France and other eighteenth-century continental systems, while faction struggles raged at court, these were largely in secret, neither corresponding to the real balance of forces in the country as a whole, nor providing a safety valve for discontent. Democracy must be seen to be done to work. Nor was debate confined to the ranks of an aristocratic and haute bourgeois élite, as in France; while the aristocracy fought to retain its influence, its real power had been diluted in the struggles of the previous century by the much larger middle class of country squires, urban merchants and professionals.

In the parliamentary maelstrom, monarch, dukes and commoners battled it out, now one gaining the upper hand, now another, none succeeding in imposing his will for long. After the reign of the Whig grandees had ended with the installation of the Hanoverians, Walpole, bourgeois, stolid, cunning, a machine politician, and his successors Pelham and Newcastle had ushered in the new political age.

In turn the newly ennobled Grenvilles and 'commoner' Pitt – 'issue politicians' in an almost twentieth-century mould – had come to dominate the stage, vying with the remnants of the old Whig aristocracy represented by the Duke of Devonshire and the Marquis of Rockingham, and the newly assertive 'court party' of George III, represented by the cack-handed Earl of Bute and, later and more successfully, by Lord North. The system embraced all dissent: it is scarcely surprising that it became the age of oratory, for rarely have political leaders felt so free to express their own viewpoints, unhindered by fear of official reprisal, or by the harsh disciplines of the party machine.

The vitality of parliamentary debate was but one of the lasting innovations of the eighteenth-century system. Another was the way in which general elections – although most of the seats went uncontested or were in the gift of political bosses – actually mattered. Governments could be undone and were unseated by the verdicts of the limited electorates in the small number of contested seats. Public opinion – however restricted the franchise – had real influence.

A third key new feature was a massive extension in the power of the press. The astonishing vigour and vitriol of press and pamphlet attacks in the eighteenth century would shame tabloid newspapers today: rarely in human history can political issues have been aired so freely, with such crude vigour and vicious character assassination.

The test case for press freedom was, of course, the struggle of John Wilkes, in his often scurrilous attacks against not just the king's favourite, Bute, but the monarchy itself. Initially dragged off to the Tower in 1763, Wilkes was freed after middle-class and 'mob' uproar, discredited, and then exiled. He returned in 1768 to secure election for Middlesex. When the government had him expelled from the Commons and fined for obscene libel, he was tumultuously re-elected while rioting spread, leading to the killing of twelve demonstrators by a company of grenadiers.

In 1769, Wilkes was again unseated, and disorder reached a crescendo, effectively bringing down the mediocre government of the Duke of Grafton, and ushering in the more pragmatic and skilful North ministry. The Wilkes agitation gradually subsided, not least because, although a gifted polemicist, he was no public speaker, nor even a real revolutionary. But his virulent journalism showed just how far the limits of press freedom now extended, and the vigour of the parliamentary debate about his fate made it impossible for him to mobilise opinion against 'the system' – even if he had wanted to do so.

The nearest equivalent of a Danton or Robespierre in England was, in the end, more of an Irish rogue than anything else, and not one to bring the constitution down. The Wilkes riots never posed the threat to the body politic that revolution did in France twenty years later. The system had shown that it could respond – indeed Wilkes brought down a government – and the challenge gradually faded, after securing its greatest triumph: the right to report parliamentary debates in the press.

If Clive's Britain was politically vibrant and mature, it was also endearingly and dottily obsessed with precisely the same sorts of issues that preoccupy the British chattering classes to this day. The conduct of the royal children was a national obsession. Aristocratic scandals were highlighted by the press, from the trial of the Duchess of Kingston for bigamy, to that of Lord Baltimore for rape (he was found to have been set up by the victim's family), to the rakish life of Lord Lyttelton, and to the indiscretions of the dazzling young Duchess of Devonshire.

The fashionable woman, in 1775, was criticised by the *London Magazine* for her tendency to 'rise at ten, throw herself into a hurry, dress before she goes out, fly away to the exhibitions of painting and models and wax, and a thousand other things: take a peep at a play to encourage a poor player on his benefit night – fly to the Pantheon [the hugely fashionable new gathering place on Oxford Street] to hear Agujari sing – whisk from thence to Ranelagh, to meet dear Lord William, and adjourn with the dear creature to Vauxhall to finish the evening with a glass of burnt champagne: then, yawning on her return, assure her dreaming lord, that she cannot support it; it is too much; the human spirit will not endure it, sink dead as a flat into her bed, and rise next morning in pursuit of similar follies'.

The historian Paul Langford points to the

apparently limitless desire for new sensations. The ideal social event, both from the commercial standpoint, and for those who attended, was one which carried an air of exclusiveness while exhibiting to the public at large an extravagant spectacle. The Thames regatta, patronised by princes of the blood, met this criterion. So did elaborate public gardens and firework displays, though some of the latter caused much annoyance in the new suburban surroundings in which they were located. One of the more influential innovations of the period was the fête champêtre, the most celebrated of which was held on the marriage of Lord Stanley at his Surrey House, the Oaks, in June 1774 . . . Stanley took full advantage of the rage for rural fantasy. There were shepherds and peasants, druids and dryads, fairy lights, rustic sports and games. The occasion cried out for a Hogarth to display its ironies.

In 1787, there was a royal pronouncement against vice and immorality after a long campaign to restore family values, which inveighed against drinking, swearing and gambling. There was vigorous debate between those like the Derbyshire poet Erasmus Darwin, who advocated bringing up children without discipline, and those who urged mental control and physical punishment. Measures were enacted to improve the lot of poor children, keep them off the streets and regulate their use as chimney sweeps, (which had increased as a result of the new narrow chimneys on Georgian terraced houses).

Animal and even vegetable rights were championed. Fox-hunting was criticised. Travel, and travel-writing, became middle-class obsessions. Women's fashions were characterised by plunging necklines and provocatively protruding bottoms. Debate raged over the 'masculine' roles of active women and the need to keep them attending to home and children. Sexual mores were chewed over relatively openly, and books such as *Fanny Hill* fed the public's appetite for the nascent industry of pornography. A prominent playwright, Samuel Foote, was ruined by his homosexuality.

Rich young men indulged in the 'macaroni' pursuit of foreign fashions and deriding English tastes. Capital punishment, penal reform and poverty were earnestly debated. Aristocratic decadence and irresponsibility were satirised and demonised while George III and Queen Charlotte came to represent the essence of bourgeois respectability taken to prudish extremes.

As Langford, the best modern chronicler of the period, points out:

It has been argued, none the less, that Georgian England was an essentially aristocratic society. This view mistakes appearance for reality, and consequence for cause. Blue blood and rank, without property, counted for very little in late eighteenth-century England, and rendered their possessors objects of pity rather than envy. It was wealth which brought power and prestige. Inherited wealth was a large proportion of the whole in a society which resisted direct taxation and social reconstruction by the state. The great landowner, with or without title, was guaranteed his share of power and prestige. But the base of propertied society was broadening and diversifying in the late eighteenth century ... The feeling that aristocratic influence was getting stronger during this period was probably mistaken. If peers controlled more constituencies at the end of the eighteenth century, when reformers first began conducting systematic surveys, it was as much a result of the deliberate expansion of the peerage in the 1780s and the 1790s as of a tendency to electoral oligarchy.

In fact, Clive's England represented the triumph of the middle classes well before the arrival of the Victorians: if the latter have been identified with bourgeois values, it is because the problems of industrialisation became much more acute during the nineteenth century, exciting both criticism and a response from the middle classes. If more extensive social reforms were passed during the nineteenth century, it was because the conditions which required them had not yet materialised during the eighteenth century. But the middle classes during the eighteenth century showed just as much sensitivity to social conditions as their descendants. The triumph of the respectable bourgeoisie had already taken place during the eighteenth century, overlaid as it was with an aristocratic veneer.

No period in British history could have been more agreeable for the well-off. Scientific innovation, following in the footsteps of Newton earlier in the previous century, abounded; intellectual and philosophical discourse raged. It was the era of a renewal of the British literary tradition – epitomised by the fashionable obsession for Shakespeare, popularised by the great actor-producer of the age, David Garrick – and such writers as Samuel Johnson, whose *Dictionary* was published in 1755; Henry Fielding, whose *Tom Jones* was published in 1749; and, later, Goldsmith, Gibbon and Sheridan.

Clive's immensely wealthy neighbour, Sir Watkin Williams Wynn, was patron to Garrick, who was godfather to his son Charles, who in turn patronised his friend the poet Robert Southey, while Reynolds, Hudson, Lawrence and Hoppner painted his family. A member of the Dilettanti Society along with Sir Thomas

Hamilton, consul at Naples and husband of the wayward Emma, Williams Wynn embodied the artistic and intellectual pursuits of the aristocracy in the late eighteenth century.

In architecture the Palladian fashion had been succeeded by the neo-classical and, later, by the Gothic revival. Robert and James Adam, James Wyatt and William Chambers scattered their beautifully proportioned gems around England. In art, Hogarth's acerbic and idiosyncratic brilliance was succeeded by the finest generation of British painters – Gainsborough, Stubbs, Constable, Hudson, Ramsay, Zoffany, Lawrence, Turner, Hoppner and Reynolds. The Royal Academy and the British Museum were founded.

The Grand Tour to Italy became de rigueur for wealthy Englishmen, who called on Venice, Florence and Rome, travelled to Naples to experience eruptions of Vesuvius, and, in the case of the wealthiest, had their portraits painted by Pompeo Batoni. Clive was also to go. It was the greatest flowering of art, literature and architecture in British history.

The Britain of 1760 was also the hub of a new empire. The previous few years had seen the most staggering victories in a catalogue of imperial expansion under the 'patriotic' ministry of Pitt. Gaudeloupe had been conquered in the Caribbean, the French fleets defeated at Cape Lagos and Quiberon. The forts of North America had fallen one by one. French Canada had been captured, all the way from Louisburg to Quebec. In the east the French had been defeated in India and Clive had conquered Bengal.

It was an age of artistic elegance; of intellectual discourse and innovation; of freedom, debate and political criticism; of religious tolerance and humanity; of prosperity; and of British self-confidence and triumph abroad. Such was the Britain Clive returned to in 1760, having made his name and a fabulous fortune, the former ruler of a state four times larger and more populous than Britain, now bent on political success to match in his homeland. He could little have guessed that the new moralism, the new priggishness, the new responsibility, would claim him as its first victim.

He wasted no time in using his new wealth to project luxury and political power. He endowed his father with enough to retire from business and keep a coach, writing off a debt of £9,000 for the old man; he paid out about £500 to his old comrade in arms, Stringer

Lawrence, who grudgingly accepted (although in fact he had a fortune of his own of around £20,000). He embarked on rebuilding the tiny manor at Styche into a large dwelling, and decided to rent a London residence and a country house appropriate to his new station, while he looked for a more permanent country seat to buy.

He found a London abode on the west side of fashionable Berkeley Square to rent from Lord Ancram at £600 a year. It was a fine gentleman's house in one of the smartest squares in London. In the country he rented Condover, a magnificent Elizabethan mansion about five miles south of Shrewsbury, which had belonged to the Owen family. Margaret, with her rather more modern, suburban tastes, described it as 'just like a church . . . windows from top to bottom but not a sash, all dismal casements'. However, she enjoyed its pleasant, formal gardens and extensive park; the house itself was reckoned to have around 100 rooms. Thus equipped with the essential accoutrements of a local magnate, he secured the nomination to be one of two members of parliament for Shrewsbury.

Yet that autumn he fell ill again, crippled by gout or rheumatism, as well as his old abdominal pain. A curious kind of nervous prostration also struck him, which seems to have been more severe, although less misery-inducing, than his old depression. The illness put him out of action for most of the next six months. He spent much of his time going off to Bath, where the waters improved his health.

According to a contemporary, he lived there 'in little pomp, moderate in his table, and still more so in equipage and retinue'. The simple habits of the soldier, which dwelt so incongruously alongside his love of extravagance and finery, apparently died hard – or perhaps Clive was just feeling too wretched to indulge in shows of display. He bitterly lamented that his illness impeded him from tackling more serious problems, both in England and the Company. 'If health had not deserted me on my first arrival in England, in all probability I had been an English peer, instead of an Irish one, with the promise of a red riband,' he lamented to a friend. 'I know I could have bought the title (which is usual), but that I was above, and the honours I have obtained are free and voluntary. My wishes may hereafter be accomplished.'

His prospects still seemed rosy enough by the spring of 1761, when a general election was held in March. Clive's political patron in Shropshire was the Earl of Powis, one of the oldest and biggest territorial magnates not just of Montgomeryshire, but Shropshire, who secured his nomination against the interests of the powerful Earl of Bath. The Earl of Powis also secured the election of Richard Clive for the pocket borough of Montgomery, across the border in Wales, near where his own seat, Powys Castle, was based.

Richard Clive, the impecunious, hard-working, crotchety old lawyer from an insignificant family of minor gentry, was now ending his career and life as an MP and confidant of kings – thanks to his son's dazzling success. One of Robert Clive's more attractive characteristics – the mirror image of his animosity towards his enemies – was his loyalty to family and friends. He had gone out of his way to reward a father who once thought of him as a scapegrace, but had worked ceaselessly for him since.

Clive also secured the nomination for the city of Worcester nearby for his old friend John Walsh. Down in Penryn in Cornwall, Clive furthered the campaigns of two more candidates, his brother-in-law, Mun Maskelyne, and cousin, George Clive, spending some £10,000 on them. This was a serious business, undertaken with the same energy and commitment as displayed in India; with five seats in his interest, Clive would have had a small voting block to rival those of the large landowners, if not the very greatest political dynasties and ducal houses. In fact he was soon to ally with the cause of Pitt and Grenville.

Clive's two Cornish candidates were, however, defeated; but he still had three votes. Judiciously used in the factional politics of the mid-eighteenth century, when governments were made or unmade by political barons and their supporters changed sides with bewildering speed, he now had limited, but real, political clout – which he was determined to use shrewdly.

CHAPTER 20

The Innocent

C live was soon thrown into an agonising dilemma. The politician he was closest to, who had almost approved his proposals for India and had acclaimed his triumphs to the House of Commons, was Pitt, the Great Commoner, the dominant leader of the age, whose administration had just presided over a dramatic revival in Britain's overseas fortunes.

However, in October 1760, just three months after receiving Clive, George II, a bluff, straightforward old man who could hardly speak English and resisted the temptation to meddle much in English politics, died. His son, vigorous, impetuous and young, was determined to restore some of the Crown's status through intrigue – a prescription for disaster, the exact reason why the Stuart dynasty had been rejected in favour of the Hanoverians, who could be trusted to take no interest in British politics.

George III promptly determined to have his favourite, the Earl of Bute, a narrow-minded northerner who was intimate with the king's mother and had captured the young prince's imagination, brought into government. Pitt hated this didactic, middle-aged man, and resisted his ascent, just as he opposed the re-entry of a meddlesome and politically active monarchy less than eighty years after most Englishmen believed it had finally been put in its place. Crowds pelted Bute's carriage, ignored the king's and cheered Pitt's. However, the arch-intriguer of the age, and Pitt's oldest enemy, the Duke of Newcastle, saw his chance to replace the Great Commoner, and moved over to become the monarch's candidate for prime minister, promising to support Bute for the highest positions.

Clive was faced with the dilemma of backing his old champion, Pitt, in opposition, or supporting the winning side – the same Duke of Newcastle who had blocked his election to parliament six years before. Clive was determined not to be on the losing side again.

With the duplicity he believed he had learned at Plassey, Clive switched sides and backed the more powerful force, that of the Duke of Newcastle – for a price: not an English peerage, which Newcastle said he could not deliver, but the next best thing, an Irish peerage, as Baron Clive of Plassey, after a small estate in Ireland which he had bought and renamed (as the title had to be derived from an actual place in Ireland).

He was also promised the first vacancy as Knight of the Bath, the monarch's most prestigious order. Although an inferior kind of peer, he would have direct access to the court, and the queen served as godmother to his latest daughter, who to their great joy was born in good health.

Early in 1761, in spite of Clive's illness, his prospects seemed rosy: controlling three seats in parliament, promised a peerage and the order of the Bath, on the side of the Crown and the government, he had everything to look forward to; he had cynically sold himself to the most promising bidder in British politics.

Little did he guess that in a matter of months his enemies in the East India Company would launch a ferocious campaign to deprive him of his main source of income and that instead of conquering the citadels of power in England by throwing his small band of supporters from one side to the other, as he had among the princes of Bengal, he would once again be cast into the political wilderness. He had abandoned the principled Pitt for the scheming Newcastle. His new ally was to prove unreliable – and was anyway soon to be dumped for the king's favourite, the disdainful Bute.

The episode was to illustrate the tension between Clive the brilliant, decisive pragmatist and Clive the romantic. We have seen how Clive was slowly sucked into Bengal's heart of darkness, and how in a society dominated by the values of conquest, corruption, plunder and politics, he slowly became their prey.

The dashing young commander in his twenties had become the devious, brilliant political tactician of his thirties. In turn, his masterstroke at Plassey had begotten the military dictator-emperor figure who had ruled and consolidated a huge nation with verve and improvisation, but had also become increasingly corrupted by violence and greed. The raging conflict within himself was resolved by the decision to return home, where he would have to start again at the foothills to conquer the infinitely higher summits of British politics.

He had made his first throw well. But an extraordinary thing was to follow; he was to be confronted with a choice between his old romanticism and his new-found cynicism, between hanging on to his old Indian creation and advancement in British politics. He was to make the wrong choice for the best of reasons. He found himself outmanoeuvred by the pushy, puritanical, scheming spider of Leadenhall Street, his political ambitions all but destroyed, fighting for his financial life.

The issue in question was simple. The treaty which had ended the seven-year war in Europe with the French restored their Indian possessions as at 1749, including those won by Dupleix. At a stroke, the efforts of the British in India against the French were to be unravelled.

Clive was appalled, concluding, probably rightly, that the British negotiator, the Duke of Bedford, had been bribed by Dupleix and de Bussy. With all the impetuousness of the younger man and none of the caution of the older, he declared, 'the King of England has no right to give away the Nawab's dominions without his consent'. He believed he had to act as the spokesman for the British in India. However, he was taking on the government itself.

Bute, now prime minister, made intense efforts to change Clive's mind. He was offered the British peerage he had craved. His cousin George was offered a £6,000-a-year government sinecure. Almost certainly, if he had played his cards right, he would have secured government support in his impending battle against the East India Company.

Instead, Clive reverted to becoming a man of principle and defender of India, revelling in the support and admiration of his Indian followers, glowing in his sudden reversion to being his own master again. The former Emperor of Bengal would not, after all, grovel for place; the liberator of the Carnatic would not abandon his people again to the French. He declared roundly, 'I still continue to be one of those unfashionable kind of people who think very highly of independence, and to bless my stars, indulgent fortune has enabled me to act according to my conscience.'

It was the action of an honest man, one raised above the need to compromise with his peers by immense power and wealth from another country – and an arrogant man, one without the necessary humility to work his way up the parliamentary ladder. It was also a ferociously self-inflicted wound; for not only had he made an enemy of Bute and the government; his deadly rival, Sulivan, with exquisite cunning, had chosen to support the government.

In thus apparently betraying India's interests, the Company chairman had in fact skilfully connived in private with one of the chief ministers, the Earl of Shelburne, to renegotiate the terms of the agreement and thus deprive Dupleix once again of his old conquests. Sulivan now had the tacit support of the government in his campaign against Clive. In a single, recklessly romantic move, Clive had found himself as surrounded by enemies and bereft of allies as at Plassey. What followed was one of the first and greatest corporate takeovers in history, which was to absorb eighteenth-century England much more than the sterile posturing in parliament.

Sulivan now made his move. Taking Clive aside, in the role of candid friend, he informed him that his income of £27,000 a year for the Company's rent of the lands around Calcutta, awarded to him by Mir Jafar, might come under challenge. The Nawab had not met his obligations under the treaty anything like in full, so the Company had some technical and moral justice in doing this.

To Clive, now embarked on a course of acquisitions of country estates and parliamentary interests, which were expensive to run and yielded a rent of no more than around 5 per cent a year, it would result in a halving of his income and influence, both in politics and outside. He embarked on a ferocious defence of a privilege he had better never have acquired. In fact, although he had bought his way into politics, he might have enjoyed more political success humbly working his way up the parliamentary ladder than through a naked defence of his self-interest and money.

Although rich by the standards of an eighteenth-century grandee and fabulously so for a man of fairly humble origins, he now lamented his lack of independence and poverty. 'Of all places in the world, dread your native country the most if you are obliged to return to it in a state of dependence . . . he must be a philosopher indeed, and master of all the passions, who can live upon a little in England.' 'Little' was hardly a fair description of his fortune!

Initially Sulivan's threat had the desired effect. Clive reined in his opposition to the Company chairman. 'I would not think it prudent to risk it by quarrelling with Mr Sulivan, although he should not pay that attention to my recommendations which I have a right to expect . . .' But he was soon incensed by Sulivan's refusal to promote Carnac and Forde. He now enlisted the support of the new chairman of directors, Thomas Rous, formerly a placeman of Sulivan's. The great civil war of the East India Company at last broke out.

It is hard not to conclude that Clive's love of wealth and finery had gone to his head. His political ambitions – so promising just a few months earlier – were now subordinated to his desire for an income sufficient to reimburse him for his loss of the luxury and pomp of his life in India.

While this desperate fight was about to take place, Clive at last had found the enormously expensive country seat appropriate to him – Walcot Hall, belonging to a family of the same name, a 6,000-acre estate in western Shropshire with a fine gabled house that Clive was to redecorate lavishly into a delightful and airy eighteenth-century palazzo with one of the finest gardens in England. Walcot had the added advantage of controlling the seat of Bishop's Castle nearby, which was to become immediately vacant, permitting Clive to add to his parliamentary interest. He was also engaged in negotiations to buy his rented Berkeley Square town house from the Ancram family.

The war with Sulivan broke out in earnest early in 1763. The battleground consisted of 2,000 stockholders of the East India Company, substantial men, more than a third of whom lived in London and the Home Counties. Clive could no longer conceal his hatred for 'this treacherous, deceitful fellow', 'this mushroom of a man'. Both Clive and Sulivan resorted to buying up East India stock, and increasing the number of voting shares on either side by 'splitting' those of others – anyone with a share over £500 was entitled to vote. However, much of the stock remained in the hands of those who belonged to neither side.

In March, the first vote took place, Clive making a strong and major speech in defence of Rous, who had opposed the treaty. Sulivan, a bookish, waspish man, was not a natural speaker, and failed to answer most of Clive's points. One of the latter's friends told him, 'Mr Sulivan, Sir. Stand up and answer for yourself. I have been informed that you did propose to give up the whole Coast of

Coromandel to the French.' While denying this, Sulivan admitted that he would be prepared to give up the whole coast for one inch of the Company's possessions in Bengal. 'You did say! And pray, Sir, if you give up the Coast of Coromandel, how are your ships to get to Bengal?'

The retort brought the house down. Clive's party went on to win by 61 votes. However, having won the vote, Clive lost in the next round – the election of directors. Sulivan promptly ordered payment of the jagir stopped, claiming that the emperor had not approved it – an entirely bogus argument (although Clive's nominal claim rested, equally speciously, on his nominal rank in the Mogul's army). Clive promptly began legal proceedings, and sought the formal approval of the emperor; but meanwhile the jagir was frozen.

Towards the end of the year, however, Clive eventually caved in and moved away from opposition to the government towards negotiation with a more acceptable prime minister, a compromise between Bute and Pitt – Pitt's brother-in-law, George Grenville, whose sister had the added advantage of being married to the most powerful territorial family in North Wales, the Williams Wynns, confidants of Clive's patron, the Earl of Powis. Grenville agreed to use his influence to get the directors to pay Clive his 'Black Jagir' for a year or two, and said he would also try to secure a peerage for Clive.

Clive's choice of political patron, George Grenville, was not as incongruous as it might seem. Grenville has gone down in history as a dullard, the man who lost Britain the American colonies through the introduction of the Stamp Act in 1764, the first real taxing measure on the Atlantic possessions, which aroused a storm of opposition under the cry 'no taxation without representation': he was to resign in ignominy shortly afterwards. Grenville was later described by Edmund Burke as thinking 'better of the wisdom and power of human legislation than in truth it deserves. He conceived, and many conceived along with him, that the flourishing trade of this country was greatly owing to law and institution, and not quite so much to liberty.' Punctilious to a fault, highly competent, a skilful and experienced parliamentarian, he appeared to be the legalistic antithesis to the temperamental, intuitive Clive.

Yet Grenville, like his eloquent brother-in-law, Pitt, had many appealing aspects. He was a man of integrity and strength of character; he had no time for meddling in politics by the king's favourites. He was the first of a new breed of high-minded professional politician who considered that the Crown and the old Whig oligarchy had had their day in politics; and unlike Walpole, Newcastle and Pelham, he did not rule through patronage and corruption.

He believed in good, disinterested government. He was the father of all that was best about the British system of government, both in politics and the civil service. The Stamp Act was but one of a whole series of long-considered measures intended to put the colonies so recently enlarged on a sound legislative and financial footing, and he enjoyed the support of virtually all shades of opinion.

Grenville himself came from the second generation of a family that had risen to considerable wealth in a short time. The Grenvilles, a relatively well-do-do family in Buckingham, had married into the family of the enormously wealthy and successful Viscount Cobham, a family titled since the days of Charles I. The Cobham estate passed over to them and they were propelled to the financial front rank, owning a magnificent house at Stowe (now the school).

The eldest son of the couple became Richard, Earl Temple. He turned out to be a brilliant administrator of the family fortunes and the leader of the Grenville interest in parliament as First Lord of the Admiralty and Lord Privy Seal. A leader of the opposition under George II, he was detested by the monarch, who wrote that 'he was so disagreeable a fellow, there was no bearing him, that when he attempted to argue, he was pert, and sometimes insolent; that when he meant to be civil, he was exceedingly troublesome, and that in the business of his office he was totally ignorant'. He was arrogant and independent-minded, and in 1759 persuaded Pitt, his brother-in-law, to threaten to resign so that the king would give him the Order of the Garter. The king is said to have thrown the garter at Temple when he was installed the following year.

His more agreeable, politically sharper brother, George, was equally contemptuous of royalty. However, Temple broke with him when he accepted the job of prime minister following the fall of Bute, who had been partly brought down by the Wilkes affair, Wilkes being one of Temple's followers. The new prime minister treated the young George III rather like an errant schoolboy and

8. The Conspiracy: William Watts concludes the treaty with Mir Jafar and his son, Miram; after the painting by Benjamin Wilson.

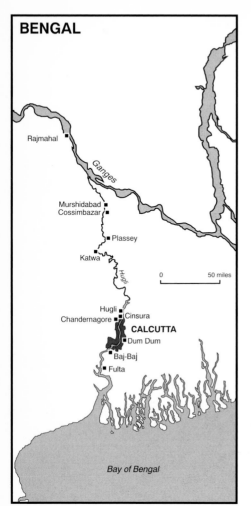

BENGAL

Rajmahal

Ganges

Murshidabad
Cossimbazar

Plassey

Katwa

Hugli

0   50 miles

Hugli
Chandernagore   Cinsura
                 CALCUTTA
                 Dum Dum
                 Baj-Baj
                 Fulta

Bay of Bengal

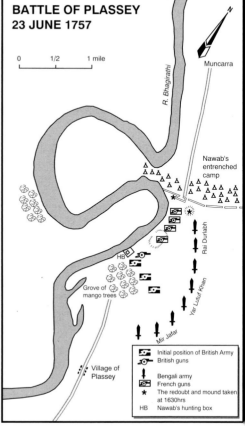

BATTLE OF PLASSEY
23 JUNE 1757

0   1/2   1 mile

N

R. Bhagirathi

Muncarra

Nawab's
entrenched
camp

Rai Durlabh

HB

Yar Lutuf Khan

Grove of
mango trees

Mir Jafar

Village of
Plassey

Initial position of British Army
British guns

Bengali army
French guns
The redoubt and mound taken
at 1630hrs
HB   Nawab's hunting box

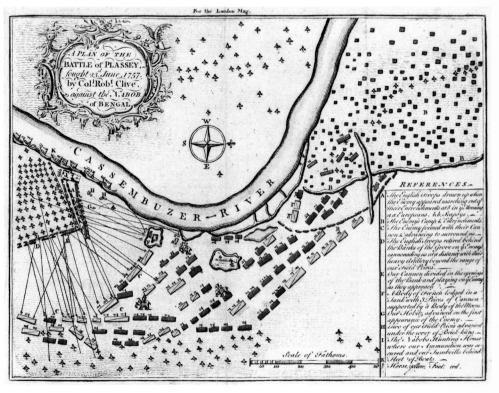

9. The Battle of Plassey – a contemporary map, the London Magazine, 1760.

10. Britain's Caesar: Emperor Clive in Roman dress, by Peter Scheemakers.

11. Clive's Bugbear: Sir Eyre Coote by John Thomas Seton.

12. Disastrous successor Henry Vansittart. Probably by John Zoffany.

13. Benares shortly after the time of Clive, showing the palace of Raja Abal and the Mosque of Aurungzeb, by William Hodges.

14. Founding of the Raj: Clive receives the Diwani from the Emperor Shah Alum, by Benjamin West.

15. Clive's pride and joy: Walcot.

16. Clive's creation: the lake and amphitheatre at Claremont.

17. The benefactor: Clive
hands on the Nawab's
grant to his fund for
destitute veterans and their
families, by Edward Penny.

18. The successor: Warren
Hastings, by George
Romney.

constantly attempted to undermine Bute, the power behind the throne, at length getting the crabbed old Scot virtually excluded from court.

George III's revenge was swift in coming: he dismissed Grenville and installed a comically inept and inexperienced administration of Whig grandees 'from the stud to the state' under the Marquess of Rockingham. This soon fell apart, although Rockingham to his credit in turn quarrelled with 'the King's Friends'. In the end, although the king flatly refused to have Grenville back, he had to send for the towering figure of William Pitt, related to the Grenvilles through his marriage to Hester, sister of Temple and George.

Thus Clive had allied himself with the most prominent political family of the third quarter of the eighteenth century, and his own political failure can in part be ascribed to their downfall. When at last the king secured a more congenial and able minister in Lord North, he was to remember Clive's connection with the hated Grenvilles.

The next generation of Grenvilles, like the Pitts, were to have a further moment of political glory early in the nineteenth century under the wise, skilful and immensely rich Thomas and William, who was to head the Ministry of All the Talents. Their sister, Charlotte, one of the great letter-writers of the age, married Clive's Welsh landed neighbour, Williams Wynn. Their elder brother, George, first Marquis of Buckingham, was to be a larger-than-life spendthrift, rake and minor politician, exceeded in his excesses only by his elder son, the first Duke of Buckingham, whose extravagance was eventually to help bring about the fall of the dynasty.

Walsh, and others of Clive's Indian friends, were appalled by his 'betrayal' in joining Grenville. Walsh said he was unwilling 'slavishly to follow the weaknesses of a master, not affording a sensible and manly support to a friend'. However, Clive seems to have persuaded him, and his small party supported the government as it began its epic prosecution of the contemporary mischief-maker John Wilkes. The story was put about how, obsequiously, Richard Clive met the king and told him his son was 'coming to town, and then Your Majesty will have another vote'.

Had Clive's career been cut short at this stage, he would have cut a sadly reduced figure in history. Although his youthful triumphs were undeniable, and his conquest of Bengal and subsequent vigorous consolidation of it would undoubtedly have earned him a major place in history, his reputation in England three years after his return was little short of disastrous, even comical. He had first sought advancement by siding with the government, then, in an admirable burst of principle, turned against it. Now, for reasons of material self-advancement, he had supported it again.

He had achieved nothing in politics, not even a minor job. He had dedicated two years to securing his own colossal source of income from the East India Company's own funds. Sulivan, although a personality entirely lacking in Clive's qualities – indeed by all accounts an extremely unpleasant man – had outmanoeuvred and, for the moment, defeated him.

At the age of 37, the dashing young warrior no longer, Clive had been made to look slightly ridiculous – immensely wealthy in most people's eyes, yet concerned mainly to protect that wealth. The only political issue he had shown himself passionately concerned about, after his admirable opposition to the peace treaty, was the defence of his own income. His British public career was spectacularly dead in the water. The chattering classes of the time, best exemplified by Horace Walpole, had him in their sights.

As far back as 1760 Walpole had written, 'General Clive is arrived, all over estates and diamonds. If a beggar asks charity, he says "friend, I have no small brilliants about me".' Walpole kept up the attack. The Annual Register ludicrously estimated the Clives' fortune at about £1.5 million. In fact, even if Clive had possessed a capital sum capable of yielding an income as large as the jagir, he could have been worth no more than £500,000. Yet the damage to his reputation had been done. Drake had been buried at sea, Raleigh had been executed, Marlborough had been fabulously ennobled, Wolfe and Nelson were martyred on the field of battle, Wellington became prime minister – but Clive was being immortalised as a rich man fighting to double his income.

Nor were the East India Company and the gossip columns of the time the only ones to sneer at Clive. In spite of his wealth and the steady expansion of his landed estates, he remained outside the ranks of fashionable society. The king and the prime minister, of course, dealt with him and received him in the course of their official duties. But Clive never made it into the ranks of the aristocracy.

There were several reasons for this. One, which he strongly believed, was that he lacked the necessary peerage. Clive was also a new phenomenon – one of Britain's very first self-made men. Previously people had joined the aristocracy through royal patronage or appointment: Elizabeth I's elevation of the bourgeois Robert Cecil to found the Salisbury dynasty is a classic example. Now the powers of the Crown in patronage were considerably diminished.

Although some city traders had amassed large fortunes, by and large they were despised by the great ducal and noble families of England, whose wealth was founded on land. Very few people had the necessary wealth to buy into their ranks except through trade – until Clive came along, an object of curiosity because he had done so through a feat of arms. In the nineteenth century, large fortunes were to be created by the industrial revolution, and although the old families accorded them second-class status, in practice they intermarried with the former, which were often in need of money, and became more or less assimilated.

At Clive's time, social status was static, more than before or since; royal patronage was gone, the new wealth had not yet arrived; and he was not admitted. The first citizen of India was considered an upstart in eighteenth-century England. Not that either Clive or Margaret made much effort to become fashionable. Unlike in Calcutta, they held no balls and kept away from the salons of London, preferring to hold court socially in the country with a small number of friends from British India, while making business and political excursions to London.

Clive himself, moreover, was the very reverse of the fashionable dandy, fop or wit. 'He would sit in company quite sluggish, while there was nothing to call forth his intellectual vigour; but the moment that any important subject was started, for instance, how this country is to be defended against a French invasion, he would rouse himself and show his extraordinary talents with the most powerful ability and animation.' He probably did care about his social exclusion – as his unflagging hunt for a title with a seat in the Lords suggests – but he affected not to show it. He was the first nouveau riche from British India – and suffered accordingly.

Loud, vulgar, ostentatious, gauche, awkward in society, a bore – all these epithets were to be applied to him. In fact he was no more ostentatious than anyone endowed with substantial wealth at the time, and his numerous houses were to be distinguished by taste and elegance more inspired by the simplicity and elegance of the colonial style in India than over-ornamentation. Yet much of the mud stuck, at the time and for later generations.

Clive's wealth and ostentation were put into perspective by his Welsh neighbour, Williams Wynn, who owned some 500,000 acres, as well as resources of coal, lime, lead, tin, copper, corn and timber, and who was part owner of the turnpike roads running through his property. Among his residences were the colossal Wynnstay in Denbighshire, with its own theatre, the elegant Llangedwyn in Montgomeryshire and a fine house in St James's Square in London. When the young Watkin Williams Wynn came of age, 15,000 guests were entertained, consuming 30 bullocks, 50 pigs, 50 calves, 80 sheep, 660 fowl, 73 hundredweight of bread, 125 plum puddings, 60 barrels of pickled oysters and 18,000 eggs.

Or take the Grenvilles. According to a maid present at the visit of King George's daughter, Princess Amelia, to the Grenville family seat at Stowe: 'nothing can exceed the grandeur and order by which everything was conducted. Twelve gentlemen, well dressed, waited at table, and twenty-four in livery waited in the next room, and in the grand hall near the dining room was a grand concert of music; the same evening, and every evening during Her Royal Highness's stay, the state apartments were illuminated with 120 wax lights . . . I never saw any entertainment conducted with more care, order, and decorum in all my days, every one endeavouring to outdo another in their places appointed them by their noble master and mistress.' Beside this, Clive was modest. He lived in an age of showing off, and he was by no means the showiest.

Clive's experience in England demonstrated one thing: that while he was a beached whale there, in India he was a kingfish. Even in England it was always Indian matters – the peace treaty, the break with Sulivan – that dominated his time. Once again, events in that far-off continent now stirred to tug at his destiny.

BOOK THREE

STATESMAN, 1764–1771

CHAPTER 21

The Cesspit

F or once, to say that all hell had broken loose after Clive's departure from Calcutta would not be wide of the mark. As with the fall of the city, a staggering succession of blunders by the British in Bengal soon threatened to undo everything Clive had achieved – and even imperilled continued British dominance there; the firm hand of the dictator-emperor had been sorely missed. The two main ingredients of the disaster were to be the cupidity of the settlers, who regarded Bengal as no more than a treasure house for plunder; and the arrival of a new, young and intellectually arrogant governor in the shape of Henry Vansittart.

The greed of the British colonists seemed to know no bounds. It was responsible for the bitter unpopularity into which British rule descended; such goodwill as had existed among the majority of professional people – the lower castes counted for nothing – was soon dissipated. The Hindu middle class, the backbone of Bengali society, which had viewed the British seizure of power from the Moslem aristocracy with indifference, even with sympathy, was soon to be wholly alienated. Clive's elaborate construction of a system of divide and rule – keeping the Moslem aristocracy and the Hindu merchant class suspicious of one another – was soon eclipsed by their mutual hostility towards the British.

The main British abuse was informally to extend a monopoly of trade to Company agents not just for exports but in all internal commerce. They were exempted from the high customs imposed through the use of duty-free passes – which in theory were intended only for the use of official Company trade, not the private transactions of the British colonists themselves. In fact the colonists remitted very little to the Company in Britain, starving it of revenue and forcing it to buy from them at prices they themselves set.

Meanwhile the Company was having to support the huge cost of maintaining an army in Bengal. The directors' response was furiously to demand more money from the settlers; their reaction was to find yet new ways of extracting revenue from the Bengalis to pay off their nominal masters in London and increase their own profits. It was classic colonialism of the most profiteering kind.

As these practices spread, much of the Hindu merchant class went out of business. In their place a large parasitic class grew up consisting not just of Company agents but of Indian crooks and middlemen, foreign adventurers and others who went about under a British flag with small parties of sepoys, plundering the countryside, compelling farmers to give them their products, forcing them to sell salt, tobacco, and betel at low prices, and then reselling these at vastly inflated prices to the local population. These were the gamashtas, of whom Clive was later to write, 'They swarm like so many bees and all have sepoys in their service . . . it is really very shocking to think of the distress of the poor inhabitants.'

These abuses generated bitter resentment of English rule in Bengal. It was to take more concrete form as a result of the singularly inept judgement of a man who had risen far above his abilities, Josiah Holwell, and of the inexperience of the young Vansittart. Between them they decided that the best way to extract yet more money from the government of Bengal, which was still behind in its payments, was to seek to replace Mir Jafar, or at least make him more pliable. The Nawab was seen to be a stubborn and weak old man, forever frustrating the British and indulging in minor conspiracies against their rule. Worse, he appeared to be deeply under the influence, in his haze of drink, drugs and women, of his venomous son, Miran, who from the start resented British dominance. However, fate was first to intervene on the side of the British and against Miran.

At the time of Clive's departure, Shah Alum, the Shahzada, the tough-minded heir to the Mogul throne, once again decided to make a direct attack on the western front of the British dominions in India. Major Caillaud had been despatched with troops to reinforce Ramnarayan, once again, at Patna. Miran insisted on accompanying the British force with a large army. Ramnarayan, thus encouraged, attacked the Shahzada's forces and was badly mauled, himself being wounded. But Caillaud's rapid advance compelled the Shahzada to withdraw before he could capture Patna. On 22 February the two armies met, Caillaud's army attacking the Shahzada on one flank, the latter concentrating the bulk of his forces against Miran's large but incompetently led force on the other side. Miran's army was forced back, but Caillaud's men went to its help and drove off the Shahzada's force in disorder.

Miran, however, who had been slightly wounded, refused to pursue them – to British disgust – and the Shahzada rallied his forces. Meanwhile his father, the Mogul Emperor, had been murdered in Delhi. On hearing this, the Shahzada proclaimed himself Emperor – Shah Alum – King of the World – and, with support from the small French force still headed by Jean Law, once again attacked Patna. This time Caillaud's and Ramnarayan's forces charged out of the city and decisively defeated him.

Caillaud, like Clive before him, decided to pacify the border province by razing the villages that had supported the new emperor. Miran refused to take part, only to be killed in extraordinary circumstances. Some alleged that Caillaud had him murdered, although there is no evidence for this. The official story is that he was struck by lightning in his tent; one witness said that his body was found full of holes, with his sword melted by his side.

So perished yet another opponent of British rule in India, albeit a deeply unsavoury one; whatever the truth, it was poetic justice for the man who had ordered the murder of Siraj-ud-Daula. What was immediately apparent was that the death of Miran knocked the stuffing out of his father.

With the departure of some ten members of the council in Calcutta to enjoy their new-found wealth in England, the self-important Holwell had been left in charge. He quickly decided that it would now be easier to depose Mir Jafar and for the British to rule Bengal directly. Clive had previously rejected such an option, because he believed the British lacked sufficient forces to control the whole province.

Caillaud, the British commander, rejected Holwell's view, and succeeded in blocking his plans until Vansittart arrived to take up his post as governor. Just 28 years old, an aristocrat by the standards of the British in India, foppish, vain and good-looking, offending local tradition by insisting that his wife and her friends accompany him on meetings with senior Moslems, who kept their women well away from men's business, Vansittart espoused Holwell's rash idea – with a difference.

The new governor's plan was to replace the incompetent, obstinate and ailing Mir Jafar with a more pliable ruler who, in addition, would agree to substantial further concessions to the British, to appease the Company directors in Leadenhall Street as well as further to enrich the colonists. The Nawab's brother-in-law, Mir Kasim, had long been pressing his claims. He insisted that Mir Jafar was implacably hostile to the British and that he, Mir Kasim, would do their bidding. He also bribed Holwell lavishly.

Deeply suspicious, Caillaud argued that Mir Kasim should instead replace Ramnarayan as governor of Bihar province, where he would be remote from the centre of power. However, Caillaud's own candidate for the succession to Mir Jafar, Rai Durlabh, had been closely identified with the infamous Miran. Vansittart sent for Mir Kasim in the summer of 1760. On arrival in Calcutta, the latter asked the British to install him as Nawab. This they refused to do, but agreed to make him the Nawab's chief minister and thus the obvious successor to Mir Jafar should he die – in exchange, of course, for lavish promises of money and territory to the British when he took power.

The conceited Vansittart and the self-important Holwell had entirely misjudged their man. Mir Kasim, by contrast with most of the senior Bengali rulers at the time, was energetic, extremely clever and ambitious – as well as being possessed of the psychopathic ruthlessness of a Siraj-ud-Daula or a Miran. Vansittart and Holwell believed that having an energetic and more intelligent Nawab would render the task of ruling Bengal easier than under the doddery Mir Jafar.

In fact, a weak ruler was in the British interest; a strong one extremely dangerous. It has been suggested that Vansittart was in fact an enlightened figure who sincerely believed, 200 years ahead of his time, in returning Bengal to local rulers; there is little to support this. All the evidence suggests he was deceived and bribed by Mir Kasim into believing he would be more pliable.

Vansittart and Caillaud set out in October with a large force of European soldiers for Murshidabad. There they found Mir Jafar implacably opposed to the idea of having his brother-in-law as chief minister. Almost certainly, the old man believed he would be murdered as soon as British backs were turned. There were rumours that Miran had, in fact, been assassinated on Mir Kasim's orders. The Nawab had been a shadow of his former self since his son's death.

Caillaud resorted to strong-arm tactics, surrounding the Nawab's Motijhil palace and insisting that Mir Kasim be installed as chief minister. At length Mir Jafar capitulated – and astonished the British by abdicating provided they agreed to give him protection from his successor. Mir Kasim was promoted to Nawab, while the befuddled old man was taken to Calcutta under British escort. Thus ended the career of the man whom Clive had elevated to Nawab – or so it seemed.

Carnac was horrified: 'I should have been extremely sorry to have had a hand in bringing it about, and I think it will vex Colonel Clive sorely. We can never expect to be trusted again, after having sacrificed the man we had so solemnly taken by the hand. I would not be prevailed upon to see, and the shock would have been too great for me to behold his downfall, the person whom Mr Clive had been the sole instrument raising.'

The next step for the British was to secure the indispensable seal of approval for the new Nawab from the emperor. At this stage, Vansittart conceived an extraordinary fantasy, instructing Caillaud to open negotiations with Shah Alum with the intention of giving British support to his campaign to take over the throne of Delhi. The idea was to emulate Clive and rule all of northern India through a puppet emperor.

There were two obstacles, however: Shah Alum remained hostile to the British, and the new British commander, Carnac, Clive's old confidant and a realist, realised there was no prospect of negotiation. Accordingly he launched a largely successful attack on Shah Alum's forces, capturing Jean Law and most of the French party at last, and seeking the emperor's *firman* when Shah Alum was forced to sue for peace.

Vansittart stubbornly revived his grandiose policy of an alliance with Shah Alum, under which British troops would install him on the throne in Delhi. The enterprising young man now readily agreed. The whole idea was pure folly: the success of such an expedition so far from supply lines from Calcutta was anything but certain; and to strip Bengal of its defences in pursuit of this alternative would have been to invite a seizure of power by Mir Kasim.

Fortunately, Mir Kasim was himself so enraged by the proposal that he failed to reach this conclusion himself. He saw the British aim as being to install one of their own placemen in Delhi who would then strip him of his authority in Bengal. He would not support the proposed British expedition, refused to swear allegiance to the emperor, and recalled his army from Carnac's command.

The British commander was enraged, but Vansittart pursued his policy of appeasement towards Mir Kasim. However, the directors in London had appointed Clive's old sparring partner, Sir Eyre Coote, as the new commander of British forces in Bengal, and he now arrived in Patna to take up this post. Coote, cussed and obstinate as ever, insisted that Mir Kasim come to Patna to swear his allegiance to Shah Alum. The Nawab, encamped outside the city, refused to do so. Lacking his backing, Shah Alum eventually left for Delhi without British support, scuppering Vansittart's ambitious plan to bring all of northern India under indirect British rule.

Furiously, Coote demanded an audience with Mir Kasim and, when this was denied, rampaged through the camp 'in a great passion, with his horsemen, peons, sepoys, and others, with a cocked pistol in each hand . . . uttering God-dammees into my tent', as the Nawab later complained. At long last Mir Kasim was persuaded to swear allegiance to the emperor.

Based in Calcutta, Vansittart seethed at this disrespect shown by Coote to the new Nawab and at the failure of his plan to march on Delhi, which he blamed on Coote's insubordination. In fact Coote, like the other British commanders, had seen through Mir Kasim.

The new Nawab had won half a battle: the proposed collaboration between the British and the emperor had failed. He now sought to oust the old enemy of central power in Bengal, Ramnarayan, Governor of Bihar, who had been so loyal to the British. The ridiculous Vansittart was persuaded, and possibly bribed, to suspend Ramnarayan from his post. Coote was appalled, writing from Patna that he was 'heartily tired of being employed for a service where there is so much corruption and villainy'.

Ramnarayan, one of the staunchest allies of the British, had his wealth stripped from him and was then murdered. The message was clear. The British were prepared to deliver up their Hindu allies to the new Nawab. Clive's subtle power structure of checks and balances – the regional noblemen checking the central authority, the Hindu merchant class balancing the Moslem aristocracy – lay in ruins.

Mir Kasim now embarked on a reign of terror in Murshidabad. All potential enemies were placed under surveillance. The Hindu merchants were watched closely. The Seths were placed under house arrest. The seething cauldron of conspiracy that was Murshidabad under both Mir Kasim's predecessors was taken off the boil by his ruthlessness. Mir Kasim switched his capital to Monghyr, away from possible plots.

The new Nawab dispensed with the sprawling Bengali army and began to recruit a much more effective one consisting of European mercenaries and deserters; his right-hand man in this task was a former French sergeant, by trade a butcher, Walter Reinhardt, under the Indian alias of Sumru.

Thus equipped, Mir Kasim began to challenge the power of the British at their weakest point: the grotesque economic exploitation under their rule. In May 1762 his soldiers began to stop ships bearing the Company flag and to search British trading agents. The notorious agents retaliated, beating up the Nawab's officials on a number of occasions. Mir Kasim complained angrily to the British, and Vansittart sought to meet him halfway: in this matter, at least, the Nawab held the moral high ground.

The governor met him at his new capital of Monghyr in December 1762, and agreed on a new regime of tariffs, as well as the right of the Nawab's officials to decide disputes. Vansittart and his cronies also accepted a substantial bribe, estimated at around £200,000. On his return to the capital, he found the whole British community up in arms at this act of appeasement and apparent sellout. The council refused to ratify the agreement.

Angrily, Mir Kasim promptly announced that equal duties would now be levied on everyone, including Company agents, and in March announced that duties would be removed altogether. This was immensely popular among the miserably oppressed peasantry and merchants, but it was a final slap in the face and declaration of independence from the British, most of whose profit came from these levies.

Vansittart immediately sought talks with him, but he announced that he would receive British envoys only if they were unaccompanied by soldiers. Meanwhile those old British allies, the Seths, were arrested in Murshidabad and brought to Monghyr. The two British envoys, Hay and Amyatt, were insulted and at length only the latter was permitted to leave Monghyr. In July Hay and his few retainers were set upon outside Murshidabad and he was killed, his head being presented to the Nawab.

Mir Kasim hurried his armies up to Patna. There was talk that he had forged a pact with the most powerful prince in north India, the Nawab of Oudh, the de facto ruler in Delhi. The British commander outside Patna, William Ellis, staged a pre-emptive strike, seizing the city. However, while his force was engaged on a punitive expedition outside Patna, the Nawab's forces seized it back. Ellis's small army was surrounded and forced to surrender.

Matters had now almost reverted to what they had been at the time Siraj-ud-Daula seized Calcutta six years before, in advance of Clive's conquest: a state of undeclared war existed between the British and the ruler of Bengal. The difference this time was that the British had a good and well-commanded army in the field. Of the five powers that ran Bengal after Clive's departure, four – the directors in London, the governor, the council and the Company agents – were all either venal or incompetent or both. Only the soldiers were to save the day, displaying both tactical ability and political good sense.

In early July, the council at last declared war on Mir Kasim, and Mir Jafar was nominally reinstated as Nawab at Murshidabad. To the colonists' intense relief, it was quickly apparent that Mir Kasim, for all his energy, brutality and shrewdness, had overreached himself militarily. A considerable British force under Major Thomas Adams marched on Monghyr, winning a series of engagements against Mir Kasim's forces, which while much more effective than the giant Indian armies of the past, were ill-trained and ill-motivated by comparison with the British troops and their sepoys. In August Adams secured the redoubt of Undwa Nala, defended by 40,000 men, and took 100 cannon.

Mir Kasim retreated to Patna as the British force approached, taking the Seths with him; on the way he had them beheaded –

partly to impress the British, partly because they were part of a plot against him. Thus ended the career of the Banker of the World and his brother, possibly the richest men in India, who had played so crucial a role in Clive's seizure of power and subsequent government of Bengal. Ramnarayan was drowned by Mir Kasim's men in the Ganges with a bag of sand tied around his neck.

The following day, Mir Kasim's chief military commander was also executed, almost certainly because he had been implicated in the plot with the Seths. The ruthlessness of the man Vansittart and Holwell had naively installed as Nawab had not yet reached its apogee. Early in October he reached Patna, just as Adams, after a string of victories, captured Monghyr itself.

Out of revenge, Mir Kasim ordered the British troops and civilians captured at Patna to be executed. Reinhardt – alias Sumru, his right-hand man – ordered his troops to surround the prison on 6 October. There then followed a massacre much less well known but even more horrific than the Black Hole of Calcutta in numbers, in the premeditation with which it was carried out – Mir Kasim had directly instructed Sumru to do the deed – and in its method.

The three senior Britons were summoned to Sumru's presence and promptly cut to bits, their remains being thrown down a well. The remainder were then attacked with swords and other weapons, prompting a furious fight by the doomed men using the few pieces of wood and bottles that came to hand. Every one of around 100 soldiers and 50 officers and civilians was slaughtered.

This atrocity against a European power was unprecedented. But the political reverberations were to be far smaller than the Black Hole, which had been used as a cover both for the English humiliation in Bengal and for Clive's subsequent conquest of the country. It was an atrocity that shrieked to the very gates of hell.

As Adams's army advanced remorselessly against what Carnac labelled the 'most obstinate resistance infinitely above whatever was made by a black army before', Mir Kasim abandoned Patna which, after a ten-day siege, the British successfully stormed. The British commander then turned his attention to pursuing Mir Kasim – but stopped at the border of the British dominions – the Karamnassa river between Bihar and Oudh – which he refused to cross without authorisation from Calcutta. To pursue Mir Kasim was one thing; to declare war on Oudh another. Soon afterwards the formidable Adams was taken ill and had to return to Calcutta, where he died.

The ever-resourceful and vicious Mir Kasim now entered an alliance not just with the Nawab of Oudh, but with the former fierce enemy of them both, Shah Alum, the young Mogul Emperor. The danger of a united front between the three was a serious one for the British, particularly because of the reputation of the Nawab of Oudh, who was effectively the ruler at Delhi and a far more impressive warrior and statesman than either the bold but ill-supported emperor, or the vicious Mir Kasim.

By January 1764, lacking proper leadership, the European forces, some of them French, who had captured Patna under Adams were mutinous. Some defected to the enemy, the remainder being bought off. This prompted a mutiny by the sepoys, who similarly had to be remunerated. Carnac, in the nick of time, arrived to take control. He advanced over the river a short way to Buxar, reluctant to extend his lines further.

His caution proved all too sensible. The swollen army of the three Indian allies moved around his flank into Bihar to cut him off. He fell back swiftly to avoid this, attracting fatuous criticism from the armchair generals in Calcutta. On 3 May 1764 a ferocious battle was fought lasting all day, on which the survival of British rule in Bengal hung by a thread, and the Indian army was at last pushed back. But Carnac did not have the strength to go in pursuit, and the loyalty of his troops was also in doubt. In Calcutta, the council was furious at his 'inaction', although any hot pursuit could have ended in a military disaster for the British – which so far had been avoided by the narrowest of margins.

More worrying still, Mir Jafar himself had begun to intrigue against the British as of old, probably out of fear that he might be toppled in a plot, and insisted on the appointment of the unsavoury Nundcomar as his chief minister. It was soon reliably reported that the latter was negotiating with the three Indian allies. The prospect of the triple alliance against the British being joined by an internal insurrection within Bengal was alarming. Carnac was treading on very thin ice indeed. Clive's empire was tottering.

Under the barrage of ill-informed criticism from Calcutta, Carnac, who was seen as Clive's stooge, was recalled and a Scottish soldier of quite formidable toughness and ruthlessness, Major Hector Munro, was despatched to try and quell the desperate threat in the west. It is possible that Carnac lacked the necessary steel; but his tactical retreats had at least held the line. Like his friend Clive, there was no element of savagery in him.

The same could not be said of Munro; the desperate nature of the threat, particularly in the absence of Clive's military genius, may have required a harsh response to counter Mir Kasim. Within a short time of Munro's arrival, a nearby garrison mutinied. The new commander promptly seized twenty-eight of the mutineers and court-martialled them.

Eight were tied over the muzzles of cannon, which were then fired – an old Indian method of punishment, but one which had a devastating effect on those that witnessed it. Munro wrote with satisfaction, 'there was not a dry eye amongst the [English] marines who witnessed this execution, although they had long been accustomed to hard service; and two of them had actually been on the execution party which shot Admiral Byng in the year 1757'.

The remaining twenty were executed at different military outposts, as examples. The mutinous tendencies of these front-line border troops disappeared overnight. The danger to them of disobedience was greater than that posed from the front by the enemy.

In October 1764, Munro, with his strengthened and disciplined forces, at last advanced on Oudh against the three allies – the powerful Nawab of Oudh, the audacious Shah Alum, and the vicious Mir Kasim. Unlike Clive at Plassey, Munro had done little to strengthen his position through intrigue. His army was only twice the size of Clive's – around 900 European troops, 900 Indian cavalry and 5,000 sepoy infantry.

The army of the three Indian allies was around 40,000 strong, about the same as Clive's opposition at Plassey. They included 5,000 legendary Rohilla cavalry, and had not been suborned and divided through conspiracy as at Plassey. The Battle of Buxar lasted from dawn to dusk on 24 October. It was fought with scarcely believable ferocity before the Indian army finally fled. The sepoy infantry was described as 'a wall which vomited fire and flames' against the approaching cavalry.

A large part of the rump was surrounded and slaughtered

because it could not get across a river whose bridge had been destroyed on the orders of the Nawab of Oudh to discourage retreat. It was a harder fought engagement than Plassey, and involved much greater slaughter, which only served to underline Clive's skill in avoiding a full-scale engagement in his own battle. The stakes were not quite as high – the three allies would still have had to conquer all Bengal had they won.

But it decisively tilted the scales against the triple alliance, and strengthened the precarious British position after Clive's departure from India. It was certainly the most important battle that had been fought by the British in India after Plassey. The grim, ferocious Munro deserves the credit for a remarkable victory. Shah Alum was the first to recognise this, congratulating Munro and saying that he had been no more than a prisoner of the Nawab of Oudh, which may have been partly true.

Mir Kasim fled, and this vicious and formidable antagonist of the British in India was reduced to wandering poverty. As late as 1776 he surfaced, writing to Warren Hastings that Sumru and Mir Jafar had connived in the execution of the British prisoners. He died destitute in a tent at Paliwal near Delhi a year later; his last shawl was sold to provide a winding sheet. Bloodthirsty and ruthless though he was, he deserves some credit as the first Indian ruler who had tried to throw off the British colonising yoke, and one who was a much more effective soldier and intriguer than either Chanda Sahib in the Carnatic or Siraj-ud-Daula in Bengal; unlike them, he escaped with his life.

The Nawab of Oudh, refusing to surrender Mir Kasim to the British, fled to the west where, with depleted forces, he sought the help of the Marathas who for a time made him their virtual stooge. Munro meanwhile pushed his way forward like a steamroller through battle after battle and had seized Allahabad by February 1765.

The goal was Benares, the sacred city that was the capital of Oudh. The council at Calcutta, always wildly over-optimistic, assumed that Munro's successes meant that the huge kingdom of Oudh was theirs for the taking. They demanded that Benares be given over to the British and that Mir Kasim and Reinhardt be handed over. They offered Oudh to Shah Alum in exchange for the revenues from Benares.

The young emperor was by now firmly on the British side. But the Marathas, with the Nawab of Oudh as their reluctant leader, launched one last ferocious attack. Carnac, who by now had been restored to the British command, defeated them in a short, furious fight on 3 May, and the Nawab surrendered himself to the British. The Marathas were driven out a couple of weeks later after another battle. The Nawab claimed that he had been an unwilling tool of the Marathas and, like the emperor before him, pleaded for reconciliation with the British.

What had happened in Clive's absence was a relapse into corruption and incompetence on the part of the colonists which had almost resulted in the loss of Bengal; only the extreme toughness and ability of the British military commanders in the field had averted disaster. The success of men like Carnac, Coote and Munro in the field proved that Clive's military exploits against Indian arms could be repeated. What had been sadly missing was his common sense, political genius and administrative skills.

The stupidity and cupidity of his political successors had very nearly lost the empire he had won; and that was to prompt his return. With extraordinary difficulty the empire had been just maintained in his absence; but politically it was rotten to the core. The wretched Vansittart was replaced by a governor hardly less incompetent. Clive's empire had been saved only through superb soldiery. The whole structure of a mercantilist council, presided over by an incompetent governor astride a subculture of venality and greed was no foundation for a permanent colonial structure.

As reports of the chaos in Bengal filtered back to England several months later, Clive, his domestic political fortunes at a low, bogged down in his fight for the jagir, found himself increasingly drawn back to the affairs of the continent where he had made his name. He had backed Vansittart at the beginning, who had shone with 'so peculiar and bright a lustre'. He had opposed Coote, Vansittart's enemy. He was indulgent towards Vansittart's 'one false step' of installing Mir Kasim.

He was then absurdly snubbed by the vain young governor. When Clive sought to make a present of an elephant to the king, Vansittart had two shipped in to George III in the early hours of the morning without informing Clive. Clive began to realise that Vansittart was resentful of his predecessor and in league with Sulivan. He wrote to Walsh that the new governor was 'a very dirty fellow'.

The chaos in Bengal had played into Clive's hands. As the East India Company's shares fell by some 14 per cent, Clive proposed that he should return to India with exceptional powers to save the situation. He wanted to be avenged on his enemies in the country and to restore good government to his terrifyingly ill-governed and abused conquests. This marked a turning point in his career. Up to then, his greatest ambition had been to achieve political power in England. India had been but a springboard, in terms of both money and reputation. After his return in 1760, he had never intended to go back to Bengal. Now, bitterly frustrated at home, he sought to revisit the scene of his first glory, once again as absolute ruler.

On 12 March 1764, at the general court of proprietors, it was proposed that Clive return as governor amid tumultuous acclamation. Clive said he would do so only if the directors fully backed him – in other words, if Sulivan was removed as chairman. Clive published a furious attack on his opponent – *A Letter to the Proprietors of the East India Stock*, some sixty pages long.

On 12 April the election was held, with Clive winning six directors, Sulivan six, while twelve were uncommitted. Sulivan, however, failed to secure the chairmanship, and Clive's ally Rous secured the post. By nearly 200 votes, the general court of the East India Company voted to extend his jagir by ten years, while a slightly ridiculous statue of Clive in Roman dress was erected in East India House.

Clive also succeeded in laying down his terms for a return to Bengal. They included dictatorial powers over the council and a minimum standing army of 3,000 European troops. For his part he promised 'not to enrich himself by one farthing by any pay or emolument he might receive' – a bow in the direction of pressure from the grass roots of the Company. But his pledge also marked the advent of an older and wiser Clive, who would lack for nothing now that he had secured his jagir. Clive was appointed a Knight of the Bath at last – although still not an English peer. He claimed that his return to India constituted 'a very great sacrifice and a point of honour against my own natural inclinations'.

Yet as he prepared for his third and last tour of duty there, he contemplated departure from a country where in spite of his magnificent houses, estates and wealth, he was politically a third-rater, mere lobby fodder for the forces ruling England at the time, sneered at by many of his contemporaries, with no prospect of significant advancement. In India he would once again become a virtual dictator, the first citizen in the land at a crucial turning point in the continent's history, the potential saviour of British interests which were now threatened for a third time.

The greatest misery was to leave his children, Ned, now 10 and just starting at Eton, Becky, Charlotte and the tiny Margaretta; all three girls had been born since his return. Miserably, Margaret agreed to 'follow the fortune of my first and best friend, my husband . . . contributing towards making my Lord's stay in India less afflicting to him in such a separation from his children'.

But renewed pregnancy intervened at the last moment and, almost certainly to her great relief, she had to stay behind. Clive, now embarking on his own, wrote sadly, 'God only knows how much I have suffered in my separation from the best of women.' It was the first prolonged break in their married life, although there had been shorter ones while he was in Calcutta and she in Madras, and her relationship with him had long been conducted in the curious hubbub of a virtually ceaseless public existence.

Clive's first letter to Margaret on board ship suggests a hint of reconciliation after marital discord. 'Nothing could afford me greater pleasure than to find you reconciled to my departure in a manner consistent with that good sense which I know you to be mistress of, and consistent with that superior duty which you owe to our children.' It is hard not to believe that there had been considerable anguish between them – whether in her disapproval of his decision to go back to India, or her disappointment at not being able to leave, or his disapproval of her failure to accompany him.

Clive's letter was, for him, unusually long and thoughtful. He wrote extensively to her on the journey, a sign of how difficult the break must have been. He himself was accompanied by Mun, her brother, and his aide-de-camp and a newcomer to his entourage, Henry Strachey, his private secretary, a protégé of George Grenville. In addition Clive travelled in style as usual, taking an assistant secretary, a steward, a valet, a groom, a French chef and four musicians – truly the retinue of a potentate.

By contrast with his speedy last voyage, the *Kent*, which left Portsmouth in June, took more than four months just to get across to Rio de Janeiro. The journey, as Clive amusingly described it, was plagued by one Mrs William Sumner who 'seemed possessed of every disagreeable quality which ever belonged to the female sex without being mistress of one virtue (chastity excepted), to throw into the opposite scale'. She insisted on the windows being kept open, and played the same tune on the harpsichord for four hours a day.

At Rio, the ship put in for nearly two months and Clive's musicians all deserted him to join the Rio Opera. He was furious, writing childishly with the implied threat of attack to the Portuguese viceroy that he was 'too sincere a friend to the Portuguese nation to deprive her capital settlement of any of its defenders, especially in its present weak and almost defenceless condition'.

In fact Clive enjoyed the tropical heat and extraordinary beauty of the town, with its backdrop of mountains cascading to the sea, and was far from unhappy with his sojourn there. A month after sailing, as the winds turned favourable, he reached Cape Town. After a further five months, he arrived in Madras, where he learnt of Munro's victory at Buxar.

By now he had wearied of months of inaction and wrote feverishly to Rous in England of his plans. 'See what an Augean stable there is to be cleansed. The confusion we behold, what does it arise from? Rapacity and luxury, the unreasonable desire of many to acquire in an instant what only a few can, or ought to, possess . . . in short the evils, civil and military, are enormous, but they shall be rooted out.'

Once again briefly ensconced in that scene of his youthful glory, Fort St David, he immediately reassumed the mantle of man of action, dictator, Emperor of India, Clive the all-powerful. The frustration of his limited political power in England, of his inability to make an impact there, of his struggles with the armchair generals in Leadenhall Street, devious directors and scurvy politicians, slipped away.

At nearly forty years of age, Clive was a man with a mission again – the most challenging of his entire career. He was about to declare war not on another native prince, but on his own countrymen, his colonial successors, those who had nearly squandered his achievement in conquering Bengal. That they would be harder to fight than his old Indian opponents, he had no doubt. His task was nothing less than the establishment of good government in India. 'Alas, how is the English name sunk,' he lamented. He would raise it again to new heights.

It seemed a terrible irony that Clive, who had enriched himself more than any single individual through his conquest of Bengal, should now persecute his fellow countrymen for doing the same. But that can be ascribed to his greater maturity and vision in middle age. He was no longer an ambitious young adventurer out to make his fortune, but a statesman who saw that the Indian empire would have to be consolidated if it was to survive at all.

The time for plunder was over. The time for good government, for placing what was to become the Raj on firm foundations, had arrived. It was a formidable task, and he could by no means be certain he would succeed. If he failed, British India was doomed at birth; if he persevered, he could claim the credit not just as a great military commander and conqueror, a shrewd diplomat and politician, but as a true statesman.

On this third tour of India, Clive had arrived with some of the fury and reforming zeal Oliver Cromwell had displayed in England 100 years before. The two men could not have been less alike in some respects: in particular, Clive lacked a sense of divine mission and was overfond of the good life. But in his energy, fearsome determination and – now – radical reforming instincts, Clive had returned to India as Cromwell once had to his quarrelsome parliament, to dissolve his own creation and commonwealth because it had proved unworthy of him.

Clive had set the British to rule over Bengal, and they had failed him. He must come back as military dictator, sweep the whole rotting structure away and start afresh. 'Take away this bauble,' Cromwell had said in disgust, seizing the mace of the House of Commons. Clive's temper was hardly better when he arrived at last down the familiar, sluggish, steamy stretch of the Hugli river opposite the elegant Georgian sprawl of Fort William at Calcutta.

He had never expected to see it again. As he was brought ashore in indignity on a porter's back, he was greeted by a respectful council headed by John Spencer, who had succeeded the wretched Vansittart. He was accorded every pomp and deference – practices instituted by the vainglorious Vansittart – a European bodyguard decked out in white and gold, mace bearers and no fewer than 100 servants to attend him in his magnificent house on Fort William's main promenade, to which he soon added two large wings.

He cut a magnificent figure in full uniform, at the height of his energies, tall, with the no-nonsense gait of command, an ample stomach and a gaze of ferocious determination that intimidated his fellow countrymen, not to mention the terrified Indians he came into contact with. No longer nagged by domestic concerns and a wife to bring him down to earth, he was power and energy incarnate.

On the day he arrived, he took his seat in council and asked to be informed of events during his absence. He received his old sparring partner, Jean Law, now reinstated as governor-general of the French trading post, and Vernet, still in charge of the Dutch possessions. He greeted a small crowd of dignitaries. He took to bed paper and candles so that he could continue to work all night.

Clive learnt that after Mir Jafar had returned to the throne, the British had imposed a staggering demand of £530,000 on him as compensation for the ruin and atrocities inflicted by Mir Kasim – whom the British had themselves installed. A further £250,000 was demanded as a gift for the army and navy. The old man could only pay by instalments, and was forced to disband a large part of his army to raise the money; Mir Kasim had helped himself to most of the treasury.

Meanwhile the abuses Mir Kasim had tried to resist had returned with a vengeance. The system of tariffs and duty-free passes for the British had been reinstated. They and their agents would quite openly plunder whole villages of their produce. As the situation declined alarmingly, Mir Jafar had died at last on 5 February.

The council had chosen as his successor his exact opposite, a plump, uninspiring youth, Najm-ud-Daula, son of Mir Jafar by a dancing girl. The aim was to set up a puppet king. The council under Spencer and its most dominant personality, John Johnstone, imposed its terms: the Nawab's army should be reduced to the status of a bodyguard, along with a police force for keeping public order and raising taxes. The British would appoint his ministers – and his chief minister was to be Muhammad Reza Khan, an old ally of the

British. Nundcomar, the old Nawab's chief minister, the devious brahmin who had attempted to frustrate the colonial power at every turn, resisted this, but was stripped of all his offices. Only Rai Durlabh, the last veteran of the original Bengali cause at Plassey, remained.

Johnstone, himself a veteran of Plassey, was a tough-minded, obstinate man with a large bald head, a determined brow and huge eyebrows. He ruthlessly imposed the British terms upon the unfortunate young man. The new Nawab was forced to make the council a further gift of £140,000 – which Johnstone claimed to have been spontaneous, but the boy was later to assert had been extracted from him. Only a month before, an edict had arrived from the Company in London forbidding employees to accept gifts of more than 4,000 rupees. This Johnstone and his colleagues blatantly ignored.

Clive commented bitterly in a letter to Carnac on the mess he had inherited. 'I arrived here this morning to take possession of a government which I find in a more distracted state, if possible, than I had reason to expect.' He was truly appalled as he caught up on his papers the following day. He found 'evils' shocking to human nature. 'What do we hear of, what do we see, but anarchy, confusion, and, what is worse, an almost general corruption.'

He flung himself upon the council like an avenging tornado. He summoned it to tell it that its powers had been superseded by himself and a select committee of three – including his friend Carnac – appointed by the directors in London. One young council member asked a question, and was brutally cut short by Clive.

Johnstone rose and suggested that the select committee's powers were in fact limited. Clive fixed a furious stare upon him and asked if he was dissenting from the formation of the new committee. Johnstone, disconcerted, replied that this was not the case. 'Upon which,' in Clive's words, 'there was an appearance of very long and pale countenances, and not one of the Council uttered another syllable.'

From the first, Clive considered Johnstone the prime instigator of the general corruption in Bengal. He had been in partnership with William Bolts, perhaps the most notoriously venal and oppressive of Company servants, and had made a colossal fortune in just two years. Within weeks Clive had the evidence he needed. The young

Nawab came to see him, and claimed that Johnstone had extorted the £140,000 present from him.

Clive promptly arrested two of Johnstone's servants as witnesses, and reported him to the directors in London. Johnstone resigned, and in retaliation sought to find legal reasons why Clive should not draw on his jagir. Clive had made a bitter and powerful enemy: one of Johnstone's brothers was under the protection of the Bath estate. Another, an MP, had previously supported Clive in his disputes with the Company in the hope of getting John Johnstone reinstated after an earlier dismissal by Vansittart.

Not only did this not happen, but Clive relentlessly persecuted the man. Johnstone petitioned the directors. Clive scathingly wrote to them, 'I hope you will not forget Mr Johnstone's minute and that you will make such discoveries as may enable you to give that gentleman such an answer as his impertinence and principles deserve.' In Bengal Clive's word was law. Matters were to be much more complex in England.

Chapter 22

Statesman at Last

C live's greatest concern was to reach a settlement that guaranteed the western borders of Bengal; most of these had already been secured by Carnac. Taking advantage of his immense prestige among the Indian princes, Clive set out in style to overawe that most ostentation- and magnificence-loving of peoples. On 25 June he left Calcutta in his splendid budgerow – a luxurious houseboat – and accompanying craft.

Mun Maskelyne and Strachey were with him, as well as a string of servants including his butler and valet, manservants, chef, pastry-cook, hookah bearer, betel-nut attendant, shaving barber and wig barber. An elephant, horses, hawks, and even a pack of English hounds were specially brought; on the way he also acquired a tiger. In an oriental luxury that perhaps no Englishman has ever flaunted, before or since, the party made its way upriver, stopping first at Murshidabad. There he stayed in a palace by the Pearl Lake endowed with magnificent gardens.

He greeted the young Nawab as ruler to subject. The British were given control of revenue collection from Bengal, Bihar and Orissa and handed the proceeds necessary to the Nawab to govern his province and maintain his city. The boy would retain 50 lakhs for his own household. However, he would also formally continue as governor of the province, to whom other Europeans would pay their respects.

Thus the Nawab was reduced to the status of constitutional monarch, having no power, not even that of raising revenue. He would administer his province in name alone. The young man was, Clive believed, overjoyed at having so large an income placed at his disposal, 'to squander away among whores, pagy fellows, etc. "Thank God," he exclaimed, "I shall have as many dancing wenches as I please." '

Clive continued on his triumphal progress to Patna, where he was due to meet with the troublesome but brave young Mogul Emperor and the fearsome Nawab of Oudh, Shuja-ud-Daula, to conclude a definitive peace treaty. But they had not yet arrived. On 1 August Clive's enormous cavalcade moved into the stunning Hindu holy city of Benares, with its 1,400 temples, many dating from before Christianity, which he was seeing for the first time.

As he arrived on the fabulous and macabre waterfront, with its funeral pyres and floating corpses, he was greeted by his old and dear friend Carnac – and at last by Shuja-ud-Daula. The latter was a remarkable-looking man, entirely different from the languid and dissipated princes of Bengal. Tall, enormously strong, in a long tartar dress that fell to his ankles, with a large fur cap on his huge head, his piercing gaze and broad, stiff black moustache gave him the appearance of an avenging tribesman.

Although past his prime, he delighted his guests with his party piece of slicing off a buffalo's head with a single stroke of his sword. Clive recognised that this was a man the British needed to ally with to secure the frontier, not a weak and devious leader of the Bengali kind. The two men instantly liked each other; and the peace agreement was a formality. Clive decided to be generous and to give Shuja-ud-Daula back all of Oudh except for Allahabad and Korah, which were to become the private fiefs of the Mogul emperor; in exchange he would have to pay the relatively small sum of 50 lakhs to the Company, and the British were to be allowed to trade duty-free in Oudh. His kingdom and Bengal were to be bound by an alliance.

The agreement was, in fact, a skilful piece of statecraft. Only a few years before, Clive had tantalised Pitt with the prospect of conquering all of northern India. Now he was determined that the British should not overreach themselves, but consolidate their hold on Bengal. He had bitterly criticised British penetration into the subcontinent as far as Allahabad – 'a march I highly disapprove of. I mean absolutely to bound our possessions, assistance and conquests to Bengal.'

Now he added: 'To go further in my opinion is a scheme so extravagantly ambitious and absurd that no governor and council can in their senses adopt it, unless the whole system of the Company's interest be first entirely new-modelled.' He was undoubtedly right. The British could not possibly have held on to Oudh as well as Bengal in the long term, and would probably have lost both if tested at this juncture.

It had been Vansittart's grandiose folly even to consider this. Clive's modest hope was that his treaties would bring 'a peace for two or three years'. In fact the Nawab respected the treaty for eight years, and Oudh was to provide a sometimes unsatisfactory buffer state for the British Raj for almost a century.

Clive's decision was a model of far-sightedness, restrained ambition and good judgement. His next appointment was with the emperor, who languidly declined to come forward to meet him, sending him ludicrously inconsequential letters instead. If the Mogul could not go to Clive, Clive must go to the Mogul, and he set off to Allahabad on 9 August to meet the largely powerless figure with the greatest family prestige on the subcontinent, a man who approved every princely appointment yet commanded barely any real forces or territory – except those the British were about to give him.

As the Shahzada he had been one of Clive's most persistent and troublesome foes; he was far from being the usual decadent holder of his throne. He had proved himself strong-willed, a good and tenacious fighter, not excessively given to cruelty, and something of a tactician and a statesman, carving out for himself a role from the very poor hand he had been dealt as the son of a puppet, however distinguished.

Clive found him a young man, very dark, with a 'grim deportment bordering upon sadness'. He repeated his old ambition for the British to restore him to the throne at Delhi, which Clive politely declined. In exchange for the *diwani* – his seal of approval for British tax collection for Bengal, Bihar and Orissa – he accepted the two provinces of Oudh that were offered him and an income from Bengal of 26 lakhs.

The following day, in a slightly ludicrous ceremony in Clive's tent, the lugubrious young man was placed on a throne consisting of a draped armchair on a dining-room table, and formally awarded the *diwani* to Clive, his subject, beneath him. Thus occurred the formal beginning of the British Raj in India.

Clive stayed on another three days at the court of his nominal imperial master, before being driven by 'bugs and flies' to leave. He left behind a brigade of European troops in Allahabad to protect the Mogul Emperor in his 'palace', a bungalow, where he retained a 'shabby sort of grandeur, continuing to implore the British to fight to reinstate him to Delhi'. In later life he briefly regained this, only to be defeated by the Rohillas. Blinded, so that he could not see the treasure he allegedly concealed from his conquerors, he had to seek British protection again.

Clive returned downstream in his luxurious river procession, taking just a fortnight. He wrote sweetly to Margaret on the way: 'It would amaze you to hear what diamonds, rubies and gold mohurs have been offered to Lady Clive because she has not signed covenants. However, I have refused everything . . . Action, as formerly, agrees better with me than indolence and laziness . . . I am as happy as a man at such distance from his wife and family can well be. I have the testimony of a good conscience to support me in the most arduous task that ever was undertaken, no less than a total reformation in every branch of the civil and military departments, never was such a scene of anarchy and confusion, bribery, corruption and extortion seen or heard of . . .'

He also handed out an admonition against Philadelphia Hancock, the doctor's wife Margaret had made such a close friend in Madras, who had become a close confidante of Vansittart and his wife, and had then had an affair with Warren Hastings, bearing his son. 'In no circumstances whatever keep company with Mrs Hancock for it is beyond a doubt that she abandoned herself to Mr Hastings, indeed, I would rather you had no acquaintance with the ladies who have been in India, they stand in such little esteem in England that their company cannot be of credit to Lady Clive.'

Margaret was evidently furious at Clive's comments, and crossed out the lines referring to Philadelphia Hancock. It was another sign of what seemed to be a subterranean rift between the two. She had failed to accompany him to India at the last moment for the best of reasons – her pregnancy; and now defended her friend against his priggish admonition – which was surprising for one who had had a relaxed attitude towards sex during his youth in India.

His royal progress along the Hugli to the heart of India seems to have gone to his head a little. He claimed that the *diwani* would provide extra revenues for the Company of around £1.7 million 'without oppressing or overwhelming the inhabitants'; his reforms, he said, would generate well over £2 million a year – a wildly optimistic forecast, although it was true that significant additional revenues were transferred from the Nawab's tax collectors to the British. The expense of the government of Bengal, which Clive reckoned at around £600,000, turned out to be nearly £1 million.

Undoubtedly the *diwani* helped the Bengali government significantly – but at considerable expense. While it limited the amount the Nawab and his court could cream off the revenues, it depended upon the exactions of the *zemindars* – tenants-in-chief – from the peasants. Naturally, so as not to be out of pocket, these raised their rents to meet the required amounts from the British. Worse, Clive set up a sepoy troop called the *pargana* battalion to enforce the payment of taxes brutally and often corruptly.

Moreover, Clive continued to rely on the inefficient and corrupt advisers of the Nawab, whose authority was now minimal. The governor had no alternative: he had far too few advisers to administer his huge realm. But the Nawab's government, devoid of the necessary force and funds for bribery to keep the government going, deteriorated, losing authority and plunging Bengal into a state of nature.

It might be easy to see in Clive's achievement an almost classic morality tale of the destruction wrought by colonisation. An established local structure of administration was being gradually undermined by the seizure of its revenues. Yet a generation later the vacuum was to be filled by that master-administrator, Warren Hastings. Clive certainly undermined the foundations of what in reality was a longstanding system of colonial rule by an Islamic upper class. But a much stronger political system was soon to be imposed and arguably this was less despotic, if no less colonial, than that of the old nawabs.

Clive exulted ludicrously at achieving the *diwani*: 'Fortune seems determined to accompany me to the last; every object, every sanguine wish is upon the point of being completely fulfilled, and I am arrived at the pinnacle of all I covet, by affirming the Company shall, in spite of all envy, malice, faction and resentment, acknowledge they are become the most opulent company in the world, by the Battle of Plassey; and Sir Hannibal Hotpot shall acknowledge the same.' Hotpot was Sulivan, who had been defeated in the 1765 election of directors.

Clive now plunged with furious rigour into reform; after trying to put the Company finances on a sound basis he tackled what he saw as one of the worst abuses of the system. The Company's agents were merchants whose prime motive was the amassing of large fortunes for themselves. It was unsurprising that abuse occurred on the large scale that it did, because their role was that of profiteers – a legacy of the days when the Company controlled a string of trading posts, not a territory the size of France.

Clive tackled the problem frontally. He established the Society of Trade, to replace the worst abuses in the commerce of salt, betel nut and tobacco, charged a 15 per cent levy for the salt monopoly – about half the previous level for Bengalis – and used its revenues for the first time to pay for a properly salaried civil service – in place of the previously nominal pay that Company servants, who were supposed to make up the bulk of their income from trade, had received. The governor was to receive £17,500 a year, council members £7,000 and so on down the scale.

Clive's bold and imaginative idea for setting up a new salaried official class, funded by a monopoly that had long existed in the past and was levied at a tolerably low level, was to be rejected by the directors in London – but reinstated by Warren Hastings. It was the embryo of the Indian Civil Service, the backbone of the Raj later on; yet it was soon to result in opprobrium being heaped upon Clive.

His lesser reforms consisted in ordering the first land survey of Bengal, founding a postal system and chipping away at the exploitation inflicted by the settlers. He also tried to force Company employees to stick to the new limits on accepting presents, most of which were not bribes but, worse, had been extorted.

He grimly stuck to his guns before the council. As one member wrote, 'Clive is really our King. His word is law and . . . he laughs at contradictions.' His chief opponents there, after Johnstone's departure, were a young man, Ralph Leycester, and George Gray. The latter's Indian agent was notorious for oppressing and robbing the local people, and Clive had him formally accused of extorting money from the prostitutes of Calcutta – to which Gray imaginatively replied that he had intended to set up a hospital for their 'loathsome distempers'. Leycester, more hotheaded, accused Clive of trying to set up a military dictatorship, whereupon he was suspended from the council. Gray returned home shortly afterwards.

Clive now had a majority on the council, as well as his control of the select committee. Undoubtedly his rule was arbitrary and despotic. On the other hand his end was just – to control the excesses of the colonists, and was probably the only means available under the circumstances. His detractors compared him to Henry VIII. Vansittart's younger brother, George, accused him of being 'guilty of so many acts of violence and oppression that his name will forever be abhorred in Bengal'.

Another council member, the unstable William Billiers, who had been notorious for repressing the population at Patna when he was its chief, was placed under investigation by Clive. He killed himself, stabbing himself thirteen times. Clive is said in private conversation to have told Carnac, 'General, had I been in Vansittart's place, I would soon have gained the majority, for I would have sent you in arrest and then voted you away to the army.' Clive the dictator had no time for constitutional niceties even as he pursued the cause of good government in Bengal. It was the great irony of his third and last tour in India.

There were now four council vacancies. Clive refused to nominate new members from Calcutta, and sent instead to Madras for supporters: he had had enough of the 'children and fools, as well as knaves' of Calcutta. This caused a group of them under a 23-year-old, William Mahendie, to occupy the council room and block proceedings, while appealing directly to the directors in London against the injustices of Clive's rule.

Clive promptly dismissed Mahendie, as well as George Vansittart, another of the protestors; duty-free passes for their supporters were cancelled, causing them to lose their trading privileges. He wrote despairingly to Margaret:

The public business is become a burden to me and if anything endangers my constitution it will be my close application to the desk. I am no longer walking about the room talking politics or dictating Persian letters to Nabobs, Rajahs etc. I am no longer making preparation for campaigns and fighting. My whole time is taken up in introducing economy and subordination among the civil servants, in reforming most notorious abuses, and sometimes, when I am dared and compelled to it, in detecting frauds and bringing to shame individuals. In short I will pronounce Calcutta to be one of the most wicked places in the universe. Corruption, licentiousness, and a want of principle seem to have possessed the minds of all the civil servants. By frequent bad examples, they are grown callous, rapacious and luxurious beyond conception, and the incapacity and iniquity of some and the youth of others here obliged us to call from Madras four gentlemen to our assistance. With their assistance I expect to bring this settlement to some order, although the gentlemen here all mutinied upon their being sent for. However, they shall be brought to reason and ruled with a rod of iron until I see a reformation in their principle and manners . . .

In short, I have undertaken the most disagreeable and odious task which my honour obliges me to go through with. I am become the slave of the Company and the detestation of individuals, and my constitution cannot bear it long if I am not relieved by the Madras gentlemen.

Within three months, the mini-rebellion had petered out.

The vigour and zeal with which Clive sought to stamp out corruption had a dramatic effect. It laid the foundations of the moral administrative approach later to be adopted by the Raj. Starting as an unashamed plunderer at a time when there were no inhibitions against this, Clive was ending his career as a colonial warden determined, first, to limit the greed of his fellow country-men; second, to create a new governing class of public-spirited and uncorrupt civil servants; third, through regulating and legitimising the British presence, to endow the British with the authority to rule in India; and, finally, through a policy of incorruptibility, to secure the support of the local people.

He moved rapidly too to revive his old divide-and-rule policy, keeping the feeble Nawab and his chief minister on the defensive by favouring the Hindu merchant class again, in particular the sons of the murdered Seths. In the short term, Clive was not to succeed. However rigidly his policies were applied at the centre, abuses continued unabated in the countryside, and for a while after he departed it seemed he had never been.

Yet he had blazed a trail; for the same policies were to be pursued by Warren Hastings and his successors, and were to underpin nearly two centuries of British rule, a remarkable achievement of colonial administration over so large and diverse a continent. Clive had started out as a warrior. He was bowing out as a gimlet-eyed reformer, setting goals of probity which other men were to follow.

Within weeks of his putting down the 'puerile' rebellion on the council, Clive was faced by potentially the most serious crisis of his career. Those who believed he had become a cantankerous, luxury-loving middle-aged colonial administrator were soon to be surprised: for he was to show that he retained the speed, courage and cool-headedness that had characterised his early career. The crisis threatened to rock the very foundations of Clive's rule – his control of the military – and in the process place British control of Bengal at severe risk.

The crisis erupted on Clive in Murshidabad, where he had gone to receive the revenues of the tax collectors. Departure from the capital had provided the excuse for a deep-seated conspiracy to be rid of him. He had travelled upriver in style, as always, with a budgerow for sleeping in, one for dining in, and as many as 40 lesser vessels in support. His destination was the palace at Pearl Lake.

There, at the end of April, he sat beside the Nawab as the tax collectors made their submissions. In the evenings there were exotic dancing and tiger fights. As he withdrew from one of these he was met by Sir Robert Fletcher, one of his three principal commanders, who told him that all officers below the rank of major throughout Bengal had resolved to resign their commissions unless Clive rescinded his decision to abandon the 'double batta' – a payment initially made to officers by Mir Jafar which had become institutionalised. The directors had insisted that it be cut, although Clive tried to compensate by increasing officers' expenses.

This mass desertion was unprecedented; worse, an army of 50,000 Marathas was said to be advancing on Allahabad, the furthest reach of British power. A revolt of this kind, if it became known, could also spark off a major insurrection within Bengal. It was as if the kind of plotting so natural to the court at Murshidabad had spread to the British army, fatally undermining its authority.

Clive's three main commanders were Fletcher, Robert Barker, a sturdy soldier, and Dick Smith, brave if highly strung. Each commanded a brigade made up of a European battalion, artillery, a troop of Indian cavalry and six sepoy battalions. Fletcher's was quartered at Monghyr, Barker's at Patna and Smith's at Allahabad. Now all were apparently in revolt, in a well-organised plot co-ordinated by Clive's civilian enemies and the traders whose livelihoods he had encroached upon, who had close friends in the army.

In reality, the conspiracy was more serious and complex still. The rebellion had been instigated by none other than the vain and ambitious Fletcher himself. He had accurately calculated that Clive, in alienating the civil authority, now had only the backing of the military to enforce his will. An army revolt would demonstrate how exposed he was: if he gave way over the issue of the double batta, Fletcher and the army would dictate policy. Naked military dictatorship now threatened to leave Clive a puppet.

Clive, awoken from his indolence enjoying the dancing girls and tiger fights, responded as if he had been called to arms again. He volleyed orders to his commanders to arrest and despatch mutinous officers to Calcutta. He sent for officers from Madras to replace them. He bade farewell to the young Nawab, who was struggling from an infection that was to kill him four days later (his half-brother, Saif-ud-Daula, was placed on the throne) and set off for Monghyr, the centre of the mutiny.

It was the Clive of old. The officers had threatened to desert on 15 May. Clive furiously forced his small forces through ferocious heat, letting them sleep only three hours a night. Some of his men dropped dead along the way. He was blocked for a time by a river which had flooded, and failed to arrive in Monghyr until the 15th itself, by which time many of the rebels had left.

On their departure, part of the European force had mutinied, but had been bought off and threatened by sepoys under one Captain F. Smith pointing muskets at them while a band played the 'British Grenadier' to rally the men. The garrison at Monghyr was only just under control. Clive was told of a plot to assassinate him on his arrival. He took no notice. He insisted on entering the gateway to the fort in the company of only a major. There he faced an armed battalion of European troops.

Coolly, he ordered them to place their guns on the ground. They obeyed. 'Now I am satisfied you are British soldiers and not, as I was erroneously informed, assassins,' he told them. He had proclaimed as he approached the gate, 'I must see the soldiers' bayonets levelled at my throat before I can be induced to give way.' In the event it was not necessary. The loyal sepoys, who looked on Clive with something approaching veneration, were rewarded with two months' double pay (which cost rather more than the double batta). The rebel officers, who had camped outside Monghyr, were ordered back to Calcutta to be shipped home.

He marched on to Patna, where the mutineers submitted without a struggle. There he raised reinforcements. The Nawab of Oudh, now his ally, gave him a necklace for Margaret, which, unusually, he accepted. At Allahabad, learning that Clive was coming, most of the mutinous officers soon yielded. Only the ringleaders were arrested. Through his personal decisiveness and courage, Clive had shown that he could crush his own rebels more effectively than any Indian prince.

He then displayed his old moderation and magnanimity. Many of the officers facing deportation were promised reinstatement. This was granted for all but those at the very peak of the conspiracy, provided they signed three-year contracts which rendered them liable to the death penalty if they repeated their offence.

Clive had been informed by the rebels at Monghyr that Robert Fletcher had been the instigator of the revolt, persuading them to resign their commissions. He had already contradicted himself by first saying he had known of the plot since January, then only since April. In his late twenties, good-looking, petulant, arrogant and ambitious, he had already once been dismissed from his command for insubordination in the Carnatic. A protégé of Sulivan's, he was corrupt, a plunderer and a falsifier of expenses.

Confronted with the evidence, he claimed he had tried to penetrate the conspiracy from the inside. He was arrested in July, found guilty of mutiny and cashiered – although by rights he should have been executed for so serious an offence and for endangering the British position in Bengal. Meanwhile the chief rebel officers were forced aboard ships at Calcutta at gunpoint by sepoys. The most prominent, Captain John Stainforth, who had 'uttered threatening expressions against Clive and proposed to assassinate him', was merely cashiered, Clive insisting benignly that he 'bore a very good character, was recommended strongly to me by some friends, and is nephew to the Bishop of London'. He was reinstated in 1770, and went on to a distinguished eleven-year career, dying in India at Cawnpore in 1781.

It had been a remarkable performance. Clive had displayed unflinching courage and firmness in dealing with this challenge to his authority – and also clemency, perhaps too much so, for mutiny was usually a capital offence at that time, and his enemies were far from grateful. But Clive was never one to lust after blood. When he had first arrived in Bengal on this tour, he had insisted that all death warrants in Bengal should be shown to him – not the practice before – in an effort to limit the number of unnecessary executions.

Clive's last great challenge in India was over: he had crushed a dangerous military mutiny and a major challenge to the civil authority. His nearly 20 months of frenzied activity in Bengal as its dictator against his own countrymen was far from being a joyless affair, however. His last months in India were marked by his continued love of partying, pomp and pageantry.

His 'fandango' to mark the peace treaty with the Nawab of Oudh lasted four days, involving a dinner for 300, a ball, fireworks and fights between such exotic animals as a buffalo, a tiger and a camel, as well as an elephant and a rhinoceros. One elephant went wild after a fight with a rhinoceros and killed several spectators. Two days later, two elephants fought fiercely, their riders being thrown and killed, until they were separated with fireworks exploded under them.

At his palatial and now extended house, he would produce the best European wines (he had brought nearly 150 bottles of claret with him from England). His table served the best French as well as Indian dishes. One of his severest detractors paints a perhaps not wholly inaccurate picture of him at this time: 'If he was in good humour, he would encourage a free circulation of the bottle and by intervals stimulate mirth and jollity; but he soon relapsed in his natural pensive mood, and was after silent for a considerable time. His conversation was not lively, but rational and solid. As he seldom drank freely enough to be seen without disguise, he was impenetrable excepted to a few confidants to whom he entrusted the execution of his schemes and designs.'

The same source, the journalist and polemicist Charles Caraccioli, claims that Clive indulged himself in a succession of undignified advances to women, some successful, others not. In fact, Clive spent most evenings at his country retreat, Dum Dum, just outside Calcutta, with his two chief aides-de-camp, Mun Maskelyne and Strachey, and Samuel Ingham, his doctor, leading a quiet life.

Clive followed up his ruthless house-cleaning with two acts of administrative dignity and self-abnegation. Left a substantial legacy by Mir Jafar, who seems to have had a genuine affection for him, possibly because he had extended British protection to him at various crucial moments, Clive turned this into a fund for his soldiers' widows and invalid officers.

Second, he formally took an oath as governor not to engage in trade in exchange for a concession of one-eighth of the Company's revenues; it was another step on the road to setting up a salaried, independent colonial administration. Clive also ensured that his own nominee, Henry Verelst, would succeed him by discrediting the deputy governor, William Sumner, who had proved ineffectual and had apparently taken a large bribe from Mir Kasim. Clive also detested his wife – his companion on board ship two years before.

In November the governor fell ill again and plunged into a deep depression accompanied by the old abdominal pain and malaria; once again his constitution was catching up with the furious explosion of activity and overwork of the past two years. He wept and ranted. Carnac wrote to Margaret:

It grieved me beyond measure to see a person endued with such extraordinary firmness so oppressed in his spirits as to exceed any degree of hysterics I was ever witness to. I was more shocked as I had never seen him so before, but Mr Ingham [Clive's doctor] informs me he had a like attack or rather worse, in England, and he, who from his long attendance upon his lordship must be well acquainted with his constitution, has never judged him to be in any danger. It was thought proper to move my lord to Barasut, where we keep him clear of business, and from the change of air with the help of the bark the bile is wholly thrown out of his blood.

He began to revive only after the New Year.

On 1 February he sailed for the last time from the scene of his conquests, glory, trials and magnificence, leaving that exotic Palladian mirage on the Hugli. Carnac accompanied his master. Himself hugely rich, he was soon to be married to Elizabeth Rivett, celebrated as the prettiest woman in England. They called in at Madras, that other most elegant and rebuilt of forts whose fate had fashioned his early adulthood, and then set sail for England with a large menagerie of exotic animals and a dazzling display of jewels, cash and swords, some of them presents from Indian princes to the king of England, to arrive on a cold July day in 1767.

CHAPTER 23

The Plutocrat

C live on his arrival in England was still only 42 years old – on the face of it with a long career ahead of him. He was fêted now as the man who had cleared up the mess in Bengal and established the East India Company on a new financial footing. His allies among the directors, notably the chairman, Rous, had crushingly defeated Sulivan at the last election.

Within two days of his arrival he was received by the king and queen, to whom he handed a large array of exotic presents, including two diamond drops for the queen from Muhammad Ali, which entranced her. Even the catty Horace Walpole, who loathed Clive, for once shared in the general admiration for his achievement in Bengal: 'Lord Clive has just sent us the whole kingdom of Bengal, which the Great Mogul has yielded to this Little Mogul without a blow . . . and when all expenses are paid, there will be remitted to England yearly a million and a half – we may buy another war in Germany, and subsidise two or three electors.'

Of the presents to the Crown Walpole hissed, 'Lord Clive is arrived, has brought a million for himself, two diamond drops worth twelve thousand pounds for the Queen, a scimitar, dagger and other matters covered with brilliants for the King, worth twenty thousand more. These baubles are presents from the deposed and imprisoned Mogul, whose poverty can still afford to give such bribes.' In fact the Mogul had for the first time been granted his own small territory by Clive.

The returning statesman remained a subject of widespread public admiration. The directors were still his allies – although somewhat miffed at having to raise their dividend because of the expectations caused by his achievements in Bengal; he later suspected them of belittling him, but they were concerned that the value of East India Company stock should not reach unrealistic levels.

His success had prompted the government, now once again led by his old ally, William Pitt, elevated as Earl of Chatham, to set up a committee of inquiry with a view to the administration taking over the revenue and the running of Bengal – Clive's old idea, and one which inspired deep mistrust of him among the directors. There were rumours of an agreement between Chatham and Clive that this should happen in exchange for government support of an extension of his jagir for another ten years. In the event, Chatham in 1767 suddenly fell victim to a manic-depressive illness not unlike Clive's, and the Duke of Grafton became prime minister. The agreement, if there was one, was shelved and forgotten.

Clive's journey ended with his being reunited with Margaret after nearly three years' separation. She had lived at Westcomb, near Blackheath, so as to receive news of her husband from London more quickly. There her little coterie continued to surround her. Jenny Latham, her lively young cousin, had recently lost her husband. Ned Maskelyne had become Astronomer Royal and was based at nearby Greenwich. She busied herself with music and learning Italian.

Clive had written infrequently but tenderly to Margaret. He told his son, Ned, 'You have laid the foundation of that knowledge which alone can make you the gentleman, and distinguish you from the herd of your fellow creatures ... Attend diligently to your studies and to the advice of your Tutor but above all follow the instructions of your mother, let her excellent example be your guide and you will render yourself truly worthy of that great fortune which Providence seems to have designed for you.'

She had continued to write adoringly. 'Language is ever too weak to express the feelings of a tender heart,' she gushed. She had given birth to a beautiful baby girl, Elizabeth, but again tragedy had followed. The infant contracted smallpox and died, the fourth child to do so. Margaret had the consolation of Ned, just going to Eton, and the three surviving girls.

Soon after Clive's return, he fell ill. Margaret was exposed again to the worst side of his character, which tended to come to the fore when he was in England. His absolute authority in India had gone to his head once more. In his home country, where it was by no means so easy to get others to do his bidding, he tended to behave with command and brusqueness. This was all very well for servants and inferiors, but was deeply trying to his family and equals. The very trappings of his wealth contributed to the delusion that he was more powerful in England than he really was.

In particular, he treated the directors, who were by no means ill-disposed towards him, with thinly veiled contempt. His great friend, Scrafton, now himself a director, warned him that he should appreciate the efforts being made for him. He responded with regal disdain. 'Know, Scrafton, I have a judgement of my own, which has seldom failed me in cases of much greater consequence than what you recommend. As to the support which you say was given to my government by the Directors, they could not have done otherwise.'

When it was suggested he become a director himself, he responded loftily, 'The being a Director may be an object to the Directors, but not to Lord Clive.' Scrafton had underestimated the extent to which Clive despised the Company and sought to bring India under direct government control. His hauteur had reached manic and self-damaging proportions. The decision to approve the extension of the jagir was railroaded through with the reluctant acquiescence of the directors, winning Clive no friends and much unpopularity. Most considered he had enough wealth without the jagir, and gave it their 'unanimous though languid' approval.

Clive treated the directors as though they were his underlings, and complained alternately about them as 'mean' and 'sneaky' or 'timid and irresolute'. In fact they now sought eagerly to do his bidding on most Indian matters, including the appointment of officers, but Clive's illness and psychological state prevented him meeting them halfway.

He had by now become an emperor without clothes in a country with hundreds of years of constitutional development, an autocrat in a land where he had money but little power. All his old illnesses, physical and psychological, had returned to plague him with a vengeance; nor did England's cold and wet climate suit his constitution.

He travelled from house to house, estate to estate, as though visiting his far-flung dominions in India. He spent long periods in Bath, apparently the only place that agreed with him. From there he travelled to Birmingham where he fell ill. He was by turns gloomy, restless, hypochondriacal, constantly proclaiming himself at death's door. When he recovered, the long-suffering Margaret declared 'to all our family and friends. If all the bells are set a-ringing, I'll pay the ringers what they please.' There he sat up 'very hearty . . . forming schemes of future good behaviour as to eating and drinking and keeping quiet and in great spirits'.

He had an acrimonious squabble with Vansittart, whom he had taken care to cultivate, in spite of having had to pick up the pieces of his disastrous rule in Bengal. Vansittart indicated he wanted to return as governor there; Clive said he would try to help him return as governor of Madras – where he would cause less trouble. Vansittart then claimed Clive had promised to back him for Bengal.

Clive exploded, calling Vansittart 'the greatest hypocrite, the greatest Jesuit and the meanest, dirtiest rascal that ever existed'. It also became known that Clive had amassed a dossier of evidence of Vansittart's acceptance of presents – which, however, he refused to release out of consideration for his old protégé. Vansittart, who had already been Sulivan's friend, now became Clive's deadly enemy.

Yet the conqueror of the Indies' reputation – if not his health – was still riding high when he was advised by his doctors to go on an extended tour of France. He was accompanied by his 'court' – Margaret, her brother Mun, Strachey, his secretary, Ingham, his doctor, Jenny Latham and a host of servants. It proved to be a roaring success, for both his health and his psychological state.

The couple visited a succession of churches and chateaux, spent a fortnight in Paris sightseeing and attending operas and plays, and travelled to Fontainebleau, Dijon and Nîmes, before settling at a delightful country house at Montpellier. Clive seemed in excellent spirits, playing cards and chess on an Indian set resplendent with elephants and camels.

Margaret, as had happened with Carnac, developed a fixation with Strachey, a man nearly her own age – 33. When he left the French party unsuccessfully to stand for parliament in England, she bombarded him with teasing letters. 'What, you think to be written to again and again?' Margaret's interest in other men was entirely forgivable: Clive was older, had an impossible temperament for much of the time, and was always the public man, affording the two of them little privacy. If he resented her flirtations and relationships, there is no evidence for it – indeed Strachey, like Carnac, enjoyed his own closest favour.

Subsequently Clive's most scathing detractors – in particular Caraccioli – suggested that, as in Bengal, Clive's progress through France had been a string of sexual relationships with the locals. Yet however vigorous his sexual appetite in his youth, there is no evidence to suggest that Clive was unfaithful to Margaret; and his relationship with her remained real enough, for she became pregnant again the following year.

After the sojourn in the south of France, the party returned to Paris, visiting Versailles and Brussels and meeting with Clive's ablest and most capable adversary, de Bussy, before returning to England in September. Clive wrote sadly to Strachey, 'I suffer in the manner I did on board the *Britannia*, both from the bile and my former nervous complaint, but not more; which convinces me the roots of both disorders still remain, and I much fear I must be unhappy as long as I live, though I am certain there is nothing mortal in either of them and in all probability I shall drag on a miserable life for fifteen or twenty years longer as I have already done ever since the year 1752.'

Yet he was now plump, could ride for 15–20 miles, and had given up opium. He had had time to reflect on his ambitions in early middle age, and it was soon apparent that he had abandoned his goals in British politics. Rather, he preferred to perform two roles: as a wealthy country magnate and as a kind of godfather of Indian affairs, keeping his eye on events there and seeking to influence them his way.

It seemed a recipe for a gentle decline into comfortable obscurity – well deserved after his astonishing feats in India. Although still only in his early forties, his lifetime of responsibility and illness made him appear much older. The dynamo in India was now becoming a portly, sometimes cheerful, sometimes grumpy, country gent. But the controversy that had dogged his career was not about to leave him yet, and was to return in a backlash of blinding fury.

At the beginning of 1768, the horizon still appeared tranquil. Clive had succeeded in securing the election of three more MPs – his younger brother William as member for Bishop's Castle, Carnac as member for Leominster, and Strachey as member for Pontefract. Together with his father Richard, his cousin George, John Walsh, and Edmund Maskelyne, he now had eight MPs to represent him in his still somewhat languid dabblings in politics.

The issue of the day was John Wilkes, the roguish MP and the father of the modern tabloid newspaper. His scurrilous journal, the *North Briton*, had mercilessly satirised the king's favourite, the Earl of Bute, with such force that Wilkes was charged with sedition and expelled from parliament in 1764. It was he who made the famous riposte to the Earl of Sandwich; after being told, 'I am convinced, Mr Wilkes, that you will either die of the pox or on the gallows,' he replied, 'That depends, my lord, on whether I embrace your mistress or your principles.'

Wilkes went on to contest and win the following election, and was repeatedly expelled. But Grenville, Clive's patron, had moved into opposition and supported Wilkes. Clive found himself in the unlikely position of allying with the radical politicians, even attending a dinner held at the Thatched House Tavern in Pall Mall in honour of Wilkes's martyrdom. Wilkes, who had once attacked Clive, was now grateful to his plutocratic supporter.

But Clive's prime concern remained India. He regarded the directors as hopelessly incapable of running its affairs, while the government continued to take only a limited interest, preferring to extend the 1767 agreement for five years rather than take over the direction of the Company. With foresight, Clive remarked, 'Our wide and extended possessions are become too great for the Mother Country or our abilities to manage. America is making great strides towards independency, so is Ireland. The East Indies also I think cannot remain long to us, if our present constitution be not altered.'

The bickering within the Company continued. In 1769, Clive's enemies, Sulivan and Vansittart, were elected back on to the board of directors, largely through borrowing and buying stock. The new chairman, Sir George Colebrook, a lightweight although good company, kept the balance between the two main factions – those of Sulivan and Clive, although the latter remained the more powerful. To Clive's further dismay, Sir Robert Fletcher, the unpleasant, arrogant head of the mutiny against him, had managed to persuade Clive's old friend Stringer Lawrence that he had been unjustly accused and was reinstated as a colonel and elected to parliament, then sent to Madras.

The first rumbles of real trouble – but they were only distant ones – came when, following Clive's departure, the news from India began to turn bad again. The new governor, Verelst, a stolid, likeable man, was far less decisive than Clive. Dick Smith, the senior military commander in Bengal, was soon quarrelling with the council.

Clive's chief Indian agent, Nubkissen, his closest Indian intimate, who had been created a maharajah and set up a magnificent palace under Clive's patronage, had been accused of robbery, rape and abusing women in Clive's name – a move engineered by the latter's enemies in Calcutta now that the emperor was out of town. Johnstone told the general court of the Company that Nubkissen was known among his fellow Hindus as 'the Catamite' – a slur designed to rub off on Clive. However, Nubkissen was soon cleared of all charges, which had clearly been trumped up. A more formidable challenge soon emerged.

In mid-1769, Hyder Ali, a ferocious common soldier who had seized power in Mysore, marched on Madras, laying waste to the countryside. British troops were sent to fight him, but were forced to retreat after a series of clashes. It was the first time in recent history that the English had shown themselves to be vulnerable to Indian attack, and East India Company stock sank by more than 30 points – incidentally ruining both Sulivan and Vansittart, who had borrowed the money they needed to purchase stock to secure election to the board of directors.

Faced by this crisis, a temporary truce was arranged by Colebrook between Clive and Sulivan, who both recommended that a governor-general be appointed to run all British possessions in India. Sulivan insisted upon the wretched Vansittart for the post, and Clive would have none of it. Finally it was decided to send three 'supervisors' – Vansittart in Sulivan's interest, Scrafton in Clive's, and as a neutral, but in reality a close friend of Clive, his old fighting colleague, Forde.

The frigate *Aurora* set sail carrying the triumvirate in September. After leaving the Cape in December, it was lost with all hands. The incompetent Vansittart was no more, but nor were Clive's two great friends, Scrafton and Forde. Some investors blamed Clive for inflating the East India Company stock price – and for his rashness in selling £100,000 of his own stock when it peaked. But Clive could weather these minor irritants.

Meanwhile he pursued his interests, buying land and estates, improving his houses and suffering occasional bouts of dreadful depression and fatigue. Styche had been almost wholly rebuilt as a comfortable country house. His now frail father, Richard Clive, still dwelt there. Walcot had been elegantly and unostentatiously refurbished.

His other Shropshire estate, only 15 miles away, was more modest, but it was a fine and beautifully positioned house nevertheless. Oakly was set spectacularly in lush parkland overlooking the River Teme beneath the bustling and elegant town of Ludlow, long guardian of the borders against the wild Welsh to the west. Clive had substantially altered it, spending much of the summer there. The river, a fast-flowing, impressive current, cradled the house in a loop. On a steep rise above, Oakly was a picture of eighteenth-century elegance and tranquillity, surrounded by huge, ancient trees set in a park that rolled away towards sloping hills beyond.

Clive's third mansion was his London house, Number 45 Berkeley Square, on its west side, bought from Lord Ancram for £10,500. It was a fair-sized gentleman's house with a Palladian façade and a fine staircase. Furnished, according to Clive's wishes, 'in the richest and most elegant manner', with two drawing rooms whose walls were covered in scarlet damask and ceilings in gilded foliage, it also temporarily housed the art collection intended for Claremont. The American painter Benjamin West was preparing a magnificent set of paintings of Clive's exploits in India.

Claremont, near Esher in Surrey, bought by Clive for £25,000 in 1769 from the widow of his old enemy the Duke of Newcastle, who had died the previous year, had already one of the most distinguished and lovely gardens in England. The estate, originally owned by Sir John Vanbrugh, had been sold to the Duke, for whom Vanbrugh built an enormous and attractive house between 1715 and 1720. Vanbrugh and Charles Bridgman, the foremost garden designer of his time, tried modestly to break away from the French concept of rigid formal gardens and symmetry which were supposed to contrast with unpleasingly untamed nature beyond. The garden boasted a magnificent belvedere, a round pond, and a steep and elaborate decorative turf amphitheatre.

This daring approach was developed further by the famous William Kent in the 1730s. His speciality was to create gardens that, although highly contrived, appeared to all intents and purposes natural, just like the fashionable eighteenth-century landscape paintings of the time, with their decorous copses and ruins tucked picturesquely away. Sir Thomas Robinson wrote in 1734 that Kent's method was 'to lay them out and work without level or line . . . This method of gardening is the more agreeable as, when finished, it has the appearance of beautiful nature, and without being told, one would imagine art had no part in the finishing. The celebrated gardens of Claremont, Chiswick and Stowe are now full of labourers to modernise the expensive works finished in them ever since everyone's memory.'

The round pond became a lake with an island. A pavilion and a menagerie – the ancestor of the modern safari park – were built, the boundaries of the garden that gave on to nearby green fields were blurred, trees were planted more haphazardly and informally, and a picturesque grotto was created. Horace Walpole in 1763 described a fête in the garden: 'From [the Belvedere] we passed into the wood, and the ladies formed a circle of chairs before the mouth of a cave, which was overhanging to a vast height with woodbines, lilacs and laburnums, and dignified with tall stately cypresses. On the descent of the hill were placed French horns; the abigails, servants and neighbours wandering below by the river; in short, it was Parnassus, as Watteau would have painted it.'

After Clive bought it six years later, he invited the next giant of landscape gardening, Capability Brown, to do away with the rambling old house, on the grounds that the land around it was damp and low-lying, and replace it with a more compact neoclassical edifice on deeper foundations. Brown also sought to do away with what remained of the formal garden, including the amphitheatre (fortunately he was not successful). Brown was unhappy about tampering with the work of his predecessors, as well as the restricted size of the garden, and did not get on well with Clive. He was instructed against his will to set up a high fence around the estate to keep Clive's exotic animals in. Clive created Britain's first safari park there: a herd of antelope, Cape geese, guinea hens, cyrus birds and a pair of nylghau were among the more exotic species. There can be no doubt that Clive intended Claremont to be his main residence for the rest of his life, a fitting ducal seat – which makes his death, if it was suicide, all the more bizarre.

A garden designed by the very greatest designers of the classical age of English landscape gardens – Vanbrugh, Bridgman, Kent and Brown – Claremont was to enjoy an equally distinguished history after it was sold by Margaret in 1775. Forty years later it became the residence of George IV's daughter, Princess Charlotte, who, however, died in childbirth a year later. Her grief-stricken husband, Prince Leopold of Saxe-Coburg, was later to become father to the notorious King of the Belgians during the bloody and dark period of that country's colonisation of Africa.

Leopold frequently entertained his niece, the young Princess Victoria, and as queen she was to recall her happy days there with affection. After his death she in turn lent it to the exiled French king, Louis Philippe, and his wife, before it was passed on to the Duke of Albany, the queen's youngest son, and his wife, parents of Princess Alice, Countess of Athlone, who lived there into the 1920s. It is now a recently restored National Trust property.

Clive had smaller houses as well: apart from his old, renovated family house at Styche there was a town house at Bath bought from his old political patron, the Earl of Chatham, and several minor estate houses.

Margaret erected her own defences against her husband's erratic moods, retreating into her own world of music and learning languages, as well as – like her brother – becoming increasingly obsessed with astronomy. She entertained a little salon of intellectuals as well as her old confidants, in particular Jenny Latham, who in 1770 had married Margaret's favourite among Clive's retinue, Strachey. Maria Ducarel became Margaret's other close companion, and Clive found her something of an old bore.

The Clives only occasionally entertained in a grand style, holding the odd ball, and continued to be snubbed by the eighteenth-century aristocracy. However, his Indian cronies remained loyal and frequent visitors. Apart from Strachey, there was Walsh, Carnac and Clive's old companion, 'Daddy' King. Only Dalton seems to have fallen out with Clive, while the dejected Orme complained, wrongly, that Clive neglected his old friends. In Orme's case, this was understandable.

In September 1770 Clive suffered another ferocious attack of depression, falling over on several occasions. Sometimes he felt ecstatically well, sometimes at death's door. Three months later he travelled to Bath where he learned that his political patron, Grenville, had died. At about this time he engaged the services of an able but sardonic and somewhat disillusioned Scottish lawyer, Alexander Wedderburn.

Clive continued in his role as great magnate. He estimated his own worth at £555,000 (about £11 million in today's values). He bought estates in Radnorshire and Monmouth, in the Welsh hills, Shropshire, and as far as Okehampton in Devon, which gave him an additional seat in parliament. He was an enlightened landlord, repairing his tenants' fences and improving their land. In 1771 he bought the magnificent Oakly estate near Ludlow, which had belonged to the Earl of Powis, and began to convert the house. He also bought the Earl of Chatham's house in Bath, which he assiduously restored.

The year was tinged with sadness. Richard Clive, so earnest a promoter of his son's interests, fell ill. Clive promptly sent him 'a hogshead of the best port wine which can be bought for money', but he died in May. His mother also soon passed away.

The same year Clive became an avid collector of paintings, relying on an American painter, Benjamin West, and the Scottish expert William Patoun to advise him. Clive made some poor choices, but bought a magnificent Veronese 'Visitation', a 'Cephalus and Procris' by Claude, and a Poussin, 'The Family of Moses', hanging most of them in Berkeley Square. Later, he bought two Vernets. Clive's taste was not spectacular and he was reliant upon expert advice; but he must have had something of an eye for a good picture.

He also paid a visit to Spa in France in 1771, and felt much recovered. Apart from the bouts of illness, life was pleasant although not active enough for this most mercurial of men. He faced decades of tranquil prosperity ahead unless his energies were once more required by his fellow countrymen.

Britain in 1771 was on the threshold of a new, altogether more serious age. The effervescence of the eighteenth century and its light, airy, exuberant art, architecture, literature and criticism were about to be replaced by the ponderousness of responsibility. The string of colonial victories was now coming to an end, as the threat of rebellion loomed in America. The huge Indian empire acquired by Clive's buccaneering adventurism in the finest tradition of the English gentleman amateur now brought searing responsibility. Above all, the new supremacy of the middle classes, based on prosperity, a flourishing entrepreneurial spirit and technical and business innovation, was about to give way to the new mass period of disfiguring urbanisation and industrialisation.

Major change was perceptibly creeping across the land. It was the age of speed, travel, and the end of the first generation of bright young things since the Restoration a hundred years before. Clive would have observed the revolution from his luxurious carriage as he travelled rapidly between his estates, on the roads and along the rivers, in the fields, on the approaches to the expanding metropolitan centres and in their new main streets. The next 50 years wrought more change to the British landscape than the previous 500.

As Clive's liveried carriage hurtled along, it would have overtaken others belonging to wealthy noblemen, the ultimate status symbol, as well as public hackneys and stage-coaches with their relatively well-off passengers huddled inside and the poorer ones freezing on top. But Clive's own fast-moving vehicle would have been passed not just by hard-riding, mud-spattered couriers but by dandified figures in light post-chaises taking advantage of the new network of 'turnpike' roads.

Speed astonishing by the standards of previous generations was now possible. As late as 1740 it still took around six days to travel from Chester to London. By 1780 it took just two days. The time from London to Gloucester was slashed from two days to one. A journey from Bath to Oxford would take only 10 hours, at a miraculous speed of seven miles an hour.

The novelist Richard Gaves had one of his characters comment in 1779 that 'the most remarkable phenomenon which he had taken notice of in these late years, in his retirement, was the surprising improvement in the art of locomotion, or conveyance from one place to another. "Who would have believed thirty years ago," he says, "that a young man would come thirty miles in a carriage to dinner, and perhaps return at night? Or indeed, who would have said, that coaches would go daily between London and Bath, in about twelve hours, which, twenty years ago, was reckoned three good days journey?"

Others tut-tutted about the new craze for speed. The novelist Charles Jenner had one of his characters denounce 'flying, a practice with which he always found great fault. He has often observed to Norris, that it was a great pity there was not some officer whose business it should be to stop every man travelling post, and inquire whether his business was such as could justify killing a horse or two, risking the necks of half a dozen post-boys, throwing three or four servants into fevers, from excessive exercise in keeping up with their master's chaise, and forty other like accidents, which happened more or less every day, from the fashionable mode of travelling [for] the mere satisfaction of saying at York, I was in London this morning.'

For Clive, the speed must have been more reminiscent of his furious rides between Trichinopoly and the coast than his stately progresses by barge up the Hugli. Accidents and congestion had become major problems, as was the new corruption of morals as landowners neglected their estates for the bright lights of the city and young ladies descended on the towns, making new acquaintances among fellow-passengers on stage-coaches.

As Clive's own coach clattered inexhaustibly from Shropshire to Bath to his estates in the West Country and then to London and Kent, he could reflect on the new roads that made the speeds possible. In stark contrast to the muddy tracks of the past, the roads were paved, properly maintained and run to make money. In Clive's youth, during the 1730s, there had been only 25 turnpike acts; between 1750 and 1770 there were 340.

By 1770 turnpike roads, which had barely linked Birmingham, Chester and Manchester with London 20 years before, criss-crossed the whole country in an intricate gridlock from Truro to Aberystwyth, Holyhead, Glasgow, Edinburgh, Berwick-upon-Tweed, Hull, Norwich and Dover. By 1765 there were an astonishing 20,000 private coaches on the road, excluding stage-coaches and hackneys for public transport. The proliferation of private transport broke down rural isolation and local commercial monopolies, bringing local prices tumbling.

As Clive gazed out on the busy highway, he would also observe the other revolutionary communications enterprise under way – the canals snaking across Britain. This had begun with the waterways constructed to bring cheap coal to Liverpool and Manchester in the late 1750s. By the 1780s a hugely improved canal system permitted the economic transport of bulk goods the length and breadth of England, transforming local economies and making possible the development of cities well away from the coast or from ready sources of raw materials. It was this colossal public investment, harnessing private capital, that permitted the industrial revolution to get seriously under way.

As Clive peered out over the fields of England's green and pleasant land, he could not but observe that a revolution was under way there too: enclosures, by which individual farmers took over common land, were spreading rapidly. The land not owned by the big estates was being privatised. Nearly 4,000 enclosure acts were passed between 1750 and 1810, affecting roughly a fifth of all land in England and Wales.

The old village communes were replaced by a class of prosperous middling farmers, while the poorer rustics became seasonal labour dependent on the farmers' whim. There was some hardship caused, but the employment offered by the new agricultural improvements was also considerable. 'Engrossing' permitted the amalgamation of small tenant farms into bigger units, driving many peasant small-holders off the land. Farming banks sprang up around the country, financing the new prosperous farms to stockpile their produce and drive up prices.

The novelist Frances Brooke summed up the impact of the changes in her *History of Lady Julia Mandeville*: 'It is with infinite pain I see Lord T— pursuing a plan, which has drawn on him the curse of thousands, and made his estate a scene of desolation; his farms are in the hands of a few men, to whom the sons of the old tenants are either forced to be servants, or to leave the country to get their bread elsewhere. The village, large and once populous, is reduced to about eight families; a dreary silence reigns on their deserted fields; the farm houses, once the seats of cheerful smiling industry, now useless, are falling in ruins around him; his tenants are merchants and engrossers, proud, lazy, luxurious, insolent and spurning the hand which feeds them.'

There was a breakdown in the old privileged relationship between landowner and farm labourer: many of these became the fodder for the new industries. It is wrong, though, to see enclosures as a cause of the industrial revolution, except in that they released some capital. Industry did not spring up to absorb surplus labour: rather, the new unemployed were lucky that industry expanded at about that time to provide them with work. Even farm workers with settled employment were attracted by the supposed comforts and wages of the new industries.

Arthur Young, on his travels, heartily welcomed the new trends, complaining of the 'sleeping, dronish state of vegetation in which so many landlords are ever content to drawl on, and not raise rents because their grandmothers did not'. He urged that Salisbury Plain be enclosed: 'What an amazing improvement would it be, to cut this vast plain into farms, by inclosures of quick hedges, regularly planted with trees as best suit the soil.' Today's countryside, with its hedges, large fields, copses of trees and occasional villages is largely descended from this era: the isolated smallholder with his field or two and the heavily populated village cultivating common land were becoming a thing of the past.

Even so, the image of a countryside near to social breaking point under the impact of commercial change and the exactions of the rich is wide of the mark. The naturalist Gilbert White wrote: 'As to the produce of a garden, every middle-aged person of observation may perceive, within his own memory, both in town and country, how vastly the consumption of vegetables is increased. Green-stalls in cities now support multitudes in a comfortable state, whose gardeners get fortunes. Every decent labourer also has his garden, which is half his support, as well as his delight; and common farmers provide plenty of beans, peas, and greens for their kids to eat with their bacon; and those few that do not are despised for their sordid parsimony and looked upon as regardless of the welfare of their dependents. Potatoes have prevailed in this little district, by means of premiums, within these twenty years only; and are much esteemed here now by the poor, who would scarce have ventured to taste them in the last reign.'

As Clive's carriage passed through Birmingham or reached the outskirts of London, he would have appreciated the enormous, self-confident expansion of urban Britain. London, from around 500,000 inhabitants in 1700, had nearly doubled by 1800. Even more impressive in relative terms was the fourfold growth of Birmingham, Manchester and Leeds between 1700 and 1770. At the beginning of the century only seven towns – Newcastle, Bristol, Yarmouth, York, Exeter, Norwich and Colchester – had more than 10,000 people; by 1800 the number was more than 50. The urban population jumped from around a fifth in 1700 to around a third in 1800, or about 2 million of England's 6 million people.

The second half of the eighteenth century also at last saw a concerted drive for urban improvement: the dingy, higgledy-piggledy, crack-paved, open-sewered streets of Clive's youth were no more. In 1754 Westminster was paved and lighted. Drain-pipes replaced spouts. Jutting house signs were replaced by numbers. Piped water was introduced, as celebrated by George Keate in 1779: 'The good order preserved in our streets by day – the matchless utility and beauty of their illumination by night – and what is perhaps the most essential of all, the astonishing supply of water which is poured into every private house, however small, even to profusion! – the superflux of which clears all the drains and sewers, and assists greatly in preserving good air, health, and comfort.'

Slums and appalling conditions continued to thrive in the approaches to London and other major cities. But the cramped industrial kennels of the Victorian era had not yet sprung up. For the most part Clive's England was a joyous combination of the best of the old with the vigour, dynamism and change of the new before the latter's ill-effects were to sink in. Clive was himself to be partly responsible for one other major contribution to the industrial revolution: the capital from empire that was to produce the spark that fired Britain's economic engine.

To Clive, then in his mid-forties, the 1770s offered a combination of excitement, vigour, elegance and intellectual challenge. It was good to be alive. He was immensely rich, powerful and widely respected. Four years later, he was dead, denigrated, despised and probably the most detested man in England.

CHAPTER 24

Typhoon

T he first sign that Clive was about to face the final drama of his lifetime came in 1771. His old enemy, Laurence Sulivan, broken and destitute, had left the board of directors in 1770. But Lord North, the new prime minister, who had taken a shine to Sulivan (Clive was still in opposition), persuaded the proprietors to re-elect him. Clive saw Sulivan as no threat at all.

At about the same time, however, there arrived the news of the awesome famine of 1769–70 that wiped out one-sixth of Bengal's population. R. J. Minney writes, 'People gnawed at the barks of trees for nourishment. Mothers fed on their dead infants. Children ate their dying parents . . . Hundreds of villages were left without a single survivor.' An eyewitness wrote: 'The Hugli every day rolled down thousands of corpses close to the porticos and gardens of the English conquerors, and the very streets of Calcutta were blocked up by the dying and dead.'

The country's wealth seemed endangered for ever. One poetic witness, Lord Teignmouth, wrote in words that still resonate in India today:

> Still fresh in Memory's eye, the scene I view,
> The shrivell'd limbs, sunk eyes and lifeless hue;
> Still hear the mother's shrieks and infant's moans,
> Cries of despair and agonising groans.
> In wild confusion, dead and dying lie:
> Hark to the jackal's yell, and vulture's cry.

The Company had just appointed a new governor in place of the three supervisors lost at sea – Warren Hastings, who had served his apprenticeship with Clive, but had since become Vansittart's intimate. Both Clive and Sulivan had approved the nomination.

Hastings, Clive claimed, had 'the opportunity to become one of the most distinguished characters of this country'.

He wrote patronisingly, though with genuine insight, to Hastings that he must face difficulties 'with cheerfulness and confidence, never entertaining a thought of miscarrying till the misfortune actually happens; and even then you are not to despair, but be constantly contriving and carrying into execution schemes for retrieving affairs, always flattering yourself with an opinion that time and perseverance will get the better of everything'.

Clive still seemed loftily unconcerned that Sulivan, with his fierce, workaholic personality, was once again in control of the board of directors and that Hastings was his nominee. Clive's deadliest, most unforgiving enemy was in control of the Company just as total disaster struck in India. Clive had no idea of the typhoon that was about to be unleashed against him.

Hastings's first action had been to unravel the system of government set up by Clive – the 'dual system'. He assumed direct responsibility for raising revenue and displaced the Nawab's chief minister, Muhammad Reza Khan, as effective ruler of Bengal. He also ended the tribute to the Mogul, in order to save money.

Clive considered this to be a double mistake. He pointed out that Hastings would be unable to police all of Bengal with the small British force at his disposal and, as the British were now legally responsible for the administration of the country, which was no longer formally in Bengali hands, the British government could argue it would have to assume responsibility for the country (this was in direct contradiction to Clive's old view that the government should take over Bengal from the directors).

But Clive's advice was ignored. For the Company itself, spurred on by Sulivan, was about to make him the scapegoat for every ill that had occurred in Bengal since his departure. To achieve this, Sulivan probably – although there is no decisive evidence – connived with the embittered colonists Clive had waged war upon during his last trip to India. They joined forces to destroy the man who had curbed their own brutal blood-sucking operations in India.

John Johnstone's influential brother, George, published an anonymous booklet attacking Clive; he and Ralph Lycet, whom the former governor had forced off the council in Calcutta, worked together to spread stories about Clive. At the same time Johnstone's former partner William Bolts, responsible for many of the atrocities perpetrated against the Bengalis, began to spread malicious gossip. He argued in a ferocious and untrue article called 'Considerations on India Affairs' that Clive had set up the salt monopoly purely to enrich himself (he had unwisely invested a small amount in it).

Clive was also accused of buying stock on 'insider' information – he had made a profit of a meagre £1,000 on stock bought in Madras before arriving in Bengal. He was charged with manipulating the coinage to make a fortune for himself, which was entirely untrue, and even of murdering Najm-ud-Daula, the unhappy puppet boy king, for which Clive had not the slightest motive.

Alexander Dow, one of the officers involved in the mutiny against Clive, followed these accusations up with a vicious attack on Clive in his preface to the third volume of the *History of Hindostan*. Another officer, John Petrie, also involved in the rebellion, furnished evidence to the directors about Clive's alleged corruption. The press now carried ferocious attacks on him – as an opium addict, an extortionist and a whorer.

It would be interesting for those who grumble about the excesses of the modern tabloid press to consider the insults heaped upon Clive in those pre-libel days. According to various scurrilous tracts put about anonymously but almost certainly financed by his enemies from Indian days, Clive, when not indulging with Covent Garden prostitutes, was flitting between the beds of actress Peg Woffington, the mistress of actor David Garrick, Kitty Clive, the ex-wife of his cousin, and George-Anne Bellamy, the mistress of his friend, the lawyer George Wedderburn. On one visit to Paris, according to the same sources, he had affairs with the Marquise de Courtanvaux, Mlle Clairon (mistress of his old adversary in India, the Marquis de Bussy), and indulged in homosexual orgies dressed as 'the Prophet Mohamet' with others disguised as the Holy Roman Emperor and Pope Honorius I. He was also initiated into the 'Sacred Fraternity of Glorious Pederasts', with the honorific title of King of Sodom, joined in a homosexual ronde and indulged himself with the Comte de Mirabeau, later to be celebrated in the French Revolution.

Later attacks were to include fictitious 'journals' allegedly written by Clive's doctors. One, by the supposed surgeon in Fort St David,

Dr John Rae, suggested that Clive had acquired a demonic libido after being circumcised as a young man in India. He and his colleagues were also 'raped' by a gang of wild Indian women. There is no record of a Dr Rae having lived in India at the time.

According to 'Dr Ingham's journal', 'If opportunity offers, his Lordship will indulge his desire for laced mutton; if not he will content himself with her ladyship or retire to his toilet-room and masturbate. 'Tis no exaggeration to say His Lordship hath one of the most abused membrums in Europe, for that he is affected with priapism (satyriasis, persistent erections and excessive desires) and must spend his semen or go out of his wits.' Clive's friend and doctor in later life was indeed called Ingham, but he had died several years before many of the entries in his 'journal'. This gives some flavour of the squalor of the attacks upon Clive – which may have been remotely based on his reputation as a womaniser in his youth. He certainly appears to have had a healthy sexual appetite – but there is no firm evidence that it extended to anyone other than Margaret after his marriage.

He was denounced as 'the great wicked lord that sold his soul to the devil', 'the king of vice and corruption', a 'monster mogul' and 'vice nabob'. Walpole claims facetiously to have asked Clive, 'Is it true that in India money grows on trees? I have just got wind of a so-called pagoda tree, which yields golden fruit, and that to shake the pagoda tree is to harvest a rapid fortune. Pray tell me more of this fabulous growth.' To which Clive is supposed to have retorted, 'My dear sir, you wonder why Britons have dirty ears. You've been talking in them for twenty years!'

However, even the leaders of respectable opinion joined in the condemnation of the state of Indian affairs. Chatham spoke of 'that rapacity, plunder, and extortion which is choking to the feelings of humanity and disgraceful to the national character . . . India teems with iniquities so rank as to smell to earth and heaven.' Burke was carried away: 'The Tartar invasion was mischievous, but it is our protection that destroys India . . . There is nothing before the eyes of the natives but an endless, hopeless prospect of new flights of birds of prey and passage, with appetites continually renewing for a food that is continually wasting. Every rupee of a profit made by an Englishman is lost forever to India . . . the golden cup of abominations – the chalice of fornications, of rapine, usury and oppression – which was held out by the gorgeous eastern harlot, was drained to the very dregs.' These speeches reflected a genuine groundswell of opinion; significantly, however, both men were to back Clive in his later trials.

It was bad enough for Clive to be subjected to an assault from his old Indian enemies. But opinion among the educated classes, which had once viewed India as a jewel in the Crown, had been revolted by the famine and astonished by the fall in East India Company stock, as well as the sudden reversal in British fortunes there. A myth grew up that the famine, which in fact was caused by drought, had been the result of exploitation by the Company.

Certainly its servants had been responsible for terrible abuses which had damaged agricultural production, but Clive had sought energetically to counter these, and they were not the cause of the famine. This was too subtle for public consumption. The ever snide and sarcastic Walpole continued to make mischief. 'The groans of India have mounted to heaven, where the heaven-born general Lord Clive will certainly be disavowed. What think you of the famine in Bengal, in which three millions perished, being caused by a monopoly of the provisions, by the servants of the East India Company?'

The 'chattering classes' of the time were, in addition, affected by a wave of social envy. After Clive returned with his ostentatious wealth, a whole succession of other men with new fortunes from India had followed. Many Clive himself had persecuted on his last tour of duty. They were derided and reviled as 'nabobs', the familiar corruption of Nawab.

Samuel Foote's satire, *The Nabob*, opened in 1773. Its villain was Sir Matthew Mite, who, 'from the Indies, came thundering amongst us; and, profusely scattering the spoils of ruined provinces, corrupted virtue and alienated the affections of all the old friends to the family'. Mite has social ambitions and has to be taught by a waiter 'the oaths and phrases that are most in use at the club'. He seeks to enter the House of Commons, bribing his opponent with a jagir. He is frustrated at last by moralisers who point out that, 'corrupt as you may conceive this country to be, there are superior spirits living, who would disdain an alliance with grandeur obtained at the expense of honour or virtue' . . . 'The possessions arising from plunder very rarely are permanent; we every day see what has been treacherously and rapaciously gained, as profusely and full as rapidly squandered.'

Richard Batwell, a venomous opponent of Clive, was as rich as the latter when he retired. Francis Sykes, an old lieutenant of Clive's, was worth around £400,000. Thomas Rumbold and Paul Benfield made colossal fortunes in Madras. Dick Smith, the military commander, enriched himself hugely. Smith and Sykes both bought big houses near Basildon. Both were disdained in polite society for their humble births, although Smith was in fact from a farming background, not the son of a servant, as was put about.

These men represented the first wealth independent of both the state itself and the urban merchant class of the big cities. They were vastly richer than most of the gentry class. By 1774 they controlled 26 seats in parliament and ten years later no fewer than 45. Small wonder a tide of envious educated gentry and middle-class opinion soon flayed the nabobs for their excesses and vulgarity. That Clive himself had fought to control these excesses went unnoticed; that he had left India long before the Bengali famine began was equally disregarded. He was by far the most famous prince of the Indian-enriched plutocracy, and the three furies of jealousy, snobbery and humbug battered against his door.

Cruelty, extortion from the native Indian aristocracy, oppression of the masses, greed, bad taste – all were blamed on Clive, although he less than any had been guilty of them. The greatest irony was that his worst critics were the representatives of the nabob class that he had persecuted during his last tour of duty.

The great whirlwind of moral indignation and vituperation, whipped up by score-settling enemies, now set upon Clive with unparalleled force. Macaulay for once was not exaggerating:

> He was, in fact, regarded as the personification of all the vices and weaknesses which the public, with or without reason, ascribed to the English adventurers in Asia. We have ourselves heard of men, who knew nothing of his history, but who still retained the prejudices conceived in their youth, talk of him as an incarnate fiend. Johnson always held this language. Brown, whom Clive employed to lay out his pleasure grounds, was amazed to see in the house of his noble employer a chest which had once been filled with gold from the treasury of Moorshedabad, and could not understand how the

conscience of the criminal could suffer him to sleep with such an object so near to his bedchamber. The peasantry of Surrey looked with mysterious horror on the stately house which was rising at Claremont, and whispered that the great wicked lord had ordered the walls to be made so thick in order to keep out the devil, who would one day carry him away bodily.

Clive gave every indication of being genuinely bemused by the ferocity of the attacks. Apart from his bouts of depression and illness, he had seemed settled in the role of powerful country magnate and political broker. His following of eight MPs was one of the largest for an individual in the House. He could still entertain ambitions for government office or another generalship. He was rich, powerful, feared, respected and famous.

Now he was being battered by waves of criticism from his many enemies – but nothing, he believed, against which he could not defend himself. His appearance at this time was arousing comment: he was prematurely aged, his faced lined and careworn, his hair fast receding under his wigs, his teeth broken and yellowing. Yet these were the consequences of a life expended at a furious pace under extreme conditions as much as of the stress brought on by his critics. He was at his best under attack.

In May 1772 he at last had his opportunity to defend himself. The Company sought to forestall the wave of public clamour for the excesses in India to be brought under control by insisting on the 'better regulation' of the colonies. Sulivan initiated the debate in the House of Commons, while the Earl of Chatham, a pale shadow of his former self, watched.

After a few speeches, Clive was called. Considered no orator in the House before, he held it spellbound with a detailed and fluent defence of his last tour in India. He described how he had never indulged himself in corruption, or flinched from opposition to him within the Company.

Three paths were before me. One was strewed with abundance of fair advantages. I might have put myself at the head of the government as I found it. I might have encouraged the resolution which the gentlemen had taken, not to execute the new covenants which prohibited the receipt of presents; and although I had executed the covenants myself, I might have contrived to return to England with an immense fortune infamously added to the one before honourably obtained. Such an increase of wealth might not have added to my peace of mind, because all men of honour and sentiment would have justly condemned me.

Finding my powers thus disputed, I might in despair have given up the commonwealth and left Bengal without making an effort to save it. Such conduct would have been deemed the effect of folly and cowardice. The third path was intricate. Dangers and difficulties were on every side. But I resolved to pursue it. In short, I was determined to do my duty to the public although I should incur the odium of the whole settlement. The welfare of the Company required a vigorous exertion, and I took the resolution of cleansing the Augean stable.

It was that conduct which has occasioned the public papers to teem with scurrility and abuse against me, ever since my return to England. It was that conduct which occasioned these charges. But it was that conduct which enables me now, when the day of judgment is come, to look my judges in the face. It was that conduct which enables me now to lay my hand upon my heart and most solemnly to declare to this House, to the gallery and to the whole world at large, that I never, in a single instance, lost sight of what I thought the honour and true interest of my country and the Company; that I was never guilty of any acts of violence or oppression, unless the bringing offenders to justice could be deemed so; that, as to extortion, such an idea never entered into my mind; that I did not suffer those under me to commit any acts of violence, oppression or extortion; that my influence was never employed for the advantage of any man, contrary to the strictest principles of honour and justice; and that, so far from reaping any benefit myself from the expedition, I returned to England many thousands of pounds out of pocket – a fact of which this House will presently be convinced.

He concluded, in a blaze of cold indignation:

The Company had acquired an empire more extensive than any kingdom in Europe, France and Russia excepted. They had acquired a revenue of four millions sterling and a trade in proportion. It was natural to suppose that such an object would have merited the most serious attention of the administration; that in concert with the Court of Directors they would have considered the nature of the Company's charter and have adopted a plan adequate to such possessions. Did they take it into consideration? No, they did not. They treated it rather as a South Sea Bubble than as anything solid and substantial. They thought of nothing but the present time, regardless of the future. They said, let us get what we can today, let tomorrow take care of itself. They thought of nothing but the immediate division of loaves and fishes.

Nay, so anxious were they to lay their hands upon some immediate advantage that they actually went so far as to influence a parcel, of temporary proprietors to bully the directors into the terms. It was their duty, Sir, to have called upon the directors for a plan; and if a plan, in consequence, had not been laid before them, it would then have become their duty, with the aid and assistance of Parliament, to have formed one themselves. If the administration had done their duty we should not now have heard a speech from the Throne intimating the necessity of Parliamentary interposition to save our possessions in India from impending ruin.

The speech went down superbly. Chatham dubbed it 'one of the most finished pieces of eloquence' he had ever heard in the House of Commons. One newspaper wrote, 'Had his voice not suffered from the loss of a tooth, he would be one of the foremost speakers in the house. In fluency he has scarcely an equal; in a speech of three hours hesitating less than any person could imagine. His delivery is bold, spirited.'

Yet the wider press onslaught against Clive continued unabated. After the second reading of the India Bill, the government proposed that a parliamentary committee of 31 be set up to inquire into the affairs of India. The chairman was Major-General 'Gentleman Johnnie' Burgoyne, a loud-mouthed, self-confident blusterer who had eloped with the daughter of an earl, amassed huge debts in his twenties, and was later to prove a disastrous general in the wars of American independence. Clive's bitter enemies, George Johnstone, a coarse-mouthed killer and frequent dueller, older brother of John, as well as another brother and a nominee of Sulivan's, were members.

Clive, although himself a member, had the support of only Strachey. The rest were neutral.

The committee was nothing less than an inquisition into Clive's career. His past governance of India had effectively been put on trial; if some of the allegations against him were proven, it might yet be a prelude to his impeachment. Lacking the backing of a powerful parliamentary faction now that Grenville had died and Chatham was retired, Clive was effectively on his own. It seemed extraordinary that this cantankerous and bilious personality should be capable of making a reasoned defence against the huge forces arrayed against him. But once again, cornered by huge odds, he rose to the occasion.

What followed was one of the most dramatic, if shortlived personal confrontations in the history of the House of Commons, as one of its most eminent members was effectively put on trial. The argument raged backwards and forwards, first against Clive, then in his favour, then against. At no stage were his prospects of victory certain; indeed for much of the time his indictment seemed certain. The trial of Charles I in nearby Westminster Hall had been more celebrated; the trial of Warren Hastings was to be much longer and better remembered. But Clive's was as dramatic as either.

His latest scene of battle was just off the elegant eighteenth-century chamber of the House of Commons, smaller, more relaxed and even rowdier than its gloomy Victorian counterpart. It was, however, crushed and malodorous when fully attended, well-lit by Georgian windows by day, but ill-lit by lamps at night. Peppered by faction and the independence of its members, poorly controlled by government, it was rowdy, easily persuaded by oratory, capable more than at any other stage in its history of being swayed by a fine speech or a rush to judgement.

Clive's parliamentary enemies were led by a legion of embittered Indian foes: Sulivan, Vansittart and his brother Arthur, two of the Johnstone brothers and Sir Robert Fletcher. There were many other old Indian hands present too: Eyre Coote, Hector Munro, Thomas Rumbold, George Pigot, Francis Sykes and ·Luke Scrafton.

Johnstone insisted that the scope of the investigation should be pushed back as far as 1757, and Clive himself was one of the earliest witnesses in what was to be a lengthy and fierce cross-examination which he likened to being treated as a sheep-stealer. The conspiracy against Siraj-ud-Daula, the deceit of Omichand, the deal with Mir Jafar – all were raked up in minute detail. Clive defended himself articulately and coolly, although his memory sometimes failed him.

Clive was relentlessly cross-examined. His starting point was that 'Indostan was always an absolute despotic government. The inhabitants, especially in Bengal, in inferior stations are servile, mean, submissive and humble. In superior stations they are luxurious, effeminate, tyrannical, treacherous, venal, cruel.' Burgoyne probed mercilessly: why had Omichand been deceived? 'Because one and all considered him in the light of a public enemy, a traitor to the cause.'

Clive admitted he had thought up the plan for the treaty 'when Mr Watts . . . informed me that Omichand had insisted upon 5% of all the Nabob's treasure and threatened, if we did not comply with that demand, he would immediately acquaint Siraj-ud-Daula with what was going on and Mr Watts should then be put to death . . . I thought art and policy warrantable in defeating the purposes of such a villain. I therefore formed the plan of a fictitious treaty, to which the Council consented. I never made any secret of it. I thought it warrantable in such a case, and still think so, and would do it again a hundred times.'

Clive was brazen about the decision to forge Watson's signature. 'I gave Mr Lushington leave to sign Admiral Watson's name to the fictitious treaty; and to the best of my remembrance, Admiral Watson gave Mr Lushington leave to sign his name to the fictitious treaty . . . I should certainly not have declared that Admiral Watson had consented to have his name put to the fictitious treaty if I had not understood so from Mr Lushington. But I would have ordered his name to be put, whether he had consented or not.'

As to the jagir: 'What injustice was this to the Company? What injunction was I under to refuse a present from him who had the power to make me one as the reward of honourable service? I know of none. I surely had a particular claim, by having devoted myself to the Company's military service and neglected all commercial advantages. What . . . pretence could the Company have to expect that I, after having risked my life so often in their service, should deny myself the only honourable opportunity that ever offered of acquiring a fortune without prejudice to them who, it is evident, would not have had more for my having had less? . . . I never sought to conceal it, but declared publicly in my letters to the Court of Directors that the Nabob's generosity had made my fortune easy.'

Clive was asked, 'Should a servant be the lord of his master?' He replied pithily: 'I call upon the Court of Directors to declare whether they think, without the Battle of Plassey and its consequences, the East India Company would now be in existence.'

Pressed upon his rewards, he made his most famous, impassioned speech. He described his temptation:

When I entered the Nabob's treasury at Murshidabad – with heaps of gold and silver to the right and left, and these crowned with jewels – being under no kind of restraint but that of my own conscience, I might have become too rich for a subject . . . The Hindu millionaires, as well as other men of property, made me the greatest offers – which are usual upon such occasions – and had I accepted these offers, I might have been in possession of millions which the present Court of Directors could not have dispossessed me of. But . . . preferring the reputation of the English nation, the interest of the Nabob, and the advantage of the Company to all pecuniary considerations, I refused all offers that were made me . . .

Am I not rather deserving of praise for the moderation which marked my proceedings? Consider my position. Consider the situation in which the victory at Plassey had placed me. A great prince was dependent on my pleasure. An opulent city lay at my mercy. Its richest bankers bid against each other for my smiles. I walked through vaults which were thrown open to me alone, piled on either hand with gold and jewels. [He struck his forehead theatrically.] By God, Mr Chairman, at this moment I stand astonished at my own moderation.

Burgoyne was relentless, talking of 'crimes which shock human nature even to conceive . . . I look upon the deposing of Siraj-ud-Daula and the bringing about of a revolution in favour of Mir Jafar, to be the origin of all the subsequent evils which have operated to the temporary distress, if not total destruction, of the Company.'

Clive shot back,

I am accused of not having observed the rules of ethics in my dealings with a notorious scoundrel such as Omichand. It was my duty as a politician to deceive so great a villain. If the whole transaction were to be repeated, I should again enact what the gentlemen are pleased to term forgery or fiction; for so far was I from repenting the part I took in that revolution, that I glory in it as an act in every way conformable to my duty as a servant of that Company whose existence was preserved by the very means I am now to be censured for adopting . . .

Certain people would have me punished for the negotiations leading to the victory of Plassey and making it possible . . . Let future generations judge how it is possible that the victor of Plassey should be treated like a sheep-stealer by his own countrymen. The Baron of Plassey has acquired for the Company an income of four million sterling and a trade in proportion! If the authorities had done their duty, the spectre of ruin would not now be hovering above our Indian possessions.

Now a scapegoat is sought. And who has been chosen for that? I, who cleared out the Augean stable of corruption – and Bengal was nothing less than that – regardless of the fact that I was drawing the enmity of a whole class of people upon myself, those very men who thought they could plunder a nation of thirty millions with impunity . . . I pushed away the hands full of gold which were stretched out towards me, damned the flood of corruption which was submerging the country . . .

It was nothing but my duty. The committee have criticised my actions with spiteful meanness, and subjected me to a merciless cross-examination. I have acknowledged all the artifices which I have used; and I say frankly that I am not ashamed of any of the means which I have employed, and that I would use them again today under the same circumstances.

The committee raked over all the supposed misdemeanours of Clive. A huge number of witnesses were called – virtually all the major players in Bengal that were still alive. Very little of the mud could be made to stick. He emerged unscathed from the allegations about the salt monopoly and the supposed murder of Najm-ud-Daula. Only the Omichand affair continued to rumble.

Nevertheless, Clive could be satisfied: he had escaped the inquiry in reasonably good shape, and he had reason to believe that the controversy would now die down. That June he was installed a Knight of the Bath. Lord North, who wanted his support in parliament, installed him as lord lieutenant of Shropshire after his old patron and friend, the Earl of Powis, had died.

In the summer of 1772 Clive, attended by these marks of official favour, had reason to feel confident. The press campaign against him rumbled on. His enemies fumed. But he had been largely exonerated by parliamentary inquiry. Yet he had failed to take account of three things: first, the increasingly precarious finances of the East India Company – which required a scapegoat. Second, his increasingly isolated and exposed position in parliament: his political patron, Grenville, was dead; his hero, Chatham, incapacitated.

The king and his supporters looked on the upstart from India with some distaste as an unreliable ally and, worse, a supporter of the hated Wilkes during the rioting and troubles he had provoked. Lord North had no great regard for him. Clive was regarded as a maverick, a loose cannon beholden to no one, too often prone to do his own thing. The opposition parties – the Whig grandees who looked down on him, and the more radical elements who regarded him as an exploitative plutocrat – held him in no high esteem. In spite of his backing for Wilkes, Clive was a man of many enemies and few friends.

But he suffered from a greater disadvantage still. Clive had emerged from his last tour of India as the principal colonial reformer in the land, a man unafraid to defy not just the implacable opposition of the colonial settlers in India, but his own parent company, in an effort to impose good, stable and permanent government on Bengal. He had long pressed for Indian decisions to be taken out of the hands of the grasping and incompetent East India Company for the British government to administer directly itself – a wish which was soon partially fulfilled.

In so doing – even though he was right – he had antagonised virtually everyone involved in Indian affairs. He stood for realism and moderation in colonial expansion, good government, honest administration and the favourable treatment of colonial peoples. He seemed the natural person to apply incorruptibility and common sense to the American empire, now plunging into a dangerous crisis. The alternative approach was more simple-minded: to extract whatever material gain was possible from empire, and to rule with a heavy and corrupt hand.

Yet the king and government were deeply apprehensive about entrusting this most critical of problems to so independent a figure. Clive was known to view American independence as all but inevitable. Worse, he was believed to subscribe to the view of his old political hero, Chatham, who had emerged a morose and implacable opponent of the government's policies on America – a view in which he was to be fully vindicated.

The main force behind Lord North's American policy – which the prime minister himself only half-believed in – was George III and his crusty old sycophant, Lord Bute. In Clive, Bute and the king discerned a threat, a possibly very influential opponent of policy on America if he were not, indeed, to be appointed British commander there. For many influential figures in government, it was essential to discredit Clive.

The pleasant and calm summer of 1772 was to prove utterly deceptive for Clive. For India was about to be plunged into a fresh crisis: both the East India Company and the government had need of someone to blame. Worse, the Indian crisis actually provided a distraction from the far more serious and imminent American crisis; and Clive was regarded as far too dangerous and honest a man to be allowed near the latter. To Lord North and the government, Clive was expendable: he could be thrown, like Admiral Byng, to the dogs of opposition to keep the critics at bay. He was now to be politically assassinated, with government connivance, as effectively as though he had been physically shot. The government's cynicism combined with a furious fit of public moral outrage into a lethal brew. He had few allies and the king's friends in parliament – the largest block in the governing coalition – distrusted and disliked him.

It was the cynical decision by the government to turn against Clive that threatened suddenly to strip the ex-emperor of Bengal not just of his wealth but of his good name and even possibly his life. He was the latest major figure to be tossed to the wolves to divert the government's enemies at a moment of acute crisis. In practice, if George III had had an ounce of good judgement, he would have looked to the commonsense Clive and the Cassandra-like prophecies of Chatham to rescue him from utter humiliation in America. Both Chatham and Clive believed a much more liberal attitude to the colonists was the only way of averting disaster in the Americas – and were bitterly opposed by the government.

*

Chatham was to break his silence at last in bitter denunciation of the American policy just after Clive's death, in oratory that resonates down the centuries for both its language and its prescience:

> An hour now lost may produce years of calamity – I contend not for indulgence but justice to America. Resistance to your acts was necessary as it was just. The Americans are a brave, generous and united people, with arms in their hands and courage in their hearts; three millions of them, the genuine descendants of a valiant and pious ancestry, driven to those deserts by the narrow maxims of a superstitious tyranny. Of the spirit of independence animating the nation of America, I have the most authentic information. Destroy their towns and cut them off from the superfluities, perhaps the conveniences of life . . . and they would not lament their loss whilst they have – what, my Lords? – their woods and their liberty.
>
> To such a united force, what force shall be opposed? A few regiments in America and 17,000 or 18,000 men at home? The idea is too ridiculous to take up a moment of your Lordships' time. Laying of papers on your table or counting numbers on a division will not avert or postpone the hour of danger. It is not repealing this act of Parliament, it is not repealing a piece of parchment, that can restore America to our bosom: you must repeal her fears and resentments; and you may then hope for her love and gratitude . . . To conclude, my Lords, if the ministers thus persevere in misadvising and misleading the King I will not say that they can alienate the affections of his subjects from his crown; but I will affirm that they will make the crown not worth his wearing. I will not say that the King is betrayed; but I will pronounce that the kingdom is undone.

Chatham's condemnation of the ministry was Olympian in its contempt:

> This bill, though rejected here, will make its way to the public, to the nation, to the remotest wilds of America . . . I am not much astonished, I am not surprised, that men who hate liberty should detest those who prize it; or that those who want virtue themselves should endeavour to persecute those who possess it . . . The whole of your political conduct has been one continued series of weakness, temerity, despotism, ignorance, futility, negligence, and the most notorious servility, incapacity and corruption.

On reconsideration I must allow you one merit, a strict attention to your own interests: in that view you appear sound statesmen and politicians. You well know, if the present measure should prevail, that you must instantly relinquish your places . . . Such then being your precarious situations, who should wonder that you can put a negative on any measure which must annihilate your power, deprive you of your employments, and at once reduce you to that state of insignificance for which God and nature designed you . . .

You may traffic and barter with every little pitiful German prince that sells and sends his subjects to the shambles of a foreign prince; your efforts are forever vain and impotent . . . your own army is infected with the contagion of these illiberal allies. The spirit of rapine and plunder is gone forth among them. But, my Lords, who is the man that, in addition to these disgraces and mischiefs of our army, has dared to authorise and associate to our arms the toma- hawk and scalping knife of the savage? . . .

It is not the least of our national misfortunes, that the strength and character of our army are thus impaired: infected with the mercenary spirit of robbery and rapine – familiarised to the horrid scenes of savage cruelty, it can no longer boast of the noble and generous principles which dignify a soldier . . . Besides these murderers and plunderers, let me ask our ministers, what other allies have they acquired? . . . Have they entered into alliance with the King of the gypsies? Nothing, my Lords, is too low or too ludicrous to be consistent with their counsels . . .

Whilst this is notoriously our sinking condition America grows and flourishes . . . You have been three years teaching them the art of war: they are apt scholars . . . My Lords, if I were an American as I am an Englishman, while a foreign troop was landed in my country I would never lay down my arms – never – never – never!

Had a general of the calibre of Clive been allied to Chatham, the government and its American policy would have been in dire straits indeed. But Clive was dead, Chatham on his last legs (he expired a year later). It was to Lord North and Burgoyne that George III entrusted his policy on America and the former, at least, had the sense to extricate himself from it as soon as he reasonably could – but not before the utter humiliation of British arms.

BOOK FOUR

THE FALL,
1771–1774

CHAPTER 25

The Last Battle

I n the late summer of 1772 a series of financial collapses were triggered off by the failure of a Scottish bank. This had a knock-on effect on the East India Company, whose revenues had dropped to £174,000 in the year following the famine, while military spending continued at a rate of more than £600,000 a year. The Company had to borrow £1 million from the government, a reversal of the position two decades before. In September 1772 the directors had to take the drastic step of stopping the payment of dividends. Company stock fell overnight from 219 to 160. The directors had to seek a further government loan of £1 million – which now enabled the latter at last to intervene decisively in the affairs of the Company.

The Regulatory Act was passed soon afterwards, providing for a measure of government control and an attempt to correct abuses at home and abroad. An independent court of justice was set up for Bengal and the Company's small proprietors were stripped of their voting rights. Clive gave the government his own memorandum on the subject. Some of his ideas were adopted, including that of establishing a single governor-general with a large salary – £25,000 a year – and a council of five to regulate him. These were old ideas floated in the past with Chatham, who was in agreement with the need for reform.

With the dismal nature of East India Company finances now open to public scrutiny, the directors had need of someone on whom to pin the blame. To Sulivan, Clive presented himself once again as the obvious target. A series of charges against him were raised, and the press was again merciless in its attacks. Sulivan was, however, himself ejected from the board in April.

When the Regulatory Act came up for debate the following month Clive made a second speech which confirmed the House in its impression that it had an orator of genius hidden in its midst. He was forthright and to the point. He defended himself against the accusation that he had made money from the salt monopoly by pointing out that there was no living European in Bengal not trading in salt. Of his stock exchange dealings he claimed, 'The transaction was neither illegal nor dishonourable, yet I say, Sir, I should not have given my enemies even this slender twig to hold by.'

Clive, always regarded as a direct and serious speaker – although in private he could be cheerful and entertaining – then displayed a remarkable show of wit. Sulivan, he remarked with devastating accuracy, had been 'so assiduous in my affairs that really, Sir, it appears he has entirely neglected his own'.

As to himself, he had been examined like a sheep-stealer. 'I am sure, Sir, that if I had any sore places about me, they would have been found. They have probed to the bottom. No lenient plaster has been applied to my sore, they have been all of a blistering kind composed of Spanish flies and many other provocatives. At the India House, Sir, the public records have been searched from top to bottom as to charges against me.'

He remarked that as the Jacobite heads on Temple Bar had been removed, they should be replaced by his own, with Sulivan and Colebrook on either side – an allusion to the anti-India witchhunt at the time. The House burst into laughter and applause for several minutes. He went on to portray the directors as 'devouring the turtle and all kinds of viands out of season and in season, and swilling themselves with whole hogsheads of claret, champagne and bur-gundy'.

This brilliant, self-deprecating defence earned the approval even of Walpole. 'It was not a piece of regular and set oratory, but the artful effusions of a man, master of his cause, of himself, and of the passions of others, which he raised, interested or amused, as he found necessary . . . his allusions and applications were happy, and when he was vulgar he was rarely trivial . . . while the Ministers and the Parliament sunk before him, he shone eminently as a real great man, who had done great things, and who had the merit of not having committed more (perhaps not worse) villainies.'

Clive's wit certainly earned him friends in the House, although it only whetted the appetite of his opponents on the scandal sheets, who wrote of his 'low buffoonery' and now whipped up a campaign to make him suffer 'pains and penalties'.

Clive's opponents began to gather in an ominous attempt to ruin him financially and bail out the East India Company with his jagir. The self-important and dim-witted Burgoyne now seems to have taken it upon himself personally to press the case against Clive – perhaps because he discerned a possible rival for an important command in dealing with the rebellious American colonies. Indeed, the whole object of the witchhunt against Clive may have been to discredit him and his high-minded colonial policies as a possible commander of British forces in America.

Edward Thurlow, the attorney-general, a tough former enemy of Clive's, became his chief parliamentary prosecutor. Wedderburn, the Scottish advocate, was his defender. The government, under Lord North, remained neutral, but was in fact hostile. The largest faction in the administration, the 'king's friends', took against Clive. The king himself had criticised the 'fleecing' of India.

Of the two main opposition groups, that supporting the Marquess of Rockingham, one which included Edmund Burke, was on Clive's side, while the other, supporting the Earl of Shelburne, a friend of Sulivan's, was hostile. Most of the radical leaders, led by Charles James Fox, were hostile to Clive. There seemed a clear majority against him.

Burgoyne opened the parliamentary trial of Robert Clive on 10 May 1773, declaring powerfully, 'We have had in India revolution upon revolution, extortion upon extortion. In the whole history of mankind, I defy mankind to produce such a continued history of oppression.' His main attack centred round the Omichand affair and the forgery of Admiral Watson's signature.

He made three proposals: that all territorial acquisitions made by British subjects should belong to the Crown; that it had been illegal for the revenues from such possessions to be given to private individuals; and, third, that such revenues had in fact been stolen. If this resolution passed, Clive would lose all he had taken from India and, having acted illegally, would be subject to impeachment. If the motion were passed, he faced at the least financial ruin, at worst stiff penalties or even a sentence of death.

Wedderburn replied for Clive with an eloquent and well-argued speech. Clive spoke only briefly and hesitantly. For once he appeared to have been caught off-balance by the ferocity of the attack. 'I cannot but lament the abuse that has been made of the public press and the methods resorted to of slandering the character of all orders of men without distinction. For my own part, I have been called a villain, a thief, a forger, an assassin, and names without number; but I need not complain, as even Majesty itself has not escaped this implacable fury. What I regret is that the cause of virtue and public spirit must inevitably suffer if this abuse be permitted to go unpunished, since the greatest inducement to men of superior talent to stand forth and distinguish themselves in their country's cause is the hope of fair fame and just applause.'

Burgoyne replied pompously,

The task of a public accuser is never a pleasing, but is sometimes a necessary one. Envy and malignity are the vices of little minds, and I disclaim them. The House, in its movements, have only followed the cry of the public. Instances of rapacity and injustice have occurred in our Eastern possessions, that are known to all the world. An inordinate desire of wealth has had full play, and has led to transactions which have stigmatised those immediately concerned in them and affected even Britain's name. It is the duty of the House, as guardians of the nation's honour, to apply a remedy; and as the vice has been general, so must the punishment.

It is a case in which no partial or limited censure will suffice to remove the evil, or to wipe off the stain from the country . . . It is therefore necessary to point out who the persons are who have acquired property, and the particular circumstances under which it has been acquired . . . In the revolution of 1757, effected by Lord Clive, great stress has been laid on its necessity; but every succeeding revolution has been sustained on the same ground, a ground that will never be wanting . . . Let it be remembered, that the revolution of 1757 [in Bengal] was the foundation and the model of all the subsequent revolutions. Our vindictive justice must go back to the origin of the evil.

The tiger was wounded at last. Thurlow launched a devastating attack on Clive, and the members who flocked to the ten o'clock vote, having listened to none of the speeches – the debate was unwhipped – voted for Burgoyne's motion to get home in good time. Clive was now censured in principle and in extreme danger.

Two days later, on 19 May, Burgoyne returned to a more specific attack. In a tedious and uninspiring speech he argued that Clive 'had illegally acquired the sum of £234,000 to the dishonour and detriment of the state'. The debate was tiresome, but Clive defended himself effectively, if no longer with languid humour. 'After the long and painful services which I have rendered the state . . . I did not conceive it possible that a motion could ever be brought into this House to deprive me of my honour and reputation. I am sure the House will not accuse me of vanity . . . they will not accuse me of presumption for stating to the House what those services are . . .'

Over Omichand he showed no remorse. 'Where the lives of so many people were concerned, and when the existence of the Company depended upon it, I would not have scrupled to put Mr Watson's name to the treaty even without his consent. I said so in committee, I say so here.' He appealed movingly and somewhat pathetically at the end.

Do I stand condemned by an ex post facto resolution for approving deceipts in presents sixteen years ago? . . . I can never bring myself to believe that this House will ever adopt such a horrid idea as to punish a man for what he could not be guilty of . . . I may be distressed, I may be ruined, but as long as I have a conscience to defend me, I will always be happy.

After certificates such as these, am I to be brought here like a criminal, and the very best parts of my conduct construed into crimes against the State? [He had only a paternal inheritance of £500 a year.] On this I am content to live; and perhaps I shall find more real content of mind and happiness than in the trembling affluence of an unsettled fortune. But, Sir, I must make one more observation. If the definition of the Hon Gentleman [Colonel Burgoyne] and of this House, that the state, as expressed in these resolutions, is quoad hoc, the Company, then, Sir, every farthing I enjoy is granted to me.

But to be called upon, after sixteen years have elapsed, to account for my conduct in this manner, and after an uninterrupted enjoyment of my property, to be questioned, and considered as obtaining it unwarrantably, is hard indeed; it is a treatment I should not think the British Senate capable of. But if such should be the case, I have a conscious innocence within me that tells me my conduct is irreproachable.

Frangus non flectes [you may break, but you shall not bend, me].
My enemies may take from me what I have; they may, as they think,
make me poor, but I shall be happy. I mean this not as my defence,
though I have done for the present. My defence will be heard at that
bar, but before I sit down I have one humble request to make to this
House: that when they come to decide upon my honour, they will
not forget their own.

The same night, Clive wound up his defence with the famous
declamation, 'leave me my honour, take away my fortune'. Cries
of 'Hear! Hear!' resounded in his ears as he left in tears, the first time
he had ever been seen in such a state in public. He took his carriage
from Westminster to Berkeley Square.

Many members were also crying. Burgoyne, sensing the mood of
the House was going against him, watered down his motion. It now
suggested that Clive had not obtained his £234,000 illegally but that
he had 'abused the powers with which he was entrusted, to the evil
example of the servants of the public'. A supporter of Clive
proposed that the motion should be reworded so that it should
simply record that he had received £234,000.

The eloquent Charles James Fox, who had lost £150,000 gambling
by the age of 23, made a ferocious and sanctimonious attack on
Clive, calling him 'the origin of all plunder, the source of all
robbery'. Lord North, the prime minister, in Burke's caustic comment, 'blew hot and cold, and veered round the whole thirty-two
points of the compass of uncertainty and indecision'. Burke himself
spoke movingly in favour of Clive, as did a bluff old soldier,
Admiral Sir Charles Saunders, who said that Clive was being
abused as badly as Sir Walter Raleigh.

Although the Rockingham faction was now solidly backing Clive,
the previous motion had still passed the House, and he remained
probably in a minority. But the ranks of the shires, the country
gentry, which had viewed Clive as a hero, and one hard done by at
that, had made its views felt in the ten days between the two
debates. Clive's own defence had swayed many MPs: could they
really do down a man who had achieved so much for his country?
The official inquiry had exonerated Clive on almost all points.

His real crime – like that of all the nabobs – was to have secured
enormous wealth through conquest. At the time such conduct had

been regarded not just as acceptable but admirable. Many of his accusers were themselves men who made their fortunes in India far more blatantly and viciously – and had turned on Clive because during his last tour of duty he had sought to control them.

With remarkable coolness, Clive had supper with a coterie of friends at Berkeley Square and went to bed at midnight, asking to be woken if he had won, and to be allowed to sleep on if he had not. His supporters decided to sit up all night until dawn fingered the elegant, wide, tree-lined square. Margaret, with them, did not know whether she would wake up a pauper in the morning, or indeed whether Clive might be arraigned as a common criminal. The former emperor of India faced ruin, humiliation and punishment.

In the empty square, in the cold light of the early morning on 22 May, a carriage could be heard approaching. Strachey, Clive's secretary, emerged. The amendment by Clive's friends rendering Burgoyne's resolution harmless had been carried solidly by 155 votes to 95. At the last moment the 'king's friends', the bulk of government supporters, had shifted to Clive, rather than running one of Britain's greatest heroes into the ground. Wedderburn had then moved that 'Robert, Lord Clive, did at the same time, render great and meritorious service to this country'. This motion was overwhelmingly passed.

The magnetic Burke remarked, 'Lord Clive has thus come out of the fiery trial much brighter than he went into it. His gains are now recorded, and not only not condemned, but actually approved by Parliament. His reputation, too, for ability, stands higher than ever.'

Macaulay's verdict on the judgement of the Commons is fair:

The result of this memorable inquiry appears to us, on the whole, honourable to the justice, moderation and discernment of the Commons. They had indeed no great temptation to do wrong. They would have been very bad judges of an accusation against Jenkinson or against Wilkes. But the question respecting Clive was not a party question; and the House accordingly acted with the good sense and good feeling which may always be expected from an assembly of English gentlemen, not blinded by faction . . . The Commons of England . . . treated their living captain with that discriminating justice which is seldom shown except to the dead.

They laid down sound general principles; they delicately pointed out where he had deviated from those principles; and they tempered the gentle censure with liberal eulogy.

Clive could now afford to shrug off such missives as the one written by his embittered military opponent, Sir Robert Fletcher, after his exoneration by parliament:

> Though you have escaped the punishment of deeds the very report of which could not be made by Colonel Burgoyne without the strongest marks of abhorrence and indignation, you will remain a blasted monument of the legislature's clemency instead of having been made an example of its justice. This great inquest of the nation, though not productive of the satisfaction the injured and oppressed had a right to expect, has however, opened the eyes of the public and brought down the mighty conqueror of Plassey and his confederates on the level with a gang of freebooters and lawless speculators.

Clive's reputation, although not wholly vindicated, had been allowed to return to that on his return from India, before the persecution began. He had secured the approval and even the accolade of his peers; he could be proud. His enemies had been confounded. He had fought his corner vigorously and with un-expected oratorical brilliance. To those in Britain like Walpole who saw him as some primitive conquistador and colonial plunderer, it became apparent how sophisticated and complex a man he was. The reasons for his success in India became more obvious.

He was an extraordinarily gifted man. In parliament he had shown himself capable of eloquence and statesmanlike common sense; had his qualities emerged at Westminster earlier, he might indeed have enjoyed the meteoric political career he craved in his youth. Arrogance, idleness and his obsession with wealth had blighted his political career.

He was still only 47, far from retirement age for a general. Because of his wealth, though, he had no need to seek an active career again. As Britain's greatest living general, he might have responded to a call to lead Britain's forces in America. He was the natural choice.

However, for the moment, the prospect was one of great luxury, the vigorous development of country estates, ceremonial occasions, intrigue within the East India Company – and no more. It was a gilded anti-climax for the man who had conquered and ruled a continent.

His health was less of an obsession these days. 'I am so well acquainted with my own constitution at present that I think I may venture to say with care and attention that I may make the rest of my days tolerably easy,' he remarked in April 1774. He had come through his final and greatest ordeal with controversy, but also with honour. He was hardly one to feel crippled by the attack upon him; he had faced much greater military challenges.

Yet he was affected by the general snobbishness towards his nouveau riche status, the continuing sense that people regarded his wealth as ill-gotten, the failure to recognise his staggering achievement for the country. Both king and country seemed strangely indifferent to the empire he had created. The main reason, he knew, was that the immense wealth he had accumulated made people sceptical as to his motives. Yet to Clive wealth was the other side of the coin to conquering India for the British. They were far from irreconcilable.

There is no sign that, following his acquittal in parliament, Clive was unusually depressed. He was invited to stand for election in Liverpool, where he was popular. He went to the Portsmouth naval review in June. He took an active part in the debate on the Regulating Bill, and he tried to see that his influence in the Company was perpetuated through a bright young protégé, Philip Francis.

The bill set up the disastrous system by which the governor-general – Hastings – was controlled by a three-man council, which was to institutionalise conflict at the top in India. Two of the three, General Sir John Clavering and Philip Francis himself, a brilliant, cynical, tough young man, were friends of Clive, and influenced by his view of India. They set themselves against Hastings.

Clive openly sought to influence Francis, inviting him to Walcot and Oakly for a fortnight, where he made a hit with Margaret, she once again delighting in the company of a young man, he enjoying the contrast from his modest house in Margate. Firm friends now, he brought his wife on his next visit, and they became constant visitors to the Clive houses. Clive became a mentor to the young man, seeking to influence him on all Indian matters, handing down his views to a new generation and criticising Hastings. Clive was also now dominant on the board of the East India Company.

Clive departed on a 'grand tour' of Italy, where he met the Pope in Rome, visited Naples briefly, and bought pictures, including a Tintoretto. Although he suffered a bout of depression in Naples, he stayed another three months in Italy, visiting Bologna and Venice. He went on to Geneva, arriving in England in 'high health and spirits'.

Margaret had not accompanied him, ostensibly because of the children, or perhaps because she preferred the company of the Francises. Philip in fact left for India just before Clive's return, leaving Margaret distraught. When she proposed a toast to the absent Francis, she burst into tears. Clive was reportedly furious.

At the end of June, Clive went up to Shropshire and took part in a general election campaign that increased the number of seats he controlled to seven – an almost ducal figure. He was now support-ing the government and had a substantial following in parliament, although he seemed curiously indolent in making himself felt there, except in his own defence. His only ambition was, according to Strachey, 'a British peerage'.

None of these were the actions of a morbid or suicidal man. There was nothing to indicate that he had been unbalanced by his near-escape in parliament. However, at the end of October, he caught a bad cold standing by the river at Oakly, and within a week was visibly ill, full of catarrh and finding it difficult to swallow. He travelled to Bath, where he stayed a fortnight, his condition deteriorating, so that he could not eat or swallow.

After a hellish journey to Berkeley Square, he lamented to the distraught Margaret and the family that he was dying. He arrived on the night of 20 November, suffering acutely and taking large doses of opium. His old abdominal pains had returned with a vengeance. He must have been a terrible and trying patient, by turns weeping, hysterical, shouting, morose and despondent. With-in two days he was dead.

What exactly was Clive suffering from? According to Strachey, his secretary, he had a very painful dyspepsia, accompanied by vertigo, which in turn caused acute depression. Chaudhury believes he was suffering from porphyria, the same disease as was to afflict George III: in its hepatic form, it causes abdominal pain and nausea, as well as hysterical and indeed psychotic behaviour. If that behaviour included aggression, this could have had a bearing on the circumstances of Clive's death.

By an extraordinary irony, Clive was suffering from symptoms similar not only to those of his monarch later, but of his political hero, Chatham, who had succumbed to a major depressive illness seven years before. In addition to his main illness, Clive is thought to have suffered from a stomach ulcer, gout and kidney trouble. These were ailments of stress and excess. He might have seemed an unusually unlucky man – yet many of his contemporaries in India had died as young men from tropical diseases.

Although blessed with remarkable determination and not morbid by nature, it may be speculated that the combination of pain, depression and mania this time had a far greater humiliation to feed upon than any that had previously occurred in Clive's life. When healthy, the ferocious personal attacks rained upon him during the past few years could be easily withstood. When ill, even two years after his acquittal, they may have assumed massive proportions in his mind.

Yet Clive was not a man to be afraid. He had brushed contemptuously with death more often than a platoonful of front-line soldiers: when swept overboard off Brazil as a youth; in the ditch outside Pondicherry when a bullet went through his hat; outside the fortress of Devikottai, when he was nearly cut down; in the foolhardy attempt to seize the French guns outside Arcot, when another man took the bullet destined for him; in his constant exposure along the walls of Arcot; during the ambush at Kaveripak; during the astonishing fracas at Samiaveram, when he was first slashed by enemy swords and then two others took the fire intended for him; at Budge Budge, when he was nearly cut down by enemy horse; in the morning mists of the Battle of Calcutta when he stumbled into the Nawab's camp; in the front line at Plassey itself; in exposing himself to the assassin's bullet at Monghyr. Death had been his constant companion, and he showed no fear of it. Perhaps his frequent exposure to danger was itself a symptom of a death-wish. It was living unhappily which he feared most, and was least bearable.

Yet there is no reason to believe he felt the slightest remorse or regret for the actions of his eventful life. His defence in the House of Commons had been robust, eloquent and unyielding. By his account, he had nothing to be ashamed about. Towards his long parade of vanquished Indian enemies, he felt only the contempt of the victor: the ghosts of inexperienced, rash Raza Sahib, of his murdered father Chanda Sahib, of butchered Siraj-ud-Daula, of deceived Omichand, of biblically avenged Miran and of destitute Mir Kasim held no terrors for him.

For his defeated French foes – Dupleix, Jacques Law, Jean Law, de Bussy, Lally – he felt the comradeship of old adversaries-in-arms. For his British foes – Sulivan, Vansittart (now dead), the Johnstones, Fletcher – he felt bitter contempt for men he despised as short-sighted, venal and incompetent. No, Clive felt no torment. He was not a man troubled by self-doubt or anguish.

The only real psychological baggage he carried was a relatively new one: the realisation that neither his king nor his countrymen felt indebted to him for his staggering achievements in India. In spite of his exculpation by parliament most people, high and low, regarded him as tarnished after the furious personal campaign waged against him in England; some of the mud had stuck. Allied to this sense of the ingratitude of his fellow countrymen may have been the feeling that his life's work in India, even after his cleansing of the Augean stables, was again unravelling: that he had created nothing of permanence there. He could not have guessed or expected that the empire he founded was to expand greatly and last the better part of two centuries.

The sense that his achievement was unrecognised, and that it was doomed, when magnified by his mental state and wealth of physical infirmities, may have proved unbearable. But this must be pure conjecture. For in no published writing do the wounds of hurt pride or of a sense of failure show through. Rather the reverse: he brushed aside his English enemies, showed indifference to what the public thought of him, scorned scurrilous press attacks, and keenly studied events in India to see how his legacy could be strengthened.

Unless this was only a bold front for the tortured soul inside – for which there is not the slightest evidence – if he did kill himself, it could only have been because 'the balance of his mind was disturbed'. His actions had caused him no despair or remorse in later life because he still felt them to be fully justified. It was illness, physical and mental, that brought on misery, and may have magnified his sense of failure.

Previous bouts of ill-health had not caused him to attempt to take his own life. This time, the administration itself, spearheaded by George III and with Lord North's tacit support, had joined the malicious offensive against one of Britain's greatest sons. This may have tilted the balance in that strong, but proud and sensitive mind after illness had stripped it bare of its defences. If it was suicide, it was homicide too, the perpetrators being the monarch and the state he had served so well – as well as public opinion, in one of its earliest outbursts of ill-informed, wrong-headed moral indignation.

How did Robert Clive die? His last major British biographer, Mark Bence-Jones, states unequivocally that 'in a paroxysm of agony, he thrust his penknife into his throat'. Equally unequivocally, an earlier biographer, R. J. Minney, states that he 'definitively' established that Clive died of an overdose of opium and that the theory of suicide was a 'contemptible slander'. In view of the torrents of abuse heaped on Clive in his last years, this might not seem improbable. In fact, though, there is remarkably little evidence for either view, although the balance of probability is that his throat was cut.

The key point about Clive's death is that it was assiduously and comprehensively covered up. There was no post-mortem, no inquest, no death certificate, no official explanation for his death. Even for a family of immense wealth and influence at the time, this flouting of legal norms was extraordinary. The family said nothing, a tradition which has persisted to this day (the video of his life at the Clive Museum in Powis Castle makes no mention of how he died). To the extent that there was no legal explanation of an untimely death, officialdom must have connived with the Clive family in the cover-up.

More remarkable still, Clive's body was rushed up to Styche in Shropshire the very afternoon he died, and then, highly unusually, buried the following evening at dusk in well-attended secrecy in an unmarked grave from which it could not be exhumed. His resting place has not been definitely established to this day, although it seems highly likely to have been inside the church, as the commemorative plaque put up by his family suggests.

Chaudhury suggests that the plaque could have referred to the 'boundary walls' of the church, but that strains credulity. If Clive was buried on consecrated ground, as the plaque makes clear, it would have been extraordinary not to have interred someone of his eminence inside the church. All of this is testimonial to the astonishing lengths gone to in order to ensure that the manner of Clive's death remained secret, and that his body should not be seen by anyone outside the immediate family.

To Minney, the reason for such inordinate precautions was 'the desperate desire of the family to elude the prying eyes of a gloating public'. This is not as improbable as it might seem. Clive was the most hated man in England, and his funeral might have been an occasion for a public demonstration by his detractors – but surely not to the extent of desecrating his grave, particularly if located inside a church. Nor does this version explain why no death certificate was issued. The question remains: why the cover-up?

The view that he died of an accidental overdose of laudanum (a mixture of brandy and opium) or even naturally, of a fit, seems the most implausible. This was certainly the version the family initially wanted people to believe, and the one given to respectable newspapers at the time. The *Morning Post* wrote on 24 November: 'On Tuesday evening, of an apoplectic fit, died Lord Clive at his house in Berkeley Square.' Two days later, the *General Evening Press* suggested he had ignored his doctor's orders not to take 'opiates . . . and was found dead the next day'. The *London Evening Press* said he 'was taken with a fit of apoplexy as he was in his dressing room' and expired a few hours later. All of these accounts are contradictory, although they imply natural or accidental causes. The timing of the first two reports has since been established as wrong.

Horace Walpole, himself a walking, if not especially accurate, newspaper, wrote the day after Clive's death, citing the Lord Chancellor – who should have been a reliable source – 'Lord H [Hertford] has just been here and told me the manner of Lord Clive's death. Whatever had happened, it had thrown him into convulsions, to which he was very subject. Dr Fothergill gave him, as he had done on like occasions, a dose of laudanum, but the pain in his bowels was so violent, that he asked for a second dose. Dr F. said, if he took another, he would be dead in an hour. The moment Dr F.

was gone, he swallowed another, for another, it seems, stood by him, and he is dead.'

However, Hertford, as the nation's top law officer, must have been in on any official decision to exempt Clive's death from the normal legal formalities, and his indiscretion in talking to the country's foremost society gossip looks remarkably like an early version of the modern calculated 'leak'. Hertford's story was clearly the one officialdom wanted the country to believe.

Another support for this theory was a letter written by Robert Pardoe, a lawyer at Lincoln's Inn, who for some reason was regarded as an authority on the matter, although it is not clear why. Written three days after Clive's death, the missive was prominently displayed in the Powys papers. He stated: 'I am very sorry for the death of Lord Clive, which was sudden. He had been taking opium for many years, and finding the disorder in his bowels very painful, he took a double dose against advice, and died in a fit. He had several of those fits before, some friends of mine have seen him seized with them in the Rooms at Bath. So that the little surmise of his dying unnaturally is without foundation. I mention this for fear it should reach the country.' Again, this letter from a lawyer who must have been close to the family bears the hallmark of an inspired leak.

None of this is very convincing. The newspapers were clearly floundering in the dark. Walpole was in any event an unreliable source and Pardoe's own informant is unknown. More important, there can have been no reason for obscuring the cause of death, for hurrying the body away from London to an immediate funeral, or for keeping the whereabouts of the grave secret, much less for the family to persist in the conspiracy of silence, if Clive had suffered an accidental or natural death.

The available family papers give no clue as to the cause of death. Clive's son, Ned, gave full access to the papers to Sir John Malcolm, his first posthumous biographer, who passed over the issue of Clive's death in silence. A later biographer, Sir George Forrest, who also had access to the family papers, records that 'Clive died by his own hand'. Certainly this view was quick to gain currency in the days after his death.

One fashionable, reliable and formidable contemporary, Lady Mary Coke, who was visiting Lady Hertford in Grosvenor Square at the very time of Clive's death, at first heard the same story of the double dose of opium that her hostess's husband had given Walpole. By 28 November she had heard from the Duchess of Montagu: 'It is strongly reported that Lord Clive had not died a natural death, and there is one circumstance that looks very suspicious; he was put into his coffin a few hours after his death.' The following day she wrote, "Tis said now that 'tis certain Lord Clive kill'd himself, and the reason given for this unhappy action is the horror of his mind.'

Lady Mary's account of how Clive is supposed to have killed himself is especially graphic and revealing: 'The method he took to deprive himself of life was, I believe, what nobody ever thought of before; he cut his throat with a little instrument that is bought at the stationers to scratch out anything upon paper; I don't know what it is calld, but 'tis so small he must have been some time before he could affect his purpose, and must have been very determined to proceed when he was giving himself such terrible pain: reason there can be none for such action, but I wish to know what it was that could have given him so dreadful a thought.'

A week later, Lady Mary had further details: "Tis reported that Lady Clive was the first person who found her Lord weltering in his blood; 'tis no wonder the horror of the scene should have such an effect upon her spirits as to deprive her of her senses, and throw her with a fit, but 'tis fortunate she remained in it so long, that when she came out of it, her ideas were so confused with regard to that terrible scene, that she believed to have been a dream what was but too real, and spoke of the shocking dream she had had of her Lord. She was encouraged in this notion, and was told he was dead of an apoplectic fit.' Lady Mary was intelligent, extremely well informed, and could hardly have made up so improbable an instrument of death.

Most strikingly, though, her account ties in uncannily with one handed down by Jane Strachey, who was in the house at the time, to her son, Sir Henry Strachey, who in turn as an old man dictated an account to his nephew, amending it in his own hand:

Lord Clive had long been ill – in a very nervous state – and had been warned by his physician against taking laudanum, but he would and did take it. Mr and Mrs Strachey and Miss Ducarel were at Lord Clive's house in Berkeley Square. Lord Clive went out of the room, and not returning, Mr Strachey said to Lady Clive, 'You had better go and see where my lord is.' She went to look for him and at last, opening a door, found Lord Clive with his throat cut. She fainted, and servants came. Patty Ducarel got some of the blood on her hands and licked it off. After the event Mrs Strachey remembered having seen Lord Clive, when at her house some days before, take up a penknife from the inkstand, feel its edge, and then lay it down again.

Sir Edward Strachey commented: 'The family of Lord Clive were not unnaturally desirous that it should be believed that he died from an overdose of laudanum, taken under medical advice, rather than by the act of his own hand; and we suppose that it was out of respect for this still existing feeling of the family that Sir John Malcolm passed the matter over in silence in his Life of Lord Clive, written from the family papers.'

Clive's biographer Gleig, writing in the 1840s, is believed to have taken this account from another witness – presumably indirectly, since she can hardly have been still alive – Patty Ducarel: 'Clive had great pain on the twenty-first, and was driven to take strong doses of opium for relief. This continued on the next day. At about noon or a little later, a lady who was on a visit at his house [Patty Ducarel] came into his room and said: "Lord Clive, I cannot find a good pen; will you be so good as to make me one." "To be sure," replied he, and, taking a penknife from his waistcoat pocket, he moved towards one of the windows and mended the pen. The lady took it back with thanks and left the room. Some time shortly afterwards a servant entered the room and found Clive dead. The weapon with which he killed himself was seen to be the same penknife.'

Lord Stanhope, in his History of England, relates at second hand an account given by the Earl of Shelbourne which is remarkably similar, although different in important details: 'It so chanced that a young lady, an attached friend of his [Clive's] family was then upon a visit at his house in Berkeley Square, and sat writing a letter in one of its apartments. Seeing Lord Clive walk through she called him to come and mend her pen. Lord Clive obeyed her summons and, taking out his penknife, fulfilled her request; after which, passing on to another chamber, he turned the same knife against himself.'

Two points stand out from this coincidence of reliable sources: first, there seems no reason why Jane Strachey, loyal to Clive, should invent the notion of suicide; much less why Patty Ducarel should do so. Second, it seems striking that no fewer than four reliable sources, two of which can be traced to first-hand witnesses, and two contemporary to Clive's death, should concur on the extremely unusual alleged instrument of death.

Suicide – in particular in this excruciatingly painful and bloody manner – helps to explain several of the mysteries surrounding the death: the absence of an official cause; the spiriting away of the body; the furtive burial; and the secret grave. If the family had initially sought to cover up the cause of death, it would obviously not have wanted it to be possible for Clive's body to be seen or exhumed, to reveal so obvious a wound. Suicide was at the time a cause of deep shame, even repugnance. Dr Johnson was to reflect a general prejudice when he remarked that Clive 'had acquired his fortune by such crimes, that his consciousness of them impelled him to cut his own throat'.

A suicide could not be buried on consecrated ground; it is clear that Clive was buried on consecrated ground, almost certainly inside a church. The whereabouts of the grave might have been concealed because the burial had been in violation of canon law, to make it more difficult to give offence or for the bones to be removed; but again, this is unsatisfactory and implausible. Chaudhury is convinced that Clive committed suicide, and cites the fact that Lady Mary Coke played cards for three hours with Clive's intimate, Lady Powis, on the day after the death. The subject was not mentioned, presumably out of delicacy. But that would have applied to any unexpected death, not just a suicide.

A third hypothesis must be examined: that he was killed by another person. The evidence for his death by overdose or suicide rests primarily on hearsay, handed down. There is not even that to support the theory that he was killed. But there is strong circum-stantial evidence in its favour, and it does provide the only explanation of all the mysteries surrounding his death.

It chimes in, first, with the fact that while Clive certainly suffered from depression, pain and illness shortly before his death, he showed no hint of morbidity or suicidal tendencies, however wretched he may have felt, throughout his life after his early unhappiness in Madras. He wrote histrionically to Strachey a few weeks before his death, 'How miserable I am. I have a disease which makes life insupportable and which the doctors tell me won't shorten it one hour,' but that was hardly a death-wish. Once absolved by parliament, he had shown vigour and zest for life, embarking on the refurbishments at Oakly and Claremont with characteristic energy – until his last illness. It is hard – although not impossible – to believe he was plunged into such deep melancholy and pain within a few weeks as to stab himself to death in the most painful manner conceivable.

To do so with a penknife, which in its original incarnation was very small, required a degree of strength, effort, application and heedless-ness of pain of an almost superhuman kind (one conceivable explan-ation is that Clive was suffering from porphyria, a quasi-psychotic illness; and he was capable of great feats of endurance). It would be far more in keeping with Clive's background, and quicker, easier and less painful, if he had shot himself, as he is supposed to have attempted to do in youth. But, extremely difficult as it is to cut one's own throat, it is much easier to cut someone else's, either in self-defence or attack.

If Clive was killed, why was this not made known? Clive certainly had a formidable list of enemies who wished him dead. Few public men have been so intensely hated, before or since. Many regarded him as the cause of their financial ruin. The ruthless new governor of Bengal, Warren Hastings, had become his enemy. Sulivan, the Johnstones, Fletcher and others detested him. An attempt had already been made to eliminate his reputation, possibly to remove him as a likely commander of British forces in America. It is in fact far from inconceivable that an assassin could have been paid to get into his house, posing as a servant or tradesman, and murdered him in those days long before the tight security that surrounds modern public figures. A more remote, if romantic, possibility is that an Indian servant did the deed.

But if so, why the cover-up? Conceivably because Clive's murder would have had huge public repercussions in a country which had so recently pilloried one of its greatest heroes. If killed by an Indian patriot, his death might have provoked an uprising in Bengal. That would account for the need not to let people see the body – and explain why it was permissible to bury Clive on consecrated ground. Yet this theory seems just as unsatisfactory as the rest: if he had been assassinated by one of his enemies, the family would surely have insisted eventually on setting the record straight.

A fourth possibility exists: that Clive was killed by an intimate in a fit of personal exasperation or temporary distraction, or by someone in self-defence. We have Carnac's report that Clive, when ill, was deeply disturbed. Laudanum was notorious as a stimulant to greater excitability, as well as a sedative later; the story of his double dose may have been true in that respect. It is clear that Clive, in one of his fits of illness and depression, was an almost impossible man to live with, being self-centred, complaining and boorish. Margaret Clive makes this clear in her revealing remarks six months after his death, in a letter to her brother: '. . . now that I feel less anguish, I feel renewed my former sensations of love, of gratitude, of the softest affection for my own dear Lord, whose qualities had almost ceased to present themselves to my mind for the few days that it was so distracted in London.' It is highly unusual to admit thinking ill of a loved one immediately after his death.

An intimate could have got close enough to inflict the wound or surprise Clive without his offering any resistance (on one account Clive was on the lavatory when it happened). The strangeness of the weapon would also be explained: while a penknife is a curious and painful choice of suicide implement, it would be an obvious chance weapon to hand in a fit of passion, unreason, in a quarrel or by someone under assault at close quarters.

Self-defence or an attack by a close relation or friend whom the family wanted to protect would perfectly explain the family's obsessive desire for secrecy; the removal of the body without an examination; the burial in a secret grave from which the body could not later be exhumed; and the fact that, as he was not a suicide, he was buried in consecrated ground. Such a death would explain the continued and excessive secrecy even centuries later. To protect the tragic perpetrator, silence and even rumours of suicide would be preferable to exposure – particularly if Clive was viewed as more to blame for the tragedy than his killer.

Who might have been the assailant, on this hypothesis, is pure speculation. Those known to have been present in the house, apart from Clive, were Margaret, the Stracheys and Patty Ducarel. If the perpetrator had been a servant, the story would almost certainly have come out. One could hypothesise that the strains of looking after Clive proved too much even for Margaret, normally cool-tempered, intelligent, gentle and devoted to him. As we have seen, their marriage was an unusual one, with its ups and downs, lengthy partings – most recently on his grand tour to Italy – and favourites on both sides, as well as the strains of his illness. There had clearly been a major row between them over her fondness for Philip Francis, who had taken Carnac's place in her affection.

On two accounts, she was the first to find Clive, alone, and herself blacked out. Small in stature, and perhaps frightened, it might have been natural for her to strike up at his neck in the middle of a violent domestic row, for example. Suicide would have been a natural immediate cover story for the servants. Her amnesiac breakdown afterwards also fits the theory. Yet such an action would seem remarkably out of character with everything else we know about this self-possessed, intelligent, slightly eccentric, sweet-tempered woman.

The loyal and dependable Strachey makes an unlikely murderer, and hardly one to use such a weapon. The 35-year-old Jane Strachey had been through a wild period in her youth – as demonstrated on her visit to Bombay in 1755, when she seemed quite out of control and may have been experiencing a psychotic attack. But she was heavily pregnant at the time of Clive's death – not that that would have stopped someone really determined or alarmed. Yet the only documented accounts suggest that both the Stracheys and Margaret were in the same room when Clive left, failing to return. If these accounts are to be believed, only Patty Ducarel, out of the room, or conceivably Margaret, who left to look for Clive, could have done the deed.

Patty Ducarel was the last person to see Clive alive; certainly her reported action in licking his blood off her hands was hysterical – and deeply symbolic – but perhaps understandable in view of the horror of the scene. According to one account, Clive came into her room; according to another, she into his. The eighteenth century was far less prudish than the Victorian; even so, it must have been unusual, on whatever pretext, for a man to enter a young lady's room or vice versa. Clive was said to have found her tiresome. Could her reason have snapped when faced with his irascibility, or could she have acted in self-defence against a psychotic or laudanum-induced attack or unwanted advance? The five occupants of that house have carried the secret to their graves.

A household tragedy of the kind outlined above, however improbable and melodramatic, would go a long way towards explaining the extraordinary and immediate cover-up and secrecy surrounding his death, then and since. There is no direct evidence to support this version, but then there is none for any other explanation. A domestic tragedy fits all the circumstances; suicide – which is also supported by hearsay evidence – fits some, although not all, of the circumstances; while murder by an outsider or a natural or accidental death seem the least plausible explanations.

Margaret was in shock for a while, and Jane opined that 'she will never again be what you and I have known her'. Yet Margaret remarked only six months later that 'my health and spirits are much better'. She was still only 39 years old. She was to live to the ripe old age of 82, beyond the victory at Waterloo, well into another century, the nucleus of a large circle of friends and family, an alert and remarkable old lady. In the prime of the industrial revolution, she was to witness her family ascend to the highest ranks of the aristocracy, a feat that had eluded Clive throughout his lifetime.

Her eldest son, Ned, was created Earl of Powis on the death of the second earl, whose daughter, Lady Henrietta Herbert, he had married. Although formally a new creation, it was virtually unprecedented for a succession effectively to pass to a man through the female line. Almost certainly this was a belated act of contrition by the Crown for the lack of recognition displayed to Clive when he was alive: Ned's family seat became the splendid Powis Castle, with its tiered gardens. Ned was to enjoy a distinguished career in India, becoming Governor of Madras.

The descendants of Ned's younger son were to marry into the illustrious Windsor family, and become Earls of Plymouth. Another daughter of Ned's was to marry the fifth Sir Watkin Williams Wynn, the 'prince of North Wales' of his day. The arriviste, the nouveau riche, the 'nabob', shunned during his lifetime by the swells of British society, pilloried by his fellow countrymen, thus absorbed two of Britain's most aristocratic dynasties, and married into a third.

His three great houses remain enduring monuments today to his wealth and taste: the Earl and Countess of Plymouth still live in Oakly, magnificently refurbished after Clive's death. Walcot is beautifully tended by the extensive family of Michael and Billa Parish, worthy successors of Clive. Claremont's lovely garden is now a National Trust property, recently opened to the public.

CHAPTER 26

The Legacy

W hat of British India, his most spectacular creation? The administration of Warren Hastings, Clive's successor, was to show how fragile his conquest was. It was Hastings's terrible destiny to act as the consolidator of Clive's conquests; and he did this with intelligence, patience, vigour and such staggering lack of scruple in pursuit of his ends as to offend both his English contemporaries and successive generations, and to cause his own impeachment, although subsequently acquitted.

Hastings was not a soldier or romantic. He was far more devious, unprincipled and cruel than Clive. His role was to set the Indian empire on a secure footing. His rule was also to confirm three of his predecessor's achievements: first, that he had created an enduring empire with only a handful of men; second, that he had created the institutional and legal basis for British rule in India; and, third, that he had been a remarkably humane and tolerant man for a conqueror and absolute ruler. Hastings was to rule by guile, ruthlessness and statesmanship; Clive had ruled through natural brilliance, soldiery, deceit, courage, humanity and total indifference towards the men who challenged him.

A quick glance at Hastings's career bears this out. He quickly abandoned Clive's system of rule through local puppets. The chief minister of Bengal was Muhammad Reza Khan, an old ally of Clive's, while the Nawab was the infant son of Mir Jafar. Reza Khan was as loyal a servant of the British as had ever ruled Bengal; but as was usual with Bengali rulers, he failed to deliver the necessary revenues.

This, and his closeness to Nundcomar, the brahmin who had so often intrigued against the British under Clive but always survived, led to his downfall. The directors in London issued orders for Muhammad Reza Khan to be removed. Hastings, who saw the chance to rule Bengal directly, promptly obliged, surrounded Reza Khan's palace with a battalion of sepoys at midnight and had him arrested. The British now assumed direct responsibility for administering Bengal, assigning nominal control to the infant-king. Muhammad Reza Khan was soon set free, and Nundcomar, who had long aspired to take his place and hated Hastings after earlier clashes of personality, was set aside.

Hastings next turned his attention to raising money. Bengal had always shown great promise of revenue, but disappointed expectations. He stopped the country's tribute to the Great Mogul and occupied two border provinces, Allahabad and Corah, that belonged to him, selling them off to the Nawab of Oudh, Bengal's most powerful neighbour.

Hastings then entered into a dreadful compact with the Nawab, Clive's old friend, Shuja-ud-Daula. The latter had long coveted the territory of the Rohillas, dwelling in the spectacular valley of Ramgunga, where they administered one of the most well-run and enlightened princedoms in India. The Rohillas were of Afghan descent and formidable fighters.

Shuja-ud-Daula in effect bought the British, at a staggering cost of £400,000, to act as mercenaries to destroy the Rohillas. The British fought the war. The Nawab's army took the spoils and laid waste to this beautiful and peaceful land. Villages were razed to the ground and some 100,000 people were forced to flee their homes. But Hastings had his money; he had now increased Company revenues by £500,000 or so and obtained a capital sum of £1 million for his immediate purposes.

In spite of his successes by fair means and foul, the East India Company, partly at Clive's instigation, had decided to send out a committee to curb his powers. It consisted of four men, one an ally of the governor, the others implacably hostile: they included Francis, the brilliant, acerbic protégé of the Clives who was almost certainly the author of the mid-eighteenth century's bitterest polemic, the *Letters of Junius*, published anonymously.

Francis and his two colleagues staged a coup, seized power from Hastings, and with the vigour of eager young men just out of England, began to maladminister Bengal. Nundcomar now stepped forward to provide evidence of corruption by Hastings, his deadly enemy, which the new council was delighted to take seriously.

Hastings promptly offered his resignation as governor, while at the same time engineering a prosecution by the supreme court in Calcutta against Nundcomar for forgery. The brahmin was found guilty and sentenced to death. Hastings then implacably saw the death sentence through, defying the pressure of the majority on the council and the population as a whole. Macaulay sets the scene:

> The day drew near; and Nuncomar prepared himself to die with that quiet fortitude with which the Bengalee, so effeminately timid in personal conflict, often encounters calamities for which there is no remedy. The sheriff, with the humanity which is seldom wanting in an English gentleman, visited the prisoner on the eve of the execution, and assured him that no indulgence, consistent with the law, should be refused to him. Nuncomar expressed his gratitude with great politeness and unaltered composure. Not a muscle of his face moved. Not a sigh broke from him. He put his fingers to his forehead and calmly said that fate would have its way, and that there was no resisting the pleasure of God. He sent his compliments to Francis, Clavering, and Monson, and charged them to protect Rajah Goodras, who was about to become the head of the Brahmins of Bengal. The sheriff withdrew, greatly agitated by what had passed, and Nuncomar sat composedly down to write notes and examine accounts.
>
> The next morning, before the sun was in his power, an immense concourse assembled round the place where the gallows had been set up. Grief and horror were on every face; yet to the last the multitude could hardly believe that the English really purposed to take the life of the great Brahmin. At length the mournful procession came through the crowd. Nuncomar sat up in his palanquin, and looked around him with unaltered serenity. He had just parted from those who were most nearly connected with him. Their cries and contortions had appalled the European ministers of justice, but had not produced the smallest effect on the iron stoicism of their prisoner. The only anxiety which he expressed was that men of his own priestly caste might be in attendance to take charge of his corpse. He again desired to be remembered to his friends in the Council, mounted the scaffold with firmness, and gave the signal to the executioner. The moment the drop fell, a howl of sorrow and

despair rose from the innumerable spectators. Hundreds turned away their faces from the polluting sight, fled with loud wailings towards the Hoogley, and plunged into its holy waters, as if to purify themselves from the guilt of having looked on such a crime.

Thus Hastings, through an act of vengeance against an always unprincipled man, instilled terror into the people of Bengal. The governor then proceeded to regain control of the government. Although formally dismissed by the East India Company, he ignored the order, obtained the backing of the supreme court, and put his opponents in a minority. It was an early example of rebelliousness by a colonial leader against his nominal superiors far away in London.

The supreme court, under Judge Impey, Hastings's erstwhile ally, now began to exercise its powers and throw its weight around Bengal, terrorising subjects and those who got in its way. Hastings turned the council against it – and was promptly served with a writ, which he ignored. He set free many of those wrongfully arrested by Impey in the past. The court, which had served Hastings so well against the council, was placed under the latter's control. Francis, now in a minority there, sought out Hastings for a duel, which the latter accepted. Francis was shot, but not mortally wounded.

Hastings, thus spared, turned his energies to the most ferocious Indian leader the British had yet encountered, Hyder Ali, King of Mysore. In the space of a few months, supported by the French, Hyder Ali's huge army left Mysore to ravage the Carnatic and terrorise the British community of Madras back into Fort St George. The British armies, led by Baillie and Sir Hector Munro, were put to flight. The French now proposed to help the Indian attack on Fort St George. Hastings promptly despatched a large army under Sir Eyre Coote, Clive's old bête noire, now grown much older but still a good soldier, to relieve Madras. With extraordinary leadership, he defeated Hyder Ali.

Hastings returned to the business of plunder. His next objective was the remarkable and beautiful holy city of Benares, whose rajah had supported Francis. He rained huge financial demands upon him, eventually receiving £500,000 as a ransom against being handed over to the Nawab of Oudh.

The cocksure Hastings, with just 50 men, went to see the rajah and had him arrested. But the latter escaped, and laid siege to Hastings

and his tiny band, now trapped in his palace. One man coolly
bluffed his way out to the large British force that was waiting
outside Benares, which attacked and defeated the rajah's men. The
relief of Benares followed; Hastings had obtained a further £200,000
for the Company's coffers.

Hastings now moved his armies to Oudh where Shuja-ud-Daula
had died. This formidable ruler had been succeeded by his son, Asaph-
ud-Daula. Hastings first threatened the new ruler, then entered into an
agreement to despoil Asaph and his grandmother, the Begum of
Oudh, of their huge estates and fortunes. By thus stripping them of
their money and confining them to the large palace at Fayzabad,
Hastings secured another huge sum for the Company.

The contrast between Hastings and Clive could not have been
starker. Hastings had immense achievements to his name – giving
Bengal its first real British government, fending off a serious threat
to British dominion in India through the combination of Hyder Ali
and the French, sweeping away the practice of rule by surrogates in
Bengal, pacifying the frontier provinces (although largely in order to
exact money from them). Above all, he placed Bengal on a secure
financial footing.

But he was cruel, rapacious, tough and relentless. Where Clive
was romantic, intelligent, bold and visionary, Hastings was essentially a calculating and intelligent thug. Without him, Bengal could
not have been consolidated for the British, nor Madras saved. He
was, like Clive, incredibly popular among the Indian population in
his lifetime, although not later.

Clive's destiny had been to establish the empire through military
victory and astute diplomacy. Hastings, the first real administrator
of British India, succeeded through one act of ruthlessness and
rapacity after another – although always acting on behalf of the
Company rather than himself. No military commander, but a tough,
tenacious, astute and unscrupulous governor, Hastings was the
perfect successor to Clive. Clive created, magnificently; Hastings
consolidated, often ruthlessly and squalidly. Yet the British were far
from being the possessive imperialists of popular imagination. In
1825, just seven years after Hastings's death, Charles Williams
Wynn, president of the Board of Control, which now administered
India in place of the Company, wrote to his friend Bishop Heber of

Calcutta, querying 'if it be desirable to retain the government of India till the day shall come when it may safely be left to itself. Whenever that day shall arrive, as come it will, though I think not in our time, I have no doubt that we should find India independent more beneficial to us than in her present state.' This was a remarkable statement, coming 122 years before the end of the Raj, and in conformity with the enlightened and benevolent tradition begun by Clive during his last tour of duty.

Robert Clive should be judged by posterity on four levels: as a private individual; as a British politician; as a military leader; and as ruler and effective emperor of much of India.

As an individual, Clive emerges as overwhelming, larger than life, a swashbuckling, bubbling volcano of a man. From youthful awkwardness – yet displaying integrity, daring and courage even as a boy – by his twenties he had become overbearingly self-confident and generous, with a huge coterie of family and friends, self-indulgent, a fount of hospitality and a lover of the pleasures in life.

He was loyal to his friends and supporters, vindictive and petty towards his enemies. Incredibly tough and driving towards his subordinates when he needed to be, he was equally unsparing on himself – a man of colossal energy who through his own example brought out the best in people. Time and again he appeared to lapse into idle enjoyment of the good things in life, and time and again rose to a further challenge, fighting back with a spartan vigour and determination.

The driven, angry, idealistic Clive and the hedonistic, fun-loving man were all part of the same complex personality. His furious determination was leavened by his love of the good things in life; his seriousness was ameliorated by his sense of fun and pleasure. When well, he was unfailingly kind to those he loved, and towards his subordinates. He behaved with contempt and rebelliousness towards his superiors, with leadership and respect towards those beneath him, a mark of greatness.

His downside was his mania and depression – whether arising from temperament, illness or overwork – and the impact upon those closest to him. His rare acts of martial cruelty occurred when he was at his most vulnerable. Overpoweringly self-centred, self-publicising and self-justifying, sometimes whiningly sensitive, with a ferocious temper, yet often the most expansive and cheerful of men, he was capable of inspiring men on a Churchillian scale. Indeed, his look of pudgy determination and vulnerability bears an astonishing resemblance to Churchill's.

To reach the top in British politics was probably Clive's central ambition; at first India was just a staging post. Yet he made little impact on the House of Commons, failed to realise the need to secure patronage initially on his way to the top and, when he did, showed a remarkable capacity for backing the wrong horse or – endearingly – taking a stand on principle to the detriment of his own career.

He was too passionate and principled a man to climb to the top of the greasy pole of eighteenth-century British politics. His years of absolute power in India poorly prepared him for the necessary compromises and ingratiation necessary to achieve his ultimate goal.

Yet where the names of most eighteenth-century politicians are forgotten, his will live on for ever. India was to be the source of his greatness, and was his greatest obsession, yet for long he regarded it as a sideshow to his principal ambition. Perhaps because running Bengal was never the summit of his ambitions, as it might have been for a lesser man, he did the job extraordinarily well, being some-times capricious, never despotic.

He only emerged as one of the House of Commons's finest orators when his back was to the wall during the Indian inquisition. He refused to compromise enough, or debase himself to the sordid world of politics; nor, either out of indolence or illness in later life, was he prepared to devote the time necessary to a successful political career. He never achieved an office of any kind in govern-ment. If he had devoted himself to a House of Commons life, he might have reached the top, but he had too much hauteur, too little application, and had succeeded in a far more challenging environ-ment.

As a soldier, Clive has been denigrated by many military historians who, half-patronisingly, half-sneeringly, refer to him as one of the first great guerrilla leaders. If this is a swipe at his energy, his daring attacks where the enemy least expected them, or his ability to cross hundreds of miles of territory and to spur his men on at great speed, it is a flattering portrait by comparison with the staid, headquarters-bound commanders of his day. In the sense that Clive was an improviser, a man of huge skill in coping with adversity, capable of engaging the enemy on its own territory and seizing the initiative through forced marches behind enemy lines, he was indeed a guerrilla leader.

In the set-piece battles – whether defending Arcot, laying siege to Trichinopoly, or turning the tables at Kaveripak – he showed he was an entirely effective conventional commander – and perhaps more so because of his imagination and courage. Plassey itself was a masterful set-piece effort, overlooked at the time because the British appeared to win so easily. Yet the outcome was far from certain most of the day; but for Clive's elaborate intrigues before the battle, it would certainly have been lost. Wellington's victory at Waterloo is not deemed the less because he was supported by Blücher – like Mir Jafar, late in the battle, but at least not on the enemy side.

That victory at Plassey was won with so little carnage was a credit to Clive, and can hardly be held against him. His tactics on that occasion were a model of propriety and imagination. Clive never fought a truly bloody set-piece battle, which has damned him in the eyes of many of the more basic military historians; but that can hardly be held against him. He secured his triumph through courage, intelligence and improvisation as much as sheer professionalism. His bravery, energy and leadership were of the very highest order.

He won a remarkable succession of victories and never lost a battle, although he had a few close calls, Plassey included. Even the initial farce of his expedition up the Hugli was soon replaced by the grudging admiration of his colleagues, as he succeeded, time and time again. As with Churchill, setbacks were simply a spur to success.

To dismiss the Indian armies he overwhelmed is unfair on both. He was far from certain at the time that his small force could prevail against such overwhelmingly superior ones often accompanied by contingents of well-trained and experienced European troops always sustained with modern cannon and guns. Unwieldy and ill-disciplined they might be; but, supported by French advice, troops and often artillery, they usually had a well-trained core far larger than Clive's small forces. Hyder Ali was later to show that Indian armies could be extremely effective. Chanda Sahib and Siraj-ud-Daula were formidable adversaries.

Clive also fought against well-disciplined European armies – the French and the Dutch, usually in superior numbers – and he never lost a single battle to them either. Clive's military career may be judged as one of the most effective in British history, whether judged by results, courage, imagination, leadership or tactical skill.

He was no good at shuffling flags about on maps back at headquarters or watching the progress of a battle from a hill in the distance. He was despised for being insufficiently aloof, too hotheaded, getting into the thick of battle too readily, as at Plassey; yet there is no sign that his forays into action warped his overall judgement. He was perfectly capable of restraint when the occasion demanded. He was one of the very greatest generals Britain has ever produced, the finest judge of the calculated risk.

Clive's career as a ruler – an emperor, a dictator of his huge swathe of India with unparalleled powers – provides for an unambiguous judgement. It is here that his greatness, exceptional as he was in other fields, truly lies. The reckless young soldier showed a remarkable gravitas and sense of purpose when given responsibility for administering an empire and millions of subjects. Placed in charge of Bengal, he could have degenerated into a native ruler himself or simply plundered the country, as some of his successors did.

Instead, he was restrained, pursuing policies of divide and rule, governing through the local Moslem élite while encouraging their Hindu subordinates to keep them in a state of paralysis. He refused to stretch the boundaries of his Indian empire beyond what he believed to be controllable, in spite of intense pressure on him to do so. His governance was on the whole popular, fair and enlightened, resisting the excesses of his own financially rapacious, native-despising followers.

Clive's humanity is reflected in the fact that he personally insisted on reviewing all capital cases under his jurisdiction; and that, as a nineteenth-century observer wrote, 'in a lifetime spent among scenes of blood and suffering, he has never been accused of a single act of cruelty'.

In fact two actions of pure revenge were laid to his door: in each there was small loss of life. Both were dictated by the need to secure

territory through military victory and discourage further insurrection by the local people – as well as, in the first case, to erase the
esteem held by the French in southern India. The plundering of the
villages showed a dark side to his nature, but occurred at a time
when Clive was clearly in one of his most manic-depressive phases.
This is not to excuse him, but to understand him.

It was during his last tour in Bengal that Clive laid the foundations for his claim to greatness and to be the initiator of all that was
best about the British in India. He showed a Caesar's unconcern for
the unpopularity he attained among his fellow countrymen in the
relentless pursuit of good government and the stamping out of
malpractice and corruption. In so doing he laid the ethos of Indian
colonial administration for two centuries to come.

He could have joined in the excesses or he could have simply sat
on his hands; he did neither. He attacked the abuses of his fellow-
countrymen with the same vigour as he had fought to conquer the
Carnatic and Bengal years before. He was utterly unafraid of the
consequences – in the event, a ferocious campaign against him that
was almost to destroy his reputation, fortune and freedom.

Clive established the legal basis of the Indian empire, as well as
defensible borders for his conquests, and put into place the beginnings of modern administration there by eliminating the old
anomaly that the Company's servants were both administrators
and profiteers. Henceforth, they were to be paid civil servants.

Finally, with audacity and strength of character, he crushed an
officers' revolt against him through bravery alone, establishing the
supremacy of the civilian over the military authority – even though
much of his own rule in Bengal had been based on the reverse. He
then displayed the magnanimity towards his opponents of a truly
'big' man. No leader is more impressive than when he moves
against his own friends and companions in defence of good
government; he suffered appallingly from the backlash later.

So to the verdict of history, the charges laid against him in his own
lifetime, fuelled by high-minded Victorians and twentieth-century
anti-colonialists. Was his life not one colossal morality tale of pride,
greed and vainglory finally getting its come-uppance? Was he not
the high priest of one of the most evil chapters – imperialism – in
British history?

The detailed allegations against Clive were examined in his inter-rogation before the House of Commons and, as concluded already, he must be exonerated of all but the extent of his accumulation of wealth, which at the time was not considered excessive, certainly for a man who had become ruler of a fabulous empire, either in Indian or British terms. Only his acquisition and dogged pursuit of the jagir must be laid against him as an act of greed and misjudgement.

In Clive's time no one thought it strange that a European should seek to enlarge his country's territorial dominion or his own wealth through conquest. This was impossible in Europe because of the existence of strong rival military powers; the further parts of the world therefore beckoned. By modern standards this ethos was cruel and amoral; but it was the measure of a man's success at the time.

The India that Clive conquered was itself under the despotic foreign rule of the Mogul princes – although the empire itself had broken up. In many respects the Hindu upper class – although caste-conscious beyond belief and hardly kind to those below – regarded British rule as no worse, or better, than Mogul rule. Clive surely cannot be faulted for not having foreseen the anti-colonial backlash of the twentieth century.

Moreover, in that he was one of the very few that sought at once to control the excesses of economic colonialism, he was well in advance of his time. For there were to be good things about empire, as well as bad: the dedication of many civil servants to good government; the attempts to control the greed of traders and settlers; the efforts to improve conditions and educate the people. All these were later developments; but Clive – first trader himself, then soldier, then reforming administrator – took the first steps.

The hidden tragedy of his death – perhaps more understandable today in an age where human psychology is better understood and people more forgiving – has also served to obscure the fact that Robert Clive, Primus in Indis, was one of the most remarkable, fascinating, humane – for his age – far-seeing and spectacularly achieving men that these islands have ever produced. He deserves to take his place along-side Drake, Cromwell, Marlborough, Nelson, Wellington and Churchill.

He lies today in an unmarked, unknown grave within the walls of an obscure church in a village barely worthy of the description, Moreton Saye, reached by tiny lanes near the nondescript town of Market

Drayton in eastern Shropshire. Those abandoned bones beneath the parquet floor returned to that remote hamlet from an adventure beyond every schoolboy's dream: daring escape from the French, the brilliant seizure of a citadel from behind the enemy's back, the defence of that fortress for nearly two months against overwhelming odds in what was perhaps the greatest siege in British military history, a series of barely believable battles against huge odds and the brutal reduction of a colossal army at Trichinopoly.

These Boys' Own achievements were exceeded by a tale out of Rider Haggard – of how one man with a tiny army tricked his overwhelming opponents into dividing themselves, won a battle with only a handful killed, installed a monarch, beheld a treasure the like of which few have ever seen, and departed downriver with a large part of it. Over the next few years he ruled over a colossal country as dictator, emperor and military chief, securing its boundaries and founding its administration. Later, he returned in person to quell abuses and a mutiny among his own supporters.

Only a handful of men in world history have done so much – Alexander the Great, Tamerlane, Napoleon. Few authors of fiction would have the imagination to encompass such an adventure. Whatever the judgement, the achievement is undisputed. He rests, anonymously, in well-deserved peace after labours of a Herculean kind.

Bibliography

Abdul Majed Khan, *The Transition in Bengal*. Cambridge 1969.

Bence-Jones, Mark, *Clive of India*, London 1974.

'Bengal, Past and Present', Journal of the Calcutta Historical Society, various.

Cambridge, R. O., *Account of the War in India*. Dublin, 1761.

Caraccioli, Charles, *Life of Robert, Lord Clive*. London 1777.

Carnac, Major John, Letters in the British Library.

Chaudhury, N. W., *Clive of India*. London, 1975.

Clive, Robert, Lord, Clive collection on loan at the National Library of Wales, Aberystwyth.

Letter to the Proprietors of the East India Stock. London 1764.

Speech of March 30, 1772.

Coke, Lady Mary, *Journal*. Edinburgh 1896.

Davies, A. Mervyn, *Clive of Plassey*, London 1939.

Dodwell, Henry, *Dupleix and Clive*. London 1920.

Nabobs of Madras. London 1926.

Edwardes, Michael, *The Battle of Plassey*. London, 1963.

Clive, the Heaven-Born General. London 1977.

Feiling, Keith, *Warren Hastings*, London 1954.

Forde, Lionel, *Lord Clive's Right-hand Man*. London 1910.

Forrest, Sir George, *Life of Lord Clive*. 2 volumes. London 1918.

Francis papers in the India Office Library, London.

Gleig, G. R., *Life of Clive*. London 1848.

Grenville Papers, London 1852–3.

Gupta, B. K., *Siraj-ud-Daula and the East India Company*. Leiden 1966.

Hill, S. C., *Bengal in 1756–7*. London 1905.

Holt, Peter, *In Clive's Footsteps*, London 1992.

House of Commons, Report of the Select Committee, 1772.

Ives, Edward, *A Voyage from England to India in the year 1754*. London 1773.

James, Laurence, *Raj, The Making and Unmaking of The British Empire*. 1998.

Johnstone, John, *A Letter to the Proprietors of East India Stock*. London 1776.

Langford, Paul, *A Polite and Commercial People*. Oxford 1992.

Lawrence, Stringer, *Narrative*. Cambridge 1761.

Macaulay, Thomas Babington, *Essay on Clive*. London 1840.

Malcolm, Sir John, *Life of Robert, Lord Clive*. London 1836. 3 vols.

Martineau, Alfred, *Dupleix*. Paris 1931.

Minney, R. J., *Clive of India*. London 1931.

Orme, Robert, *History of the Military Transactions of the British Nation in Hindostan*. London 1763–78.

Orme papers in the India Office Library, London.

Powis Collection on loan to the India Office Library, London.

Ram Gopal, *How the British Occupied Bengal*. London 1963.

Scrafton, Luke, *Reflections on the Government of Indostan*. London 1763.

Sinha, N. K., *Economic History of Bengal*. Calcutta 1956,.

Spear, Percival, *The Nabobs*, London 1932.

India, a Modern History. Michigan 1961.

Twilight of the Moguls. Cambridge 1951.

Strachey, Henry, *Narrative of the Mutiny of the Officers*. London 1773.

Sulivan, Laurence, Papers in the Bodleian Library, Oxford.

Sutherland, Lucy, *The East India Company in 18th Century Politics*. Oxford, 1952.

Thompson, Virginia, *Dupleix*. New York 1933.

Thornton, Edward, *History of the British Empire in India*. 6 vols. London 1841–5.

Vansittart, Henry, *Narrative of the Transactions in Bengal from 1760 to 1764*. London 1766.

Verelst, Harry, *A view of the Rise, Progress and Present State of the English Company in Bengal*. London 1772.

Verelst papers at the India Office Library in London, including letters from Clive

Walpole, Horace, *Letters*, Oxford 1903–8 and 1918–25.

Watts, William, *Memoirs of the Revolution in Bengal*. London 1764.

Williams Wynn, Arthur, *Charles Williams-Wynn*. London 1932.

Woodruff, Philip, *The Men who Ruled India*. London 1953.

Index